DISASTER PREPAREDNESS AGAINST ACCIDENTS OR TERRORIST ATTACK

DISASTER PREPAREDNESS AGAINST ACCIDENTS OR TERRORIST ATTACK

(Chemical/Biological/Radiological)

PRASANTA K RAY

Emeritus Medical Scientist
National Institute of Cholera and Enteric Diseases
Indian Council of Medical Research
Government of India
Kolkata, India

Formerly

Director Industrial Toxicology Research Center
CSIR, Government of India, Lucknow

Director, Bose Institute, DST, Kolkata

Director, Chittaranjan National Cancer Research Centre
Government of India, Kolkata

NEW AGE REFERENCE

An Imprint of

NEW AGE INTERNATIONAL (P) LIMITED, PUBLISHERS

LONDON • NEW DELHI • NAIROBI

Bangalore • Chennai • Cochin • Guwahati • Hyderabad • Kolkata • Lucknow • Mumbai

Visit us at **www.newagepublishers.com**

Published by New Age International (P) Ltd., Publishers
First Edition: 2006
Reprint: 2017

GLOBAL OFFICES

- **New Delhi** **NEW AGE INTERNATIONAL (P) LIMITED, PUBLISHERS**
  7/30 A, Daryaganj, New Delhi-110002, (INDIA)
  Tel.: (011) 23253771, 23253472, **Telefax:** 23267437, 43551305
  E-mail: contactus@newagepublishers.com • Visit us at www.newagepublishers.com
- **London** **NEW AGE INTERNATIONAL (UK) LTD.**
  27 Old Gloucester Street, London, WC1N 3AX, UK
  E-mail: info@newacademicscience.co.uk • Visit us at www.newacademicscience.co.uk
- **Nairobi** **NEW AGE GOLDEN (EAST AFRICA) LTD.**
  Ground Floor, Westlands Arcade, Chiromo Road (Next to Naivas Supermarket)
  Westlands, Nairobi, KENYA, **Tel.:** 00-254-713848772, 00-254-725700286
  E-mail: kenya@newagepublishers.com

BRANCHES

- **Bangalore** 37/10, 8th Cross (Near Hanuman Temple), Azad Nagar, Chamarajpet, Bangalore- 560 018
  Tel.: (080) 26756823, **Telefax:** 26756820, **E-mail: bangalore@newagepublishers.com**
- **Chennai** 26, Damodaran Street, T. Nagar, Chennai-600 017, **Tel.:** (044) 24353401, **Telefax:** 24351463
  E-mail: chennai@newagepublishers.com
- **Cochin** CC-39/1016, Carrier Station Road, Ernakulam South, Cochin-682 016, **Tel.:** (0484) 2377303, **Telefax:** 4051304
  E-mail: cochin@newagepublishers.com
- **Guwahati** Hemsen Complex, Mohd. Shah Road, Paltan Bazar, Near Starline Hotel, Guwahati-781 008,
  Tel.: (0361) 2513881, **Telefax:** 2543669, **E-mail: guwahati@newagepublishers.com**
- **Hyderabad** 105, 1st Floor, Madhiray Kaveri Tower, 3-2-19, Azam Jahi Road, Near Kumar Theater, Nimboliadda Kachiguda, Hyderabad-500 027, **Tel.:** (040) 24652456, **Telefax:** 24652457
  E-mail: hyderabad@newagepublishers.com
- **Kolkata** RDB Chambers (Formerly Lotus Cinema) 106A, 1st Floor, S N Banerjee Road, Kolkata-700 014
  Tel.: (033) 22273773, **Telefax:** 22275247, **E-mail: kolkata@newagepublishers.com**
- **Lucknow** 16-A, Jopling Road, Lucknow-226 001, **Tel.:** (0522) 2209578, 4045297, **Telefax:** 2204098
  E-mail: lucknow@newagepublishers.com
- **Mumbai** 142C, Victor House, Ground Floor, N.M. Joshi Marg, Lower Parel, Mumbai-400 013
  Tel.: (022) 24927869, **Telefax:** 24915415, **E-mail: mumbai@newagepublishers.com**
- **New Delhi** 22, Golden House, Daryaganj, New Delhi-110 002, **Tel.:** (011) 23262368, 23262370, **Telefax:** 43551305
  E-mail: sales@newagepublishers.com

ISBN: 978-81-224-1742-5
C-17-01-10114

Printed in India at Glorious Printers, Delhi.
Typeset at Goswami Associates, New Delhi.

NEW AGE INTERNATIONAL (P) LIMITED, PUBLISHERS
7/30 A, Daryaganj, New Delhi-110002
Visit us at **www.newagepublishers.com**
(CIN: U74899DL1966PTC004618)

This volume is dedicated to the memory of thousands of innocent victims of terrorist attack and/or of accidents

Preface

Terrorism is the most common word being discussed, talked about and read all over the world these days. Almost every day, the terrorists strike various parts of the world. The Terrorist's acts or deeds are always associated with a large number of killings of innocent people, wounding several thousands at the same time. This is also associated with huge financial losses. Plenty of time and money is needed for the reconstruction, replenishment and rehabilitation.

Thousands of families become the victims of circumstances. Most of the families have lost the *only earning member* of theirs during the number of massacres took place in the past. Terrorism always brings in a lost of despair in the mind of the kiths and kins of the victims. The miseries, the sufferings and the agonies of the bereaved families are unbearable.

I am the eyewitness of two major disasters of the world—1. The infamous toxic chemical disaster, which occurred in the Union Carbide Factory in Bhopal, India. 2. The notorious Twin-Tower (WTC) disaster, which leveled off major financial and business center of the world on September 11, 2001. I cried along with the victims' families. I shared their mental agonies. I experienced the sufferings and troubles of the aftermath of the disasters that the people had to go through. Since that time, I felt a deep sense of mental pressure that I must do something to make people more aware so as to cope with the situations in a better way. The anxieties for survival I have witnessed on the faces of the people, who were running out for their lives in Manhattan, moved into my heart severely. The cries of the nearest and dearest ones of the victims, who died during the incident, still linger in my memories. The helpless faces, the wet eyes with sobbing sound, the endless sorrows of the families touched the deepest core of my heart. I decided to help them out by preparing a book, which every individual may like to read for better preparedness and for taking all necessary precautionary measures, including survival skills, treatment procedures etc. The present volume is the result of that initiative.

As I mentioned above, I prepared this volume from an eyewitness's point of view. I have witnessed the two major disasters so far occurred in the world—first was the **Bhopal gas tragedy,** which took place due to an accident, and the other was demolition of the **WTC (World Trade Center) in New York.** These two highly horrifying experiences prompted me to prepare this volume.

In March 1984, when I took over as the Director of Industrial Toxicology Research Center (ITRC), Council of Scientific and Industrial Research, Government of India, Lucknow, India, I never thought that a few months later on December 3, 1984, I should have to deal with one of the greatest chemical disasters in history. The incident took place in the Union Carbide Factory at Bhopal, Madhya Pradesh, India. Believe me! I was never ready for that, but I had to do what I was required to.

In the early morning of December 3, 1984, one of the 40-ton capacity storage tanks of the deadly gas, *methyl isocyanate*, exploded and released in the atmosphere. The released pressure forced it up in the sky, as a ballooning structure. Soon it was flown in the direction of the wind, killing thousands of people on the way. Several thousand livestock, poultry, birds, aquatic and soil flora and fauna got destroyed. The trees turned brown, as they have been burnt, and scorched in the temperature generated, perhaps as a result of some exothermic reactions or because of the direct toxic chemical reactions. Being the Director of ITRC, I lead to organize a team of multidisciplinary scientists and technicians. The team was equipped with all the necessary instruments, laboratory chemicals and gadgets. The team was sent to Bhopal (about 500 km from Lucknow) to establish temporary laboratories and conduct multidisciplinary study, planned and designed by me.

At the aftermath of the disaster, the study was conducted for a period of three months, and it continued periodically as a follow-up study for a period of three years. We noticed and also experienced the sufferings of the exposed victims, the agonies of the survivors and the severe after-effects among them who survived longer. There was no time to take precautions and to leave the place and go to safer places. There was also no time to bring in any kind of help by the Government machineries. It started all of a sudden, that people had no other option than dying haplessly. Most people died on their beds. Those who slept keeping their doors and windows open were the major victims. And those who kept their windows and doors shut from inside, showed significantly less casualties. The children, pregnant women, the elderly and those who had asthmatic and other cardiopulmonary problems, suffered the most. With in no time, Bhopal turned into a dead city. The entire country and the neighbouring counties were simply stunned in the morning as soon as they came to know about the mishap. The people of the world started mourning, right from the morning of December 3, 1984.

It was an unprecedented sight! When our team was proceeding towards the city of Bhopal, in the early morning hours, they found hundreds of cars, taxis, buses, lorry, tempos, rickshaws, bullock carts, thelas etc. were going out of the city, carrying crowds of people. Some were standing and some were sitting on the floor of the vehicle even. Some were just hanging in even at the risk of getting dropped on the way. They were all fighting with a menace. What they have seen, what they have gone through during the early morning hours, remained in their minds as a horrible experience. This episode would be tingling in their memories for many years to come. Of course, it is there in my mind even after a pretty long time of 20 years.

As the news spread far and wide, people started pouring in the city by all means from all over the world. Representatives from various governments, diplomats, representatives from UN and its constituent agencies, WHO, IPCS, IRPTC, NIH, NIOSH, BIBRA and many others came to Bhopal offering help and assistance. Representatives from various newspapers, photographers from all around the world came in to cover the story. Writers, environmentalists, philanthropists, scientists, doctors and engineers arrived from various parts of the world to investigate and collect information of various kinds as per their own needs and requirements. The history labelled it as one of its worst chemical disasters, the world had witnessed so far. It had been recorded as the most horrible nuclear disaster next to Hiroshima and Nagasaki of Japan.

It just happened that I became almost an eyewitness of the 9/11 Twin-Tower Disaster in the New York City, USA. In 2001, I was associated with the Albert Einstein College of Medicine at Bronx, but my laboratory was in St. Lukes Roosevelt Health Sciences Center, in one of their affiliated buildings of Beth Israel Medical Center, Manhattan, at 455 W 58th Street. I was on the way to my lab as usual on that fateful day of September 11, at around 8:30 a.m. in an underground metro from Bronx. Just a few minutes earlier, we would have arrived our destination, one of the passengers brought to the attention of others that some huge amount of spiraling black cloud formation is there, over the Manhattan Island. At that point, the train was moving through the open surface areas of an unknown place. Everybody was anxious to see it. Some commented that there must be a big fire somewhere. Some said, "it must be something else". But no body could even guess that it was the result of a terrible terrorist attack. Within no time, the train came to a halt without any announcement. Soon it was realized that it would not go any further. When asked, one of the station employees said, 'no train will move in either directions'. Like everybody else, I came up to the stairs at the street level, but only to see an unprecedented sight I saw never before.

Panic-driven people were howling, shouting, sobbing, crying and running to the opposite direction of the heart of the city. Some people were drenched in water. They were all muddled. On enquiry, I came to know that America was attacked by its enemies. Twin Tower at Manhattan, the major business center of the world was demolished by two flying planes coming from two opposite directions. People were terribly panicked. Everyone out of them was trying to reach home safely. Anyhow, people were moving out of the city, riding on overcrowed buses, vans, cars, SUVs etc. A havoc was spread in the city of New York. I was walking in a direction quite unknown to me, but of course following others only to go away from the city as far as possible, without knowing where I was going.

Walking for a long time, and taking ride to some distance, I had to walk across a bridge in Harlem. I did not know that place. I did not know even how to go to my place from that point. Asking people while riding in buses, finally I reached my home safely around 2:00 pm. My wife was obviously very anxious. She appeared to be relieved seeing me back at home. She got the news already from a telephone call from my sister-in-law from New Delhi, who wanted to know about our whereabouts. Up to that point of time, my wife did not know anything. Telephone calls started pouring in from India and also from various parts of the USA, from my friends, relatives and two of our sons, living in two different places in the USA.

As my wife switched-on the TV, there was a series of news about what had happened. Soon it was realized, it was the design of a terrorist organization activity called AL QAIDA. The organization was located in Afghanistan. The terrorists had a deep-rooted plan to strike the White House, the American President's official residence, and also the Pentagon Headquarters, the site of the American Military might. Whereas by that time they could hit a portion of the Pentagon Building, but the attempt to go toward Washington D.C was failed because of the heroic sacrifice of several Americans who were boarded on one of the aircrafts, and intercepted the terrorists while in air and got killed in the process. When they realized that they are going to die anyway, they managed to divert the direction of the aircraft toward another direction, only to crash-land somewhere in Pennsylvania.

Now it has become quite clear that such type of disasters can take place either due to an accident, due to fire, chemical spills, compressed gas release, power failure, by bomb explosions, radioactive spills, terrorist's activities, biohazards and chemical emergencies, and of course during the warfare. It is required to keep in mind that where high explosives or inflammable materials are stored in large enough quantities, those areas definitely have strong disaster potential. Those installations are required to be guarded properly and an appropriate security arrangement should also be made around it, round the clock.

The purpose of this volume is to critically apprise the readers about the various types of disaster-associated situations, which the world had seen and experienced already, and to suggest a rational program for anticipation, abatement, and management of chemical, biological and radiological disasters. While going to do this, I shall point out the lacunae in the field, responsibilities of each of the persons involved, preparing a coordinated action plan, focusing attention on preventive and protective aspects of it. I shall also discuss about a proforma for inventory control, which can be used as a part of the action plan. It is recommended that mock-drills may be performed from time to time to keep people alert and also to ensure that trained people are always available, and instruments necessary for abatement are in stock and in good functional order.

The basis of this document is to some extent the personal experiences of the author, gained first from the "Bhopal episode (1984)", and recently from the "Twin Tower Disaster" and "Anthrax Mail" disaster in 2001 at New York, New Jersey and some other states of USA.

By now, the 'Disaster Management Plans' are already implemented in various industries. WHO-IPCS, Geneva also has an abundance of such literature. A large body of International literature also provides a lot of information, which have been consulted/utilized in various sections of this volume for the benefit of all sections of readers, avoiding jargons as far as possible, and presenting the matter understandable to everybody.

Thus, the overall objective of this volume has been to put together a document for everybody's information. Knowledge and benefit to make him/her aware about the potential of various disaster-prone situations and suggest a strategy for preparedness, prevention and containment of hazardous substances—chemical, biological, and radiological.

I have seen, I have witnessed and I have experienced the troubles, the problems, and the sufferings of disaster victims. The agonies of people who are hard-hit in that kind of circumstances are far-reaching. It touches everybody's mind. The helplessness of the innocent people, their panic-stricken and shocked faces, was fully shadowed by despair. It still reminds us that we need to do something, to show solidarity with those who suffered. We all should prove that we are with them. Let us proclaim that, "we are here to help you, to share your grief, to extend our handkerchiefs towards you to wipe out tears from your faces". A few words of sympathy worth often more than millions of dollars.

I decided to prepare a document to make people aware about the aftermath of such kind of disasters and the preparedness it needs to safeguard one's own self and the family. Some details on the preparatory measures for prevention and protection are also discussed in this volume. Disaster management and disaster control has been given special attention, including diagnosis of the hazardous chemical/biological/radiological exposure of victims, and the available treatments etc. It has also been pointed out that counseling and rehabilitation are also very important aspects of management of the aftermath of the disasters.

For long two and a half years, I read various books extensively, the magazines, the newspapers and searched the pertinent literature, and surfed extensively the Internet to collect data and information. In public interest and to help the mankind, I have drawn heavily from the available published information. I have very humbly acknowledged them and also referred their works in the references and also under "Further Reading" section. If by chance, I may have forgotten to properly refer anybody, any organization, institution etc., it should be considered as purely a mistake, and was totally unintentional. In any case, I beg to be excused if there is still found any.

I am especially grateful to my wife, Khana, two of my sons Partha and Amartya, and my daughter-in-law, Tania, for their patience and sacrifice they contributed for the past two and a half years, when I had to spend relentless hours of time in a speechless manner, totally engrossed in thinking, typing and copying just sitting before my computer. At times, I became sleepy while working for long. Khana woke me up from time to time, sometimes asking me to go to bed, if it was too late at night, while some other time sitting on the sofa just behind me knitting a sweater just to give me company. She reminded me many times regarding my deadline. She has been the big inspiration for me in this work. My sincere gratitude is for her. Tania, a Ph.D. in Chemistry, helped me collecting some photographs from the Internet. Partha, an M.D., kept his eyes firmly focussed on the various medical aspects dealt with in this treatise. Amartya, B.A. in Computer Science and English, helped me in proofreading and also fixing my computers from time to time, sometimes giving instructions over the telephone sitting at a greater distance.

In addition, I am indebted to Prof. Manish Chakrabarty, M.D., Ex-Director, School of Tropical Medicine, Kolkata, for his critical reading of a portion of this manuscript. I am also thankful to Dr. Rajagopal Chattopadhyay, Ph.D., a scientist at the Bose Institute, Kolkata for the preliminary reading of some sections of the manuscript and for shaping-up the structure of this treatise. Thanks to Dr. Tanya Das, Ph.D. and Dr. Gauri Sankar S.A., Ph.D., both scientists at Bose Institute, Kolkata for their help in the computer work, especially to sort out pictures, transfering materials etc. Thanks are due for the Indian Council of Medical Research, Government of India, especially its Director General, Prof. N. K. Ganguly, for awarding me an Emeritus Medical Scientist position, which enabled me to put the final touch on the manuscript.

Last but not the least of importance, my heartfelt gratitude to Mr. Saumya Gupta, Managing Director, New Age International (P) Limited, Publishers New Delhi, for their interests to come forward to publish this volume. I also acknowledge the interests shown by Dr. S.K. Bhattacharjee, M.D., Director, NICED, Dr. Pradip Das, Ph.D., Head Parasitology Department, NICED, Mrs. K. Ray, the librarian, NICED and my students Sudakshina and Sudip for offering various types of help.

My thanks are due for all those readers also who would read this volume with interests. I tried my best to prepare a document for everybody's use, starting from a *lay person to students to workers and practitioners of medicine, microbiology, life sciences, chemistry, toxicology and environmental sciences, nursing, management, law and order personnel and other civic authorities, fire fighters, police and military, scientists, technicians* etc. The major part of this volume is for the common people. There is something for almost everybody. I would consider my efforts a great success if the readers find it helpful and useful as a practical guidebook.

I have taken every precaution to check the typographical errors, both manually and electronically. The readers may still find some unavoidable mistakes or omissions here and there. Once again if some references are omitted or inadvertently missed, the author is apologetic about it. It is purely unintentional. The author does not have any intention whatsoever to hurt anybody's feelings, or of any nation, or religious groups, whose references had to be brought in for historic reasons and in public interests. It is definitely not to cast any shadow or reflections on anybody or on any organizations. It is not the purpose of this document to tarnish the image of anybody or of any organization whatsoever. For the sake of benefit to the vast humanity I prepared this volume with open mind. I strongly hope that it would serve that purpose.

Prasanta K. Ray, Ph.D., D.Sc., FIBIOL (LOND)
Emeritus Medical Scientist
Indian Council of Medical Research,
National Institute of Cholera and Enteric Diseases
Government of India
Kolkata, India
E.mail: pkray2000@yahoo.com

Contents

"A prudent man foresees the difficulties ahead and prepares for them; the simpleton goes blindly on and suffers the consequences."—Proverbs 22:3

1 Introduction

"... and he that will not apply new remedies must expect new evils; for time is the greatest innovator ...."

—The Essays by Sir Francis Bacon, 1601

1.1 INTRODUCTION

In the twentieth century, the world witnessed the enormous power of the Atomic Bomb and various other sophisticated weapons. The nature and extent of devastation, which are caused by an atomic explosion, was witnessed in Hiroshima and Nagasaki. The loss involved not only in instantaneous killing of hundreds and thousands of human, plant and animal lives, but also in the thousands of associated casualties in people who suffered from loss of their eyes, limbs, severe burns and different chronic ailments due to radiation continued for many more years later. As stated above, the devastations were so grave that thousands of people embraced death almost instantaneously. Cities and towns were leveled off within minutes. Everything was burnt into ashes. A vibrant city was turned into a city of "Dead" just in the twinkling of the eye. The entire world became speechless and was taken aback to see such a weapon of mass destruction (WMD) for the first time in history. The people were stunned and terrified. The awesome nature of devastation had gone beyond the imagination of any rationally thinking persons.

Soon the people of the world realized that this has to stop. The production, procurement and use of WMD have to be stopped. From various corners of the world people started raising their voices, protesting against such WMD. The cry soared high and the voice of both the rich and the poor were heard from all quarters. Dissents, processions, and public meetings decrying the use of WMD were witnessed in every part of the world. So much so that The United Nations (UN) came forward to pass resolutions for International Treaties to restrain all nations of the world from producing, storing and using WMD. The two superpowers at that time, USA and USSR came closer to sign an agreement to destroy and reduce stockpiles of such WMD within a specific period of time, which was mutually agreed upon. The sentiments of the so-called 'cold war' melted down and gradually came to a halt. The people sighed relief.

The goodness and virtues of major policy-makers over-powered the madness and cruel intentions of those, which may have governed its production at the first instances.

The collective power of the people was soon realized. Political and economical picture of the world changed soon. After thirties and forties in the 20th century, political upheaval within many Nations up-rooted the foreign colonial powers. Sovereign and independent states came into being. They were run by the people, of the people and for the people. Democracy was the preferred form of Government, although some feared at the rise of democratic power of the people. It was overwhelming to witness the fall of the foreign rule, and the rule of autocratic powers one after the other. Happy, joyous and freedom loving people were seen all around.

Soon, many of those new Governments realized that a tough task was ahead of them. They will have to reconstruct their nations from the ruins, which have only been left out. The people faced the harsh realities of life. The Governments realized that they have to grow more food to feed the millions, provide at least the minimum of health care, education, shelter and above all jobs to the millions of jobless. They also understood that they needed to protect the sovereignty of their nations and above all maintain law and order to protect their hard-earned liberty and freedom. The world social order almost got changed within a span of just 25-50 years.

Many countries suffered from the initial shock and euphoria and had even faced a setback for want of enough of experiences to rule a country. Soon power transferred hands and the autocratic, authoritarian or military rulers grabbed it. What was initially thought was not fulfilled. The dreams of the people did not get converted into real opportunities. The wealth of the nation started concentrating within a few who ruled those countries. The poor became poorer, and the rich richer. Grievances of the people started accumulating and gradually came to a point to burst out in the form of massive uprising, looting, and rioting. Killing became the order of the day. Thousands died. Thousands went underground to form militant outfits to launch Guerilla warfare, while some organized Nationalistic Movement against their rulers.

1.2 SCIENCE AND TECHNOLOGICAL DEVELOPMENT

Soon after World War I and World War II, almost around the time when all those societal transformations were taking place, unprecedented development in the area of Science and Technology was observed in different parts of the world, especially in the countries of the Northern hemisphere. Some of the nations which were lagging behind initially, soon started catching up. To extract the benefits of the discoveries and inventions in the field of Science and technology, some massive developmental programmes were undertaken. Educational level rose high slowly but steadily. Health care and nutritional standards improved considerably. As a result, the child mortality rate decreased to a considerable extent. Large number of new industries came up. New forms of agricultural policies and technologies were adopted. Green revolution was witnessed in many parts of the world, including India. Later came the white revolution also. The buying power of the people started improving. Women education was on the top of the agenda in most of those countries. Women were given equal status in the society, and the power was shared with them in many countries. All those prompted rapid growth and development of many nations of the world. Thus science and technological development helped in the rapid societal change, economic advancement, bringing in prosperity among the people, and the taste of modern living in many countries of the world.

Life-styles of people got upgraded considerably. It went up to such a level that the middle class, or even a section of the poor in some instances, could afford to have a house, and at least a second hand car, a radio, a television, telephone, cooking range, washer and a dryer etc. Provisions for the jobless, the poor and the elderly of the society for providing them food and shelter was also made. More and more people started traveling by air than traveling by the road or by train.

Speedy aeroplanes initially brought the world and its people closer than before. Mutual co-operations, cultural exchanges, trade and commerce increased considerably among the nations. In the midst of all these, industrial revolutions took place. Large number of new industries almost in every sector was set up. Hundreds and thousands of new openings for jobless were created. There were so many choices that the people could find their preferred jobs easily. A healthy competition in the market could bring in quality products at a cheaper price. New gadgets for everyday life started pouring in the market. Refrigertaors, deep freezers, cooking range, ovens, washing and drying machines, stereo and photographic equipment, gas and electric heating systems, all kinds of luxury cars, electric trains etc. brought in a lot of comfort for the modern men and women. Standard of living of the people started rising sharply, especially in the advanced countries of the north, while the conditions of the poor and the middle class remained almost where they were in the developing countries of the world. A difference got created, bringing in indirect jealousy, hatred, and anger in the minds of many.

A critical analysis of those achievements point out to the fact that the countries which could rapidly develop their economy were those which had stable governments, open competitive economy, a craze for applying the know-how of science and technological advancements to obtain the best, and a continuous effort to engage in research for further and further improvements to make things improved and better. Most of these nations followed democratic norms and practices, had an increasing educational rate, and an increasing order of sharing of economic and political powers between the two sexes. Side by side, those nations initiated plans for the poor and elderly. Social Security programmes, welfare programmes, Medicare and Medicaid programmes for the poor and elderly were run for the poor and the destitute. Soup kitchen, food coupons, and homes for the homeless and destitute were initiated in different parts of those countries. All these brought in a new social order in those countries.

While progress and development were the two key words heard all around, computer era and space age came into being with a host of useful gadgets, such as Fax, Mobile phones, Cell phones, e.mail, e-commerce, supersonic jets etc. It changed the entire life vis-à-vis working style of the people, brought in more productivity especially in the developed countries of the world.

1.3 REVOLUTIONS IN MODERN BIOLOGY

Better health care, proper nutrition and hygiene led to greater longevity of the people, especially in the Northern nations of the world. There has been a North-South divide as far as the more advanced and less advanced countries were concerned. Countries in the Southern hemisphere, except for Australia, Japan, China, India, Singapore, Philippines, South Korea, South Africa and a few others remained basically poor. Countries in the Northern hemisphere except for a few, most of them developed faster than others. These were all possible because of the great scientific and technological achievements in those countries. Production of high yielding varieties of wheat and rice, a better understanding about nutrition, growing consciousness about the proper maintenance of hygiene, production and use of effective vaccines and drugs for the treatment against a large number of deadly diseases were responsible for spectacular results in providing better health and increasing longevity of the people. Many deadly diseases were under control. Child mortality index sharply fell and at the same time longevity of people started increasing. Somehow such growth and developments were mainly limited to the developed Northern countries of the world.

The tools and techniques of Molecular Biology brought in a revolutionary change in Genetic Engineering, cloning of genes, gene insertion and its expressions in foreign hosts, creation of transgenic super bugs and high yielding plants, cells with new properties, test tube babies, cloned animals etc. These discoveries provided mind boggling and awe-inspiring promises for an unimaginable type of progress and developments in the near future.

First generation and second generation vaccines, correction of genetic disorders by way of implants of proper stem cells, designer proteins and peptides, use of synthetic nucleic acids, synthetic Nano-molecules etc. will offer a host of new avenues of treatments of various ailments. It will provide greater productivity, better life, and an extended longevity to the future generations of the world.

One has to understand that growth and development does not fall from heaven. One has to achieve it. One has to earn it. A lot of planning, sincere efforts, imposition of restrictions, strict regulatory measurers, major controls and disciplines, and above all hard work are necessary to see rapid growth and development of any nation. Simply talking will not do. Only desire will not create miracles. Of course one major and essential need is investment of adequate funds.

Many less developed and developing countries of the world could not afford to have such a magnitude of investments as were necessary. On the contrary, it was often observed that whatever they could even invest was not done in the most judicious manner. On many occasions, money earmarked for developmental work had gone to corrupt pockets. Wrong policies of various Governments, poor education of the majority of people, poverty, poor health, lack of sincere efforts, prevailing corrupt practices etc. did not permit many nations to witness much progress and could not accrue its benefits.

Since the world came closer because of Telephones, Television, Fax, Computers, Satellite technology and e.mails, the people in the poor nations came to realize how their counterpart in rich countries live and what is their standard of living. Consumerism and affordability of the common man to buy things of their choices baffled the eyes of the people. The result was an increasing order of frustrations in the minds of many people. They began to ask the question if the people of those nations could do it, they must have done it at their expense, by exploiting the poor nations, by extracting their wealth, and/or by siphoning out their money, directly or indirectly.

1.4 TERRORISM

The developmental picture was not at all rosy everywhere. Many nations of the southern hemisphere could not come up to the mark. Their standard of living appeared to be in sharp contrast to that of what existed in the rich northern nations. Poverty, immature deaths, unemployment, injustice, suppression and oppression of people caused both by the Government and the powerful and rich of the society, brought in restlessness, anger, jealousy, and hatred in the minds of the people. Soon it became the hotbed of Terrorism. Many turned into terrorists to take revenge. The sentiments to become a terrorist grew rapidly and were carefully nurtured by the opportunists to satisfy their ulterior motifs. The burning anger in their minds was converted into deep hatred towards those who are more powerful and those who are better off. They considered their sufferings as an injustice to humanity. People from such strata of the society produced revolutionaries, freedom fighters, Guerillas and Terrorists, depending upon the needs, circumstances and the tasks they had to perform (87).

1.4.1 Emergence of Terrorism

People in the twentieth century had witnessed a lot of terrorist activities in as much as the world had gone through a great deal of mistrust, misrule, disparity between the haves and have-nots. This led to growing discontent, and chaos in different parts of the world. When sufferings reached at its maximal level, people became restless and daring. Many of them took guns in their hands. They wanted to take revenge and soon embarked upon violence and killings of people. Thus, terrorism emerged in the world. Terrorism has a deep root within the downtrodden class of the society. Terrorism was considered to be the weapon of the weak, an outlet of the growing frustrations and a satisfaction of the brewing grievances and hatred.

In some parts of the world, political upheavals, chaos and anarchy helped the small but organized groups of underground Revolutionaries, Guerillas, Freedom Fighters or Terrorists to organize and engage themselves to counteract the merciless killings, inhuman acts of the superstitious Government by imposition of draconian rules and regulations on the innocent people. Suppressive regimes were causing severe hardships and extreme sufferings for the common man. Poverty stricken millions died without any food. At the same time concentration of wealth was observed within a few families at the top, especially those who were running the Government. Funneling out of funds in the names of family members and relatives, maintenance of secret account in foreign banks, siphoning out national wealth leaving behind an almost empty treasury angered the common man. Disparities between the poor and rich increased, which led to growing disenchantment in the minds of common people. As a result, mass agitation, strikes, chaos, looting, breaking of law and order resulted in an overall anarchy, including attempts to overthrow people in power. Sometimes parties from outside the state accentuated such situations existing within the nations. Hatred obviously started brewing against those outsiders as well. So terrorism no longer remained a local activity, it became International.

The terrorists are desperate people. The concept of human-bomb killing innocent people here and there, derailing and damaging train lines and killing innocent passengers, destroying aeroplanes with bombs and explosives killing innocent civilians, bombing or laying mines on train lines, underground metros, bridges, places of mass gathering or worship etc. are some of the tactics used by the terrorists. Their intentions are to create terrors in the minds of the people.

Terrorist activities cost lot of money. So they have to take recourse to earning that money in a relatively easy way. So the terrorist organizations keep close touch with the suicide bombers, paid killers, smugglers, abductors, drug Mafias etc. to obtain funds. Sometimes they themselves are engaged in such activities. They also earn a lot of money from the sympathizers, sometimes by sponsoring Governments, political opponents of their targeted countries, religious fanatics and organizations etc. As has been said above, since any type of terrorist attack or activities cost a lot of money, they have to generate their own sources of funds. They need to accumulate lot of funds in order to finance various groups of people who become members of their organizations so that they can support their poor families. Incidentally, one terrorist organization keeps close touch with similar such organizations both within the country and outside the country. This helps them to procure arms and ammunitions, enter into international crimes, smuggling, drug and flesh business etc.

1.4.2 Some Examples of Terrorist Attacks

A report from the Center for National Security Studies published in 1995, had stated under International Terrorism in the U.S that according to an FBI (Federal Bureau of Investigation,

USA) estimate, in the past eleven years, there have been two major international terrorist incidents in the United States.

The FBI defines an International terrorism incident as one committed by a group or individual that is foreign-based and/or directed by countries or groups outside the United States or whose activities transcend national boundaries. One of the two incidents was the notorious bombing of the World Trade Center in February 1993. The other was not even directed against the U.S. and is hard to characterize as a serious incident: in April 1992, five opponents of the Iranian regime occupied the offices of the Iranian Mission to the United Nations in New York City. All the five were caught. They pled guilty and were sentenced to three months in jail.

1.4.3 Domestic Terrorism in the USA

According to the statistics maintained by the FBI, in 1994, there were no terrorist led attacks in the United States. One set of suspected terrorist incident was reported in the New York City. Some improvised explosive devices were discovered in two locations of the city. Incidentally, the devices did not detonate. The people behind it left behind a note where they criticized the Government of Israel as being too liberal. The 'McCabe Squad'and the 'Shield of David' signed this note. The case remained unsolved to date. This incident proves that sometimes to draw just the attention of the authority, some terrorist organization may also be involved in such activities as may be otherwise destructive.

In 1993 there were 11 terrorist cases in the USA. Nine of those eleven occurred in the same night and was caused by the animal rights activists who placed a small incendiary device in four Chicago departmental stores that sell furs. According to FBI the most active terrorist group in the U.S. have been the 'animal rights activists' and "skinheads".

In recent years (up to 1995), the number of terrorist incidents in the U.S. has been described as follows by the FBI-

Year	*Actual*	*Prevented*	*Suspected*
1994	0	0	1
1993	12	7	2
1992	4	0	0
1991	5	4	1
1990	7	5	1
1989	4	7	16

As noted above, all but one of the incidents under 'actual' was domestic in nature. According to available statistics, International terrorism was on the decline, but the lethality of incidents was on the rise.

The incidents reached a peak in 1987. However, the terrorist incidents were declining at the global level. In 1992, the State department recorded 365 incidents, down from 666 recorded in 1987. In 1993, the total incidents increased to 427. This increase was caused by a campaign of 150 attacks carried out by the 'Kurdistan Worker's Party' against Turkish interests in Western Europe on two separate days, in June and November, with about 75 attacks each day. In 1994, the terrorist incidents fell to 321; anti-U.S. attacks fell to 88 in 1993, down from 142 in 1992. Anti-U.S attacks fell in 1994 to 66, by comparison. There were 204 attacks against Americans in 1987. According to U.S. State department records about 21% of all terrorists attacks are against the U.S. targets.

In 1993, 109 people were killed and 1,393 were wounded in terrorists' incidents worldwide, the highest casualty total in five years. Six of those killed and nearly thousand of those wounded were Americans, all as a result of The World Trade Center Bombing. Prior to that, the most deadly attack against Americans was the downing of PAN AM 103, in which 189 Americans were killed. In 1992, 2 Americans were killed and one was wounded in terrorist incidents. In 1991, there were 7 American fatalities and 14 other casualties. In 1990, 12 Americans were killed and 11 injured in incidents worldwide.

Killing of President Anwar Sadat of Egypt, President John F. Kennedy of USA, Prime Minister Indira Gandhi and Rajiv Gandhi of India, Oklahoma city Disaster, Twin Tower Disaster, downing of several 747/757 Jumbo jets carrying hundreds of innocent passengers over the Atlantic ocean and elsewhere, bombings of US Embassy in several countries of the world, bombing of the US Navy tanker in Amman, Attack on American Center in Calcutta, India, Bombing on a Church in Pakistan, attack on the Parliament Building in New Delhi, India, repetitive killing of innocent civilians by bombing and mining attack in Jammu and Kashmir of India and in North East Frontier regions of India, abduction of tourists and news men in different parts of the world and many others are only a few of the major examples which are thought to have been master-minded by the terrorists. In the recent past there is again an upsurge of terrorist activities in different parts of the world.

Keeping behind all the previous statistics and the severity of terrorist-led incidents, 9/11 incident on the Twin Tower of the United States of America appeared to be the largest and most devastating of such operations, in terms of its planning, articulation, execution and direct and indirect loss of human lives and his property. Downing of the Twin Towers in the New York City was happened on that ill-fated day of September 11, 2001. Two Jumbo Jets 757 took off one after the other, at about 10 minutes interval, in the early morning of September 9 from the Logan Airport at Boston. They were to go in two different directions. But the terrorists diverted them in the air and asked the pilots to go toward Manhattan, New York. The first aircraft along its passengers, the pilot and the crewmembers and of course the terrorists came flying only to hit deliberately one of the Towers It hit at a strategic location high above the land. A big bang caused a huge explosion high up in the air. In the backdrop of the clear blue sky, deep black smoke, dusts and a huge amount of fire spiraled up causing massive crack and explosion. While people were watching from the streets, curious and surprised, came in another Jumbo Jet airliner before their eyes and penetrated directly into the other Tower. It resulted in a massive fire and destruction. Before the people in the First Tower could even realize as to what had happened, both the towers started sinking down, just like a child's wax house melts down in fire. The incident killed more than 3500 people, wounding several thousands who had undergone different types of treatments in a large number of hospitals both within and outside Manhattan. Several minutes later news came that another plane in the mean time hit one of the wings of the Pentagon Building on the same morning, while another Jet crash-landed somewhere in Pennsylvania. Apparently, this one was targeted for the "White House"- the official residence of the President of the United States of America.

It is an astounding but horrible example of the high-tech method masterminded by the terrorists. The incident had also shown the extent of devastation, which can be caused by such an attack. Such huge operations were very carefully planned, crafted and coordinated for several months or years to make it a full proof operation. All intelligence of all the countries of the world failed miserably to know or even to suspect beforehand that anything like this was in the offing. It did not give anybody any time to make any precautionary measure or any preparations. It was so uniquely masterminded by some determined, dedicated and fully committed Terrorists that the entire operations were kept tight-lipped and strictly secret.

Apart from the above there are a large number of scattered examples of terrorist-led operations of various kinds from different parts of the world. These will be discussed later. Some of the recent ones are-

Spraying of a deadly neurotoxic gas, Sarin, in the underground of a Metro in Japan, took a toll of several lives and created panic in the minds of thousands of people not too long ago. On February 6, 2004 a suicide bomb attack on a Moscow Metro blasted the train, killing 40 persons, and injuring 70 others. In the early morning of rush hours, about 8-30 am, the second coach of the train moving through the Center City was hit. About 700 passengers were to be evacuated. The Terrorist's design, and Al Qaida operatives involvement was also found in the serial bomb blasts on 8 compartments of a train in Madrid, Spain, recently in the month of March, 2004, killing about 200 people and injuring more than 1500.Almost every month, hundreds of innocent people are dying in the hands of Terrorists in Jammu and Kashmir or India, in Pakistan, Nepal and in some mid-eastern nations.

When we look at the history, there is no clear-cut evidence to prove whether or not the terrorists ever used biological and chemical weapons against the people in large numbers. However, there remains a lot of suspicion that such weapons were in fact used, during the Vietnam and Cambodian war, at least to test for its potentialities. The potential to use weapons of mass destruction to make the enemies debilitated, disabled and destabilized in large numbers within a short period of time, say within overnight, appear to exist in today's troubled world. Therefore, the question of complacency does not arise at all. Recently, what was suspected at one time became very evident that nuclear proliferation is not at all a myth. It's a reality!

Various world news organizations flashed a report that the chief of the Pakistani Nuclear Power Program openly declared on camera that he and his colleagues transferred sophisticated nuclear technology to Libya, North Korea and Iran and that China was also involved in it. Soon the newspapers published another report that some terrorist organization possesses "Dirty Bomb" or "Nuclear Bomb in a brief case". If these are true, it is a matter of great concern all over the world.

1.5 DEFINITION OF TERRORISM

An act of terrorism is the intentional use of or threat to use of violence against anybody, including civilians or against civilian targets, as also the military targets, in order to attain personal or political gains. The aim of the activity is to take revenge by hook or by crook.

The terrorists remain invisible to carry out their operations very secretly just like political spies in earlier days. Oftentimes their plans are meticulous. Their science is well advanced and technology based. They keep their timing of operations very exact and strikes all on a sudden. They do not give any time to their opponents to take any preparatory measures in order to counter the attacks. The people who are directly engaged in such deadly task are totally dedicated individuals. They are fully committed to the cause and are ready to die. They move toward their targets bit by bit, but steadily, until their ulterior motif is realized. Such type of TOTAL commitment is the 'Hallmark of Terrorism'.

A violent activity against civilians that has no political quest has been defined as an act of criminal intention associated with serious repercussions. On some occasions, the violent act could simply be just an act of insanity without any motif related to terrorism. In any case, some tend to add ideological or religious objectives to the list of political aims in the terrorist activities.

Terrorism is differentiated from other types of political violence, such as Guerilla warfare, civil insurrection etc. Terrorism exploits the tremendous vulnerability of the civilians in order to create a terror or an anxiety in order to attract intense media reactions. If the perpetrators choose to attack military targets or military installations, it would be considered Guerilla warfare as against terrorist attack.

1.5.1 Distinction among Terrorism, National Liberation Movement and Guerilla Warfare

Many different terminologies are found in the literature while going to describe an act of destruction or devastation. It would be of much interest to critically examine the acts and operations with the activities of a terrorist, and that of a freedom fighter and a Guerilla fighter. It has been observed that often those terminologies have been taken as synonymous with each other, which it is not.

Attempts to legitimize terrorist activities as a part of national liberation movement has been made from time to time. It has been argued that if terrorist activities are directed against

AFTERNOON EXTRA EDITION

THE CINCINNATI ENQUIRER

FROM THE AIR

U.S. ATTACKED

Hijacked airliners lead terrorist assault on World Trade Center, Pentagon

Fig. 1.1. Terrorists of the AL-Qaida organization of Mr. Bin Laden made the unprecedented suicidal assault of the World Trade Center, at Manhattan, New York, using highjacked 747 Jumbo Jet Airliner full of passengers and members of the crew on September 11, 2001 at around 9-00 am.

Fig. 2.3. While a huge explosion causing a gulf of fire just set in the first Tower, the second Tower was hit.

the opponent enemy regime, its military installations, warehouses stockpiling arms and ammunitions, military barracks, political leaders etc., such kind of terrorist activities were often given a berth in the whole series of tactics and approaches adopted in the warfare of weaker nations to fight out the more powerful and mighty.

The following distinctions can be made between the activities of a freedom fighter or a revolutionary and the terrorist.

(*a*) A Freedom fighter or a revolutionary doesn't blow up buses or trains containing non-combatants, but the terrorists' do.

(*b*) A Freedom fighter or a revolutionary never attack innocent Children, school and colleges, the terrorists' do.

(*c*) Usually no freedom fighter deliberately attacks the innocent people. They have never killed small children, passers-by on the street, foreign visitors, newsmen or other civilians. Such concepts may be considered as groundless and confusing when terrorism is included as a part of the freedom movement, especially by the weak opposition and against a foreign ruler. If their strategy includes uprooting them by hook or by crook, the freedom fighting might take a different turn at that time.

According to the above definition normally the freedom struggle do not involve violence or threat of violence. Non-violent protests, general strikes, peaceful demonstrations, mass agitation, non-cooperation movement, pen-down strikes, dharna, tax revolts etc. are not in the agenda of terrorist activities, but all these are included in the programs of the freedom fighters. The non-cooperation movement of Mahatma Gandhi for freedom and independence of India, the movement against Apartheid of Mr.Nelson Mandella in South Africa, the Civil liberty movement of Mr. Martin Luther King in USA, all falls in the category of Freedom Movement.

1.5.2 Guerilla Warfare

In the past century the world had witnessed many Guerilla warfare in different parts of the world. The Vietnam wars, Cambodian war, the separatist movement of Tamilians in Sri Lanka etc. are some of those examples. The Guerillas tend to fight in small groups to occupy small places at a time in order to establish their military installations. They try to grow gradually in terms of strength, increase in numbers, and mobilize equipment to fight the troops of the Government. Guerilla War is a small war and is localized in a small area. It is subject to the same rules and regulations that apply to big wars, and so it differs from terrorism.

1.5.3 What has Given Birth to Modern Terrorists?

As has been discussed earlier, with the improvement in the standard of living of people all around, and as the distance and disparities between the "haves and have-nots" increased, it resulted in hatred and jealousy in the minds of some of the people, who belonged to the class of downtrodden, backward and victims of the society. This culminated in the development of a mind-set to cause harm to those who, they think, are responsible for their misfortune. Many people have given different connotations to the cause of the terrorists to justify their motivations, heinous attitudes, and their destructive activities. However, it is the deepest hatred, which motivates one towards terrorist activities.

The terrorist leaders very often project themselves as an extraordinary human being-as the preacher of a major religious thought or of a cult. They want to create something new and astounding to glorify them. A new type of social order and/or a new cult is born in this manner. They exploit the disadvantaged, the poor, the oppressed or the suppressed, the unemployed, and the rebels of the society, and recruit them in their outfit. They subject them to rigorous training to make them totally dedicated to a 'cause'. We have seen a number of examples of that during the 20th Century, wherein a large number of people even drank poison at the behest of their spiritual leader to embrace death. Perhaps many more such incidents will emerge during the 21st century.

1.5.4 What is the Main Feature of a Terrorist?

The terrorists are just like any other person. The terrorists are usually smarter than many intellectually advanced personalities. Some times they are very well read. They have some extra mental power and strength over and above most of the people. Some may be mentally ill or deranged. Some may be of violent nature. Some others may be very cool tempered.

Sociologists noted that disliking of various social, cultural, economic and political acts or deeds of some nations, which have direct or indirect negative impacts on the lives of people from an altogether different social, cultural and economic conditions, directly or indirectly, may make the people of the latter hostile against those of the former group, who are better-off. Such feelings may percolate down to the common man. Their helplessness and despair create anger and hatred in their minds, and thus may prompt them to become terrorists.

Fig. 1.3. A massive amount of black smoke, dusts and debris spiraled through the entire skyline of the Manhattan Island of New York. Picture was taken from the other side of the Hudson River.

1.5.5 Psyche of a Terrorist: Distinguishing Features

As has been discussed above, a Terrorist's mind is like that of any other person, except for the fact that they are often restless, not satisfied with the normal work or activities, and would like to do some heroic activities of a major type to draw satisfaction out of that. The terrorists' mind roams around such avenues and an ordinary person does normally not visit rugged terrains as. They find enjoyment in such type of acts, happenings and occurrences, which are normally dared and hated by most of the people and feared by many.

Fig. 1.4. A portion of the PENTAGON Building was severely damaged by another hijacked passenger airliner used by the same terrorist group on the same day.

In fact, the make up of a terrorist mind is quite different from an ordinary person. Sometimes they may be highly educated or just a layperson. They may or may not be always sophisticated. But they are smart people and quite intelligent. They are usually soft spoken, simple, and having either very soft or very rough-looking eyes. Their looks are very sharp, sometimes of a piercing nature. They are always very alert. Today's terrorists are highly trained in using modern technology, computers, and cell phones. Some of them know how to analyze satellite imagery, can interfere and interrupt telecommunication messages, and know how to hack to dig down computer information or damage computer functions by introducing virus in it. Many of them are trained pilots, engineers, doctors and scientists.

The terrorists lose their faith and confidence against almost everything. Their anger may be directed against some individuals, some groups, and even some countries. Their revengeful minds are easily attracted by the terrorist organizations, which come forward to recruit them, train them and use them for such operations as may cost even their own lives. To take revenge is their only obsession. Some of them may often be misinterpreted as a mad man, which of course they are not.

Fig. 1.5. A close up picture of the damages caused to a portion of the PENTAGON Building.

2 Historical Perspectives on Accidents Causing Major Chemical Disasters: Deliberate Terrorist Attack: Dropping of an Atom Bomb

In this chapter we will discuss about various forms of disasters caused by chance accidents or were caused by the terrorists. Examples will be drawn from the history including the devastations, which were caused due to the dropping of the Atom Bomb on Hiroshima and Nagasaki of Japan.

Apart from terrorist's attack using hazardous chemical/biological/radiological agents or other gadgets leading to both small and large disasters, accidental explosions can also cause disasters of a very large magnitude. A quick review of some of them might help in our understanding of various aspects of a disaster. This might also help us realize as to what kind of preparedness is necessary to cope with such kind of disasters.

Smart and knowledgeable as the Terrorists are, they often generate new, novel and unconventional methods, such as car bombs, bombs placed in suitcases, luggage and shoe containing explosives etc. Besides, they very often use suicide-bombers where bombs/ explosives are wrapped around the body of the individual, which are either put to work by an impact or through a remote control detonating device.

Recent use of aeroplanes for the destruction of the Twin Towers in the New York city in 2001, and use of postal mails to transmit virulent organisms and toxins, such as anthrax and Ricin, certainly have some novelty in it. These are far from the conventional type of approach, and are very difficult to apprehend in advance, or even suspect for taking preventive measures. Normally the terrorists pick up those agents, which can transmit very quickly, very rarely seen, used or utilized, and so can not be diagnosed very easily, and whose treatment is normally not available or are available in a few places only.

Some of the potential chemical, biological and radiological agents as may be used by the terrorists have been mentioned in the next Chapter in some detail. A very short account of that is presented below:

2.1 TOXIC/HAZARDOUS AGENTS AS WEAPONS OF THE TERRORIST

Apart from the Bioorganisms and Biotoxins, which may be used by the terrorists, there is tremendous likelihood that they may choose highly toxic chemical agents as well. Among them are - Ricin, Aflatoxins, Toxic pesticides, Chlorine gas, Oleum gas, HCN (Hydrocyanic acid) gas, Potassium cyanide etc. Therefore, tanks storing them and tankers transporting them from one place to another might be the target of a terrorist attack. Details about such chemical agents are described later in a separate chapter (Chapter III).

2.2 POSSIBLE BIOORGANISMS/TOXINS AS WEAPONS OF THE TERRORISTS

Anthrax spores, Yellow fever virus, Dengue virus, Rocky mountain spotted fever virus, Small pox virus, Plague virus, Botulinum toxin, Diphtheria and Tetanus toxin and several other deadly poisons could be the potential target for use by the terrorists. This is particularly because that against most of them proper diagnostics and treatment is not available. In the event of an epidemic kind of attack or spread, it would be very difficult for most of the countries of the world, to first of all diagnose them properly and also to find proper treatment for them. In certain cases, even if the prophylactics and therapeutics are available, it may not be available in sufficient quantities as may otherwise be needed. These are the main issues and outstanding problems, which still remain as a challenge at the International level. A detailed account of several bioorganisms as potential bioweapons has been detailed in the next chapter. NIAID Biodefense Research in USA categorized the priority pathogens into three Categories, A, B, and C.

Category A

- Bacillus anthracis (anthrax)
- Clostridium botulinum
- Yersinia pestis
- Variola major (small pox) and other pox viruses
- Francisella tularensis (tularemia)
- Viral hemorrhagic fevers
    1. Arenaviruses
        (*a*) LCM, Junin virus, Machup virus, Guanarito virus
        (*b*) Lassa fever
    2. Bunyaviruses
        (*a*) Hantaviruses
        (*b*) Rift Valley Fever
    3. Flaviruses
        (*a*) Dengue

4. Filoviruses
   (*a*) Ebola
   (*b*) Marburg

Category B

- Burkholeria pseudomallei
- Coxiella burnetti (Q fever)
- Brucella species (brucellosis)
- Burkholderia mallei (glanders)
- Ricin toxin (from Ricinus communis)
- Epsilon toxin of Clostridium perfringens
- Staphylococcus enterotoxin B
- Typhus fever (Rickettsia prowazeki)
- Food and Waterborne pathogens

1. Bacteria
   (*a*) Diarrheagenic E.coli
   (*b*) Pathogenic vibrios
   (*c*) Shigella species
   (*d*) Salmonella
   (*e*) Listeria monocytogenes
   (*f*) Campylobacter jejuni
   (*g*) Yersinia enterocolitica
2. Viruses (Caliciviruses, Hepatitis A)
3. Protozoa
   (*a*) Cryptosporidium parvum
   (*b*) Cyclospora cayatenensis
   (*c*) Giardia lamblia
   (*d*) Entamoeba histolytica
   (*e*) Toxoplasma
   (*f*) Microsporidia
4. Additional viral encephalides
   (*a*) West Nile virus
   (*b*) LaCrosse
   (*c*) California encephalitis
   (*d*) VEE
   (*e*) EEE
   (*f*) WEE
   (*g*) Japanese Encephalitis Virus
   (*h*) Kysanur Forest Virus

Category C

Emerging infectious disease threats such as Nipah virus and additional Hantaviruses (the readers may consult NIAID website, updated up to June 13, 2002.

- Tick borne hemorrhagic fever viruses
  (*a*) Crimean Congo Hemorrhagic fever virus
- Tickborneencephalitis viruses
- Yellow fever
- Multidrug resistant TB
- Influenza
- Other Rickettsias
- Rabies

2.3 NIAID HIGH PRIORITY BIODEFENSE PRODUCTS

This includes design, development and testing of products specific to NIAID Category A-C priority areas.

Therapeutics

1. Antivirals, especially against smallpox and viral hemorrhagic fevers
2. Antitoxins to B.anthracis and C.botulinum
3. Narrow-spectrum antibiotics, especially for anthrax
4. Passive immunotherapeutics, including antibodies and soluble receptors
5. Broadly reactive antimicrobials

Vaccines

1. Cell-based smallpox vaccines
2. Tularemia vaccines
3. Plague vaccines
4. Rift Valley Fever vaccines
5. Novel influenza vaccine strategies, including vaccines against pandemic influenza
6 C. botulinum/botulimum toxin vaccines

Adjuvants/Immunostimulants

1. New immunostimulatory agents including adjuvants
2. Immune assessment of responses to drugs/infections/vaccines in different individuals/subpopulations
3. Products to induce enhanced innate immune protection in the lungs, gastrointestinal tract, or systemically.

Diagnosis

1. Methods for detection of NIAID Category A-C priority agents.

   Tests that evaluate the possible spectrum of antimicrobial resistance of genetic manipulation.

   High-throughput screens (*e.g.*, microchip-based platforms).

   Functional genomic tools to identify multiple organisms simultaneously.

   Novel immune assays to study human immune responses.

   Identification of novel or improved biomarkers for human immune activation.

   In vivo imaging methods and development of contrast reagents for visualization of pathogens or host immune responses in vivo.

   Clinical diagnostic tools for human eczema.

Resources

1. Vaccine delivery systems and platform technologies.
2. Software development as tools for genetic, genomic and proteomic analysis and modeling of host pathogen interactions.
3. Screening tools and services for high throughput antigen identification.
4. Appropriate standardized cell cultures and animal models for antimicrobial vaccine testing and development.
5. Validated assays to measure toxicity, safety, efficacy/immunity and other host responses needed for product licensure.

Tremendous research and developmental work is essential in all the areas mentioned above to be able to cope with rare bioorganism-related infections, terrorist acts, accidental exposures etc. Details of hazardous Biological agents, their diagnosis, and treatment etc. are described separately in another chapter (Chapter III) later.

2.4 RADIOLOGICAL WEAPONS

Although there exists a remote possibility that a terrorist in his attack against the enemies will ever use Radiological agents or Atom Bombs emanating radioactivity, nothing can give any guarantee that it will never happen. The 21st century inherited that threat from what the world had witnessed during the 20th century. Although seemingly it still appears impossible to get access to all the necessary items required for the manufacture of an atom bomb, secret nuclear proliferation is still possible. Possibility of use of "Dirty Bomb" by a terrorist, however, appears to be a strong one. Although not as devastating as the Atomic Bomb, the Dirty Bomb can still cause substantial damage to both human and animal lives, and pollute the environment around us.

Let us examine the requirements for the manufacture of an atomic device. First of all, to make an atomic bomb there is a need of many sophisticated technology, large number of highly trained manpower, secret but sophisticated installations, and huge amount of funds.

Nobody himself or any small group alone is likely to proceed in this direction. But if the State or States sponsor such programs together, the situation will be devastating.

Very recently some disturbing news appeared in the Press and Television. The Chief of the Pakistani Atomic Power Programme, Dr. Amir Qadeer Khan, confessed on camera that he and, at his instruction, his colleagues had disclosed atomic power secret, the Centrifuge Technology to purify Uranium to make it a nuclear grade material, to several countries, such as Iran, Lybia and North Korea. United States Intelligence also brought about similar such reports. The entire world, the United Nations, and the International Atomic Energy Commission got stunned in that in spite of their best efforts not to allow further escalation of atomic power capability all that happened secretly. It has also been revealed that China had initially provided to the Pakistani authorities the drawings of a design for assembling an imposition type nuclear bomb that could fit atop a large ballistic missile. "It was just what you would have on the factory floor. It tells you what torque to use on the bolts and what glue to use on the parts"- Washington Post reported (February 15, 2004). It also stated " The Chinese designs were later resold to Libya, by the Pakistani-led trading net-work that is now the focus of an expanding International probe"—the Washington Post said. The packet of documents found in Lybia, some of which were in Chinese, contained the details of that manual. This information may only be the tip of the iceberg. Certainly lot more must have been happening in different parts of the world secretly. Thus escalation or proliferation of nuclear technology has been going on directly or indirectly. Nuclear ambitions of North Korea and Iran are no longer a secret.

According to a BARC (Bhabha Atomic Research Center, Trombay, India) several countries of the world possess operable nuclear reactors (Further reading No. 2). The major ones are:

Country	*Reactors Operable as of June 2003*	
	No. of Units	*Capacity, MW (e)*
USA	104	98523
France	59	63293
Japan	53	44153
Russia	30	20793
UK	27	12082
Germany	19	21141
Republic of Korea	18	14870
Canada	14	9998
India	14	2503
Ukraine	13	11195
Sweden	11	9460

Only those countries, which have operable reactors in double-digit figures, are listed above. Besides that, countries such as Argentina, Armenia, Belgium, Brazil, Bulgaria, China, Czech Republic, Finland, Lithuania, Mexico, Netherlands, Pakistan, Romania, Slovak republic, Slovenia, South Africa, Spain, Switzerland, and Taiwan. Iran and North Korea were having one each of the Reactors under construction, having the capacity of 950 MW (e), as of June 2003.

Thus, apart from big Nuclear powers, there are several smaller nuclear power capabilities in the world. Only the United Nations and its constituent Agencies, in collaboration with all the atomic powers of the world will have to meet urgently in an International assembly, to review the present situation and enact Internal Laws, Guidelines and regulations etc. to stop and control the nuclear proliferation in the world. Otherwise it might pose severe dangers to the future of humanity

2.5 SOME HISTORICAL EXPERIENCES

2.5.1 From Chemical Accidents in Bhopal

Any chance accident like that of what happened in the Union carbide factory at Bhopal, Madhya Pradesh, India in the year 1984, between the nights of December 2 and 3, is the major one. This took a heavy toll of human, animal, and plant lives in the history of any chemical disasters. Besides killing 2500 human beings just overnight, it caused permanent health damage to several thousands of people who are still suffering long after 20 years. About 10,000 animals died. Hundreds and thousands of trees, plants and foliages were churned to death. The water curtain, which was used around the storage tank areas in an effort to contain the toxic cloud, finally drained down with the toxic washings to the nearest lake killing hundreds and thousands

Fig. 2.1. Picture of an unknown dead child among other Bhopal Gas victims.

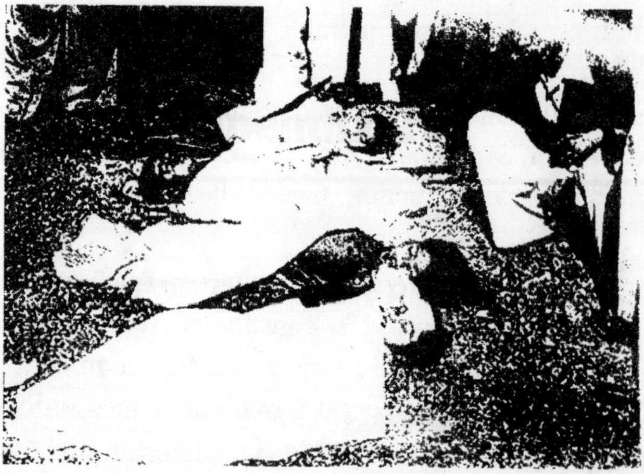

Fig. 2.2. Child victims of Bhopal Toxic gas tragedy, which killed more than 2500 people, and injured more than 10,000 due to the release of deadly Methyl Isocyanate from a 40 ton storage tank.

of fishes and destroying other aquatic animals and phytoplankton's making the water poisonous. The Bhopal Government had to declare that the water of the lake is poisonous and unsuitable and unsafe for human and animal use. So far as the health damages are concerned, severe damages had been caused in the lungs, brain, skin, immune function and germ cells. Genetic damages just like that of radiation exposure, which might continue generations after generations, were also observed in the toxic gas exposed population and in experimental animals exposed deliberately to methyl isocyanate (MIC) gas. The author of this book (PKR), has published a large number of papers on the deleterious aspects of MIC toxicity on humans which was due to their exposure to the toxic gas released during the Bhopal disaster (46, 72,86,93,101), and which resulted from deliberate exposure of animals to methyl isocyanate gas (28,32, 47- 49,73, 74, 94).

2.5.2 Experiences from the Terrorists' Attack on Twin Towers and Anthrax Mail Scare in the USA

Recent terrorist attack on Twin Towers on 9/11/2001 and that with "Anthrax Mail" later once again brought to light that, given such type of things to happen again, we are very vulnerable in such a situation. It pointed out very strongly that there should be a regular type of preparedness, as that of the fire-fighting agency, which can be utilized immediately and made functional within minutes, in order to save both the lives and properties of tens of thousands of people.

The world had witnessed an unprecedented leadership of New York Mayor Rudolf Juliani, Governor George Pataki, and President George Bush during the September 11, 2001 Twin Tower Disaster. They led the state and the nation with proper zeal, courage, wisdom and hopes, and mobilized all available technology, medical help, public support system, rehabilitation measures etc. If such disasters would have stricken elsewhere, the sufferings and loss could have become much more but for their timely actions. There is no question about it. The damages would have been severe, and it would have taken many more months, even years, to stand firm again to reorganize and rebuilt.

Mayor Juliani mobilized his men of law and order and also the fire fighters to deal with the aftermath of the disaster. As the Jumbo Jet 757 hit the first Tower most people thought that it might be a Bomb attack. But within minutes, in front of hundreds and thousands of eyewitnesses who were already out of the buildings and all those who were on the streets still watching, another Jumbo Jet airliner hit the second tower. The whole thing appeared to have melted down like a wax house. A huge amount of fire engulfed the entire area. As soon as people started realizing that something dangerous had happened, they came out of their office rooms in the towers and started running down the escalators. Some people got stuck within a running elevator, which stopped all on a sudden. There was a tremendous rush in the escalator. Finding no place to go out of the building, some people got panicky and jumped down from the window of possibly greater than 60 or 70th floor, before the eyes of thousands of people outside. Many got tired of running down the stairs. They sat there for help. Some came forward to carry them down. Some could make it, while some others not. Many people, fire fighters and security men in the mean time tried to come up to help all those who might be stuck up there. Many people and rescuers went up and could not come down. The floors collapsed before their eyes. Some were caught up in the fire while rushing out of their office rooms, when they went there trying to look for somebody. Some remained on the stairs itself and could not make it. There was a total chaos, but people did not lose their cool. They showed unprecedented amount of discipline, selflessness and brotherhood, and even sacrificed their own lives for others.

Many could run down the streets and were trying to flee. Many people witnessed the whole situation standing on the streets, footpaths, from the windows of the adjacent buildings but could not realize as to what really had happened. In the mean time, people started rushing out taking the injured people to shelter, some were looking for ambulances or taxis to take the injured to near-by hospitals.

Just before thousands of glaring eyes who were watching in the back - drop of the clear blue sky of the city, about 15 minutes after the first incidence, another 757 Jumbo Jet simply penetrated deep into the second Tower. Immediately there was an explosion. The building looked like a wax house and simply melted down. A huge cloud of fire and dusts were seen from far distance. It was an awesome sight! A horrific scenario! An unbelievable thing must have happened. Soon it was realized that the Enemies of America, have invaded the mainland USA for the first time in its history. It is only at that time that the people realized that it might be a Terrorist's design. Immediately the news went out far and near that " Enemies of America, the Terrorists, have attacked America. There might be more to follow".

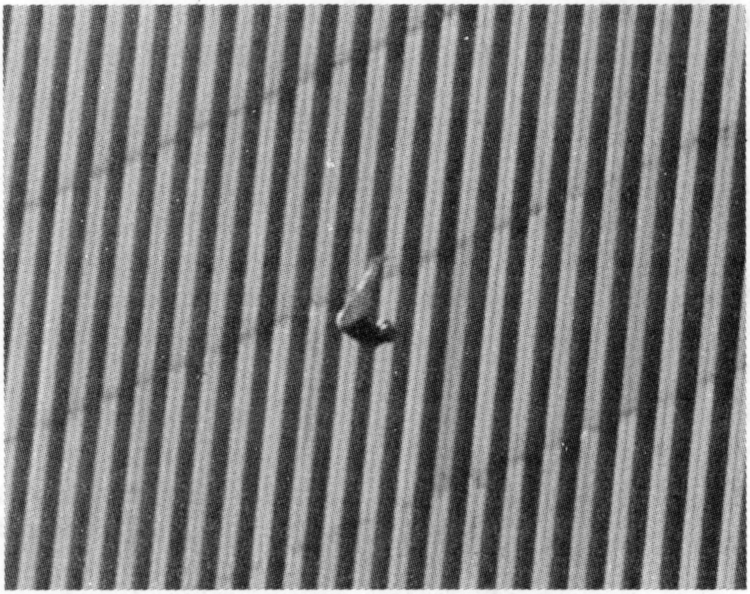

Fig. 2.4. A panic-stricken person jumped out of one of the windows of the building, high above the 70th floor, with the hope possibly to save him.

Fig. 2.5. Everything was happening before the eyes of people at the famous China-Town at Manhattan, New York.

Immediately the Government took several measures. All the airports were immediately closed. No flying or landing of aircraft was permitted. A Red Alert was given all over. Military fighter planes flew up in the sky to intercept any possible enemy planes to chase them in the sky itself. All security measures were immediately taken. President Bush, who was not at

Washington, was taken in a remote unidentified place, by diverting his plane in the sky. He was informed about it when he was visiting a children's school. Without any visible perturbation, he immediately asked about more information and left the place. The Vice President Mr. Dick Cheney took the temporary charge of the Government.

When they learnt that more planes are coming towards the "White House", all the people of the "White House" were evacuated immediately. All planes in the sky were grounded immediately. All airports and Harbors were ordered closed for any incoming and outgoing flights. Ships stopped in the mid-sea. Clear instructions were given to bring down any aircraft if they do not follow the instructions to be given to them by the patrolling aircraft in the sky. F-16 fighter jets, Tom Hawk, were engaged in the operation. It started roaming around big cities, airports, and other major sensitive and vulnerable sites of the nation in order to protect them, and also to chase any such terrorist plane, if suspected.

Fig. 2.6. Soon after the attack, the New York City was closed to all Traffic.

In the meantime news came that another plane had flown into one of the arms of the Pentagon Building Complex - the site of the Military power of the World's mightiest nation on earth. Something, which was unthinkable, and unimaginable until recently, had happened. What a big challenge, which has been thrown to this power center of the most powerful nation on earth!

Fig. 2.7. All flights from all the airports were cancelled also.

Later it was realized that another plane was headed towards Washington D.C. to hit the "White House"- the official residence and office of the President of the United States of America. But it was gathered later that because of the heroic sacrifices of some of the passengers in that aircraft, who intercepted the terrorists within the aircraft and tried to prevent them from doing such heinous crime such that the plane had to divert its journey from going towards Washington D.C and crash-landed somewhere in the outskirts of Pennsylvania. Those brave Americans died along with others by creating a history. While sitting on their seats in the aircraft, they heard the conversations of the terrorists and realized that they were planning to go to Washington, D.C. to make a major strike on the "White House", they came forward and fought with the terrorists within the aircraft.

An unprecedented and horrific happening! Simultaneously, the world had once again witnessed some exemplary sacrifices of lives of common man for some noble cause. They intercepted the terrorists to save the lives of their President and died. The world saluted such heroes. A new chapter has been written in history.

As has been said above, what was unthinkable to reach by anybody that was reached by the terrorists, not using very high-tech, but by using low-tech approaches. It looked almost like a Hollywood movie. The melting down of the superstructures of the Twin Towers almost looked like melting down of a wax house. Human bodies were observed falling down the windows of the building. Body parts were scattered all around within the huge amount of bricks, metal parts, smoke and dusts. Large amount of smoke and dusts rushed towards every direction of all the streets of Manhattan. It entered through the windows of apartments in the adjacent areas. The dust-covered people were coughing, crying, shouting, sobbing and running in any direction they could, out of fear and anxiety in their minds, only to save their lives. A man-made disaster of a very serious dimension took place at lower Manhattan, New York on the morning of September 11, around 9-05 and 9-20 am.

Fig. 2.8. A close-up view of the picture at Figure 2.3.

Soon appeared the face of the President of USA, Mr. George W. Bush on the Television screen. He declared, "America is under attack, the Democracy is under attack. The freedom and the life style of the free society are under attack. We have to remain calm and firm to deal with the situation, so that the enemies of Democracy lose and we win. Win we must".

A bewildered nation watched with tears in their eyes. A shocked world mourned. Never before in the history of the United States of America, this country was ever attacked on its mainland and main territory, except for one such attempt on Pearl Harbor, although not on the mainland. The sleeping Giant was provoked. Its wounds started causing pains. Its vanity and dignity was shattered. The feeling of supremacy and superiority were hurt. Somebody tried to make USA a fool, an under dog, in spite of so much of its might in economic, scientific and technological power.

2.5.3 What Did the World Learn Out of this Incident?

The world learnt a great deal out of this incident. That proper kind of leadership, availability of proper technology, ability to mobilize resources and above all solidarity of the people of the nation, are some of the much-needed virtues, which are a must to be able to cope with such type of disasters. In spite of such magnificent leadership and preparedness, more than 3500 human lives were immediately lost, several thousands injured. A large number of families lost their only earning member. Many lost their father, mother, sons, husbands, daughters, wives and friends. Billions of dollars worth of property damage threw a spell on the entire business world both in and outside USA. World market got shattered. So much so that it needed a considerable period of time to recuperate. American business paid a heavy toll. There was an indirect effect on the entire business communities of the world. Many of them who had their offices in the twin tower buildings and its surroundings had to close down their shutter. Some could reopen their businesses several months later, but on a different location. Small shop owners lost their businesses altogether, since the entire area was cordoned off and traffic and pedestrian movements were restricted. Although the Federal Government and the nation came forward to raise sufficient funds to rebuild and reconstruct, even after more than two years now the rehabilitation, reconstruction and rebuilding job could not be completed.

2.6 EXPERIENCES FROM BIOLOGICAL WEAPONS

Although there are differences of opinions on the official statistics available regarding the extent of damages that a Bioterrorist kind of attack can cause, that the devastations could be severe there is no question about it. In 1993, the U.S. congressional Office of the Technology Assessment made a statement that releasing 100 kilograms of aerosolized anthrax spores in the aerial environmental of a city like Washington D.C., the capital of USA, could kill an estimated number of about 130,000 to 3 Million people. Such lethality only matches with that of a Hydrogen Bomb.

In the year 2000, U.S. Justice Department revealed that discharging pneumonic plague spores, say in Denver, could make an estimated number of about 3000 or more people becoming sick, with an estimated death of 950 or more within a week.

More dangerous and devastating situations can be caused due to the release of small pox organisms, according to an U.S. Air Force exercise. It has been indicated that if small poxvirus were released in Oklahoma City, it would take less than two months to kill more than a million people all over the world. It is contagious and spreads very fast all around. Businessmen, tourists, diplomats who may visit such a place may carry these germs from one place to another or from one country to another.

Mysteries still prevail whether the recent (2001) episodes of mailed Anthrax spores and loss of several lives in Florida, New York, New Jersey, US capital and other places was related to Bioterrorist activities. Such a suspicion was obvious, because of September 11, 2001 Twin Tower Disaster which was caused and master-minded by highly sophisticated and trained 21st century terrorists led by Mr. Bin Laden, leader of the AL QAIDA organization.

During late 2003 and early 2004, some incidents of sending mails containing deadly RICIN powder to the office of the US Congressional leader took place. It created panic once again. But because of earlier preparations all due measures were immediately taken. Many people were quarantined; US congressional offices had to be closed for clean up operations. No body was allowed entry there for fear of possible contamination.

2.7 CHERNOBYL EXPERIENCE

Several years ago release of radioactive substances from Chernobyl Atomic Reactor in Russia had been witnessed by the world with chilling coolness. No body knew as to what was going to happen. It was gathered that in order to release the internal pressure, built over a period of time, it was considered necessary to release deliberately some amount of pressure to save an otherwise major disaster. It would have led to a major explosion otherwise. The released air containing radioactivity traversed through a long area in Europe, particularly throughout Eastern Europe, causing fallouts of radioactivity in a vast area on the ground. This contaminated water, soil, grass and other food materials of livestock, poultry, fish etc. As a result, milk, meat, dairy products and poultry eggs were all contaminated with radioactivity. Use of these items was banned for sometime in Europe and adjacent countries.

Unfortunately, newspapers in some countries published some disturbing reports of the presence of those contaminated foodstuffs in some of the developing countries causing local agitations etc. Whether those contaminated foods were smuggled out or deliberately given away in the name of 'aid' and channelized in some of the developing nations of the world was not quite clear. But radioactivity had been detected in some of the far-off countries on the soil and grass.

2.8 HIROSHIMA AND NAGASAKI EXPERIENCE

In order to take revenge on Japan, because of their bombing on Pearl Harbor, the US dropped Atom Bombs on Hiroshima and Nagasaki during the Second World War. The world had witnessed for the first time the severity of the damages that an Atom Bomb can cause on human lives and his property. As soon as the World heard about it, everybody became speechless. The people were stunned. Fear and anxiety gripped the entire nations of the world. And there were obvious reasons for that.

The heat and fire generated as a result of the explosion almost roasted everything it found on its way. A vast area of an entire city was devastated completely. Almost nothing was left back. The mushrooming cloud formed in the sky because of the explosion was seen from a long distance. It carried with it huge amount of radioactivity. It traveled through many miles because of the wind current. All those areas through which it passed, the people were subjected to large amount of radioactive fallouts, which contaminated the entire areas and its water, plants, vegetables, livestock feed etc. Hundreds and thousands of people died instantaneously. Several thousands, who were exposed but survived, became its long-term victims. They suffered from a variety of disorders and malfunctions - from mutational, teratogenic and carcinogenic effects to immunosuppression, neurological disorders, heart and lung troubles, bone deformations, abnormal mental behavior, abnormal childbirth and many others. Some of those health problems lingered through several generations. Children were born with deformed limbs and abnormal mental status. Abnormal childbirth was very frequent and common among the exposed women. Many people are still suffering from cancer. Abortion of the child and premature delivery is very common among those who were pregnant during the time they were exposed to radiation.

2.9 HOW REAL IS IT THAT THE TERRORISTS WILL EVER USE RADIOLOGICAL WEAPONS?

Nobody has the real answer as to whether or not the terrorists or any lunatic ruler will ever drop an atom bomb on any nation of the world. First, its manufacturing procedure is extremely difficult, and very expensive, Secondly, the amount of material required for a reasonable size Atom Bomb in order to cause a massive destruction would require sophisticated technology, highly trained scientists, huge amounts of funds, sophisticated control device for its limited tests, including the knowledge of its de-contamination.

But to-day's world there is no doubt in anybody's mind that no matter what, those devices with deadly poisons can be manufactured, stockpiled and even used when needed. Such knowledge and technology is available. Besides, international smuggling of uranium, highly sophisticated process technology for purification of uranium to make it weapon-grade radiological material, reactor technology etc. are being continued secretly, as has been recently (2004) revealed by Dr. Abdul Qadeer Khan, the architect of Pakistan's Nuclear Power Technology.

Dr. Khan himself declared on camera that he and his colleagues had divulged the nuclear secret to Libya, Iran and North Korea. In course of time it came out that there are "private network and individuals" who are also engaged in the International trade of nuclear technology and radioactive materials. Such a network has been suspected to engage private individuals in a number of countries of the world. Obviously, therefore, there remains no doubt that some people or countries are interested to empower them with the knowledge of nuclear technology. It has also come out in the Newspaper that AL QAIDA organization possesses nuclear technology and also some amount of purified uranium good for radioactive arsenals.

Now possibility exists that the terrorists may sometimes do the mischief by spraying radioactive chemicals having long half-life over an extended area. This will expose hundreds and thousands of people to the adverse effects of radioactivity. The problem is that it may be difficult even to detect it early enough, since radioactivity cannot be seen in naked eye, cannot be felt. It can neither be tasted nor smelt. Specific instruments can detect radioactive disintegrations. However, those are not available everywhere. In case the terrorists spray it, it will come to light only long after it was sprayed. If and when suspected, then only it will be measured. This poses a major threat since it might already contaminate everything - water, air, food, soil, vegetables, fish, meat, dairy products and all others in the environment.

Something of this kind we have witnessed during the Chernobyl (USSR) disaster. As a result of radioactive gas release, there was radioactive fall out in the entire Europe, and possibly in other adjacent countries as well. Dairy products were heavily contaminated. Situations were almost close when the crisis arose in the atomic power plant of "Three Miles Island" in USA. In spite of such natural disasters, everybody should take a note that Food and water may be deliberately contaminated with radioisotopes by the terrorists. All concerned should be cautious about it. Proper organizations should maintain their continuous vigil and carry out regular checking and testing of all items to safeguard the health of the people.

Please keep it in mind that Radiation exposure is dangerous. The problem is that radiation is a slow poison and a dangerous killer. It can cause cancer, mental disorders, immuological dysfunction, neurological abnormality, abortion and abnormal childbirth etc. Long-term exposure, even to small doses of radiation, could become fatal. One should take all precautionary measures to prevent any ambitious attempt to spray radioactive agents or drop Atomic Bomb by anybody or by any nations on another. It could be a self-defeating kind of situation, as nobody would be able to get out of its devastations.

2.10 AUTHOR'S OWN EXPERIENCE

I, the author of this book, have had the rare opportunity of gathering some personal experiences of witnessing and also personally dealing with two of the major disasters as have been referred to above.

2.10.1 Author's Experiences with the Twin Tower Disaster

On September 11,2001 around 8-30 am like everyday I was also proceeding toward Manhattan, New York by boarding a Metro from Bronx, New York. I was a Senior Visiting Scientist, associated with the Albert Einstein College of Medicine, New York. I had my research laboratory at Beth Israel Medical Center at Manhattan. As said above, like everyday I was travelling by the Metro on that fateful day also from Bronx. After about half an hour as the Metro was very close to our destination, somebody within the train brought our attention to the spiraled black smoke up in the sky. As the train was moving toward Manhattan it became clearer and appeared larger. All of a sudden, the train stopped without any announcement. No body knew what had happened. People suspected that there could be a big fire somewhere. I had also come out of the tunnel up on the street. Soon I witnessed something, which I have never seen in my life. It was a sight of its own kind! This will long linger in my memory. I looked around and saw that hundreds and thousands of people were running toward the opposite direction of Manhattan. They were panicky, fear driven and full of anxiety. Some of them had dusts and black smoke on their face, hair and clothes. Everybody was in a rush and was in a hurry to move out of the city.

Streams of people are normally seen to go toward Manhattan every morning. To day, the scene is totally opposite, something different. To day the people were seen running and rushing toward any direction, no matter wherever they could go but for the Manhattan itself. The pedestrians, cars, vans and buses everything showed their back toward Manhattan and was moving out in the opposite directions. In the process, many people arrived at strange places where they had never visited earlier. The underground Metros, which were moving toward Manhattan from various directions i.e., East, West, North and South, stopped all on a sudden. " America has been attacked"- heard the people! People rushed out of the underground Metros, from their offices, shops, departmental stores, restaurants etc. to go out to a safer place. When they came out on the street, they witnessed something unbelievable. Cars, Bus, Taxi over-loaded with people were all moving out of Manhattan. They had no time to stop and to talk. Everybody feared that the worst was still to come, since "America was attacked" by the Enemies. No body knew when and how the enemy attacked, what was the extent of damages, whether Bombs were dropped, how many people died, who dropped the bomb etc. After walking along the street, I reached the Harlem area and hitchhiked at least three times to come finally to our apartment at Pelham Parkway, Bronx, which is close to Albert Einstein College of Medicine.

2.10.2 Bhopal Toxic Gas Disaster—Author's Own Experience

Bhopal toxic gas disaster from a Union Carbide Factory is yet again another disaster, which occurred due to an accident. Because of some faults in the safety valve, as is suspected by many, deadly methyl isocyanate (MIC) gas stored in a 40-gallon tank under pressure, suddenly burst out in the open on the early morning of December 2-3, 1984. It created a ballooning effect with the formation of a thick cloud in the sky, and the gas traversed in the wind current more than 40-50 km. Most people who used to live in the direction of the wind current and had their windows open died overnight. The casualty was an estimated number of 2500 people who died and several thousands were injured. Many are still suffering even after long 20 years. More than 10,000 livestock and poultry died due to the exposure. Several thousand plants and trees got charred. The water of the near-by lake became toxic. Hundreds and thousands of fish died within a week's time. Several thousands of people had to be hospitalized for emergency treatment, for breathing troubles, cough, eye burns and skin irritations etc. Those who had chronic lung problems such as asthma were the worst sufferers, since it got further aggravated. Many pregnant women exposed to the toxic gas delivered prematurely or babies born of them were with limb deformities, mental disorders etc.

As the then Director of the Industrial Toxicology Research Center (ITRC), Lucknow, Uttar Pradesh, India - a National Research Laboratory under the Council of Scientific and Industrial Research, Government of India, I, the author of this Book, had to provide a major leadership. I organized a 26-member scientific and technical team to establish a temporary laboratory at Bhopal in order to undertake scientific study on the toxic gas exposed population. Immediately after receiving instructions from the CSIR, Director General, we organized our team within a very short period of time so as to be able to proceed towards the city of Bhopal early on the morning.

There was an unprecedented sight! While most of the people of Bhopal were moving out of the city in a state of panic and despair, our team was only moving into the city of Bhopal after travelling quite a long distance (from the city of Lucknow in Uttar Pradesh to the City of Bhopal in Madhya Pradesh, about 500 km). Using any type of transport, such as rickshaws, buses, lorry, vans, motorcycles, scooters, private cars and even bullock carts, bicycles etc., the people of Bhopal were going out of the city. Many people were running. Some others were walking toward the opposite direction of the wind. There were many dead bodies of livestock lying here and there. Many local people, especially those who lived in the shanty areas of the plant and had their doors and windows open, died. Thousands of their bodies, covered with cloths were lying in front of their huts. Several hundreds were being taken to the hospitals. Hospital Emergency rooms were alerted and it started operating twenty-four hours. The number of beds was increased considerably. Hundreds of Doctors were flown in from all over the country. Hundreds of Engineers, Scientists, Technicians, Fire fighters, Police and Military personnel, International experts from various foreign countries, UN, WHO, IPCS, IRPTC, UNEP and others from all around the world came into Bhopal to conduct different types of operations, analysis, diagnosis, treatments, containment and decontamination work. It was a stupendous task to burn those thousands of dead bodies or animal carcasses in an appropriate manner. Special attentions were given on maintaining proper sanitation to check any possible outbreak of diseases. Many affected people were flown out in other hospitals around the nation.

The Mayor of the city and the local administrative staff welcomed our team. Soon the necessary laboratory space was made available to us in a school by courtesy of the Mayor of the city and the laboratory was set up. In our multidisciplinary team of experts, we had Medical Doctors, Lung specialists, Epidemiologists, Botanists, Biochemists, Immunologists, Neurologists, Cytologists, Molecular Biologists, Toxicologists and Geneticists. As soon as the people knew about us, soon a large number of the exposed victims lined up in a long queue seeking proper evaluation, medical check-up and suggestions for appropriate treatment.

A series of investigations have been carried out on the exposed population, both hospitalized and not hospitalized (46, 72, 86, 93, 101). These include - Epidemiological study, Radiologic study, Lung function studies, Biochemical and Serological studies, Enzymological studies, Imunological studies, Cytological and cytogenetics studies etc. The studies were conducted immediately after the exposure for a period of about two months. They were followed up for about two years thereafter. In an attempt to find some solutions to the controversy as to whether the population was actually exposed to "Methyl isocyanate gas " or to some other compound formed in the air, after it was released from the tank in the open atmosphere of the month of December when the early morning temperature is very chilly in Bhopal.

At ITRC, Lucknow I organized controlled inhalation toxicology studies in the laboratory by exposing rats to the sub-lethal doses of the deadly MIC gas. Data on controlled inhalation studies in animals using deadly MIC gas was not available in the world literature. To carry out these studies there were so much scare in the minds of the scientists and technicians! Some of them asked me the question "If I die during the course of the experiment, who is going to take care of my family?" There was so much for fear and anxieties in the minds of people around! I had to convince them. Give them my whole-hearted support. Such dangerous studies with highly lethal chemicals were not carried out at ITRC before. Even all necessary facilities were not available. A proper type of inhalation chamber was also not there. Almost everything had to be procured new. A custom-made experimental design was made by me. Miniaturization of the inhalation apparatus in a large desiccator was locally made, with inlet tube and outlet tubes, and a Y connector for addition of chemicals during the course of the experiment and for the withdrawal of gas for testing purposes. Even a whole body suit, face masks, artificial respirator with oxygen cylinder etc. had to be purchased before carrying out the laboratory studies.

I took the active part in the animal experiment myself, wearing whole body suit, face masks, respirator etc. Since there were virtually no literature data available on the MIC toxicity, all precautionary measures were taken. I saw the sufferings of the exposed animals in my own eyes, and was thinking how much suffering the exposed human beings had to go through in Bhopal before they died.

A series of biological studies spanning across 3-6 months of time were carried out in a simulated environment. All those data were published in several monographs and reputed journals (28, 32, 47 - 49, 73, 74, 94). The Indian Journal of Experimental Biology came out with a special edition in 1988 containing a large number of papers of ITRC together. The Editor of the Journal "Chemistry International" (USA), after reviewing several publications coming out from various laboratories at that time, wrote, " The ITRC data is a landmark in the history of the Methyl isocyanate toxicity".

The above information would set an example about the role of Scientists and Scientific Research Organizations of the nation in situations like this. As the Director of ITRC at that time, I had to take part in a series of seminars, symposia and conferences on MIC, both within the country and outside. It was an eye—opening of the world. Both the Government and the people of various nations started thinking what if such thing happens in their own nations, what kind of preparedness they might need at various levels to protect them or to minimize the adverse effects of highly toxic chemicals.

The descriptions of the nature and extent of devastations illustrated above as are caused due to chemical, biological and radiological weapons of mass destruction (WMD), indicate to some extent how much responsibilities fall upon different individuals playing their individual roles to tackle various episodes associated with a major disaster. Some more details will be discussed in subsequent chapters.

3 Hazardous Chemicals/Biologicals/ Radiologicals as Potential Weapons for the Terrorists

In the previous chapter, we have discussed about the chemical, biological and radiological weapons as have the potential to be used by the Terrorists. It has also been discussed as to the extent of devastations that is caused by such weapons. Salient features of some of the recorded historical experiences, including author's own experience with respect to two of the major disasters have been discussed.

It can be stated that any chemical, biological or radiological agent could prove to be hazardous, if mishandled or improperly disposed of, as is usually the case when an accident occurs. In the industries, mishandling of manufacturing processes could be dangerous. It might lead to explosions, toxic vapor cloud formation and dispersions of hazardous chemicals both within the industrial environment and outside. It might spread over a large area around the industry. It will go toward the direction of the wind current, affecting many people along its way. In general, all chemicals, which are corrosive, inflammable, explosive or toxic, can be considered disaster prone. Up until this date more than 7000 chemical reactions have been described as hazardous (8). More than 10,000 chemicals are being produced by the industries all over the world. The number must have increased many folds by now. Thus there is no dearth of chemicals, which can cause harms to human and animal physiological systems.

3.1 SAFE PRODUCTION, HANDLING, STORAGE AND TRANSPORTATION OF CHEMICALS: SAFETY GRADING

Over the years, a considerable amount of knowledge has been advanced in the area of safe handling and storage of chemicals (81). A hazard signal system with the grading of 0-4, with increasing **Health risks, Fire hazard and Instability** and the corresponding warning labels are useful (NFPA). Thus, acetone has been given a rating of 1.3.0, whereas HCN has 4.4.2 and Xylol as 2.3.0.

Combustible chemicals are classified into 8 categories, depending on their flash points. Similarly, oxidizing agents are regulated in terms of their reactivity and amounts. Preventive measures, precautions and emergency management of hazardous chemicals in the laboratories are now well known. The "Baker Saf. T. Data" provided on labels of chemicals will help in the understanding of the hazard as well as the protective measures, which are necessary against them.

The experience on safe production, storage, handling and transportation of hazardous chemicals at the laboratory scale can easily be applied to those situations where it is used in a larger magnitude as in industries (37).

Cralley and Cralley (23,24) reiterated that small laboratory experience could be applied into the development of programs that can, in addition to avoidance of occupational and environmental problems, safeguard the society against the potential chemical and biological disasters.

Most of the basic information needed in the case of various hazardous biologicals and chemicals are available in most of the textbooks of Microbiology, in the handbook by Brown et al. (9), and in the monumental treatise of Sax (92). It is suggested that each of the manufacturing, storage and utilizing industries keep copies of such books easily available at hand. Doctors and physicians treating patients, who are the victims to the toxic exposures, should be properly trained. It is to be ensured that such books and manuals are made available to them. They should have information about the toxicity, diagnosis, clinical treatment or management of the exposed victims, follow up and rehabilitation of the victims of the chemical, biological or radiological disasters, both on a short term and long term basis are also the subject matter the attending doctors and physicians must address.

3.2 CHEMICAL DISASTERS: INTERNATIONAL EXPERIENCE

Apart from the Bhopal chemical industry disaster as has been described in the previous chapter, the literature has a large abundance of information in this area. Voluminous data have been accumulated over the past many years regarding industrial disasters. In this regard, a document prepared by the Pan American Center for Human Ecology and Health has highlighted the need and principles of evaluations of public health hazards associated with chemical accidents (99). Such a document is very useful for all those concerned with chemical toxicity.

The case history of documented and recorded accidents show that chlorine and ammonia leakage are the two most common incidents in the industrial settings and during their transport, with mortality index (Total fatalities/Total amount lost) of 0.3 and 0.02 respectively. The corresponding figures for flammable materials are 0.6 (of course in highly populated areas, the values have to be much higher).

Ammonium nitrate explosion involving 4000 tones of the chemical and claiming 550 lives in Texas City, when two ships blew up in 1947, is one of the major accidents apart from the MIC leakage in Bhopal, India in 1984.

The increasing order of use of chemicals in our society and so also their production by the industries for a variety of purposes, and obviously for meeting the growing human needs, has led to an exponential increase in chemical accidents also (17). The risk is very serious since the machinery needed to cope with such tragedies may not be in abundant supply, or even if some are available may not be able to contain the major chemical, biological or radiological disasters.

WHO, Regional Office in Europe has prepared two documents on health aspects of chemical safety- (1) Emergency Response to Chemical Accidents (111) and (2) Rehabilitation following accidents involving toxic and hazardous chemicals (30). Several other valuable reports are also available (6,11, 20,54), which furnish information on Disaster Preparedness and its management.

According to Silano (99), chemical accidents occurring from static (factory) and mobile units (railways and trucks) differ in degree and magnitude in terms of both area and people affected, organization for containment and long term clean up procedures and its effects. In either case, the hazards can be predicted by predictive approach based on know-how and retrospective data based on past experiences. By a realistic utilization of all available information, major hazards can be anticipated and necessary corrective actions taken. This information came from identifying all vulnerable points in the process of preparation, nature of chemicals, and pattern of accidents. Such an accident can be at the level 1 (operator, factory,), level 2 (local community), level 3 regional/national, and level 4 (International). WHO/IPCS guidelines (111) are available for developing emergency response at each of these Levels. Appendix I at the end of this book describes this in detail.

From the data presented by Silano (99) it is learnt that about 150 chemicals can account for more than 90% of the accidents in terms of number of spills and volume dispersed due to tank ruptures, overflow, leakage, failure of transfer system, ruptures and punctures of other containers etc. These are the common causes. A proforma has been designed to obtain necessary data to carry out a study of chemical risks in a stationary installation. This includes inflammability, explosion, and toxicity data of each one of the chemicals along with the details of their manufacturing process, regular monitoring and continuance of vigilance in safety and health care. (See Appendix II).

Among chemical accidents, explosions have been fairly well understood and proper conditions and engineering measures to minimize chances have been developed (78). Lists of various chemicals, which are capable to cause explosion, are available in the treatise of Meyer (68). Mayer has appended the symptoms and emergency treatments for different toxic chemicals or poisons including the safety chart for common solvents in his book (68). These are of great help in disaster preparedness and it's planning.

3.2.1 Toxicological Emergencies: Disaster Management

Goldfrank's (43) comprehensive handbook on Toxicological Emergencies is another useful reference manual for dealing with chemical poisoning and its management.

After reviewing the then available information, the WHO (IPCS) (110) made a document setting up the administrative guidelines for planning emergency response to chemical accidents. The health aspects of man and other species are graded as low, serious, dangerous, and extremely dangerous for all accidents and duration as short-term, long-term and permanent. The accidents are normally seen to occur at four levels- operator levels, community level, regional level, and international level. The action plan for each level of containment and remedial measures has been defined. Identification of vulnerable foci, toxic effects, protective and remedial measures, nature and amount of the chemicals spilled or spread are required to be documented for an emergency planning. (See Appendix I).

The criterion for taking action during emergency and organizational link-up are also discussed in the above document. Safety requirement for transport of hazardous materials is also outlined. Experiences from actual handling of chemical disasters, particularly that from major chlorine tanker derailment in Canada and how it was contained is described. Such experiences are always helpful dealing with such type of cases if and when happens elsewhere as well.

The document suggests that each Industry or organization where such disaster may take place either by accidents or by terrorists attack should have a contingency plan compatible with that of the local community and its own emergency services, and organizations collaborating with the community services. They should collect all information about the nature of the accidents, chemical/biological/radiological nature, caused by the hazardous agents, their volume, dispersibility, inflammabilty, reaction nature with other agents, major exposure route, possible affected organs, treatments available etc. They should inform the authorities about it as soon as they have the information. The authorities should immediately respond with its emergency/emergency management team. All resources should be mobilized immediately. Hospitals and medical centers should be alerted to render emergency medical care to the victims.

Governments should enforce the Industries and such installations to have such a disaster management plan, keep periodic vigilance on it and provide all assistance. The contingency plan should include among others, anticipatory actions, decontamination steps, risk identification, prevention and control strategies and continuous updating of information. I strongly recommend this document for everybody.

The most comprehensive treatise on disaster containment is the volume edited by Faucet and Wood (38) on " Safety and Accident Prevention on Chemical Operations". In this document a unique effort has been made to trace the hazards in each of the reaction mechanism type used in the Industry. This approach may help in identifying possible run-away reactions and their consequences. Similarly each phase of chemical manufacture from size reduction and making to transfer has been assessed for potential risks. Safety precaution at each step of the process has also been suggested. The major chances of fire in chemical plants and recent techniques to forewarn and control are also described in detail. The grading of health hazards, flammability and reactivity of each chemical, color-coded blue, red and yellow, into 0-4 scales by NFPA as given in this treatise is beneficial in risk assessment.

The most important aspect of general interest is the paper "Developing a community preparedness for sudden emergencies involving hazardous materials" by Kathleen Tierney. She has identified disaster preparedness, removing misconceptions on safety and suggests the right approach for disaster containment. The responsibility of the industry, local government departments, state administration, private relief organization, health services and community organizations in disaster control are clearly defined. A community checklist of resources and disaster preparedness has also been suggested, which is useful in all circumstances. Based on these views some suggestions are given in Appendix III.

Fawcett and Wood (38) also described various preventive and protective measures that can be adopted, and means to check disaster proneness and preparedness.

3.2.2 Disaster Response: Aftermath of a Major Disaster

Every disaster has its own characteristics. Some common, and some uncommon. Disaster arising due to toxic Chemicals will have its own nature, property, and characteristics of devastations, while biological and radiological disasters will have a different type, nature, degree and persistence of the after effects. Although there could be a lot of commonness, nature and degree difference of damaging effects are always anticipated. There are 4 distinct phases of a chemical/biological/radiological disasters:

(1) Emergency phase,

(2) Follow up phase,

(3) Clean up phase, and

(4) Rehabilitation phase.

It is suggested that the first thing one ought to know to deal with a chemical/biological/radiological disaster is the nature of chemical, biological or radiological agents, which are related with the disaster. Immediately all available data on that chemical, biological or radiological agents should be collected, or organizations who have those knowledge should be contacted for all available information, such as NIH, NIEHS, CDC, Brookhaven National laboratory, National Toxicology Program etc. in USA and similar such organizations in other countries. In India, one may seek such help from ICMR, CSIR, DBT, DST, ITRC, CDRI, BARC, and IICT. At The International level, WHO, IPCS, IRPTC at Geneva, IAEA at Vienna and IARC in Lyon, France may also be contacted for potential help and information. BIBRA in Surrey, England can serve the same purpose. In Appendix III all the possible lines of observations as might be useful in Disaster follow up has been listed.

Let us take some lessons from one of the chemical disasters, which have been systematically studied by multidisciplinary experts. This is the infamous **Sevesso** dioxin leakage disaster. The run away reaction, which led to the formation of highly toxic TCDD, leaked. As soon as its release was identified the entire premises were evacuated. A symposium presenting a series of 6 papers have described all aspects of the problem, such as its toxic effects on various forms of life, residue levels, decontamination, follow up, organizational set up and suggestions for the future (16).

Chemical explosions are among the most serious accidents, the worst being at Texas City in 1947 and Oppau in Germany in 1920, both involving ammonium nitrate. The subsequent follow up study led to the development of proper safety conditions for storage and transport of various explosive materials (67). The maximum amount of dangerous substances like explosives and corrosives that can be stored and safe distances from storage facilities for explosives maintained are listed in this volume. Safety precautions are also given. Such information on other materials is mostly lacking.

A useful monograph on safety is "Safe handling of chemical carcinogens and toxic substances" by Walters (109). Details of handling of dangerous chemicals, methods of spill containment, deactivation and disposal methods described in that book have been used in the follow up suggestions of this treatise.

In 1974, at **Flixborough**, England a major accident leading to unconfined vapor cloud explosions occurred. The incident took place due to the release and explosion of cyclohexane storage tanks. The inadequate management allowing a substandard plant modification caused the disaster. Detailed public inquiry report revealed many shortcomings in the organization of plant operations and total unpreparedness to deal with the magnitude of hazard involved.

The disaster of San Carlos dela Rapita, Spain in 1978 was an important eye opener. A tanker carrying propylene developed a leakage due to overfilling; escaping vapor ignited and the vessel burst catastophically killing around 200 people in a nearby campsite.

An authoritative article on disaster planning has been published by Geiderman and Paris (4). In this volume emergency medical management and disaster planning, casualty flow diagrams in various disasters (natural, industrial, human activity, and transport) are described. The **eight principles** in any disaster planning, which have been, identified are - **prevention, minimizing, immediate control, rescue, first aid, evacuation, treatment and rehabilitation.** Proper communication and transportation facilities, adequate medical management, disaster drills, administrative organizations and maintenance of records are essential for disaster preparedness. Of special interest is the psychological aspect of disaster at the pre impact, warning impact recoil and post-traumatic phases on the people affected. Such protocols can be used in case of chemical disaster, biological and radiological disaster also with a little bit of changes here and there.

If combustion or volatile products are involved in any accidents it may cause inhalation injury. For combustion products such as CO, CN, Cl2CO2, H2 S, HCN and many others coming from fire, explosion or leakage, health effects and their management, standard protocols for hospital evaluation, treatment, history taking and diagnosis can be used for chemical disaster inclusions also. The clinical course to be adopted during inhalation, immediate (2 hours) and progression of injury (within 2 - 24 hours), pulmonary failure, or recovery (24 hours) can be made from lung function assessment and clinical studies. These approaches along with toxicological know-how and symptomatic treatment may be useful in handling large number of victims exposed to massive amounts of noxious gases.

3.2.3 Do's and Don'ts Regardings Some Commonly Known Hazardous Substances Exposure Signs, Symptoms and Possible Treatments

Some of the most commonly known hazardous substances are:

1. Chlorine, phosgene, hydrogen cyanide, hydrogen sulphide, carbon monoxide, which are severely toxic substances,
2. Hydrogen, liquid oxygen, sodium chloride, nitrocellulose compounds etc., are highly reactive,
3. Flammable materials are hydrocarbons, organic solvents and compounds with low atmosphere boiling and flash points.

The hazards due to leakage of some of the gases such as chlorine, HCL, ammonia, acetic acid, nitrous fumes and other acidic vapors may occur due to failure of pipe line joints, choice of wrong materials for construction, failure of emergency systems, creation of back pressure in systems due to choking in the pipeline or containers. Therefore, all the operations and the devices are to be checked periodically, cleaned and repaired as and when necessary without waiting for the ultimate to happen.

3.2.3.1 *Exposure Signs, Symptoms and Treatments*

Chlorine Gas. Chlorine gas is one of the respiratory irritants. Concentrations above 3 to 5 ppm volume in air are readily detectable. The threshold limit value of chlorine is 2.9 ppm.

Exposure. Short duration of exposure of skin to high concentrations of chlorine gas is not very irritating or corrosive but this effect is perceptible only when prolonged exposure is tolerated by use of respiratory protection. Splashes of liquid chlorine on the eyes, skin and clothing may cause immediate irritation and chemical burns and severe damage to body tissues.

Chlorine gas is extremely irritating to the mucous membranes, the eyes, and the respiratory tract and causes restlessness, throat irritation, spasmodic and painful coughing, sneezing, and copious salivation. In extreme cases lung tissues may be attacked resulting in death due to pulmonary edema.

Symptoms of exposure. Chlorine leaks always get worse unless it is promptly corrected. Authorized and trained personnel equipped with suitable gas masks must investigate the leak. If the leak is extensive, the persons in the path of the gases should be warned.

Water should never be used on a chlorine leak as it always makes the leak worse due to corrosion. If a leak occurs in piping or equipment in which chlorine is being used, the supply of chlorine should be shut off and the chlorine, which is under pressure at the leakage point, should be disposed off safely.

If chlorine or chlorinated water has contaminated skin or clothing, the emergency shower should be used immediately. If the eyes have been affected with liquid chlorine or high concentrations of chlorine gas, they should be flushed immediately with running water. The swallowing of liquid chlorine is extremely unlikely. However, if a person has swallowed chlorine and is conscious she should immediately be made to drink copious amounts of limewater, milk of magnesia or fresh water if the others are not readily available. Sodium bicarbonate may be given. The victim is expected to vomit spontaneously, but no attempt should be made to induce vomiting.

Hydrochloric acid gas vapors. Inhalation of excessive HCl gas produces a severe irritation in the upper respiratory tract. Prolonged exposure to high concentrations is dangerous to life. It will cause corneal damage. The maximum allowable concentration is 10ppm for 8 working hours in a day. Water flushing is an effective antidote.

Hydrogen Sulfide. Hydrogen sulfide, H_2S (formula weight 34.08) is a colorless flammable gas which may be liquefied under pressure and which occurs in a variety of natural and industrial settings. It is present in most volcanic gases, in "sulfur springs", and as a bacterial decomposition product of protein. It occurs to some extent in most petroleum and natural gas deposits and in may mines, and therefore it is a potential health hazard in related drilling, mining, smelting, or processing operations. In other industries, hydrogen sulfide is usually a byproduct of some manufacturing process.

In air pollution incident in Poza Rica, Mexico, lasted only 20 minutes, but resulted in hospitalization of 320 persons and in the deaths of 22. About half of the domestic animals, birds, and pets living in the area also died. The poisoning was attributed to hydrogen sulfide. At an exposure dose of 1000-2000 ppm of hydrogen sulfide in the air was measured.

Exposure signs and symptoms. Clinical findings for the exposed persons included loss of the sense of smell, burning eyes, cough, pulmonary edema, nausea, vomiting, unconsciousness, severe headache, vertigo, partial paralysis, neuritis of the acoustic nerve, lingual difficulty, and aggravation of a preexistent case of epilepsy.

Of the people who died in the Mexico Disaster, 9 were dead on arrival at the hospital, four died within 2 hours, four within 6 hours, one 24 hours after arrival, and one each on the 2nd, 5th, 6th,and 9th days after hospitalization. Lasting sequel was reported for only four of the human survivors (two with acoustic nerve neuritis, and one with aggravated epilepsy and new nervous manifestations).

The most surprising finding was that even moderate occupational exposure and insidious downwind environmental exposure to a low dose of H_2S (25ppm) for some time can cause permanent impairment.

Oil refineries, sulfur plants, sewage treatment plants are some of the common sources of H_2S emission. Rescue workers must wear respirator; face masks and should not expose them even for a short while to H_2S gas.

Ammonia. Ammonia emits an irritant vapor. When inhaled it causes irritation in all parts of the respiratory system. It causes burns of eyes and skin. Anhydrous ammonia is a colorless gas with an extremely pungent odor and is very toxic with a TLV of 50ppm and 35mg./m3. It constitutes a fire hazard (flammability limits in an air is 10 to 30% volume) and is explosive. Water flushing is an effective antidote.

Acetic acid. In the acute form condensed acid vapor is a skin irritant and produces erythema, chemical burns and blisters. These vapors have a highly irritant action on exposed mucous membrane and particularly conjunctiva, upper respiratory tract and nasopharynx.

Exposure signs and symptoms. In the chronic form, workers exposed for 7 months to 1 year to high concentrations (80 to 200ppm) have been found to suffer from palpable edema, chronic pharyngitis, chronic cataract, bronchitis, and in some asthmatic bronchitis. The skin on the palm of the hands feels dry, cracked and hypersensitive. When affected, water flushing is advised.

Nitrous fumes and other oxides of nitrogen. It is a mild irritant to the eyes, nose and upper respiratory tract at 10 to 12ppm. At a concentration of 100 to 1000 ppm and above, it causes death in animals. With men, acute exposure to nitrogen dioxide causes death due to asphyxia.

Categories of several other specialized toxic chemical agents include:

- *Nerve agents*
    1. Tabun (ethyl N, N-dimethylphosphoramidocyanidate).
    2. Sarin (isopropyl methylphosphanofluridate) [This has been recently used in the underground Metros of Japan]

3. Soman (pinacolyl methyl phosphonofluridate)
4. GF (cyclohexylmethylphosphonoflurodate)
5. VX (O-ethyl- [S]-[2-diisopropylaminoethyl]-methylphosphonothiolate.

- *Blood agents*
  1. Hydrogen cyanide
  2. Cyanogen chloride
- *Blister agents*
  1. Lewisite (an aliphatic arsenic compound, 2-Chlorovinyldichloroarsenic)
  2. Nitrogen and sulfur mustards
  3. Phosgene oxime
- *Heavy metals*
  1. Arsenic [the aquifer in a large area of West Bengal, India and Bangladesh have been contaminated with Arsenic, which in turn had contaminated the drinking water sources to Millions of people, causing arsenic poisoning in those population.
  2. Lead (Lead is a poison, children are especially affected due to lead exposure. It may produce encephalitis.
  3. Mercury (Mercury in organic form) i.e. Methyl mercury is very poisonous. Mercury poisoning of coastal sea water, which thus contaminated fishes, caused severe poisoning among those who ate them in Japan. The symptoms were known as "Minamata Disease"
- *Volatile toxins*
  1. Benzene
  2. Chloroform
  3. Trihalomethanes
- *Pulmonary agents-*
  1. Phosgene
  2. Chlorine
  3. Vinyl chloride

  Incapacitating Agents:
  1. (3quinuclidinyl benzilate)
- *Pesticides, persistent and non-persistent*
- *Dioxins, furans and polychlorinated biphenyls (PCBs)*
- *Explosive nitro compounds and oxidizers*
- *Ammonium nitrate combined with fuel oil*

- *Flammable industrial gases and fluids*
  1. Gasoline
  2. Propane
- *Poisonous industrial gases, liquids and solids*
  1. Cyanides
  2. Nitrides
- *Corrosive industrial acids and bases*
  1. Nitric acid
  2. Sulfuric acid

3.3 CDC RECOMMENDATIONS REGARDING APPROPRIATE TYPE OF TREATMENTS

It is to be noted that hundreds of new compounds are being introduced every month at the International level. Therefore, treating exposed persons by clinical syndrome, rather than by specific agents, is more useful for public health planning and emergency medical response purposes, a CDC report said. Public health agencies and the first responders might render the most aggressive, timely, and clinically relevant treatment possible by using treatment modalities based on syndromic categories (e.g. burns and trauma, cardio respiratory failure, neurological damage, and shock). These activities must be linked with authorities responsible for environmental sampling and documentations. Therefore, **TREAT BY SYNDROME NOT BY THE TYPE AND NATURE OF AGENTS is** the essence of CDC suggestions.

3.3.1 Bioterrorism

After the recent "anthrax letter and Ricin letter" episode, news on birds dying of blue nile virus infection, massive flu attack during the on-set of summer months, SARS virus spread in some south east Asiatic countries, birds (chicken) Flu, periodic cholera episodes in South East Asia, diarrheal diseases due to Pseudomonas pylori in USA, Dengue virus infection in South East Asia etc. have caused quite a bit of concern in the minds of people. In case there is a deliberate attack with these or other microbes, the population at large will be definitely very vulnerable to suffer from the highest possible casualties. It is primarily because that our overall preparedness to tackle such episodes, as of now, is much less than what is otherwise necessary. Although the US and other Governments have taken the matter very seriously, and that there is an all round plan for preparedness, it will take a considerable amount of time to implement it. The scientists and technologists have to put their whole-hearted efforts to come out with useful and handy methods of diagnosis in one hand as well as prophylactic and therapeutic treatment procedures on the other.

Regarding use of highly toxic Biological agents for terrorizing purposes, several incidents in recent years may be worth reviewing. In 1984, the Rajneeshee cult in Dallas, Oregon, contaminated salad bars with Salmonella. Some 715 people developed gastroenteritis. In 1991, a ricin toxin threat was reported in Minnesota. In 1995, an individual carrying the deadly toxin, ricin, was arrested while crossing the Canadian border. Ricin powder was mailed again to the Chief of the US Congressional Office and also in his Capitol Hill address and to several other places in 2003-2004. It was suspected early enough and diagnosed quickly. No major damage was done, except for the fact that there was a scare all around, and several policemen on duty, the cleaning people and the postmen were quarantined for several days and the offices were to be closed for several days for clean up operations.

A deadly gas, called sarin, was released in the subways of Tokyo, Japan in 1994. In 1995, Iraq confirmed production and deployment of weapons containing Bacillus anthracis and botulinum toxin. In 1996, a laboratory technician in Dallas, Texas provided pastry coated with Shigella to coworkers.

In 1998, the Center for Disease Control and Prevention (CDC) were notified of 50 threatened incidents, six of which were deliberate anthrax hoaxes in Kentucky, Tennessee and California. In 1999 and 2000 more hoaxes were announced as threats to individuals and corporations. Flu season arrive every year during late fall and early winter, causing symptoms that mimicked diseases caused by some of the agents likely to be used in a bioterrorist attack.

The bombings at the World Trade Center in New York City and at Alfred P. Murrah Federal Building in Oklahoma City and the recent terrorist attacks on the Twin Towers at the New York City; the Pentagon Buildings at the Washington D.C. in 2001 shattered the myth that the United States is not vulnerable to outside attack. So people are scared. They do not consider them safe any more. A deep-rooted fear and anxiety engrossed their minds all the time, since they know that anytime anything can happen anywhere.

Thus the threat of bioterrorism has become real in today's world. If people of the United States of America cannot feel safe, one can easily understand the feelings of people of other nations, which are less advanced both scientifically and economically. Therefore an overall preparedness is a must at all levels and such information should be shared among nations.

Right from each individual to each community health care, the infrastructure should be geared up in a manner that they can tackle the situation satisfactorily. They should have trained scientists, Doctors and technicians, all available diagnostic procedures, prophylactic and therapeutic drugs or vaccines etc. Please keep it in mind that an early diagnosis would save thousands of lives. Therefore, these health care doctors should have proper knowledge of bioterrorism agents and their diagnostic techniques. Proper gadgets and laboratory facilities, self-protection device etc. should also be made available to them.

It may be noted that an unprepared community health care system may cause more harm than the crime itself. Unpreparedness may pose more threat to the safety and tranquility. Often the threat of a bioterrorism can foster terror and panic among the minds of the people. This may be the goal of the bioterrorists. Therefore the clinicians should not wait until a bioterrorist act is performed. They should be well aware and well informed about the management plan of any unusual or unexpected illness, not just those anticipated from the bioterrorism attack. The health care community must develop the capacity to deal with such events, develop good communication systems and response plans and is able to maintain peace and harmony in the locality (69).

Bioterrorism agents are chosen from amongst such potential pathogenic organisms, which can cause rapid infection, transmit from one individual to another, and also can cause severe morbidity and mortality leading to mass casualties. After all the whole purpose is to overwhelm the health care system. Some of these agents are named below-

(*a*) Variola major (small pox);

(*b*) Bacillus anthracis (anthrax);

(*c*) Yersinia pestis (Plague);

(*d*) Francisella tularensis (tularemia);

(*e*) Botulinum toxin (botulism);

(*f*) Filoviruses and arenaviruses (Viral hemorrhagic fevers), and

(*g*) Brucella species (brucellosis).

It may be noted that although some of the organisms as have been named above, the use of the organisms in a bioterrorist attack may not necessarily be always limited to the above list. The microbiologists and the clinicians should be aware of this. And all suspected cases should be immediately reported to the state health department.

Microorganisms, which have the potential to be used by the bioterrorists, exhibit characteristic properties, i. e.,

1. they must be able to be "weaponized", which means that they can be packaged and distributed in a manner that can infect a large area, with the least damage to the organism itself.
2. These organisms should be viable, stable and infectious in aerosols, so that their distribution is very efficient. Because of very poor immunity or no immunity most of the people become very susceptible to infection caused by these organisms, and they clearly produce high morbidity and mortality rates. Obviously, more casualties are seen in those areas where such organisms are rarely seen and so virtually no preparedness is available.

A bioterrorist attack may take place as an overt event and may usually precede or accompany an announcement. In this case, the disease may be recognized early, earlier experiences may help in the treatment, and emergency response from the biohazard responders, usually the first responders such as emergency medical services, public safety personnel etc.

Sometimes the covert event may take place without any announcement or the criminal operator may be days and miles away from the actual place of the incident. In this case the diagnosis takes longer time and the treatment is delayed. So more victims are dead. The first responders in covert events are the health care workers, in clinics, hospitals, private practices, and emergency rooms, because public safety and emergency room technicians would be unaware of such an event until later (69).

3.4 SOME CLUES TO POTENTIAL BIOTERRORIST ATTACK

Very often it is very difficult to determine whether or not a bioterrorist's attack may have been occurred. It may be several hours to several days that the disease may be diagnosed properly. So the casualties are often very high.

Some clues are provided below for the benefit of early diagnosis:

1. Rapid outbreak of a rare or a novel disease.
2. Rapid outbreak of a disease in a non-endemic area.
3. A seasonal disease in an off-season time.
4. Known pathogen with an unusual resistance profile or an unusual epidemiologic features.
5. Unusual clinical presentation or age distribution.
6. Genetically identical pathogen emerging rapidly in different Geographical areas.

Since any episode caused by these agents are uncommon and novel, to diagnose and treat these patients remain a challenge to the clinicians. The rapidity with which proper diagnosis can be done and treatment is given, many more lives could be saved.

Novel infection in a large number of populations may occur sometimes as a normal episode and may not have anything to do with the terrorist attack. Therefore these two should be differentiated properly.

The clinicians and infection control personnel should sit down together to recognize an increased incidence of a particular organism or a disease in a locality or in an organization and should conduct epidemiological investigations. They should document a sharp rise or fall of an organism; assess an unusual increase in respiratory or gastrointestinal sickness during a specific period of time, or large incidences of diseases or fatal cases from a single locality etc. These data together with characteristic syndromes would help in the assessment of the episode, if it were natural or due to terrorist attack. But whether natural or due to terrorist's attack, preparedness at all levels is the key-determining factor for the success of controlling the disasters.

3.5 PREPAREDNESS AT THE COMMUNITY LEVEL

It has been described previously that the local community physicians, hospitals or clinics are likely to be the first to recognize a bioterrorism related attack and also initiate a response. It is therefore necessary that the local hospitals and health care professionals must be ready and equipped with all necessary facilities, such as diagnostic gadgets, self protective suits, sera, vaccines, drugs, antibiotics etc. Appropriate preparation is a major task, because of the magnitude of such attack and the severity of the illness it may cause.

There are many in the health care system that may think whether it is cost effective to go to make such a huge preparation for an otherwise low-probability incident. But it will not be wise to take a chance and sit idle until it happens. Preparedness again is the only factor, which would reduce the intensity of the sickness and reduce the morbidity and mortality associated with it. A flow chart diagram given at the end of this volume for this purpose may be consulted.

In all community hospitals there exist an existing **Emergency Response System (ERS).** The **ERS** can form the basis of properly developing an emergency response procedure to deal with bioterrorists attack. For this purpose, the hospital administrator should appoint a proper person to deal with the bioterrorism related attacks. Such a person should be able to work with all concerned, keep him abreast of all information and contacts, and ensure that all the stocks of proper drugs and other gadgets etc. are available. He should also know the sources of their availability. Such a person should be an infection control professional, infectious disease clinician or any other physician who is fully knowledgeable as to how to deal with a preparedness agenda. Infection control officials through the web site of the Association may note for Professionals in Infection Control (APIC) at www.apic.org or at the web site of the CDC at www.cdc.gov.

3.6 PREPAREDNESS AT THE STATE AND FEDERAL GOVERNMENT LEVEL

Since in any bioterrorism related attack, the toxins or microorganisms likely to be utilized are so rare or uncommon that both the physicians and also the laboratory personnel may not have any experiences to deal with them, or even to recognize them. The clinicians may have very seldom seen infecting a patient with organisms like that of Brucella and Francisella. So clinicians are unaware of the clinical episodes. Physicians practicing in the west of Rockey Mountains of USA are familiar with Yersinia pestis than those working in the east of Rocky Mountains. Most physicians have not witnessed cases of small pox or viral hemorrhagic fever viruses. But physicians in the South Eastern Countries have dealt with a large number of small pox patients and patients having viral hemorrhagic fever.

Physicians in the Asiatic countries have a lot of experiences to deal with cholera and other diarrheal diseases. Doctors in the West find them difficult to diagnose. Moreover, Doctors in Asiatic nations can very easily diagnose malaria, tuberculosis, Leismania, typhoid organisms and know of their treatments. Doctors in western nations find it difficult, because the incidences of such diseases are few and far between.

Some of those organisms are so dangerous, that without proper training and proper laboratory facilities, it might be fatal to the persons dealing with them in the laboratory. Therefore it is suggested that such isolates, specimens etc. should be sent to a reference laboratory at the state or central level in proper package. So all microbiology laboratories should be able to have information regarding specimen selection, collection, transport, and storage. They should also know the optimal processing criteria for each of the agents. All community hospitals should know the simple clues to rule out these agents and send suspicious specimens only for proper diagnosis at the state or central level.

In his article Miller (69) has given very useful information regarding transport, storage, specimen plating and processing procedures. Laboratories dealing with them may follow such procedures.

Table 1. Specimen Selection

Disease / agent	***Specimen Selection***	***Time and Temperature***	
		Transport	***Storage***
Anthrax Cutaneous	Vesicular stage :Using sterile Swabs collect fluids from Vesicles.	< 2h RT	<24h RT
	Eschar stage: insert swab Beneath the edge of eschar, Rotate to collect the lesion Material.	< 2h RT	<24h RT
Gastrointestinal	Collect 5-10g of stool in a Clean, sterile, leak-proof Container.	<1h RT	<24h 4C
	Blood : collect just enough for routine cultures.	<2hRT	*
Inhalation	Sputum : Collect expectorated Specimen into a sterile, leak-proof Container.	<2hRT	<24h 4C
	Blood: Collect enough for the blood cultures.	<2hRT	*

(Contd.)...

Specimen Plating and Processing						
		SBA	CA	MAC	Stain	Comment
Anthrax,	Cutaneous Vascular Stage	x	x	x	Gram's stain	India ink for Capsule
	Eschar stage	x	x	x	,,	,,
	Gastrointestinal Stool	Inoculate routine stool plating media plus CNA or PEA				Minimal Recovery
	Blood	Blood culture bottles				Positive in the late stage Of disease.
	Inhalation, Sputum	x	x	x	Gram's Stain	Minimal Recovery
	Blood	Blood culture bottles				Positive in the Late stage of the disease

Disease/agent	Specimen Collection	Time and Temperature	
		Transport	Storage
2. **Brucellosis**	Serum, 10-12 ml may be colllected Acute, subacute after acute phase onset of disease.	~2hRT	– 20C
Or chronic	Collect a convalescent phase speci-men 21 days later Blood; collect for routine blood cultures	<2hRT	do not Refrigerate
	Bone marrow, spleen, or liver as per Surgical/pathology procedure	<15min RT	<24hRT

Disease/agent		Specimen Plating and Processing				
		SBA	CA	MAC	Stain	Comment
2. **Brucellosis**	Serum	Specimen should be stored And shipped at – 20C				Serologic diagnosis 1.Sigle titer >1:160 2. Four-fold rise 3. IgM

(Contd.)...

Blood	Blood culture bottles hold 21 days			Blood culture isolation varies depending on Methods and period of isolation
Bone marrow, Spleen, liver	x Hold cultures for at Least 7 days	x	x for capsule	Gram's stain India ink and add Blood Culture Bottles or enrichment broth

Disease / Agent / Specimen type / Clinical syndrome

	Food borne	Infant	Wound	Intentional release	Specimen Volume	Transport Temp.
3. **Botulism** / Enema fluid	x	x	x	x	20cc	4C
Food sample	x	x		x	10-50g	4C
Gastric fluid/	X, A				20cc	4C
Intestinal fluid	A	A			20cc	4C
Nasal swab				x	Anaerobic swab	RT
Serum	X, A		x	X	10-12cc	4C
Stool	X	X	X	X	10-50g	4C
Vomitus	X				20cc	4C
Wound/tissue			X		Anaerobic Swab or transport system	RT
Environmental Sample		X		X		RT

Disease/Agent/Specimen	*Type Specimens of choice*
	for confirming botulism : (*a*) Serum (*b*) Wound/Tissue (*c*) Stool and incriminated food

(Contd.)...

3. **Botulism**	Enema fluid	Purge with a minimum amount of sterile Nonbacteriostatic water to minimize Dilution of toxin
	Food sample	Food that support Clostridium botulinum Growths will have pH of 3.5 to 7.0; most common pH is 5.5, 6.0 - 6.5. Submit Food in original container, placing individually in Leak-proof Sealed transport devices.
	Gastric fluid	Collect up to 20 ml.
	Intestinal fluid	Autopsy: intestinal contents from various areas of the small and large intestines should be provided
	Nasal swab	For aerosolized botulinum toxin exposure, Obtain nasal cultures for C.botulinum and Serum for mouse toxicity testing.
	Serum	Serum should be obtained as soon as possible after the onset of symptoms and before antitoxin is given. A minimum of 10cc of serum (20 cc of whole blood) is required for mouse toxicity testing. In infants, serum is generally not useful, since the toxin is quickly absorbed before serum can be obtained.
	Stool	Botulism is confirmed in infants with only "pea-sized" stools. It may be noted that patients given anti-cholinesterase as in Patients with myasthenia gravis may interfere with the toxin testing.
	Vomitus	Collect up to 20cc
	Wound/tissue	Exudate, tissue or swabs must be collected And transported in an anaerobic transport system. Samples from an enema or feces should also be submitted, since the wound may not be the source of botulinum toxin.
	Environmental sample	Environmental swabs

Disease/Agent		*Specimen Selection*	*Time and Temperature*	
			Transport	*Storage*
4. **Plague**	Pneumonic	Sputum/throat : Collect Throat culture using a swab or expectorated sputum, Collected into a sterile, Leak-proof container. Tracheal washing is the Preferred specimen.	<2hRT	<24h 4C

(Contd.)...

	Specimen Selection	Transport	Storage
	Bronchial/tracheal wash : Collect it in an area identified for collecting respiratory specimens under isolation containment circumstances, such as isolation Chamber/"bubble".	<2hRT	<24h 4C
	Blood: Collect for routine blood Cultures.	<2hRT	*

Disease/Agent	*Specimen*	*Specimen Plating and Processing*				
		SBA	*CA*	*MAC*	*Stain*	*Comment*
4. **Plague** Pneumonic	Sputum/throat	x	x	x	Gram stain	Minimal Recovery. Prepare smears for Wayson (and DFA Referral)
	Bronchial/tracheal Wash	x	x	x	Gram stain	Prepare smears for Wayson Stain (and DFA referral)
	Blood	Blood culture bottles			Patients with negative cultures having a single titer, >1:10, specific to F1 antigen by Agglutination method would be enough to meet presumptive criteria	

Disease/Agent	*Specimen Selection*	*Time and Temperature*	
		Transport	*Storage*
5. **Tularemia** Pneumonic	Sputum/throat, collect throat swab or sputum into a sterile container	<2h RT	<24h 4C

(Contd.)...

	bronchial/tracheal wash. Collection should be done in an isolation containment area, such as isolation Chamber/Bubble	<2hRT	<24h 4C
	Blood: Collect for routine blood cultures	<2hRT	*

Disease/Agent	*Specimen*	*Specimen Plating and Processing*				
		SBA	*CA*	*MAC*	*Stain*	*Comment*
5. **Tularemia**	Sputum/throat	x	x	x	Gram Stain	Minimal Recovery. Add a BCYE plate and prepare smears for DFA referral
	Bronchial/ Tracheal wash	x	x	x	Gram stain Add a BCYE plate and prepare Smears for DFA referral	
	Blood	Blood culture bottles			Blood cultures have rarely been positive. A positive DFA from an ulcer/wound, tissues, and cultures Or a positive serological test would meet presumptive criteria. Whereas fo confirmation culture identification or a four fold rise in titers of specific antibodies are required.	

(Contd.)...

Disease / Agent		*Specimen Selection*	*Time and Temperature*	
			Transport	*Storage*
6. **Small pox**	Rash	Biopsy specimen aseptically collect two to four portions of tissue into a sterile, freezable container.	~6h 4C	– 20C to – 70C
		Scabs, aseptically collect the, scrapable materials into a sterile freezable container	,,	,,
		Vesicular fluid, collect fluids, from separate lesions into separate sterile swabs. Caution should be taken to collect cellular material from the base of each vesicle	,,	,,

Disease / Agent	*Specimen*	*Specimen Plating and Processing*				
		SBA	*CA*	*MAC*	*Stain*	*Comment*
6. **Small pox**	Biopsy specimen	1. A suspected case of small pox should be reported to the state health department immediately for review.				
	Scabs	2. If after review small pox is still suspected, CDC's pox virus section (404-639-2184) must be contacted seeking approval for sending a specimen for testing				
	Vesicular fluid	3. Review the packaging and shipping requirements with CDC and request assistance in coordinating a carrier for transport/shipment				

Disease / Agent	*Specimen*	*Time and Temp*		*Specimen Plating and Processing*				
		Transport	*Storage*	*SBA*	*CA*	*MAC*	*Stain*	*Comment*
7. **VHF**	Serum Collect 10-12 cc Serum for antigen capture ELISA, IgG ELISA, PCR, and Virus Isolation	~2hRT	– 4C	Specific handling conditions are yet to be standardized				

A, autopsy; BCYE, buffered charcoal yeast extract agar; C, centigrade; CA, Charcoal agar; CAN, colistin nalidixic acid agar; DFA, direct fluorescent antibody; g. grams; h, hours;

MAC, MacConkey agar; PFA, phenyl ethyl alcohol agar; RT, room temperature; VHF, viral hemorrhagic fever; *, delayed entry depends on instrument.

3.7 SAFETY MEASURES DURING TRANSPORT

An extreme precautionary measure is required during the transport of such deadly bacterial organisms and viral particles from one place to another. It should be stored and packaged in such materials, which are not easily breakable. Proper labels are also necessary so that transport people can handle it properly. It should also say that in case of any accident where to contact.

3.7.1 What to Do If You Find Out Suspicious Biological Specimens

Any controversial or suspicious specimens spotted by anybody - policemen, transport authorities, airlines, navy, rail authorities, border security, post office personnel or may be by any common man, should always be examined by the trained staff of the state or county public health laboratory, for confirmation or a second opinion. At the national level, in USA, the CDC has been designated by DHHS to lead the overall planning effort to upgrade national public health capabilities to respond to chemical and biological terrorism.

In India, ICMR (Indian Council of Medical Research, Government of India, New Delhi) is the nodal agency. It has a large number of associated Research Laboratories under its control all over the country. In New Delhi, there is an Institute for Communicable Diseases dealing with various forms of communicable diseases; National Institute of Cholera and Enteric Diseases, Kolkata, deals with Cholera, various forms of Diarrheal Diseases; Virus Research Laboratory, Pune deals with various Viruses. Besides them School of Tropical Medicine of West Bengal Government, Kolkata; Vector Control Center, Pondicherry, ICMR; Institute of Microbial Technology of CSIR at Chandigarh; Center for Tuberculosis Research, Madras; Leprosy Research Institute, Agra; Infectious Disease Hospital, Kolkata and several other Hospitals and Research Laboratories all around the Country has some limited capability to diagnose and treat some of the infectious agents and the diseases caused by them. Special measures are perhaps required to develop specific diagnostic and treatment facilities, especially of those organisms, which are potentially important from the bioterrorism point of view. Vigorous researches are going on to develop biotechnological capabilities for the production of diagnostics, suitable vaccines and other treatment facilities all over the world now.

3.7.2 Gearing up Laboratory Capabilities

In order to increase the laboratory capability, the US Government allocated CDC more than $ 121 Million in 1999 for developing:

(1) A laboratory response plan,

(2) Building a surveillance and epidemiology network around the nation for bioterrorism response,

(3) Stockpiling vaccines and other therapeutics,

(4) Developing a health alert system to enable nationwide alerting and communication system, and also

(5) To facilitate a national plan to coordinate the entire efforts.

As a result the CDC established the **Bioterrorism Preparedness and Response Program (BPRP).** Similar such programmes are necessary in other countries, at least in a modest way, taking recourse to its own requirements and resources available. CDC has also developed and implemented a strategic plan for bioterrorism preparedness, and facilitated the development of a state-wise bioterrorism preparedness planning process. In addition they have created a National Health Alert Network, and helped finance state and local public health efforts in their preparedness planning. Future funding will assist states in completing the readiness plans listed earlier.

The National Laboratory Response Network (LRN) was a part of the CDC strategic plan. A number of other organizations would work with each other and one another in these coordinating efforts. State public laboratories, the FBI (Federal Bureau of Investigation), the United States Army Medical Research Institute of Infectious Diseases (USAMRIID) and other partners will work in coordination with each other and each state will establish its own laboratory readiness.

1. Community level laboratories will be labeled as level A laboratories. They should first come out with the clues or suspicions regarding unusual and suspected type of organisms and its occurrences. They should package and transfer them to the next higher-level laboratory. The level A laboratory will also rule out any agents.
2. The state or county Public Health laboratories can be labeled as level B laboratories. They should have more capacity and equipments to deal with BSL (Biosafety level) 3 types of agents. They should have the core capacity for isolation of organisms. Presumptive level testing of suspected specimens or isolates, ant microbial susceptibility testing facilities. These laboratories are agent specific in the LRN.
3. The level C laboratory must have the capacity of level B laboratories, plus advanced capacity of rapid identification using molecular methods. It also can help in surge capacity and has much greater BSL-3 working capacity.
4. The level D laboratory should have the highest level of containment (BSL-4) and expertise in diagnosis of rare or highly dangerous agents. In USA, CDC and USAMRIID maintain such type of Level D laboratories.

3.7.3 Preparedness at the Local Community Level

Preparedness at the community level needs to look at several important factors.

One of those important factors is —**Biosafety.**

A risk analysis of the microbiology laboratory would help determine the areas most likely to have problems, should there be any critical agents encountered. Reinforce the necessity of the use of Class II biological safety cabinets, not only at the set up station, but also for storage of all associated items related to a suspicious culture until it can be safely packaged and shipped to the next level laboratory. Support the aggressive use of aseptic techniques by the laboratory technicians and suggest that the age-old practice of sniffing plate's four characteristic odors should be abandoned, because some of the agents of bioterrorism are infectious at a very low level of inoculum (1 to 10 organisms).

Education is the most important factor. The laboratory technicians should be educated regarding how to safely handle agents of bioterrorism. With the appropriate precautions, the risk of infection with working with any of these agents is small.

Communication is the third most important item, which is emphasized. The technicians should know the bioterrorism readiness plan for that institution and understand their roles in each part of the plan.

Another important aspect is to recognize **the limitations of the laboratory**. The community hospital laboratory has to play a significant role should a bioterrorism event occur. It should serve as a sentinel for the health care community. However how far to with specimen work up and when to submit an isolate or a specimen to the next higher-level laboratory is very critical. To optimize the capacity of microbiology laboratories to respond to and recognize any unusual isolate, access to a board certified clinical microbiologist of the American Board of Medical Microbiology (ABMM) or equivalent is desired.

Because these agents are so rare and the disease they produce are so unusual that the laboratories and clinicians be aware of the salient features of illness and their etiologic agents. Some of these features are summarized later. If you may go to the web site, www.bt.cdc.gov, you will get the organism-specific information. Links to some other valuable sites may be accessed at http://www.bt.cdc.gov/links.asp.

3.7.4 Preparedness at the State and Federal Government Level Ensuring Proper Preparation at the Laboratory Level

At the State and Federal (Central) Government level, advanced laboratory capacities are to be established, at the level of B, C and D described above. It should be equipped with sophisticated equipment, highly trained Microbiologists and Virologists, appropriate containment facilities and adequate safety measures and storage facilities. These laboratories will have to function both as a service laboratory and also as referral laboratories. They should organize training programs to train the technicians to diagnose the organisms properly. Training programs are also required to be organized by them for the medical Doctors to have proper knowledge of diagnosis and treatment for those rare diseases and disorders caused by various bacteria and viruses as well as their toxins.

Some major features about some of the most deleterious, but mostly rare organisms, their diagnostic procedures and available treatments etc. are discussed below-

3.8 ANTHRAX

3.8.1 Critical Criteria

Anthrax is a zoonotic disease, frequently transmitted to the humans who handle or consume contaminated animals products. The etiologic agent is Bacillus anthracis. Anthrax is a bacillus, gram positive, spore forming and encapsulated organism. The United States is normally not considered to be a highly endemic area, once in a while the disease is seen among the livestocks and some wild animals in Louisiana, Mississippi, Oklahoma, and South Dakota. The annual incidences have declined from 130 cases in the year 1900 to virtually no cases in the year 1992.

In humans there are three primary forms of anthrax determined by the mode of their transmission—Cutaneous anthrax, Gastrointestinal anthrax and Inhalation anthrax.

3.8.2 Cutaneous Anthrax

Cutaneous anthrax (malignant pustule) occurs when either the spores or the organisms enter the body through a cut or abrasion while the patient is handling contaminated wool, hides, or hair products. In most cases the patients begin to experience symptoms within 48 hours of their exposure, although a range of 2-7 days may be required in some cases. Initially before the symptoms appear, the infection may mimic an insect bite with a raised bump that is itchy. Within 2 days, the bump develops into a fluid filled vesicle that eventually ruptures to form a painless Escher about 1 to 3 cm in diameter with the characteristic black necrotic center. About 20% of the untreated cutaneous anthrax may result in death because of systemic spread of B. anthracis. With appropriate therapy death is rare. Lesions become sterile within 24 hours and resolve within weeks. The lesions may continue to evolve, however, even with appropriate therapy.

3.8.3 Gastrointestinal Anthrax

Gastrointestinal anthrax is caused by infected or contaminated meat from infected animals. Usually, within few hours of consumption of food the patient experiences nausea, vomiting, fever, loss of appetite, followed by abdominal pain, bloody emesis, and severe diarrhea. Mortality is estimated to be 25% to 60% of cases.

3.8.4 Inhalation Anthrax

Inhalation anthrax is also known as Wool sorter's disease. It is this form, which can be expected in most bioterrorist event. Because of its quick spreadibility among a large section of the people of a community, the terrorists may prefer it. Many individuals can be potentially affected by one release of an infectious aerosol. Spores, once aerosolized are inhaled, and infection is likely to occur with the inhalation of an estimated 10,000 spores or less. Reports vary in this regard. Some think that from 8000 spores to 50,000 spores are good enough to cause an infection. The symptoms appear within 1 to 6 days and are usually mild and nonspecific. Occasionally a non-productive cough and mild chest discomfort may be present. Initial symptoms may resolve briefly, followed in 3 to 5 days in abrupt, acute hypoxia and dyspnea, and radiographic evidence of mediastinal widening with pleural effusions, but not infiltrates. Fever and shock often appear 24 to 36 hours after the onset of respiratory distress. The mortality rate is usually 100%, even with aggressive therapy.

In pulmonary anthrax, inhaled spores are carried from the lungs to the lymphatic system (mediastinal lymph nodes) by macrophages, where the spores germinate, and organism multiply, and the result is a severe septicemia. In fatal cases of any type of anthrax, bacteria in the blood build to levels of 107 to 109 organisms per ml. of blood at the time of death. These numbers clearly portend a poor prognosis. The production of toxin by these organisms is the major cause of death. Even appropriate antimicrobials late in the course of the disease may be ineffective. B.anthraciss toxin is a complex, plasmid directed protein composed of edema factor (Factor I), protective antigen (Factor II), and a lethal factor (FactorIII).

Adequate knowledge about the structure of these protein factors that make up "anthrax toxin" should be valuable in the design of new drugs to counteract its lethal effects. Two of the three toxin components, protective antigen and the lethal factor, had their structures determined in 1997 and 2001 respectively.

Drum et al. completed the story by elucidating the structure of the third component, the edema factor (EF), with or without calmodulin (CaM), the protein that activates EF after entry into the host cell.

Like many infectious organisms, the anthrax bacteria disrupts intracellular signaling pathways by increasing the concentrations of a key signaling molecule-cyclic AMP-in infected cells, thus inhibiting the immune response against the bacteria. On binding to calmodulin (CAM), a ubiquitous intracellular modulator, the conformation of EF is considerably altered creating a site that can catalyze the formation of cAMP from ATP, but at a rate 1,000 fold higher than of the adenylyl-cyclase-CaM complex that has this role in the normal cells. Moreover, in the EF-CaM complex, CaM is locked into a conformation that cannot modulate other signaling proteins, as it would normally. Whether or not EF remains a good drug target remains to be seen. Only future research would throw more light in this regard. (Further reading 5,6, 31)

3.8.5 Treatment

Most B. anthracis isolates are susceptible *in vitro* to a variety of antimicrobial agents. A fluoroquinolone (ciprofloxacin, levofloxacin, or ofloxacin) or doxycycline (if fluoroquinolones are not available or contraindicated) is usually recommended for therapy. Penicillin is also useful but the therapy should be guided by the anti-microbial susceptibility test results. Therapy must begin early in the disease to reduce the risk of death. A vaccine is available and is reported to be 92.5% effective in protecting against cutaneous and inhalation anthrax combined. The vaccine has been tested in adult men and non-pregnant women. The vaccination protocols consist of three subcutaneous injections given at 6, 12 and 18 months. An annual booster dose is needed to assure continuous protection. Reactions are usually mild; 30% of recipients exhibit tenderness and redness at the injection site. Respiratory symptoms occur in less than 0.2% of vaccine recipients. In a subsequent table information on vaccines for all agents is discussed.

3.8.6 Prophylaxis

An abundance of caution is to be observed to treat people prophylactically when anthrax infection is diagnosed among some people. Considering others in the area may also have been exposed, prophylactic treatment should continue for at least 60 days and beyond. People who were exposed to B. anthracis may wish to continue antimicrobial treatment for an additional 40 days. Another option could be to receive 40 additional days of antimicrobial therapy and three doses of the anthrax vaccine. According to USHHS department secretary Tommy G. Thompson. A third option offered by Johnson was to stop therapy after the initial 60 days but to remain alert for symptoms that could indicate anthrax infection. NIAID Director, Anthony S. Fauci said that the treatment options were extended based on the results of animal studies in which B.anthracis spores were found to persist in the lungs for up to 100 days.D.A. Henderson, Director of the office of the Public Health preparedness, noted that there were no cases of anthrax in humans beyond 43 days. But it was stated that the optional precautions might be most appropriate for people who had been exposed to a large number of B.anthracis spores. Henderson, however, cautioned that people having post exposure long-term antimicrobial therapy, beyond the initial 60 days might have unpleasant experiences of adverse drug reactions. It may be noted that post exposure use of anthrax vaccine has not been currently approved by FDA. Patients who choose to be vaccinated would receive three doses over a period of one month and would also receive concurrent antimicrobial prophylaxis.

3.8.7 Laboratory Diagnosis

In Gram stains of blood the Bacillus anthracis organism can be seen as large non-spore forming rods. It can be detected in blood cultures late in the disease, by which time the therapy is most often ineffective. Spores can be detected only when the organisms have grown aerobically in the culture media. Carbon dioxide levels in the body inhibit in vivo sporulation.

It is not necessary nor is it recommended that the community level laboratories (level A) should have the capacity to fully identify B.anthracis to the species level. Always use gloves when working with a suspivious isolates, until it is proven not to be B. anthracis. At the community level the laboratory should only be able to perform the following:

1. Perform gram's stain and observe gram-positive rods. After the organisms have been grown in air, spores can be seen as unstained oval or central bodies within the cell that do not swell the cell. Organisms from clinical specimens or blood may not demonstrate spores on initial cultures or stain.
2. Recognize the characteristic colony morphology of Bacillus species. Colonies are large, flat, or slightly convex with irregular edges. A ground glass appearance will be

evident. B. anthracis colonies may have the consistency of beaten egg whites demonstrated by the ability to lift the edge of the colony from the plate surface with the colony remaining intact and standing.

3. Recognize that the B. anthracis colonies will be catalase-positive and non-hemolytic.
4. Differentiate B. anthracis from other Bacillus species. B.anthracis is non-motile. Most of the other Bacillus species, but not all, are motile as demonstrated by direct wet mount or in motility medium.

If the above characteristics are noted, no further work is needed at the Level A laboratory. The organism should be packaged properly and transported to the state public health laboratory or other designated Level B laboratory for confirmation.

The LRN facility (Level B or C) has the capacity to confirm thee species identification and perform susceptibility tests. Other confirmation options are available at the level B and C laboratory. Culturing the organism on bicarbonate medium and noting highly mucoid colonies can demonstrate the poly-D-glutamic acid capsule. The capsule is not formed optimally when grown on blood or chocolate agar. The organisms can be subjected to a simple India ink test or M'Fadyean stain to observe the capsule. The level B laboratory should also be able to confirm the identification using lysis by gamma phage and using direct fluorescent antibody stains to demonstrate the cell wall polysaccharide and capsule. Susceptibility tests, if indicated, are done only at the level B or C laboratory.

Table 2. Microbiology Biosafety

Agent	*Biosafety level*		*Specimen exposure risk*	*Precautions for level at laboratories*
	Specimen handling	*Culture handling*		
1	2	3	4	5
Bacillus Anthracis	2	2	Blood, skin lesion exudates cerebrospinal fluid, sputum, And rarely urine and feces	BSL2: clinical material collection,diagnostic Quantities of Infectious cultures. BSL3: Activities With high potential for aerosol or droplet production.
Brucella Species*	2	3	Blood, bone marrow, cerebrospinal fluid(CSF), tissue, Semen, and occasionally urine	BSL2: Collection, transport, and plating of clinical Material. BSL3 :Manipulations of cultures

(Contd.)...

Clostridium Botulinum**	2	2	Toxin may be present in food materials,clinical Specimens and Environmental samples (soil surface water).	BSL2:materials containing toxin must be handled in the safety cabinet (Class II),with a lab coat, gloves, and a face shield (as needed). BSL3: Activities with high potential for aerosol or droplet production
Francisella Tularensis***	2	3	Skin lesion, exudates,CSF, blood, respiratory secretions, Urine.Tissues from infected Animals and fluids from infected Aarthopods	BSL2:Collection,transport and plating of clinical materials. BSL3 : all activities involving manipulations of cultures
Yersinia pestis ++	2	2	Bubo fluid, blood, sputum CSF, feces, urine	BSL2:Clinical material collection and diagnostic Quantities of infectious Cultures. BSL3:Activities with high potential for aerosol or droplet production
Smallpox^	4	4	Lesion fluids,crusts, Respiratory secretions, Or tissue	BSL4: Specimen collection transport
VHF^^	4	4	Blood, urine,semen, Tissue, respiratory Throat secretions	BSL4:specimen collection transport

* Laboratory acquired brucellocis has occurred by sniffing cultures, aerosols, generated by centrifugations, mouth pipetting, accidental parental inoculations, and sprays into eyes, nose, and mouth; and direct contact with clinical specimens.

** Exposure to toxin is the primary laboratory hazard, because absorption can occur with direct contact with skin, eyes, or mucous membranes, including the respiratory tract. The toxin can be neutralized by 0.1M sodium hydroxide. C. botulinum is inactivated by 1:10 dilution of household bleach. Contact time 20 mins. If material contains both toxin and organisms, the spill must be sequentially treated with bleach and sodium hydroxide for a total contact time of 40 mins.

*** Laboratory acquired tularemia infection has been more commonly associated with cultures than with clinical materials /animals. Direct skin/mucosa membrane contact with cultures; parenteral inoculation, ingestion, and aerosol exposure have resulted in infection.

++ Special care should be taken to avoid the generation of aerosols.

^ Ingestion, parenteral inoculation, and droplet or aerosol exposure of mucous membranes or broken skin infectious fluids or tissues are the primary hazards to laboratories.

^^ Respiratory exposure to infectious aerosols, mucous membrane exposure to infectious droplets, and accidental inoculation are the primary hazards to laboratories.

Table 3. Bioterrorism Agents, Infective Dose, Manifestation Time, Duration of Illness

Disease	*Virulence factors*	*Infective dose*	*Incubation period*	*Illness duration*
Inhalation Anthrax	Exotoxin* Capsule	8000- 50,000 spores	1 to 6 days	3-5 days
Brucellosis	LPS PMN Survival	10 to 100 organisms	5 to 60 days	weeks to months
Botulism	Neurotoxin	0.001ug/kg (Type A)	6h to 10 days	24- 72 hr
Tularemia	Intracellular Survival	10 to 50 organisms	1 to 21 days	~2 weeks
Pneumonic Plague	V and W** antigens LPS endotoxin** F1 antigen**	< 100 organisms	2 to 3 days	1 to 6 days
Smallpox		10 to 100 particles	7 to 17 days	~ 4 weeks

Table 4. Bioterrorism—Agent, Mortality, Transmission, Precautions, Persistence

Disease	*Mortality*		*Person to person transmission^*	*Precautions for hospitalized^^*	*Persistence*
	Treated	*Untreated*			
Anthrax	~99%	~100%	No	Standard	Soil,40 yrs
Brucellosis	~1%***	~5%***	No	Standard	water,soil ~10 weeks
Botulism	Outbreak 1st Patient: 25% Subsequent cases: 4% Overall -5-10%		No	Standard	Food,water weeks
Tularemia	< 4%	33%	No	Standard	Moist soil Months
Pneumonic Plague	5-14%	100%	Yes (high)	Droplets^^^	Soil > 1 yr

(Contd.)...

Small pox	Variola minor: < 1% Variola major: 20% to 50%	Yes (high)	airborne^^^	Very stable
VHF	53% to 88%	Yes (moderate) airborne, contact^^^		Unstable

* B. anthacis exotoxin(s) consists of three components. The edema factor and lethal factor exert their effect within cells by interacting with a common transport protein designated, protective antigen (so named because, when modified, t contributes to vaccine efficacy). One plasmid and that of the capsule (D-glutamic acid polypeptide) mediate expression of toxic factors by a second plasmid. Strains repeatedly subcultured at 42C become avirulent as a result of losing virulence determining plasmids, which is thought to be the basis for Pasteur's attenuated anthrax vaccine used at Pouilly-le Fort in 1881.

** The V and W antigens and the F1 capsular antigens are only expressed at 37C and not at the lower temperature of the flea (20 to 25C).

*** Endocarditis accounts for the majority of brucellosis-related deaths.

^ Period of communicability: For inhalation anthrax, brucellosis, botulism, or tularemia: None, no evidence of person to person transmission; pneumonic plague: for 48 hours, following initiation of appropriate antimicrobial therapy or until sputum culture is negative; Small pox: approximately 3 weeks, usually corresponds with the initial appearance of skin lesions to their final disappearance, most infectious during the first week of rash by way of inhalation of virus released from oropharyngeal-lesion secretions of the index case; VHF: various with virus, but at minimum, all for the duration of illness and for Ebola/Marburg transmission through semen may occur up to 7 weeks after clinical recovery.

^^ Guidelines for isolation precautions in hospitals. Infect Control Hosp Epidemiol 1996; 17:53-80. www.cdc.gov/ncidod/hip/isolat.htm.

^^^ In addition to standard precautions, which apply to all patients.

3.9 BRUCELLOSIS

It is a zoonotic disease and is transmitted to humans by a variety of animals such as, cattle, goats, sheeps, pigs, rabbits, dogs and reindeer. These animals are carriers of specific species, i.e. Brucella abortus (cattle), Brucella melitensis (sheep and goats), Brucella suis (pigs, rabbits, and reindeer), or Brucella canis (dogs). Brucellosis is usually in the United States. It is a systemic infection often characterized by unusual fever pattern. About 100 cases are reported every year from around the United States, such as from California, Florida, Texas, and Virginia. The organism is highly virulent for humans, with an infectious dose off 10 to 100 organisms. Transmission occurs mostly from handling infected animals, or more likely, by ingesting contaminated milk and dairy products. The incubation period is unpredictable, usually 5 days to more than 6 months. It is very difficult to diagnose.

3.9.1 Symptoms

The various signs and symptoms, which may be associated with the disease, are—acute or insidious onset of fever, headache, anorexia, weight loss, profuse sweating (night sweats), malaise, arthralgias, and muscle and back pain. The mortality rate is less than 5% in untreated cases and less than 1% in treated cases. Death is usually caused by primary infective endocarditis. Brucellosis is the most commonly reported laboratory-associated bacterial infection. Cases have been reported in the laboratory setting by sniffing cultures, direct skin contact with cultures, and as a result of aerosol generating procedures. There is no person-to-person transmission.

The serious after-effects associated with brucellosis include- peripheral arthritis, spondylitis, meningitis, uveitis, optic neuritis, granulomatous hepatitis, anemia, leukopenia, thrombocytopenia, papilledema, and infective endocarditis.

3.9.2 Treatment

The most useful drugs of choice for treatment of this disease include doxycycline, together with either gentamycin or streptomycin. Alternatively, doxycycline plus rifampin, or trimethoprim-sulfamethoxazole plus gentamycin can be used. Immunity is acquired in humans after active infection and both cellular and humoral immunity is involved. No human vaccines are available in the United States. The RB51 strain of B.abortus is used as an attenuated, live vaccine in cattle. Although humans have been exposed to cattle and bovine tissues infected with this strain, no human cases have been reported.

3.9.3 Laboratory Diagnosis

In the laboratory, serological diagnosis is done most frequently. Acute and convalescent phase serum specimens are to be collected about 21 days apart. In addition, blood and bone marrow may be submitted for culture. The organisms may also be isolated from spleens or liver tissue. Brucella species will grow in most commercially available blood culture media, although it may take longer than the standard 5 to 7 day culture period. If the physician suspects brucellosis, the laboratory must be notified to extend thee normal incubation time.

At the community laboratory level (Level A), personnel should suspect Brucella species based on colony morphology, Gram's stain morphology, and the results of oxidase and urea hydrolysis tests. Under the microscope,

Brucella species appear to be minute, faintly staining, gram-negative coccobacilli 0.5 to 0.7 um x 0.6 to 1.5 um. Microscopically, B. melintensis is the most coccoid of the four species, rarely exceeding 1um in size, whereas B. abortus will appear more rod-like and reach lengths of 2 to 3 um. On 5% sheep blood agar media, colonies of brucella will barely be visible at 24 to 72 hours. The organisms are fastidious in nature, and colonies on blood agar are nonhemolytic and nonpigmented.

These organisms are usually oxidase positive but can be variable. All B. melintensis are oxidase positive. Ninety five percent of B.abortus and B.suis and 72% of B.canis are oxidase positive. All are capable of hydrolyzing urea. B. suis and B.canis are usually urea-positive with 5 minutes of inoculating a prewarmed urea slant. Both abortus and B melitensis becomes positive after 24 hours in culture.

There are other organisms, which are oxidase positive and urease positive including Bordetella bronchiseptica and some biotypes of hemophilus influenzae. However, B. bronchiseptica is not fastidious and X- and V factor requirements differentiate Haemophiluss from Brucella. Other similar gram-positive glucose-oxidizers, such as members of the genera Achromobacter, Acidovorax, Agrobacterium, Flavobacterium, Methylobacterium, Ochrobactrum, Pseudomonas, Riemerella, Roseomonas, and organisms reported as EO-2 and -3 and IIJ, may be confusing. Brucella species are not in the database of the commonly used commercial identification systems. Therefore, those systems may provide an inaccurate genus and species report. Updated version of the systems may likely address the identification of these organisms.

At first the specimen is to be tested in a Level A laboratory. If the level A laboratory observes tiny, faintly staining, gram-negative coccobacilli from blood or bone marrow cultures with slow-growing, oxidase positive, colonies on sheep blood after 2 to 3 days of culture, the isolates and all the associated plates and bottles should be placed into a biological safety cabinet until appropriate packaging and shipping protocols have been followed. After this the materials should be shipped to a level B or C laboratory.

A good standard laboratory at least at the Level B or C should be able to perform micro agglutination tests on the patient's serum to detect a four-fold increase in titer between acute and convalescent paired sera. Single specimen titer is positive if reported at a level of 160 or higher. Because Level C laboratory has BSL-3 capability, the personnel can perform tests necessary for confirmation and species identification, production of hydrogen sulfide, due tolerance, gel formation by B.canis in phenolyzed saline, and atmospheric growth requirements. Slide agglutination tests are also available at this level, as the phage lysis tests.

3.10 BOTULISM

Botulism is a neuroparalytic disease. It results from a potent neurotoxin elaborated by Clostridium botulinum organisms. The toxin has also been demonstrated from various other strains of Clostridium species i.e. C.butylicum, C.baratti, and C.argentinense. Seven toxin types have so far been reported-A through G, of which types A, B, E, and F are most commonly found in human disease conditions. Types C and D are mostly found in birds and mammals, and the type G are elaborated by C. argentinense isolated from the soil of Argentina.

The infective dose is estimated to be about 0.001ug/kg (Type A LD50). The incubation period of botulism is dose dependant and can be from 18 to 36 hours.

3.10.1 Symptoms

The patients are initially alert, oriented, and afebrile and have normal sensory responses. However, they may experience nausea, vomiting and diarrhea. Symptoms or cranial nerve damage begin to emerge with ptosis, blurry and double vision, difficulty in swallowing and talking, and decreased salivation. Progression to motor nerve involvement leads to a bilateral, descending flaccid paralysis, respiratory paralysis, and death if not treated. Death occurs in 60% of the untreated patients but the death rate comes down to less than 5% in treated cases.

3.10.2 Diagnosis

At first the laboratory data has to confirm the presence of botulinum toxin. The diagnosis of botulism is confirmed based on the clinical presentation and laboratory confirmation of the toxin. The local community hospital (level A laboratory) will be unable to confirm the presence of the toxin. Select level C laboratories which have such capacity. Differential diagnoses include stroke syndrome, myasthenia gravis, Guilliaan-Barre syndrome (Miller Fischer Syndrome variant), tick paralysis, atropine poisoning, or paralytic shellfish/puffer fish poisoning.

3.10.3 Therapy

The most appropriate therapy may include ventilatory assistance and supportive care, early administration of pentavalent antitoxin (Types A, B, C, D, and E) obtained from the CDC or another designated source. Antibiotics are appropriate for the infants and wound botulism. Recovery may be prolonged with a need for continual supportive care. Currently no vaccine is available for the public, but a pentavalent vaccine is available for the laboratory workers and those with work-related exposure. The vaccine requires repeated exposure to achieve immunity. Active immunity will likely not occur, because the lethal dose is below that require for an immune response.

3.10.4 Precautionary Measures for the Laboratory Personnel

In the laboratory the specimens are needed to be handled very carefully. Clinical specimens suspected of containing botulism toxin can be extremely dangerous because of the toxin's potency and the quantity present in the sample. Even very minute quantities acquired by ingestion, inhalation or by absorption by the skin or membrane contact can cause profound intoxication and death; therefore, all material suspected of containing botulism toxin must be handled with caution. Laboratory technicians should work within Class II biological safety cabinet and wear laboratory coats and gloves and face shields (as needed)

Serum is the specimen of choice to confirm botulism. However, stool or food (for toxicity testing) and samples of tissue (wound botulism) and stool or suspected food (food borne) for culture. All isolates must be sent to the appropriate level C laboratory for toxin testing. B.botulinum is a large, spore forming, anaerobic, gram-negative rod. Spores are more likely to be found after culture in the laboratory and may not be evident if organisms are observed in direct clinical specimens. Isolation of the organisms is not necessarily diagnostic without toxin confirmation.

3.11 TULAREMIA

Tularemia is a rare disease and is mostly found in the Northern hemisphere. Mostly birds are infected with it. Individuals who had contacts with wild rabbits, hares, and ticks that infect these animals may contract this disease from the animals. Mostly in the south central and western states of United States about 200 cases are reported every year. Most cases occur during the summer season when people spend their time mostly outdoors and go in the wilderness for holidaying. Another peak season is early winter when people go for rabbit hunting.

Francisella tularensis is a highly virulent bacterium, requiring only about 1 to 10 organisms to cause a disease. Like anthrax, tularemia is not spread from person to person. The fever caused by the organisms goes by different names in different States. It is called **deer fly fever** in Utah, **glandular tick fever** in Idaho and Montana, a **plague-like disease in rodents** in California, **market men's disease** in Washington D.C., **rabbit fever** in the Central United States, **Ohara's disease** in Japan, and **water-rat trapper's disease** in Russia.

There are several forms of Tularemia. Individuals who come in contact with infected rabbits and handle infected skins or meat will likely manifest on the glandular forms of the disease. Wood ticks, dog ticks and lone star ticks can also transmit the organisms throughout their lifetimes through their bites. Aerosolized organisms can infect mucous membranes and enter the lungs to cause severe, life-threatening respiratory infection.

3.11.1 Symptoms

In the pneumonic form, the incubation period is usually 3 to 5 days with a range of 1 to 21 days. The signs and symptoms of the illness are characterized by the abrupt onset of fever, clills, headache, myalgiaa, and a non-productive cough. Chest X-ray often reveals segmental/ lobar infiltrates, hilar adenopathy, and effusions. The mortality rate is up to 60% if the disease remains untreated. An early therapy may bring it down to only <10%. Differential diagnosis includes atypical community-acquired pneumonia such as that caused by Legionella and Mycoplasma, and classic streptococcal pneumonia, influenza, and pneumonia caused by Hemophilus influenzae and pneumonic plague. Unless treated the agent may be found in the blood during the first 2 weeks of the disease, and in lesions for a month from onset, and sometimes longer.

3.11.2 Treatment

The treatment of choice for tularemia is streptomycin, gentamycin, or tetracycline. Prophylaxis would include a fever watch for 7 days or the administration of doxycycline or tetracycline for

14 days if the patient were febrile. A food and Drug Administration (USA) approved vaccine is not available, although a live attenuated vaccine has been available for immunizing personnel at risk, such as research laboratory technicians in contact with large number of cultures. This vaccine is about 80% effective against a 1 to 10 (LD50) dose.

Presumptive diagnosis is accomplished either by detecting elevated serum antibody titers to F. tularensis antigen (without documented four fold or greater change) in a patient with no history of tularemia vaccination or by confirmed detection. Of F.tularensis in a clinical specimen using a direct fluorescent antibody assay. Diagnosis is confirmed by isolation and identification of the agent or by noting a four-fold or greater change in serum antibody titer to F. tularensis antigen. Both tests can be performed at a Level B and Level C laboratory.

3.11.3 Laboratory Diagnosis

F. tularensis is a minute, pleomorphic, poorly staining, gram-negative, facultative intracellular coccobacillus (0.2 to 0.5um x 0.7 to 1.0um). It is a fastidious organism requiring cysteine-supplemented media for optimum growth. It is nonmotile and biochemically inert.

This organism is dangerous and highly virulent and should only be handled in a BSL-2 safety cabinet. Laboratory acquired infection can occur through accidental aerosol inhalation or by sniffing an agar plate containing the agent or by accidental inoculation. The Level A community Hospital laboratory need only recognize characteristic s of isolates on culture media to consider the isolate suspicious. The media required for growth of F.tularensis are optimized by the addition of Cystine; cystine heart agar (CHA) is ideal but generally not available to laboratories. It is prepared by addition of 9% sheep blood and cystine to enriched chocolate agar. Because cystine is also present in the Legionella medium buffered charcoal yeast extract (BCYE) agar, F.tularensis will grow on it. On routine sheep blood, chocolate, and Thayer-Martin agars, F. tularensis will grow poorly and often not at all. It grows slowly at 35C, and poorly at 28C.After 24 hrs on these media, colonies are however too small to be seen. By 48 hrs, colonies may be as large as 1mm in diameter on chocolate and Thayer-Martin agars but are still minute on blood agar.

When a laboratory technician observes the presence of tiny coccobacilli in a gram-stained smear, only a few possible etiologic agents are likely to be considered. The most likely to be Actinobacter (oxidase negative), Actinobaccilus (colonies adhere to the agar), hemophilus aphrophilus, Bordetella or group IV organisms (inert and urea positive), or pasteurella (nonadherent but will grow on MacConkey agar). Least likely agents would be DF-3 (dysgonic fomenter), Brucella (usually urea positive in seconds to minutes), and Francisella (urea negative). Therefore, the observation of minute, gram-negative coccobacilli on Gram's stain is significant to the laboratory technicians.

At level A, if the laboratory reports a tiny, gram-negative, poorly staining coccobacillus from blood, lymph nodes, or respiratory specimens, and if there are blood culture isolates that grow slowly on chocolate agar but poorly on blood agar in 24 hours, then this organism should be immediately referred to a Level B or C laboratory for conformation.

At the Level B or C laboratory, susceptibility tests can be done by the E-test (AB Biodisk, Pisctaway, N.J.) performed on cystine-heart agar. Other confirmatory tests for identification include the slide agglutination tests with hyper immune F. tularensis serum, which is performed similarly to the salmonella agglutination test used in routine laboratories. The rapid identification will allow quick transition of the culture to a BSL-3 work area. A micro agglutination test is available for detection of serum antibodies to F. tularensis, where a single titer of at least 128 or a fourfold rise in titer in acute and convalescent sera taken more than 2 weeks apart would indicate a positive reaction. This laboratory could also provide direct fluorescent antibody staining of the isolate. In addition, enzyme immunoassays are available for the detection of antibody to F.tularensis outer membrane protein (OMP) antigen.

3.12 PLAGUE

Historically it is a disease, which has killed large populations in Asia, Africa and Europe. The black plague, or bubonic plague is a scourge in history. This organism and the disease has been used as far back as in the 14th century to foster biowarfare within the walled city, by way of throwing the diseased corpses or body parts from outside to infect those who reside within the walled city and are killed in large numbers. Plague occurs worldwide. Today, the United States averages about 13 cases each year with 15% fatality rates. Incidences are more among the Native Americans, about 30%, in the southwest. Most confirmed cases occur near the patient's residence. Fleas from hosts which include rats, dogs, squirrels, chipmunks, rabbits, and carnivores serve as the natural vectors of the disease. The infectious dose is < 100 bacterial cells.

3.12.1 Bubonic Plague

It has an incubation period of 2 to 6 days. It is characterized by sudden malaise, myalgia, fever, tender lymph nodes with regional lymphadenitis (buboes). In the bubonic form one may find a papule, vesicle, or pustule at the site of inoculation or infection. Which eventually develops into purpuric lesions late in the course of the disease. Differential diagnoses include staphylococcal and streptococcal adenitis, glandular tularemia, or cat-scratch disease.

3.12.2 Septicemia Plague

It may result from direct inoculation into the blood stream. It can be secondary to bubonic or pneumonic plague. In systemic plague, one may observe severe endotoxemia, systemic inflammatory response syndrome, shock, disseminated intravascular coagulation, and acute respiratory disease syndrome. Differential diagnosis would likely include sepsis caused by other gram-negative organisms, meningococcemia, Rocky Mountain spotted fever, thrombotic thrombocytopenic purpura (TTP).

3.12.3 Incubation Period

The pneumonic form has an incubation period of 1 to 3 days followed by sudden onset of malaise, fever, myalgia, and cough. The pneumonia progresses rapidly to dyspnea, cyanosis, and hemoptysis, with death occurring primarily from respiratory collapse and/or sepsis. Differential diagnoses include other forms of pneumonias, hemorrhagic leptospirossis, and other bioterrorism threat agents such as those causing anthrax, tularemia, and even melioidosis.

3.12.4 Treatment

The treatment of choice is streptomycin, gentamycin, tetracyclines, sulfonamides, or chloramphenicol (when meningitis or pleuritis is suspected). Antibiotic resistant strains have also been suspected. Supportive therapy follows symptomatic progression of any form of the disease. For infection control, isolation and droplet precautions for pneumonic plague should be instituted until sputum cultures are negative.

Individuals who have been exposed to infected fleas or who have been within 2 m of a coughing patient with pneumonic plague should take doxycycline, tetracycline, or trimethoprim-sulphamethoxazole for 7 days. For other close contacts, (i.e. those within 2 m) a 7-day fever watch is adequate. For pneumonic plague, persons in contact with respiratory droplets should be treated with oral doxycycline, tetracycline, or trimethoprim-sulphamethoxazole for 7 days after the last exposure.

Until recently, a killed and formalin-inactivated Yersinia pestis vaccine was only available for high-risk individuals, but not approved for general use in the United States. This formerly licensed product was discontinued by its manufacturers in 1999 and is no longer available.

3.12.5 Laboratory Diagnosis

Under the microscope, Yersinia pestis appears to be a nonmotile, non-spore forming member of the Enterobacteriaceae family, In Gram stain, it looks like a short-chained pleomorphic, graam-0negative, plump rods (0.5um to 1.0 um, a coccobacilus). The cells may appear with a characteristic bipolar stain, where each end of the cells stains more densely than the center, giving a safety-pin appearance. The Wright-Giemsa stains used in hematology demonstrate the bipolar characteristics in a better way. Other organisms

Such as Pasteurella species, Klebsiella species, Yersinia species, and Escherichia species may also show bipolar characteristics. With suspected Y.pestis an additional smear should be prepared and submitted to thee next higher-level laboratory for direct fluorescent antibody stain.

The organisms grow better at 28C than at 35C on sheep blood agar, forming only tiny colonies on solid media (i.e., blood and MacConkey agars) after 24 hrs at 35 C. When grown in broth cultures for 24 to 48 hours, cultures show suspended flocculent or crumbly particles the sides and at the bottom of the tubes, while the remainder of the broth remains clear. Y.

pestis is biochemically inert. Its profiles are found in the database of the Microscan (Dade-Micro Scan, Sacramento, Calif.), Vitek (bioMeriuix Vitek, Inc, Hazelwood, MO.), and the API 20E (bio Meriux Vitek, Inc., Hazelwood, MO.). But correct identification by these methods remains problematic. Because of the low level of suspicion of this organism the laboratory will continue to work uninterrupted. Y.pestsi is a non-lactose fermenter, oxidase and urease negative, and catalase positive. Isolates suspected of being Y. pestis should be immediately shipped to the Level B or C laboratory for confirmation.

For the community hospital laboratory three criteria may arouse suspicion that an isolate could be a potential Y.pestis. They are small, gram-negative coccobacilli from blood, lymph node aspirate or respiratory specimens; safety pin appearance in the Gram's stain (would more likely appear in Wright-Giemsa stains); a patient with a short specific period of fever with lymphadenopathy. If these criteria are met, the specimen should be submitted to the Level B or C laboratory for confirmation.

At the Level B laboratory where identification can be confirmed, a direct fluorescent antibody is available for detecting the fraction 1(F1) envelope antigen of Y. pestis. The F1 antigen is immunogenic and elicits strong and lasting antibody responses to Y.pestis, but is expressed only at 37C after 24 to 48 hrs of incubation. Antimicrobial susceptibility by E-test can be performed, as can complete biochemical confirmation, specific bacteriophage lysis for Y. pestis, enzyme immunoassay for detection of antibody to the organism, and passive hemagglutination tests (PHA) and passive hemegglutination inhibition (PHI) test for detecting antibody to the F1 antigens.

3.13 SMALL POX

The last naturally occurring case of this disease was reported from Somalia in 1977. The World Health Organization declared the disease eradicated in 1980. It was possible for the coordinated efforts of many nations and its Public Health Laboratories, who worked together in this joint venture.

Humans are the only known reservoir of variola. It is a large double stranded DNA virus. Because of the virulence and the droplet mode of transmission of this virus, in the absence of control measures, populations were infected with a mortality rate of 30%. The highly successful vaccination program was suspended after the last incidence of the disease was reported, leaving most people to day with little or no immunity. A crowded, mobile population with almost no immunity makes this organism as the choicest one for any probable future bioterrorism attack. Public health authorities all over the world should take a note of it. While there is no necessity to create an alarm about it, proper preparedness program would definitely reduce the morbidity and mortality profile.

3.13.1 Infection

The infectious dose is unknown, but is believed to be only a few virus particles. In managing smallpox, strict airborne and contact isolation of the patient must be enforced. The patient is contagious until all the scabs have separated. Public health authorities should immediately be notified to facilitate identification of other suspected cases and contacts that happen within 17 days of the onset of the patient's symptoms.

3.13.2 Treatment

Contacts, including health care workers require immediate vaccination. If vaccinated within 2-3 days of exposure, resulting disease may be prevented. If vaccinated within 4-5 days, the disease may be lessened; Passive protection with vaccinia immune globulin (VIG) should be considered for contacts and high-risk individuals showing vaccine complications such as, pregnancy, dermatoses, or immunosuppression. The vaccine is a live, attenuated vaccinia virus introduced into the skin by the multiple puncture technique with a bifurcated needle. **Smallpox immunity** from vaccination is **not lifelong**, and complications from the vaccination may occur.

3.13.3 Laboratory Diagnosis

Early in diagnosis the lesions of small pox may be confused with chickenpox; therefore, chickenpox should be ruled out by a molecular method, such as PCR (Polymerase Chain reaction) tests. Historically, the diagnosis of smallpox was largely a clinical diagnosis, sometimes with laboratory confirmation. If small pox is suspected to day, it should be immediately sent to a Level D laboratory after appropriate consultations. For most laboratories in the United States, the Level D laboratory will be a CDC laboratory. The CDC should be consulted before any shipment regarding the collection of sample, proper packaging, storing etc. In case it is suspected of smallpox, FBI will transport the specimen.

The specimen of choice would be the crust material or fluid from the base of a single vesicle placed as a droplet on a single slide and allowed to dry. One slide should be used for each lesion sampled. Each slide should be stored and shipped in a separate slide holders. Autopsy specimen must be frozen. Formalin solution is acceptable if histopathologic study is requested. Specimens should be stored at 4C briefly or at -20 to -70C when stored for a longer periods.

3.14 VIRAL HAEMORRHAGIC FEVER

Viral haemorrhagic fever (VHF) is caused by a variety of virus families including the Filoviruses (Ebola and Marburg fevers), Arenaviruses (Lassa, junin, machupo, sabia, and Guanarito fever), Bunyaviruses and Flaviviruses (dengue). Dengue is common is some USA and in some other neighboring countries. Hantavirus (a member of the Bunyaviridae) is found in several areas of the United States.No other viruses occur naturally in the continental United States. Natural vectors of these agents include rodents, mosquitoes, and ticks and are dependant on individual virus.

3.14.1 Incubation Period

The incubation period is normally between 5 to 10 days. But it may range from 2 to 16 days. Fact sheets of these diseases are available at http://www.cdc.gov/ncidod/dvrd/spb/mnpages/disinfo.htm.

3.14.2 Symptoms

Initial signs of VHF include flushing, conjunctival injection, periorbital edema, hypotension, and a positive tourniquet test. As disease progresses, fever, headache, malaise, and dizziness occur, along with myalgia, nausea, and vomiting. Later symptoms include prostration, and pharyngeal, chest or abdominal pain, along with mucous membrane bleeding, ecchymosis, and shock. Bleeding, central nervous system involvement, or a marked serum glutamic-oxaloacetic transaminase (SGOT) elevation indicate poor prognosis. Mortality rates, depending on the virus, range from 10% to 90%.

Differential Diagnosis includes typhoid fever, meningococcemia, rickettsioses, leptospirosis, falciparum malaria, vasculitis, TTP, or hemolylic uremic syndrome. Therapy is primarily supportive, with cautious sedation and analgesia. Coagulopathies must be corrected as necessary. In addition no antiplatelet drugs or intramuscular injections should be administered. Ribavirin may be effective for Arenaviruses and Bunyaviruses.

3.14.3 Laboratory Diagnosis

Like small pox the diagnosis is mostly clinical. All samples should be sent to the Level D laboratory for identification after due authorization is obtained. Normally 10-12ml of serum drawn at admission and again at 21days later for acute and convalescent analyses. Sera should be shipped cold or on dry ice in a plastic, not glass, tube. Although most tissue may be tested for the presence of the virus, the preferred tissue is from the lung, kidney, or spleen. Lymph node, heart, pancreas, pituitary, brain, or liver tissue is also acceptable. Paraffin blocks shipped at ambient temperature are preferred, but formularized tissue is adequate.

Table 5. Vaccine, Availability, Type, Efficacy

Disease/Agent	*Immunity by natural exposure*	*Vaccine type*
Anthrax	Yes*	Cell free culture filtrate of an avirulent, non-encapsulated, derivative of a bovine isolate designated, V770
Brucellosis	Yes	No human vaccine available in the United States
Botulism	No**	Pentavalent (ABCDE) toxoid***
Tularemia	Partial	Live attenuated vaccine
Plague	Partial	Suspension of killed (formalin inactivated) Yersia pestis
Small pox	Yes	Vaccinia (smallpox) vaccine grown in the skin of bovine calves
VHF	? ^	Not available

* Some degree of immunity is conferred following coetaneous anthrax. No detailed information regarding immunity following inhalation anthrax because of its low frequency and high mortality rate.

** Immunity to natural intoxication appears not to occur because of the toxin's potency; i.e., the lethal dose is below that required for an immune response

*** Distributed by the CDC under an investigated new drug (IND) protocol and used to protect high risk laboratory personnel actively working with C.botulinum or the toxins

^ Immunity to Lassa fever reinfection occurs following infection, but the length of protection is unknown.

Table 6. Vaccine, Efficacy and Comments

Disease/Agent	*Vaccine efficacy (aerosol exposure)*	*Comments*
Anthrax	Two-dose efficacy against 200 to 500 LD50 in Monkeys	Required for Level A laboratories. No lab-acquired cases. None reported since late 1950's, when the human vaccine was introduced, until the anthrax letter episodes during late 2001
Brucellosis	no vaccine	Required for level A laboratory. None available. It is one of the most commonly acquired laboratory

(Contd.)...

		infection reported so far. One of the largest reported cases involved 45 cases with one death. Protection is based on adherence to BSL-3 precautions. Immunity is acquired after active infection, both cellular and humoral immunity responses are required.
Botulism	Three dose efficacy100% Against 25 to 250 LD50 In monkeys	Required for Level A laboratories. There has been one case of laboratory acquired botulism. In food borne exposure immunity does not develop even with severe disease and its repeated Occurrence has been reported.
Tularemia	80% protection against 1 to 10 LD50 in monkeys	Required for Level A laboratories. This has been the third most common infection acquired in the laboratories. Multiple episodes of reinfection has been documented among vaccinated laboratory personnel and in unimmunized individuals.
Plague	has yet to be measured in a precise manner	Required for Level A laboratories. No laboratory acquired cases has been reported. Indirect evidence from military personnel indicate that the plague vaccine is effective for preventing fleaborne transmission of the disease.
Smallpox	Vaccine protects against Large doses in primates	Required for Level A lab. No laboratory acquired cases. If a Small pox sample has been handled in the Level A lab. within 3 days post exposure vaccination may be effective in preventing serious illness or death.
VHF	No vaccine	Required for Level A lab. No laboratory acquired cases. Skin mucous membrane exposure to virus laden material, such as blood, cell cultures, body fluids, secretions, has been responsible for most cases among humans. No data are available regarding immunity.

Table 7. Clinical Features of Various Diseases

Disease / Agent	*Clinical features*
Anthrax	All illnesses in acute form are characterized by several distinct clinical features: Cutaneous—A skin lesion evolving within 2 to 7 days from a papule, through a vesicular stage, to a depressed black eschar Gastrointestinal—Severe abdominal distress, followed by fever, and signs of septicemia, edema and fever. Inhalational—A brief prodrome resembling a viral respiratory illness, followed by development of hypoxia and dyspnea, withradiographic evidence of mediastinal widening.
Brucellosis	Acute form— < 8 weeks from onset, 'flu-like" symptoms Including fever, sweats, malaise, anorexia, headache, myalgia and back pain. Undulant form— < 1 year from onset, undulant fever, arthritis, or orchiepididymitis in young males. Chronic form— > 1 year from onset, symptoms may mimic Chronic fatigue syndrome, with episodes of depression.
Botulism	Food borne—intoxication caused by the ingestion of preformed exotoxin usually from improperly processed or canned low-acid foods contaminated with spores. Wound—Results from toxin produced by the organism after contamination of a wound site. Infant—Toxin elaborated in the intestinal tract of infants. Botulism caused by this mechanism in infants can also occur in older children and adults Inhalation—No natural occurrence, but developed as a biological weapon.
Tularemia	Ulceroglandular—Cutaneous ulcer with regional lymphadenopathy (45% to 80% of cases). Glandular—Regional lymphadenopathy without skin lesions (10% to 25% cases). Oculoglandular—Painful purulent conjunctivitis with periauricular lymphadenopathy(< 5% of cases). Oropharyngeal—Stomatitis or pharyngitis, or tonsilitis and cervical lymphadenopathy (< 5% cases). Typhoidal—(possible bioterrorism form). Septicemia with fever with no lymphadenopathy (< 5% cases). Pneumonic—(possible bioterrorism form). May be a primary or secondary pleuropulmonary disease (< 5% cases).

(Contd...)

Plague	Bubonic plague—Inguinal, axillary, or cervical lymph nodes commonly involved. Eighty percent become bacteremic with a 60% mortality rate if remain untreated. Septicemic plague—Virulent form that has a 100% mortality rate if untreated. Pneumonic plague—From aerosols or septicemic spread to lungs. Person to person transmission likely from lung infection with a 100% mortality rate if untreated.
Small pox	Prodrome phase—Incubation period 7-17 days. Acute onset of fever, malaise, prostration, headache, backache, occasional delirium, and a transient erythematous rash. Exanthem phase—Begins on face, oral mucosa, hands, and forearms, spreading to lower extremities, then the trunk over a seven-day period. Synchronous progression from macules, vesicles, pustules, and scabs. Lesions may occur on palms and soles.

3.15 BIOPREPAREDNESS DRUG INFORMATION

Monographs from the American Society of Health-System Pharmacists' (ASHP) will give pharmacists and other health professional's some

Comprehensive drug information on medications that may be needed to counter a terrorist attack.

The newly released Resource Manual contains 21 monographs that provide information on the vaccines and ant-infective medications that will most likely be used by the physicians to treat their patients who have contracted Anthrax, Small pox, or Plague. The monographs include discussions on the therapeutic roles of medications such as **Ciprofloxacin** (for treatment of **Anthrax), Gentamycin** (for the treatment of **Plague**), and **Smallpox vaccine** for smallpox.

The monographs also include information on-Drug interactions, toxicity, and cautions on Dosage and administration, Preparations, Chemistry, and stability, Pharmacology and Pharmacokinetics.

The manual includes the most current recommendations on prevention and treatment of infectious diseases from the Centers of Disease control and Prevention, the Public Health Service Advisory Committee on Immunization Practices, and others.

The Health professionals are recommended to collect that information by calling the customer service of ASHP at 301- 657- 4383 in USA or visit the web site of the society at www.ashp.org.

3.16 BIOLOGICAL AND CHEMICAL TERRORISM: STRATEGIC PLAN FOR PREPAREDNESS AND RESPONSE: RECOMMENDATIONS OF CDC STRATEGIC PLANNING WORKGROUP

Recommendations of the CDC (USA) Strategic Planning Workgroup, comprising of experts drawn from National Center for Infectious diseases, National Center for Environmental Health, Epidemiology Program Office and National Institute for Occupational Safety and Health, USA, *Moines, Iowa,* April 21,2000, pages 1-14, as has been widely disseminated through Internet for the benefit of all concerned, is summarized as follows:

In the above document, the CDC Working Group stated that the civilian vulnerability of U.S. national to the deliberate use of biological and chemical agents has been increased because of the growing increase in biological weapons development programs and stockpiling of arsenals in several foreign countries. The attempts to acquire biological agents by militants, and several high-profile terrorist attacks in various parts of the world made USA very vulnerable to such attacks. An evaluation of this vulnerability has focused attention on the role of public health in detecting and managing the probable covert biological terrorist incident. It has been realized that the U.S. local, state, and federal infrastructure were already considered to have fallen short of what was exactly needed. Moreover, other important public health problems are required to be addressed also. In collaboration with the representatives of local and state health departments, medical and public health professional associations, and other federal health agencies, CDC has developed a strategic plan for preparedness against the deliberate dissemination of biological or chemical agents. The plan also contains recommendations to reduce U.S. vulnerability to biological and chemical terrorism—preparedness planning, detection and surveillance, laboratory analysis, emergency response, and communication systems. They have also suggested that Training and Research are the two major components for achieving these recommendations. It has been pointed out that the success of the plan depends on strengthening the relationships between medical and public health professionals and on building new partner-ships with emergency management, the military, and law enforcement professionals.

In the introduction of the report, the CDC Working group illustrated that:

An act of biological or chemical terrorism might range from (1) dissemination of aerosolized anthrax spores to food product contamination, and (2) that when and how such an attack might occur is not possible to predict. Even though it cannot be predicted, the possibility of biological or chemical terrorism should not be ignored, especially in the light of events occurred during the past 10 years (e.g. the Sarin gas attack in the Tokyo subway and the suspicion and discovery of the military bioweapons programs in Iraq and the former Soviet Union. Preparing any nation to address this threat is a formidable challenge, but the consequences of being unprepared could be devastating.

The public health infrastructure must be prepared to prevent illness and injury that would result from biological and chemical terrorism, especially a covert terrorist attack. As with emerging infectious diseases, early detection and control of biological or chemical attacks depends on a strong and flexible public health system at the local, state, and federal levels. In addition, primary health-care providers throughout the United States must be vigilant because they will probably be the first to observe and report unusual illnesses or injuries, the report said.

This report is a summary of the recommendations made by CDC's Strategic Planning Workgroup entitled **Preparedness and Response to Biological and Chemical Terrorism: A Strategic Plan (CDC, unpublished report, 2000),** which outlines steps for strengthening public health and health-care capacity to protect the United States against those dangers. This strategic plan marks for the first time that CDC has joined with law enforcement, intelligence, and defense agencies in addition to traditional CDC partners to address a national security threat. Other countries may follow such guidelines adapted as per their own system of operations, requirements, availability of resources etc.

There is no denying the fact that a broad-based public health involvement is required in terrorism preparedness and planning. In the CDC working Group, staff from CDC's centers, institutes, and offices participated in developing the strategic plan. These include:

- National Center for Infectious Diseases,
- National Center for Environmental Health,
- Public Health Practice Program Office,
- Epidemiology Program Office,
- National Institute for Occupational Safety and Health,
- Office of Health and Safety,
- National Immunization Program, and
- National Center for Injury Prevention and Control.

When preparedness against Radiological Terrorism is to be effected, then National Centers and Laboratories dealing with Atomic Energy are to be included. In USA, Brookhaven National Laboratory, Radiation Laboratory at Los Alamos, CALTECH, MIT, Princeton Laboratory and any other Laboratory or Universities dealing with preventive and therapeutic aspect of radiation may be included in the team.

The Agency for Toxic Substances and Disease Registry (ATSDR) is also participating with CDC in this effort and will provide expertise in the area of industrial chemical terrorism. In this report, the term *CDC* includes ATSDR when activities related to chemical terrorism are discussed. In addition, colleagues from local, state, and federal agencies; emergency medical services (EMS); professional societies; universities and medical centers; and private industry provided suggestions and constructive criticism.

Combating biological and chemical terrorism will require capitalizing on advances in technology, information systems, and medical sciences. Preparedness will also require a re-examination of core public health activities (e.g., disease surveillance) in light of these advances. Preparedness efforts by public health agencies and primary health-care providers to detect and respond to biological and chemical terrorism will have the added benefit of strengthening the U.S. capacity for identifying and controlling injuries and emerging infectious diseases, the report stated.

3.16.1 U.S. Vulnerability to Biological, Chemical and Radiological Terrorism

Terrorist incidents in the United States and elsewhere involving bacterial pathogens, nerve gas, and a lethal plant toxin (i.e., ricin) (Further reading 5 and 6), have demonstrated that the United States is vulnerable to biological and chemical threats as well as explosives. Recipes for preparing "homemade" agents are readily available (Further reading 5), and reports of arsenals of military bioweapons (Further reading 5, 6) raise the possibility that terrorists might have access to highly dangerous agents, which have been engineered for mass dissemination as small-particle aerosols. Such agents as the variola virus, the causative agent of smallpox, are highly contagious and often fatal. Responding to large-scale outbreaks caused by these agents will require the rapid mobilization of public health workers, emergency responders, and private health-care providers. Large-scale outbreaks will also require rapid procurement and distribution of large quantities of drugs and vaccines, which must be available quickly.

3.16.2 Overt Versus Covert Terrorist Attacks

In the past, most planning for emergency response to terrorism has been concerned with overt attacks (e.g., bombings). Chemical terrorism acts are likely to be overt because the effects of chemical agents absorbed through inhalation or by absorption through the skin or mucous membranes are usually immediate and obvious. Such attacks elicit immediate response from police, fire, and EMS personnel.

In contrast, attacks with biological agents are more likely to be covert. They present different challenges and require an additional dimension of emergency planning that involves the public health infrastructure (Box 1 <http://www.cdc.gov/mmwr/preview/mmwrhtml/rr4904a1.htm>). Covert dissemination of a biological agent in a public place will not have an immediate impact because of the delay between exposure and onset of illness (i.e., the incubation period). Consequently, physicians or other primary health-care providers probably will identify the first casualties of a covert attack. For example, in the event of a covert release of the contagious variola virus, patients will appear in doctors' offices, clinics, and emergency rooms during the first or second week, complaining of fever, back pain, headache, nausea, and other symptoms of what initially might appear to be an ordinary viral infection. As the disease progresses, these persons will develop the popular rash characteristic of early-stage smallpox, a rash that physicians might not recognize immediately. By the time the rash becomes pustular and patients begin to die, the terrorists would be far away and the disease disseminated through the population by person-to-person contact. Only a short window of opportunity will exist between the time the first cases are identified and a second wave of the population becomes ill. During that brief period, public health officials will need to determine that an attack has occurred, identify the organism, and prevent more casualties through prevention strategies (e.g., mass vaccination or prophylactic treatment). As person-to-person contact continues, successive waves of transmission could carry infection to other worldwide localities. These issues might also be relevant for other person-to-person transmissible etiologic agents (e.g., plague or certain viral hemorrhagic fevers).

Certain chemical agents can also be delivered covertly through contaminated food or water. In 1999, the vulnerability of the food supply was illustrated in Belgium, when chickens were unintentionally exposed to dioxin-contaminated fat used to make animal feed (Further reading *6*). Because the contamination was not discovered for months, the dioxin, a cancer-causing chemical that does not cause immediate symptoms in humans, was probably present in chicken meat and eggs sold in Europe during early 1999. This incident underscores the need for prompt diagnoses of unusual or suspicious health problems in animals as well as humans, a lesson that was also demonstrated by the recent outbreak of mosquitoborne West Nile virus in birds and humans in New York City in 1999. The dioxin episode also demonstrates how a covert act of foodborne biological or chemical terrorism could affect commerce and human or animal health, the report noted.

3.16.3 Focusing Preparedness Activities

From the above discussion, there remains no doubt that an early detection of and response to biological or chemical terrorism are crucial. Without special preparation at the local and state levels, a large-scale attack with variola virus, aerosolized anthrax spores, a nerve gas, or a foodborne biological or chemical agent could overwhelm the local and perhaps national public health infrastructure. Large numbers of patients, including both infected persons and the "worried well," would seek medical attention, with a corresponding need for medical supplies, diagnostic tests, and hospital beds. Emergency responders, health-care workers, and public health officials could be at special risk, and everyday life would be disrupted as a result of widespread fear of contagion.

Preparedness for terrorist-caused outbreaks and injuries is an essential component of the U.S. public health surveillance and response system, which is designed to protect the population against any unusual public health event (e.g., influenza pandemics, contaminated municipal water supplies, or intentional dissemination of *Yersinia pestis*, the causative agent of plague [Further Reading 5 and 6]. The epidemiological skills, surveillance methods, diagnostic techniques, and physical resources required to detect and investigate unusual or unknown diseases, as well as syndromes or injuries caused by chemical accidents, are similar to those needed to identify and respond to an attack with a biological or chemical agent. However, public health agencies must prepare also for the special features a terrorist attack probably would have (e.g., mass casualties or the use of rare agents) (Boxes 2-5 <http://www.cdc.gov/mmwr/preview/mmwrhtml/rr4904a1.htm>). Terrorists might use combinations of these agents, attack in more than one location simultaneously, use new agents, or use organisms that are not on the critical list (e.g., common, drug-resistant, or genetically engineered pathogens). Lists of critical biological and chemical agents will need to be modified as new information becomes available. In addition, each state and locality will need to adapt the lists to local conditions and preparedness needs by using the criteria provided in CDC's strategic plan.

It has been stated earlier that potential biological and chemical agents are numerous, and the public health infrastructure must be equipped to quickly resolve crises that would arise from a biological or chemical attack. However, to best protect the public, the preparedness efforts must be focused on agents that might have the greatest impact on U.S. health and security, especially agents that are highly contagious or that can be engineered for widespread dissemination via small-particle aerosols. Preparing the nation to address these dangers is a major challenge to U.S. public health systems and health-care providers. Early detection requires increased biological and chemical terrorism awareness among front-line health-care providers because they are in the best position to report suspicious illnesses and injuries. Also, early detection will require improved communication systems between those providers and public health officials. In addition, state and local health-care agencies must have enhanced capacity to investigate unusual events and unexplained illnesses, and diagnostic laboratories must be equipped to identify biological and chemical agents that rarely are seen in the United States. Fundamental to these efforts is comprehensive, integrated training designed to ensure core competency in public health preparedness and the highest levels of scientific expertise among local, state, and federal partners.

3.17 KEY FOCUS AREAS

CDC's strategic plan is based on the following five focus areas, with each area integrating training and research:

- Preparedness and prevention;
- Detection and surveillance;
- Diagnosis and characterization of biological and chemical agents;
- Response; and
- Communication.

Those points are equally important for all the nations of the world, which are in the process of developing a Disaster Management Plan and a Disaster Response System against chemical/biological /radiological accidents or terrorist attacks.

3.17.1 Preparedness and Prevention: Role Played by CDC

Detection, diagnosis, and mitigation of illness and injury caused by biological and chemical terrorism is a complex process that involves numerous partners and activities. Meeting this challenge will require special emergency preparedness in all cities, towns and states. In USA, CDC (Center for Disease Control) will provide public health guidelines, support, and technical assistance to local and state public health agencies as they develop coordinated preparedness plans and response protocols. CDC also will provide self-assessment tools for terrorism preparedness, including performance standards, attack simulations, and other exercises. In addition, CDC will encourage and support applied research to develop innovative tools and strategies to prevent or mitigate illness and injury caused by biological and chemical terrorism.

3.17.2 Detection and Surveillance

Early detection is essential for ensuring a prompt response to a biological or chemical attack, including the provision of prophylactic medicines, chemical antidotes, or vaccines. CDC will integrate surveillance for illness and injury resulting from biological and chemical terrorism into the U.S. disease surveillance systems, while developing new mechanisms for detecting, evaluating, and reporting suspicious events that might represent covert terrorist acts. As part of this effort, CDC and state and local health agencies will form partnerships with front-line medical personnel in hospital emergency departments, hospital care facilities, poison control centers, and other offices to enhance detection and reporting of unexplained injuries and illnesses as part of routine surveillance mechanisms for biological and chemical terrorism.

3.17.3 Diagnosis and Characterization of Biological and Chemical Agents

CDC and its partners will create a multilevel laboratory response network for bioterrorism (LRNB). That network will link clinical labs to public health agencies in all states, districts, territories, and selected cities and counties and to state-of-the-art facilities that can analyze biological agents. As part of this effort, CDC will transfer diagnostic technology to state health laboratories and others who will perform initial testing. CDC will also create an in-house rapid-response and advanced technology (RRAT) laboratory. This laboratory will provide around-the-clock diagnostic confirmatory and reference support for terrorism response teams. This network will include the regional chemical laboratories for diagnosing human exposure to chemical agents and provide links with other departments (e.g., the U.S. Environmental Protection Agency, which is responsible for environmental sampling).

3.17.4 Response

A comprehensive public health response to a biological or chemical terrorist event involves epidemiologic investigation, medical treatment and prophylaxis for affected persons, and the initiation of disease prevention or environmental decontamination measures. CDC will assist state and local health agencies in developing resources and expertise for investigating unusual events and unexplained illnesses. In the event of a confirmed terrorist attack, CDC will coordinate with other federal agencies in accord with Presidential Decision Directive (PDD) 39. PDD 39 designates the Federal Bureau of Investigation as the lead agency for the crisis plan and charges the Federal Emergency Management Agency with ensuring that the federal response management is adequate to respond to the consequences of terrorism (8). If requested by a state health agency, CDC will deploy response teams to investigate unexplained or suspicious illnesses or unusual etiologic agents and provide on-site consultation regarding medical management and disease control. To ensure the availability, procurement, and delivery of medical supplies, devices, and equipment that might be needed to respond to terrorist-caused illness or injury, CDC will maintain a national pharmaceutical stockpile.

3.17.5 Communication Systems

U.S. preparedness to mitigate the public health consequences of biological and chemical terrorism depends on the coordinated activities of well-trained health-care and public health personnel throughout the United States who have access to up-to-the minute emergency information. Effective communication with the public through the news media will also be essential to limit terrorists' ability to induce public panic and disrupt daily life. During the next 5 years, CDC will work with state and local health agencies to develop a) a state-of-the-art communication system that will support disease surveillance; b) rapid notification and information exchange regarding disease outbreaks that are possibly related to bioterrorism; c) dissemination of diagnostic results and emergency health information; and d) coordination of emergency response activities. Through this network and similar mechanisms, CDC will provide terrorism-related training to epidemiologists and laboratory technicians, emergency responders, emergency department personnel and other front-line health-care providers, and health and safety personnel.

3.17.6 Partnerships and Implementation

Implementation of the objectives outlined in CDC's strategic plan will be coordinated through CDC's Bioterrorism Preparedness and Response Program. Program personnel are charged with a) helping build local and state preparedness, b) developing U.S. expertise regarding potential threat agents, and c) coordinating response activities during actual bioterrorist events. Program staff has established priorities for 2000-2002 regarding the focus areas (Box 6 <http://www.cdc.gov/mmwr/preview/mmwrhtml/rr4904a1.htm>).

Implementation will require collaboration with state and local public health agencies, as well as with other persons and groups, including:

- Public health organizations,
- Medical research centers,
- Health-care providers and their networks,

- Professional societies,
- Medical examiners,
- Emergency response units and responder organizations,
- Safety and medical equipment manufacturers,
- The U.S. Office of Emergency Preparedness and other Department of Health and Human Services agencies,
- Other federal agencies, and
- International organizations.

3.17.7 Recommendations

Implementing CDC's strategic preparedness and response plan by 2004 will ensure the following outcomes:

- U.S. public health agencies and health-care providers will be prepared to mitigate illness and injuries that result from acts of biological and chemical terrorism.
- Public health surveillance for infectious diseases and injuries — including events that might indicate terrorist activity — will be timely and complete, and reporting of suspected terrorist events will be integrated with the evolving, comprehensive networks of the national public health surveillance system.
- The national laboratory response network for bioterrorism will be extended to include facilities in all 50 states. The network will include CDC's environmental health laboratory for chemical terrorism and four regional facilities.
- State and federal public health departments will be equipped with state-of-the-art tools for rapid epidemiological investigation and control of suspected or confirmed acts of biological or chemical terrorism, and a designated stock of terrorism-related medical supplies will be available through a national pharmaceutical stockpile.
- A cadre of well-trained health-care and public health workers will be available in every state. Their terrorism-related activities will be coordinated through a rapid and efficient communication system that links U.S. public health agencies and their partners.

3.17.8 Concluding Part of the Report

Recent threats and use of biological, chemical and radiological agents against civilians have exposed U.S. vulnerability and highlighted the need to enhance our capacity to detect and control terrorist acts. The U.S. must be protected from an extensive range of critical biological and chemical agents, including some that have been developed and stockpiled for military use. Even without threat of war, investment in national defense ensures preparedness and acts as a deterrent against hostile acts. Similarly, investment in the public health system provides the best civil defense against bioterrorism. Tools developed in response to terrorist threats serve a dual purpose. They help detect rare or unusual disease outbreaks and respond to health emergencies, including naturally occurring outbreaks or industrial injuries that might resemble terrorist events in their unpredictability and ability to cause mass casualties (e.g., a pandemic influenza outbreak or a large-scale chemical spill). Terrorism-preparedness activities described in CDC's plan, including the development of a public health communication infrastructure, a multilevel network of diagnostic laboratories, and an integrated disease surveillance system, will improve our ability to investigate rapidly and control public health threats that emerge in the twenty first century. (Further Reading No. 5)

BOX 1. Local public health agency preparedness

- Because the initial detection of a covert biological or chemical attack will probably occur at the local level, disease surveillance systems at state and local health agencies must be capable of detecting unusual patterns of disease or injury, including those caused by unusual or unknown threat agents.
- Because the initial response to a covert biological or chemical attack will probably be made at the local level, epidemiologists at state and local health agencies must have expertise and resources for responding to reports of clusters of rare, unusual, or unexplained illnesses.

BOX 2. Preparing public health agencies for biological attacks.

Steps in Preparing for Biological Attacks

- Enhance epidemiologic capacity to detect and respond to biological attacks.
- Supply diagnostic reagents to state and local public health agencies.
- Establish communication programs to ensure delivery of accurate information.
- Enhance bioterrorism-related education and training for health-care professionals.
- Prepare educational materials that will inform and reassure the public during and after a biological attack.
- Stockpile appropriate vaccines and drugs.
- Establish molecular surveillance for microbial strains, including unusual or drug-resistant strains.
- Support the development of diagnostic tests.
- Encourage research on antiviral drugs and vaccines.

BOX 3. Critical biological agents

Category A

The U.S. public health system and primary health-care providers must be prepared to address varied biological agents, including pathogens that are rarely seen in the United States. High-priority agents include organisms that pose a risk to national security because they

- can be easily disseminated or transmitted person-to-person;
- cause high mortality, with potential for major public health impact;
- might cause public panic and social disruption; and
- require special action for public health preparedness (Box 2 <http://www.cdc.gov/mmwr/preview/mmwrhtml/rr4904a1.htm>).

Category A agents include:

- variola major (smallpox);
- *Bacillus anthracis* (anthrax);
- *Yersinia pestis* (plague);
- *Clostridium botulinum* toxin (botulism);
- *Francisella tularensis* (tularaemia);
- Filoviruses,
  - Ebola hemorrhagic fever,
  - Marburg hemorrhagic fever; and
- Arenaviruses,
  - Lassa (Lassa fever),
  - **Junin (Argentine hemorrhagic fever) and related viruses.**

Category B

Second highest priority agents include those that

- are moderately easy to disseminate;
- cause moderate morbidity and low mortality; and
- require specific enhancements of CDC's diagnostic capacity and enhanced disease surveillance.

***Category B agents** include:*

- *Coxiella burnetti* (Q fever);
- *Brucella* species (brucellosis);
- *Burkholderia mallei* (glanders);
- Alphaviruses,
  - Venezuelan encephalomyelitis,
  - Eastern and western equine encephalomyelitis;
- Ricin toxin from *Ricinus communis* (castor beans);
- Epsilon toxin of *Clostridium perfringens*; and
- *Staphylococcus* enterotoxin B.

A subset of List B agents includes pathogens that are food- or waterborne. These pathogens include but are not limited to

- *Salmonella* species,
- *Shigella dysenteriae*,
- *Escherichia coli* O157:H7,
- *Vibrio cholerae*, and
- *Cryptosporidium parvum*.

Category C

Third highest priority agents include emerging pathogens that could be engineered for mass dissemination in the future because of

- Availability;
- Ease of production and dissemination; and
- Potential for high morbidity and mortality and major health impact.

Category C agents include:

- Napa virus,
- Hantaviruses,
- Tick borne hemorrhagic fever viruses,
- Tick borne encephalitis viruses,
- Yellow fever, and
- Multidrug-resistant tuberculosis.

Preparedness for List C agents requires ongoing research to improve disease detection, diagnosis, treatment, and prevention. Knowing in advance which newly emergent pathogens terrorists might employ is not possible; therefore, linking bioterrorism preparedness efforts with ongoing disease surveillance and outbreak response activities as defined in CDC's emerging infectious disease strategy are imperative. *

*** CDC. Preventing emerging infectious diseases: a strategy for the 21st century. Atlanta, Georgia: U.S. Department of Health and Human Services, 1998.**

BOX 4. Preparing public health agencies for chemical attacks

Steps in Preparing for Chemical Attacks

- Enhance epidemiologic capacity for detecting and responding to chemical attacks
- Enhance awareness of chemical terrorism among emergency medical service personnel, police officers, firefighters, physicians and nurses.
- Stockpile chemical antidotes
- Develop and provide bioassays for detection and diagnosis of chemical injuries
- Prepare educational materials to inform the public during and after a chemical attack

BOX 5. Chemical agents

Chemical agents that might be used by terrorists range from warfare agents to toxic chemicals commonly used in industries. Criteria for determining priority chemical agents include:

- Chemical agents already known to be used as weaponry,
- Availability of chemical agents to potential terrorists
- Chemical agents likely to cause major morbidity and mortality
- Potential of agents for causing public panic and social disruption, and
- Agents that require special action for public health preparedness (Box 4)

A list of different categories of specialized chemical agents such as Nerve agents, Blood agents, Blister agents, toxic heavy metals, Volatile toxins, Pulmonary agents, Incapacitating Agents, Poisonous Industrial Gases, solvents, acids, and bases have been listed earlier during the dissuasion on hazardous chemicals. Those are also to be considered for proper capability building in the area of proper diagnosis and treatment.

BOX 6. Implementation priorities regarding focus areas for 2000-2002

Preparedness and prevention

- Maintain a public health preparedness and response cooperative agreement that provides support to state health agencies that are working with local agencies in developing coordinated anti-terrorism plans and protocols.
- Establish a national public health distance-learning system that provides chemical/ biological/radiological terrorism preparedness training to health-care workers and to state and local public health workers.
- Disseminate public health guidelines and performance standards on chemical, biological and radiological terrorism preparedness planning for use by state and local health agencies.

Detection and surveillance

- Strengthen state and local surveillance systems for illness and injury resulting from pathogens and chemical and radiological substances that are on CDC's critical agents list.
- Develop new algorithms and statistical methods for searching medical databases on a real time basis for evidence of suspicious events.
- Establish criteria for investigating and evaluating suspicious clusters of animal or human disease or injury and triggers for notifying law enforcement of suspected acts of biological, chemical or radiological terrorism.

Diagnosis and characterization of chemical/biological/radiological agents

- Establish a multilevel laboratory response network for bioterrorism that links public health laboratories/agencies to advanced-capacity facilities for the identification and reporting of critical biological agents.
- Establish regional chemical /biological/radiological terrorism laboratories that will provide diagnostic capacity during terrorist attacks involving chemical /radiological agents
- Establish a rapid response and advanced technology laboratory within CDC to provide around-the-clock diagnostic support to terrorism response teams and expedite molecular characterization of critical biological agents.

Response

- Assist state and local health agencies in organizing response capacities to rapidly deploy in the event of an overt attack or a suspicious outbreak that might be the result of a covert attack.
- Ensure that the procedures are in place for rapid mobilization of CDC terrorism response teams that will provide on-site assistance to local workers, security agents, and law enforcement officers.
- Establish a national pharmaceutical stockpile to provide medical supplies in the event of a terrorist attack that involves chemical/biological /radiological agents.
- Establish a national electronic infrastructure to improve exchange of emergency health information among local, state, and federal health agencies.
- Implement an emergency communication plan that ensures rapid dissemination of health information to the public during actual, threatened, or suspected acts of chemical/biological/radiological terrorism.
- Create a website that disseminates terrorism preparedness and training information, as well as other terrorism-related emergency information, to public health and health -care workers and the public

3.18 REMOTE POSSIBILITY OF USE OF BIOLOGICAL / RADIOLOGICAL AGENTS AS POTENTIAL TERRORISM AGENTS

There is only a remote possibility that anybody or by a group or by any nation will ever use any biological/radiological agents/bombs against potential enemy targets unless he is lunatic or under any spell or he is committed to perform an act of heroic nature for which he has been especially trained and then assigned this as a noble duty. The technology involved, the cost to be incurred, and sophistication, which is required to prepare those agents, is not the task of any single person or even by any small group. But you never know. Cult effect is still there in many parts of the world. Several years ago, both the Cult **GURU** and his several hundred followers died together by drinking some poisonous liquid somewhere in southern America. But today's world is becoming more and more complex, and therefore uncertain. Nothing can be predicted for sure. No body can give any guarantee that it will never happen.

It is very disturbing to see that even the United Nations is helpless when it comes to the question of imposition of certain restrictions / regulations or International law to an individual or a small group of insurgents/terrorists etc. Besides that suicide bombers and killers are now frequently available. They are being trained for carrying out heinous crimes in different parts of world. State-sponsored training camps for training the terrorists in large numbers have been reported. These people may be used for smuggling of radiochemical, weapon-grade refined uranium or plutonium ***per se, including spare parts for nuclear reactors*** **and other necessities**, which are required for the construction of atomic bomb. Several countries had stockpiled huge quantities of atomic arsenals, which are enough to destroy several planets like that of EARTH. One cannot ensure totally that at least some of them will never be smuggled out or those premises will never be bombed by terrorists. Openly several nations trade their atomic know-how, and secretly send their atomic bomb experts in other countries to help them develop atom bombs. Even though the father of Atomic Power and Atom Bomb expert of Pakistan divulged on camera that he and his colleagues had transferred the atom bomb technology to Libya, Iran and North Korea, the world bodies and the people of the world in particular have remained as silent spectators. They cannot do anything. They have no such powers to be able to do anything. This has obviously made the issue very serious. Thus it appears that from the point of "Impossibility", the use of Radio-weapons and Bioweapons have become a possibility in today's troubled world.

It is very unfortunate that if the United States of America feels very vulnerable, then where the others stand in the world is something to think about. Collective efforts are essential and collective measures are necessary to fight out terrorism from the world, if not completely at least in part thereof.

3.18.1 Preparedness Against RADIOLOGIC AGENTS

While radium, uranium and plutonium are highly radioactive, radionuclides, radioisotopes and radio labeled chemicals with high specific activity and long half-life can be dangerous if human beings are exposed to it. Depending on the extent of exposure, and the nature of radiological agents to which the individual is exposed, the nature of damages that it can cause depends. Both from minor to extremely severe type of damages are anticipated. What is of more importance is the fact that the health effects of radiochemicals can pass on from one generation to another. Radiation causes mutation at the germ cell level leading into impotency, abortion, abnormal childbirth, mental retardation etc. It can cause cancer as well. Very high level of radiation causes burns, spontaneous death.

With the technological advancement, today both fusion and fission technologies are used for the manufacture of an Atomic Bomb. Besides Hydrogen Bombs, Neutron Bombs and similar other types of high power Atomic Bombs have been manufactured and stored in several parts of the world. The devastating power of an Atomic Bomb depends on the amount (kilotons to megatons) of atomic fuel it carries. The Hiroshima and Nagasaki experiences had given the world some practical experiences regarding the severe devastation that it can cause in terms of killing of human lives and destroying his property.

No body wants it to happen any more. But still people are worried. Just in case! This is the reason why a great degree of understanding is needed as to the preparedness plan for protection of human lives, and prophylactic and therapeutic measures etc.

3.18.2 Fallout from Atomic Explosion/Implosion in any Part of the World

If nukes are ever blasted by anybody, warring participants, by accidents, during transport or accidentally during its manufacture or deliberately by the terrorists, in any part of the world USA, UK, France, Germany, India, Pakistan, Iran, China or Japan, everybody everywhere in the world would soon be in deep trouble, no matter whether you are directly involved, targeted or not.

It is to be understood that soon after any nuclear detonation taking place anywhere in the Northern Hemisphere, people living in the USA and in other countries could be having their radioactive fallout raining down on their soil. There will be a large amount of thyroid-contaminating radioactive iodine. Wind-current will carry the nuclear ashes in various directions and the nuclear fallout will be there within a few days.

On December 28,1966 the Chinese made an underground nuclear test of the order of few hundred kilotons. Interestingly, radioactive fallout was detected in most of the United States of America and in other countries as well. In a book (57) "Nuclear war survival skills" published by Oak Ridge National Laboratory, US Department of Energy, 1987,details of various aspects of it have been described.

The author of the above book, Cresson H. Kearny(57) stated about this, **now declassified incident**: Kearney wrote:

"It produced fallout that by January 1, 1967 resulted in the fallout cloud covering most of the United States. This one Chinese explosion produced about 15 million curies of iodine-131- roughly the same amount as the total release of iodine-131 into the atmosphere from the Chernobyl nuclear power plant disaster."

About 300 **kilo**ton of Chinese nuclear test explosion caused pastures near Oak Ridge, Tennessee and elsewhere to be contaminated with radioiodine. It entered in the food chain, which eventually found its way in the Cow's milk and milk products. Milk was contaminated up to 900 picocuries of radioactive iodine per liter of milk. Gamma rays were emitted from the fallout particles in different parts of the United States. This indicated that trans-Pacific fallout from even an overseas nuclear war using two or three hundred **mega**tons of nuclear material could result in tens of thousands of people suffering from various ailments including thyroid problems, according to Kearney (57).

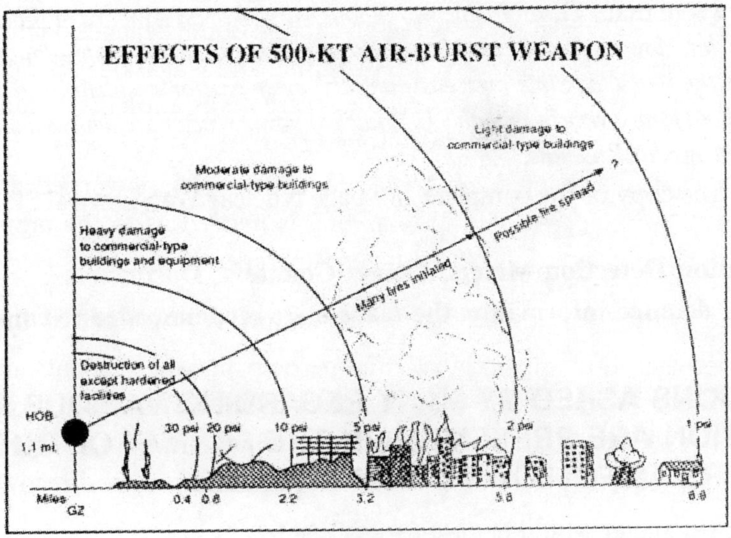

(*a*)

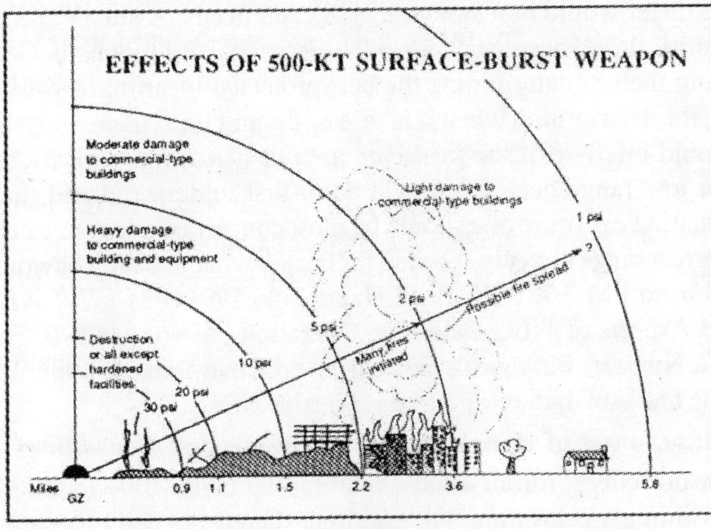

(*b*)

Fig. 3.2. Picture shows the extensive areas covered under Blast, heat and radiation, (*a*) When the blast is in the air, (*b*) When the blast is on the ground.

He had also stated "It is now quite possible that the first nuclear war casualties in the United States and other countries adjacent to the USA will be caused by fallouts from an overseas **nuclear war** in which USA may not even be directly involved. It is definitely a matter of great concern to the peace-loving people of the world that more and more countries in the Middle East, South East Asia and Eastern Europe are embarking upon nuclear programmes, which in fact poses danger not only for their own as well as to the entire world. What appears to be dangerous is that it might fall someday in the hands of the Terrorists".

Kearney wrote that *"Trans-Pacific war fallout, carried to an America at peace by the prevailing west-to-east winds that blow around the world, could be several hundred times more dangerous to Americans than fallout from the worst possible overseas nuclear power reactor accident, and many times more dangerous than fallout from a very improbable U.S. nuclear power reactor accident as lethal as the disastrous Chernobyl accident was to Russians."*

A free on-line copy of the complete 280-page Nuclear War Survival Skills book is at the FAQ.

(*ii*) **Radiation Detection Meters, Geiger Counters, Dosimeters**

(REF. For detailed information the readers are recommended to consult KI4U, Inc.)

3.19 QUESTIONS ASKED BY MANY REGARDING VARIOUS ASPECTS OF RADIATION ARE PRESENTED IN THE FORMAT OF QUESTION AND ANSWERS AS FOLLOWS (FROM KI4U, INC.)

Q: Which survey meter would be best for my needs?

Ans: The first decision in selecting a survey meter is choosing whether a high-range meter or a low-range meter would best suit your goals and needs. A survey meter will be used to help make critical decisions, such as to flee, how far, and to where. Or, to stay in-place, and if staying then in determining the best-protected location in your home or shelter. Then, later, for determining when it is safe again and until then, when and for how long someone could briefly exit the protected area to perform a critical chore, etc. Key to that high or low range decision should be to first understand and then determine the levels of radiation exposure one should be most concerned about in a nuclear emergency. Then the correct range meter best suited for the job will be readily obvious. The following is compiled from FM 3-7. NBC Field Handbook, 1994. FM 8-9. NATO Handbook on the Medical Aspects of NBC Defensive Operations, 1996. FM 8-10-7. Health Services Support in a Nuclear, Biological, and Chemical Environment, 1996. It is instructive in outlining the levels of radiation and their health effects.

Exposure dose, onset of signs or initial symptoms and dispositions

Expected health effects for an adult assuming the cumulative total radiation exposure was all received within a week's time. For children, the effects can be expected at half these dose levels.

Total Exposure	*Onset & Duration of Initial Symptoms & Disposition*
30 to 70 R	From 6-12 hours: none to slight incidence of transient headache and nausea; Vomiting in up to 5 percent of personnel in upper part of dose range. Mild Lymphocyte depression within 24 hours. Full recovery expected. (Fetus damage Possible from 50R and above.)

(Contd...)

70 to 150 R	From 2-20 hours: transient mild nausea and vomiting in 5 to 30 percent of Personnel. Potential for delayed traumatic and surgical wound healing, Minimal clinical effect. Moderate drop in lymphocyte, platelet, and Gametocyte counts. Increased susceptibility to opportunistic pathogens. Full recovery expected.
150 to 300 R	From 2 hours to three days: transient to moderate nausea and vomiting in 20 to 70 percent; mild to moderate fatigability and weakness in 25 to 60 Percent of personnel. At 3 to 5 weeks: medical care required for 10 to 50%. At high end of range, death may occur to maximum 10%. Anticipated medical Problems include infection, bleeding, and fever. Wounding or burns will Geometrically increase morbidity and mortality.
300 to 530 R	From 2 hours to three days: transient to moderate nausea and vomiting in 50 To 90 percent; mild to moderate fatigability in 50 to 90 percent of personnel. At 2 to 5 weeks: medical care required for 10 to 80%. At low end of range, Less than 10% deaths; at high end, death may occur for more than 50%. Anticipated medical problems include frequent diarrhea stools, anorexia, Increased fluid loss, ulceration. Increased infection susceptibility during Immunocompromised time frame. Moderate to severe loss of lymphocytes. Hair loss after 14 days.
530 to 830 R	From 2 hours to two days: moderate to severe nausea and vomiting in 80 to 100 percent of personnel; From 2 hours to six weeks: moderate to severe Fatigability and weakness in 90 to 100 percent of personnel. At 10 days to 5 weeks: medical care required for 50 to 100%. At low end of range, death May occur for more than 50% at six weeks. At high end, death may occur For 99% of personnel. Anticipated medical problems include developing Pathogenic and opportunistic infections, bleeding, fever, loss of appetite, GI ulcerations, bloody diarrhea, severe fluid and electrolyte shifts, capillary leak, hypo tension. Combined with any significant physical trauma, survival rates will approach zero.
830 R Plus	From 30 minutes to 2 days: severe nausea, vomiting, fatigability, weakness, dizziness, and disorientation; moderate to severe fluid imbalance and headache. Bone marrow total depletion within days. CNS symptoms are predominant at Higher radiation levels. Few, if any, survivors even with aggressive and Immediate medical attention.

It should be readily apparent now that the more dangerous levels of radiation are well beyond the capability of measurement of a low-range survey meter, such as the CD V-700, which would be maxed out at 50 mR/hr which is only .05 R/hr. (A low-range meter is better suited for verifying successful decontamination and/or checking for low-level contamination in food or water.) With that meter alone, and maxed out, you would not know if you just walked into a 1 R/hr field or a potentially fatal 1000+ R/hr environment.

Cresson H. Kearny, covers this point, too, in his book *Nuclear War Survival Skills, Chapter 10—Fallout Radiation Meters:*

Some companies sell instruments that measure only milliroentgen-range dose rates for war use. Since most people have no idea what size of radiation doses would incapacitate or kill them, and do not even know that a milliroentgen is 1/1000 of a roentgen, some people buy instruments that are capable of measuring maximum dose rates of only one roentgen or less per hour, which is far too low to be of much use in a nuclear war.

Bottom Line: Low-range survey meters, like the CD V-700, do have their place, but without a higher-range survey meter first, and initially, warning you away from exposure to excessively high levels of lethal radiation, the opportunity to later even use a low-range meter may never come!

OK, so if it were a high-range survey meter we would need first, then which Civil Defense high-range survey meter is *'the best'*?

We asked this and other important related questions in all of our conversations with the FEMA technicians and radiological officers we interviewed. They responded; #1 - Any of the high-range Civil Defense meters will work just fine IF it has been properly maintained, stored, and calibrated. Also, calibration no more frequently than every three years is normally sufficient IF shelf-bound and stored properly, but is much more frequently required if subjected to rough handling, for example, bouncing around in the trunk of a car. Also, they emphasized that the calibration needs to always be with a sufficiently strong enough radioactive source that a mid-scale meter reading can be attained for all the ranges, not just the lower ranges. #2 - Universally, when pushed to rank them, most all of them said their preference for a particular CD survey meter model was in the following order: CD V-715, CD V-717, and CD V-720. Asked to elaborate why this personal preference and most said it was for the lighter weight of the CD V-715 over the other two and the basic KISS principle in that the CD V-715 had no frill 'bells & whistles' that might invite complications in the field. Also, many were openly critical of the CD V-720 design 'feature' of its sliding beta shield for attaining beta readings. They felt it was more of marketing 'feature' than of any real practical use. They also found it required more maintenance attention as it was more prone to allow the intrusion of humidity and dirt internally. We also inquired how comfortable they were with used and visibly worn Civil Defense survey meters compared to any of the same type new and largely unused meters available there on their shelves, too. They made it clear that it didn't matter, used or new looking, just so long as it was properly maintained, calibrated, and stored until needed. If called on to respond to a radiological emergency, they would rush out the door with whatever unit, new or used, was known to them to of been properly maintained, calibrated, and stored correctly there.

The following are various FAQs publicized on behalf of KI4U, Inc. The author does not take any responsibility for these items. These are presented here only for information. The consumer may use it at his or her own risks. The author and the publisher of this monograph do not bear any responsibility in any case.

But for the convenience of the potential readers and users those are presented below:

'MREs FAQ—Military-Style Meals Ready to Eat & Sources

☒ Chemical & Biological Attack, Detection & Response FAQ
☒ Do Terrorists Really Have Nukes Here?
☒ Using CD Meters in Fallout Shelters (FEMA - 120 pg book)
☒ 'Nuclear War Survival Skills' (280 pg book) FREE On-Line Here!
☒ Nuclear War Unthinkable? (Russian & Chinese Update!)
☒ FEMA Nuclear Weapon Target Maps For Each State!
☒ Bruce Beach's Nuclear Survival Ark II Site (Updated 1/12/02!)
☒ Trans-Pacific Fallout (Don't be caught off-guard by these ill winds!)
☒ 'You Will Survive Doomsday' (A myth-busting eye-opener!)
☒ '11 Steps to Nuclear War Survival' (Canada Emergency Measures Organization)
☒ Sabotage and Terrorism of Nuclear Power Plants
☒ Lost and Stolen Nuclear Materials in the United States

4 Coping with the Disasters: Chance Accidents or that Caused by Terrorist Attack

In order to deal with any small or big accident or any disaster caused due to an attack by the terrorists, there is a need of different types of expertise. Right from the management of the law and order, mobilization of fire fighting personnel, providing immediate medical and nursing help, providing proper treatment, proper clean-up operation, rehabilitation of the people who have been injured, and providing proper rehabilitation to all those whose nearest of family members have died etc. Safety Engineering is one of the major ones.

4.1 SAFETY ENGINEERING

The job of the management, the scientists, the doctors, fire fighting agents, law and order personnel and others in disaster preparedness is to first understand the risks involved with the process of manufacture of the biologicals, radiologicals or chemicals and the run-away reactions which might cause a disaster. The scientists assessing the health risks through predictive and preventive efforts, and the industrial physicians, in case of an industry or other doctors treating them are supposed to implement it.

The responsibility of the Safety Engineer is even more important than the others. He has to ensure that under normal conditions safety is always ensured. He should even be prepared to avoid even the remotest chance of an accident leading to a disaster.

The responsibilities of the safety engineer are well delineated by Gloss and Warble (42). Safety Engineers are advised to go through this article. The principles to be followed in forwarding and controlling industrial disasters are outlined there. The corporate safety programs have been drawn out in this volume later. According to the author, each plant or operations, or events should have a fault-free system and a checklist for safety. For which proformas are given at the end of this treatise.

Ridley (88) has compiled a volume of comprehensive articles on safety at work. In the first two chapters, Bamber has outlined the principles and techniques to be adopted in effective accident prevention. It has been stated that the accident prevention is to be based on a safety policy. Such a Safety policy should address to the following areas - in design, installation, process and premises, protective and preventive measures and regular vigilance. The essentials of an ideal health and safety policy statement are also to be evolved for each unit. The organizational set up, functions of safety advisors of the plant and safety representatives of the workers are also to be ascertained. Hazard identification can be achieved by in-plant hazard-rating indices. Safety inspection is to be done through sampling survey, collection of health data and regular machine inspection. The sequel of events in controlling fires has to be anticipated and job safety analysis should be practiced. Formal and specific safety training for all the workers should be encouraged. System safety monitoring at various phases and the fault free analysis of vigilance will be beneficial to all disaster planning. Identification, evaluation, avoidance, retention, transfer and reduction of risks are conceptually discussed and these ideas are used in our disaster preparedness schedule.

4.2 DISASTER PLANNING

So far as hazardous industries are concerned, the disaster planning should include in- plant check list for total emergency action along with anticipatory action to forewarn disasters, in order to maintain and streamline disaster preparedness and should have the ability of a sudden mobilization of all forces to meet any calamity. Such a tragedy could result from fire, explosion, accident, and leakage into environment hazardous chemicals either due to normal wear and tear or deliberately by the terrorists, or even due to natural factors such as flood, earthquakes etc. Apart from implant coordination, interactions with outside agencies like the city, district, state and federal administration (fire, police, health), and voluntary organizations, such as Red Cross, Ambulance, Local Clubs, Philanthropic organization, Churches, Hospitals, clinics etc. are desired.

European Federation of Chemical Engineering has compiled the rationale for assessment and control of major hazards (EFCE, 1985). Modern methods to detect and rectify the problems with the integrity and reliability of the industrial plant, including computer systems are presented there. Mathematical models are also suggested for consequence assessment, risk analyses, and case studies under various situations. Viable suggestions for identifying processes and plants prone to accidents and for assessing potential consequences have been outlined in this document. This document also has offered information, which is useful in hazard management. The readers may try to collect such a copy, if they are interested to know more about it.

4.3 HAZARDOUS ACCIDENT: DISASTER INVESTIGATION AND RESPONSE

Apart from the above, an accident or disaster investigation and reporting is highly informative regarding the immediate and subsequent steps to be taken when an accident or disaster is reported. The proforma for recording, the proper authorities to whom each type of accident is to be reported, and an accident investigation checklist are provided. The statistical approach to accidents will be highly beneficial in disaster preparation, planning and follow up.

4.4 TYPES OF EMERGENCY ARISING OUT OF ACCIDENTS OR MAJOR DISASTERS

Challis (19) has outlined the principles in the management of a major hazardous plant as follows:

It has been described that the chemical or biological enmergencies may arise in a number of ways. Some of the most important types are as follows:

1. Disaster or explosion in a chemical plant handling or producing potentially toxic substances.
2. Accidents in storage facilities handling large quantities of various chemicals, or harmful biological.
3. Misuse of chemicals or biological, resulting in contamination of foodstuffs, the environment, the overdosing of agrochemicals etc.
4. Improper waste management, such as uncontrolled dumping of toxic chemicals, failure in proper waste management systems or accidents in wastewater treatment plants.

Depending on the quality and quantity of chemicals involved in the accidents as well as the local conditions, i.e. geography, meteorology, density of population, distribution of industry, layout of the neighboring plants etc., the emergency may be classified in a variety of ways:

1. Environmental health aspects
2. Duration of adverse effects,
3. Extent of remedial action required.

4.5 LEVEL OF ACCIDENTS/DISASTERS

The level of accidents or disasters can be classified into four different categories:

1. Level 1 (operator level)
2. Level 2 (Local/community level)
3. Level 3 (Regional/national level)
4. Level 4 (International level)

4.6 DEVELOPMENT OF A CONTINGENCY PLAN

For the development of a contingency plan the following criteria are very important:

- To know the type of operation in order to assess the probability of accident, i. e., for this one has to know and identify the weak points of operation or the processes involved.

- Probable character of the potential accidents is to be ascertained, i.e., explosion, fast release of chemicals or spread of harmful biologicals into the environment, slow release and/or dispersion of the chemicals or biologicals.
- Characteristics of chemicals or biologicals involved in possible accidents including its toxicity, volatility, persistence including its probable quantities.
- Expected concentrations resulting from the accidents, rate of its dispersion, synergistic effects, rate of oxidation etc.
- Local conditions i. e. layout and process of the plant, neighboring industries (their products and processes, settlements (residential and commercial), resources available for emergency responses, and
- Possible consequences of potential accidents i. e. the area to be affected, risks to the people of both public and workers, spread of damage etc.

4.7 EMERGENCY RESPONSE SYSTEM

The basic objective of any emergency response system is to minimize the possible adverse impacts of accidents on people, environment and property. This necessitated the establishment of a system which makes the optimal use of available resources for expeditious containment of the incident, spilled or dispersed materials, protecting the health and safety of the people, both near -by residents and workers as well as minimizing the damage to the environment and the property. The emergency response system must also provide adequate and accurate information to all relevant authorities and the public and provide ultimately for the safe rehabilitation of the affected areas.

4.7.1 System Approach to the Establishment of Emergency Response Systems

For the development of a comprehensive emergency response system, one has to go through the following steps:

1. Procure all Investigative data on all vulnerable points, unit processes and or activities.
2. Estimation of Chemical spills/emissions or biological spread out.
3. Sufficient knowledge about thee effects of the toxic chemicals, biologicals or radiologicals on a short term and long term basis.
4. Adequate knowledge regarding the availability of possible protective and remedial measures.
5. Designation of responsibilities
6. Preparation for a plan of action
7. Establishment of the liaison with the external authorities, Government Officials, Local law and order people, fire fighting people, hospital authorities, rehabilitation centers etc.

8. Mobilization of resources to handle the emergencies, and
9. Communication facilities, emergency control rooms

4.7.2 Structure and Elements of Emergency Response Systems

The establishment of a focal point, "Headquarters" at each level to coordinate emergency response activities is essential. The person named at the focal point as the chief, shall also be responsible to process, transmit and receive all necessary information to the public administration and to the public. He will facilitate the speedy provision of all necessary help. The response system should include thee following elements:

(*a*) An alert system,

(*b*) Group evaluating the situation, classifying the accidents, its nature and extent,

(*c*) Division and alerting the emergency response systems,

(*d*) Provision of information,

(*e*) Provision of external help,

(*f*) Decision on and implementation of required protective and remedial measures,

(*g*) Continuous monitoring of the post-accident situation, adoption of relevant decisions and measures,

(*h*) Maintenance of all communication links,

(*i*) Preparation of plans for rehabilitation,

(*j*) Post-accident analysis and evaluation of response activities, and

(*k*) Preparation of the final report on the accident.

It is also important to identify the level of the Emergency Response system. Normally, it may be characterized into four categories:

1. Emergency response system at the operator level (Level 1)
2. Emergency response system at local community level (Level II)
3. Emergency response system off regional or national level (Level III)
4. Emergency response system at International level (Level IV)

Each one of them will have distinctive responsibilities. The Level I will have the following duties and responsibilities:

(*a*) Development of a contingency planning,

(*b*) Assignment of responsibilities,

(*c*) Assessment of risks,

(*d*) Preparation of emergency response system,

(*e*) Approval of emergency response system, and

(*f*) Develop an information system.

The emergency response systems at the local community level (LEVEL II), regional and national level (LEVEL III), and International Level (LEVEL IV) should be comprised of all the above elements, but with much larger and greater magnitudes of support system, speedier communication and dispatch system, well trained task force, greater financial and technological facilities etc. The Level I should report to Level II, the Level II should report to Level III, and Level III should pass on all the information to Level IV.

4.8 POTENTIAL PROBLEMS AND HOW TO CIRCUMVENT THEM

In any work of such magnitude there is ought to be some problems. So one has to learn how to circumvent them. In the past century, the world had witnessed unprecedented growth and expansion in the area of Industrial expansion and technological development. The development in mining, metallurgy, and petrochemical industries and in the field of basic chemicals including agrochemicals has shown tremendous growth almost in every part of the world. Such expansion led to increased production, storage, and large-scale transport and processing of chemicals, biologicals and radiologicals. Many of those are hazardous in nature.

Although technological progress has changed the entire scenarios of our industries, accidental chances cannot be totally ruled out. The Automated processes, microprocessor controlled machineries, remote control operations, usage of robotics in hazardous operations, use of sensitive control device, highly sensitive sensors, sophisticated high precision measurement equipment etc. are some of the unique but useful instruments and control devices which of course had helped cutting down and or/avoid many chemical disasters in an industrial setting. Simultaneous development of know-how in control of occupational health problems and environmental pollution has consolidated the benefits of industrialization without compromising the productivity. The condition of safety in most of our industries are generally satisfactory, since we have the benefit of learning from each others' mistakes and experiences of more advanced countries that launched massive industrialization much earlier than others in the developing countries. Nevertheless one cannot be complacent; safety cannot be taken for granted. Accidents are accidents. It happens once in a while. It comes all of a sudden. Political upheavals continue in different parts of the world. Fanatics are still fighting on religious grounds. Self-immolation using fire, human bomb, suicide bombers, terrorist, bioterrorists etc. are frequently heard words, which cause fear and anxiety in the minds of millions. They cause devastation of innocent humanity. Hundreds and thousands of lives and billions of dollars worth of properties are lost almost in seconds as a result of terrorist attack all over the world. Plane journey, train journey, bus journey, journey in metros, visiting shopping centers and other crowded places for business purposes, pleasure trips etc. have become no longer safe. One does not know when and wherefrom a terrorist attack would come. It is also not known what type of attacks they are going to launch. In spite of advanced vigilance system, remote control cameras set up in all strategic areas, the world experiences terrorist attack once in a while. Accidents and terrorist led human catastrophes would continue, but one has to learn how to minimize the extent of damage, and how to avoid them as far as practicable.

Accidental leakage of hazardous substances in large quantities during production, transport, storage or use is a situation, which is somewhat different from routine liquid effluents and gaseous emanations. In this case the amounts involved are massive and leakage unexpected. To avoid this requires a more efficient preparedness. There have been several minor incidences of leakage, spills or fires in many industries in the entire world over. Oil refinery fire, spillage of hazardous liquid and leakage of hazardous gases, sudden explosions and flooding in mines can create problems too large to manage.

Transport of hazardous materials like gasoline, toxic gases, inflammable materials by road or by rail has to be strictly regulated. Proper vigilance and guards are to be installed. In spite of all the knowledge and precautionary measures, the world's largest Chemical Industry disaster took place in 1984 at Bhopal in India, in a Union Carbide Factory, due to the sudden release of deadly MIC gas. It killed some 2500 people just overnight and more than 10,000 cattle and livestocks also died. It destroyed many plants and trees and also caused death to many aquatic lives. The wounds lingered for many years in the minds of all those who suffered. Damages were transmitted from one generation to another.

In another major disaster, a fire in a tank car propelled the adjoining chlorine tank a goods train in Canada, leading to spillage of chlorine in the adjoining areas. Fortunately, it did not take place in crowded areas, so damages were relatively small. Such a calamity if ever to take place in a thickly populated area, it can be very serious and devastating.

5 Sponsored Terrorism: Preventive Measures at the State, Federal and Individual Level

In the modern era, it has become a major headache to the various Governments as to how to deal with "Terrorism". It has become almost an everyday affair. As you open the pages of your News papers or switch on your TV or Radio, there comes the news from some part of the world that due to terrorist attack so many people died and so many got wounded. Besides, property losses incurred were of the value of Millions of Dollars.

Terrorism is now costing many lives every year all over the world. Most of them are innocent victims. What is disturbing is the emerging fact that several countries of the world are engaged in sponsoring terrorist organizations, for their direct or indirect benefits of one kind or another. In most cases, highly trained and sophisticated leaders run the terrorist outfits. They produce trained terrorists, suicide bombers, under-cover agents, spies, paid killers etc. and supply them to all those whosoever may need them. Obviously, they charge a heavy price for that service. These outfits are internationally connected with each other. Their actions are often directed towards earning quick buck through abduction of the sons and daughters of rich people or of the rich persons themselves. They have an eye also on film and business personalities. They earn a lot of money through international smuggling, drug smuggling in particular, and also by intimidating the politicians and indulging in flesh trades. Sometimes they indulge in black mailing of Governments and / or the leaders of political parties as well.

These days the terrorists are utilized for a variety of purposes, such as to kill important political leaders, to destabilize nations, to infiltrate within the national armies of various countries in order to cause sabotage from within, to create panic in the minds of people by subversive activities. They pass on intelligence to those people who have either engaged them or are interested to get them. They plan to mobilize disenchanted people from within to train them to become terrorists. Sometimes they are engaged in raising funds in disguise of various charitable organizations, and also become active to cause panic in the minds of innocent people, by destroying places of mass assembly so that thousands die in one shot and Billions of Dollars worth of lives and properties are lost. An estimated amount of loss due to Twin Tower Disaster was about $ 30.00 Billion. There has been a horrendous indirect effect on the economy and employment in the entire USA and the world. Immediately stock markets all over the world suffered from a downward jolt. Those countries, which had very direct connection with the trade and commerce of the USA, suffered the most. The New York stock Exchange slumped down. An otherwise strong American economy was under recession. Industries one after the other had to cut down their employee strength. The unemployment rate rose sharply to double-digit figures. The Federal Reserve had to slash down the interest rates gradually to only about 1% level for term deposits. Oklahoma City Disaster comes next in this category.

Thus it appears that sooner or later, mild or severe, Terrorist attack appears to be a possibility. This has become a reality today. Terrorism is a potential weapon of undeclared war. Although we all know that it is one of those heinous crimes, autocrats, religious fanatics, lunatics and military rulers may not be spared the use of even those type of weapons in case, and as and when, they are pushed to the wall and they have had no other weapons in their hands but for an effective and dangerous one. In order to save them and/or to satisfy their revengeful evil minds, some leaders might use terrorists to accomplish certain operations to satisfy their ultimate motifs.

5.1 COPING WITH STATE SPONSORED TERRORISM

The question of state involvement in terrorist attacks has become a question of concern. On most occasions, the states involved remain in disguise and provide all the support to the terrorist organizations, providing all financial aid, ideological support, military and operational assistance etc. Sometimes the states initiate, direct, and perform terrorist activities through groups outside their own institutions. On occasions, the states may perpetrate terrorist acts abroad through their official bodies-members of its security forces or intelligence services, or their direct agents. In other words, state intentionally attacking civilians in other countries in order to achieve political aims without declaring wars. Thus one cannot rule out the possibility of future use of chemical, biological and even radiological weapons of mass destruction by the terrorists. Proper preparedness against such possibilities has become a must. It will not be prudent to wait until the extremes happen. Because the casualties will be very severe if any nation is found in a state of unpreparedness when such types of unconventional weapons are used by anybody.

Let us all pray to God Almighty that such a horror as was seen in Twin Tower Disasters are not inflicted upon the humanity again. But lunatic or mentally disturbed people still exist. Fanatics still prevail in different parts of the world. People believing in superstitions, cults and its order and practices, are still existent. Surprisingly, the control of political powers is even in some of the hands of people who still believe in that sort of things. This is very dangerous not only for those nations but also for the world. It is not impossible to take a political control over them. But what is more dangerous is that when WMD go in the hands of people who might be mentally imbalanced, it may cause havoc. People who are destined to die and have fully committed themselves toward such a utopian cause of faith and religion that they die of terrorist operations, after death they will go to heaven, they will be considered as a national hero, that it is the desire of that supreme being that should be 'martyr". Such a religious dictum is so convincing to the terrorists that nothing can stop them. Thus it once again becomes evident that Terrorist attacks, although may be few and far between, would happen once in a while.

A collective move, both at the local and International level is necessary to deal with terrorism of all kinds, including State sponsored terrorism. For this purpose, several measures are necessary. One of the first things, which have to be done, is to internationalize a definition of terrorist and terrorism, which can be utilized by everybody all over the Globe. Some possible measures are discussed in the following.

5.1.1 Legislation and Punishment

Proper type of International laws and appropriate regulations are required to be promulgated by the UN to provide the security forces sufficient training and instrument for combating terrorism. For this purpose, the definition of terrorism and its related activities are to be properly understood and illustrated so that it can be differentiated from other types of ordinary crimes. Legislative laws have to be designed to ban terrorism and assistance to terrorism, directly or indirectly, and confiscating their financial resources and supplies. The need for an accepted form of definition by the International community is there so that separate legislation and punishment for terrorism can be enacted, and is not confused with other crimes. Because of the fact that terrorism poses an enormous threat to the society and its values, to the Government in power, and also to the public at large, and due to its political dimension, as opposed to crime, suitable laws for punishment has become necessary.

5.1.2 International Cooperation

As stated above, an Internationally accepted definition of terrorism is required for the enactment of suitable laws for punishment. International cooperation is required for extradition of terrorists from one country to the other against which it was functioning. The countries where they are harboring should stop providing them with any assistance-financial, military or by any other means. They should confiscate the properties of the terrorists, and stop any commercial transactions, trading etc initiated by the terrorists.

5.1.3 Measures against States Sponsoring Terrorism

Modern terrorism is almost always dependant on the support of some nations. It cannot grow and develop without strong financial, ideological and moral support from other countries and its population groups. States sponsoring terrorism use terrorist organizations as a one of the means to their own ends. The terrorist organizations depend on the assistance they receive from some countries at the economic, military and operational levels. Some organizations are so closely dependent on the assistance of other states that they become "puppets" functioning at the initiative, direction, and with the complete support of these states. It is impossible to contend effectively with such type of terrorism without severing the close ties between the terrorist organizations and the sponsoring states. Again, for proper legislative actions, a good understanding of the act of terrorism and state-sponsored terrorism is required, so that proper actions could be taken against them at the International level.

5.1.4 Offensive Action

The states struggling against terrorism must retain the initiative and should never feel depressed since the success is slow, and very often not countable. Attempts must be made to limit the operative capacity of the terrorist organizations. To attain these aims, a continued offensive must be conducted against terrorist organizations and their activities, although diplomatic approaches, political pressures, economic sanctions etc. should be tried first. If and when all of that fails, world opinions should be mobilized to ensure International support. It is always better to go for a collective offensive. It is essential for countries struggling against terrorism to attract support, and for that also a well-accepted definition of terrorism is required.

5.1.5 Attitudes Towards the Population Supporting Terrorism

Terrorist organizations often rely on the assistance of the sympathetic civilian population. An effective instrument in the limitation of the terrorist activity is to undermine the ability of the organization to obtain support, assistance and aid from the population. Counter propaganda is essential to divert the attention of the general population that they are following an evil path, and nothing concrete can be achieved following that path. A definition of terrorism is required here too for determining new rules of the game both locally and at the International level. Any organization contemplating the use of terrorism to attain its political aims will have to risk losing its legitimacy at the International level of diplomacy, even with the population that supports its cause.

5.1.6 Public Relations

For an International campaign designed to undermine the legitimacy of terrorist organizations certain measures are necessary-1). Curtail support for them, 2). Galvanize an International united front against them, 3) Build up cooperative approaches for intelligence gathering, 4). Joint military exercises, 5). Confiscation of property, 6). Severing ties of trade and commerce, 7). Impose sanctions etc. For this purpose also, a proper definition of terrorism is required to separate these activities from other crimes.

5.2 PREVENTIVE EFFORTS AT THE INDIVIDUAL LEVEL IF THERE IS AN ACCIDENT OR TERRORIST ATTACK

If there is an accident or we face a terrorist attack, what we can do at our individual level is the question in everybody's mind. Should we sit idle and see it happen and become victims of such an attack in today's technology primed world? The answer is 'No'. An all round effort is therefore necessary to understand, educate and make everything possible to mitigate the deleterious effects of the hazardous chemicals, biorganisms or radiation released due to the accident or terrorist attack.

It is almost certain that the local community hospital or clinic and the practicing physicians will be the first to recognize a chemical/biological/radiological attack. They will have to initiate an immediate response. Therefore local health care professionals and their facilities must be kept ready and fully equipped to face such an event.

For preventive measures, proper preparedness for the procurement of anti-dotes, anti-sera, proper vaccines for immunization purposes, anti-toxins, anti-bacterial and anti-viral drugs are required. These drugs and vaccines are required to be stored in sufficient quantities. Research initiatives must be boosted where there is a lack of supply, say for example in the field of antisera and anti-toxins. The potential toxins are to be identified, and cloned to produce antidotes, such as antibodies (anti-toxin sera). Toxin mimics are to be produced having the binding abilities with the receptor molecules (anti-receptor molecules) to inhibit the natural binding of toxins on the cell surface receptors, or any such suitable detoxifying agents. Therefore, antibiotics, antibacterial and anti-toxins, and other specific anti-toxicants are to be produced in large enough quantities and stockpiled, at least by those countries which are the potential targets of such type of attacks. World Health Organizations should come forward to develop major expertise with them, so that they could help others when needed.

Perhaps not too many people are yet aware and are concerned about the potential threats of WMD, which might be used by the terrorists. Some are very optimistic that it will never happen. Some keep their fingers crossed, who knows! Some others raise their voice and show their concern and urge everybody to come forward and do something effectively. The response from many is still lukewarm, while many suffer from the highest state of anxiety.

It has already been felt at some quarters, that most of us do not know what to do in case he/she has to face such major disasters. Where to go, who to seek help from, how to get treatments etc. are the questions, which are always in their minds. It is also not known to many whether the treatments are at all available, what kind of after-effects are to be experienced and how long it will persist etc. Many are therefore advocating that at the college level some course work is essential to teach the students regarding various aspects of terrorism. In today's world such knowledge is essential at all levels of our society, such that enough of information is available at the first responders' level, if and when they might face such type of disasters.

5.3 PREVENTIVE MEASURES AT THE STATE AND FEDERAL GOVERNMENT LEVEL

After the recent episode of Sept.11, 2001 at the New York City and Washington D.C., and later the anthrax letter scare, the Government of USA, both at the State and Federal level, have undertaken vigorous efforts to safe-guard American interests both at home and abroad. The Philadelphia Governor was chosen as the Secretary of Home Safety and was given all responsibility for doing everything possible for gearing up the present machinery at all levels, and equipping further the existing machinery to the desired level of operation. In several areas complacency was noted, structural deficiencies were found, serious communication gap between

Agencies (CIA, FBI, Office of the Home Secretary, Defense Secretary, Defense advisor, President's office etc.), Even shortcomings at the level of stocking of adequate medicines, sera, vaccines, antibiotics etc. were observed. Sophisticated diagnostic methods, isolation methods, self-protection equipments etc. were far from adequate in places where it was mostly needed.

Although immediately the Federal Government allocated lot of funds for scientific research to come out with those diagnostic methods and vaccines for prophylactic and therapeutic purposes, the present state of their availability was not at all adequate. Bush administration has asked the Congress to appropriate $ 2.8 billion out of an approved $ 20 billion ear-marked for emergency spending to deal with bioterrorism. Of these funds, $ 643 million would dramatically expand the national Pharmaceutical Stockpile by purchasing additional supplies of antibiotics, antitoxins, and antidotes for toxic chemicals.

These drugs and supplies are stored near major cities, such as New York and Washington that have been or are likely future targets of bioterrorism. Attempts to increase the supply of antibiotics to treat 12 million people against Anthrax infection for 60 days are being attempted. Apart from Ciprofloxacin manufactured by Cipro, effective generic drugs are also being considered for maintaining stock.

An estimated $509 million was considered to speed the development and acquisition of small pox vaccine. The Government has only 15.4 million doses of old smallpox vaccine in its cold storage. About 300 million doses of vaccine have been planned for purchase from various companies. The CDC has contracted the London-based Cambia to produce 54 million doses of a new, safer smallpox vaccine, Dryad, with delivery pushed up from 2004 to next year. In addition, BioReliance and a number of other Contract vaccine manufacturers have been tasked to produce some of the 18 vaccines needed for the U.S. Military stockpile under a subcontract from DynPort vaccine LLC. In the research front a lot of activities have been initiated, employing Biotechnology to develop Monoclonal antibodies, enzymes to diagnose or kill organisms likely to be used as bioweapons (1,117).

Apart from the most popular ones, such as Anthrax, plague, and small pox, about 20 bioweapons have been identified which has the potential to be used in large-scale attack. But it was recognized that few vaccines exist, but their availability is limited, and diagnosis is often difficult and slow. Early symptoms mimic flu and pneumonia, and the treatment and management should be early to be effective. Although the Public Health Sector would treat the patients in such an attack, a lot of work is needed to be done by the scientists and technologists to improve diagnosis, treatment and management of such patients. Proper management of the outbreak of such a disease is yet another area which needs proper attention.

A number of research projects are underway in the areas of diagnostic and therapeutic studies and efforts to prepare effective vaccine with long-lasting immunity. Innovative ideas to train bees to recognize the scent of chemical and biological agents, approaches using sensor and electronic chips to detect if rat brain tissue had been exposed to harmful substance, development of a skin cream made of novel materials to soak up pathogens from the body or the environment.

Vaccine development research is also underway in other parts of the world, but it is not easy to develop any good and effective vaccine within a short period of time. The task is not an easy one. It is still a kind of black art. According to an estimate made by the Pentagon Advisory Panel, to make 8 vaccines against some potential Bioweapons, the cost might go up to $ 3.2 Billion plus several years of endeavors before they can be developed, tested and used. FDA approval for a new vaccine takes at least two years. Nevertheless, hectic research work is going on to stockpile more anthrax and small pox vaccine. At the Armed Forces Institute of Pathology, scientists are developing a fluorescent dye-labeled probe for detection purposes. Ami Kraft has been working on "TaqMan" probe, which spots unique microbial genes for pathogen identification during DNA or RNA amplification in a miniaturized Light Cycler (RAPID, Idaho, Technology). The instrument identifies bioagents in about 30 mins. Microbiologists are also working on an online genomic and Biioinformatics Information Resource Center. Information about small poxviruses, such as vaccinia virus and monkey pox will be kept here for the use of everybody.

5.4 ONLY REMOTE POSSIBILITY OF USE OF BIOWEAPONS OR RADIOLOGICAL WEAPONS

Many people are of the view that there are several odds for the development of Bio- and radiological weapons. So there remains only a remote possibility of its use by the terrorists. Let us examine as to what are those odds.

5.5 THE ODDS OF DEVELOPMENT OF BIOWEAPONS AND ATOMIC WEAPONS

No body should think that it is easy to weaponize any virulent organism for the purpose of using it as a Bioterrorism agent. Serious scientific and technological back up, funds, space and large number of trained manpower are required for this. Numerous steps are required to weaponize an organism to be used in Bioterrorism attack. First, the organism is to be isolated in its virulent form and successfully grown in the laboratory without losing its virulent property. Then the organism must be turned into spores, say for **Anthrax**, which is to be suspended into a solution without allowing it to be clogged when sprayed, using the right kind of spraying mechanism and device. It has to be adapted then to remain viable at the right kind of pressure. One has to ensure also that when sprayed, it gives the proper particle size, which is required for causing an infection.

Among the equipments needed for making bioweapons are - large isolated laboratory with type 3 or type 4 safety facilities, centrifugal separators, cross-flow filtration apparatus, freeze-dryers, aerosol inhalation chambers and micro-encapsulation equipment. Ecological conditions should also be just right, not too high or too low temperatures, rain, sun or wind. All could damage the effectiveness of an attack, according to Raymond Zilinskas, a senior scientist at the Center for Nonproliferative Studies, Monmeytary Institute of International Studies.

Although there are tremendous odds for the development of weapon-grade organisms for large-scale propagation in the environment, because of the sophistication it needed in scientific knowledge, research, and technology, together with huge amount of funds, one cannot rule out that it would never be built by anybody, except of course by the state.

Between 1990 and 1995, the Japanese cult Aim Shinrikyo spent millions of Dollars for developing biological and chemical weapons with the help of a few trained Biologists. The group attempted about nine biological weapons' attack with anthrax and botulinum toxin, but none of them were successful. Later they resorted to an extremely toxic, Sarin gas, and released it in a Tokyo subway station in 1995, killing 12 persons and injuring many. One attack, which involved spraying anthrax from the top of the ninth floor of a building failed because they used a nonvirulent strain.

With the knowledge available today in Genetic Engineering and Molecular Biology, creation of super-bug with more virulent properties in the laboratory, which does not normally exist in nature, has become a possibility. We do not have any immunity against them, since those organisms do not exist in our environment. Without sub-lethal exposure immunity cannot be developed. The Russians are known to possess genetically engineered Anthrax and Tularemia, which are antibiotic resistant. But it is again not that easy to develop them and needs substantial amount of money, knowledge, time and technology. According to some report, in the Russian bioweapon program alone 60,000 people were engaged. Thus it is quite understandable that such kind of program will only be seen in only a few and far between places (117).

It has been discussed earlier that there exists only a remote possibility that the terrorists will ever be able to use Atom Bomb, because of the complexity involved in its manufacture, unless of course it is sponsored by a State. At the most, the terrorists might go to use what is called a "Dirty Bomb" to create enough of scare, hardships, and nuisance for clean up operations. It has been discussed in earlier chapters. Preparatory measures to protect the health of the people will be discussed later.

5.6 VULNERABILITY OF THE UNITED STATES OF AMERICA

In the present context of geopolitical situation, fall of the Soviet Union, Emergence of an united Europe, efforts to launch an United front by the European Union, China coming up as an Economic Giant, Japan rising high as a very strong technologically advanced nation of the world, emergence of India as a scientific, technological and economically powerful nation, up-coming of Iran as a strong nation, efforts of mobilization of Arab countries together on Muslim sentiments, and disintegration of more disadvanced and poverty stricken African countries etc. will dictate the interrelationship of various countries of the world. Many countries in the Middle East and south East Asia have been reported to use terrorism as a form of diplomacy and as an adjunct to their foreign policy. Terrorism is more or less an instrument, which they are using to black mail others to satisfy their ulterior motifs.

Furthermore, Moscow's fall have brought in a lot of instability in those countries once controlled by the Soviet Union. Ethnic and nationalist movements have given way to separatists' demands often accompanied by political violence, terrorism, mass murder, increasing rate of organized crime, and civil war. The instability has spilled over into Eastern Europe. Years-long Israeli-Palestinian war continues. Many Palestinian splinter groups have considered terrorism as the only way of retaliating the militarily strong Israelis.

The fight between the weak and the strong, haves and have-nots, more advantageous and disadvantageous nations and its people appears to continue and will continue. While any major declared war is far from any realistic concept, smaller versions of it culminated in local confrontations, and limited warfare cannot be ruled out. Less powerful countries/states might resort to terrorist activities here and there by creating a "smog of terrorism" primarily directed against the United States, UK, Russia, Japan, China and India and targeted against its interests world over.

During the last several decades, many sociological experts have pointed to the social ills of the world as root causes for the intense hatred of America among the poorer people of the planet. As the richest superpower, America is viewed in the eyes of the disenchanted, disenfranchised Third World and countries of the south as imperialistic, materialistic and oppressive.

By the turn of events in the political history in the world, the United States remained as the only superpower in the present day world. Obviously, all eyes are on it. Everybody wants something out of it, or even expects that it should come forward to do something for them. In these scenarios, the responsibility and liability of the United States have increased considerably. It should act accordingly after carefully judging every incident.

In the context of the above scenario and the so-called "smog of terrorism" it is very difficult to prejudge a terrorist activity. It is all the more difficult because the terrorists act through small groups, their very close interpersonal communications, and normally hitting soft targets. Therefore, all counter-terrorism activities must be carefully evaluated and tried after assessing the intentions, capabilities, and targets of existing and future terrorist groups. One must note that predictive and preventive measures becomes somewhat easier if the strategies of operations of the terrorists could be apprehended beforehand It may be accomplished by intercepting their communication systems, by intervening into their set up in order to determine their order of approach, strategies and plan of actions.

While it is very difficult to penetrate into the terrorist's cells to acquire their strategic informations needed to mitigate or prevent an attack, no sophisticated technological arsenals of intelligence can function as the substitute for human intelligence capabilities. It is very much needed to gather information on terrorists. The whole process becomes more complicated in that the terrorists continue to change and opt for newer and newer strategies and weapons that sometimes both predictive and preventive measures may foil out and become ineffective. During the cold-war era, Moscow used to guide some terrorist activities, which were limited to bombings, hostage taking, skyjacking, and other forms of mayhem. This was almost known and could be prejudged. Those days are over. Tactics have changed, new scenarios are evolving almost everyday.

5.7 HOW TO ERADICATE TERRORISM FROM THE WORLD

So much have been read and written about terrorisms that now everybody wants to know 'What are the solutions?' In simple theory, unless Democracy is established in those nations and freedom and independence is given in the hands of the people, human rights are upheld, education is given to most of the people, improved health care is provided, and a more equitable economic, political and social balance is created, Terrorism can not be wiped out. It will stay and we have to live with it. Basically terrorism is the outcome of social evil, injustice and oppression. This has to go. But who will do it. Who has the capacity to do it? No matter how much technological advancement is there during the course of coming 50 years, when world population might touch anywhere between 8-10 billion, the opportunities for the growing populations might not be rising at the similar rate. What essentially is required is that the economic and technological development should double up to cope with the increasing requirements of the vast millions of the coming generations. Further, it should not only happen in a few countries of the world, it should happen in most of the nations, such that disparities could be brought down. A new type of social order is required for this to happen.

Only United States of America and some of its other allies may be the G-8 nations can do it. With their scientific, technological and economic might, which they have achieved during the last century, while they have to continue to progress in these areas, they have to make the system more productive and innovative to produce more. A part of that wealth will have to be invested in the social development of some of those countries, which have mostly given birth to terrorism. The job is not easy, as the existing Governments in those countries might come in the way and may not be ready to turn democratic just overnight. They would be suspicious to start with. They might not believe them. But the rich nations have to show and prove to the world that they have come forward to help them as a friend, not as the Big Brother, that their attitude is very sympathetic and intentions are clear. They should be able to prove further that their desire to build these nations on a new framework is a genuine one. As they did with Germany, rebuilding it both socially and economically after 1945, and helping them to stand on their feet again.

Such magnificent display of magnanimity and humanity has to be shown by America and its allies once again. No matter what are the obstacles, America has to continue to make sincere efforts for achieving widespread social reforms, economic balance, and stability for rebuilding some of those nations, it has to be ready to make sacrifices also while the other side, the receiving countries, will have to make a lot of efforts as well.

It may be essential to change our attitudes towards some of the social and religious doctrines, which are continuing for many years. Some of the things, which we consider as 'good things', 'good approaches', and patriotism or nationalism, may have to change in view of the new social order. No religious faith should create any fear or hatred towards others, particularly it should not close the minds of the people to think in a rational manner. The essence of all religion is "Love" and sympathy to the distressed. Once the concept of doubt can be instilled in their minds that we all are the children of one God to live in one world as brothers and sisters. We should not hate each other, but show our love and affection towards one another. If mind is open, it will ask rational questions and interpret things rationally. It would pave the way to eradicate all political, moral, ethnic and religious fanaticism i.e. the parents of terrorism, from the world.

5.8 FUTURISTIC PLANNING

One of the ways to prevent chemical/biological/radiological disasters caused by an accident or by terrorist activities is to have futuristic planning within the industry sites and also across the country, at State level, city level, county level, district level and community level, bridging them together through a central body, and empowering them with all regulatory powers to take measures as per the law of the land. Violators should be punished. Strict legislative measures are to be imposed, wherever required. Organizations or persons found at fault or connected with terrorist activities, directly or indirectly should be brought to justice.

So far as the futuristic planning is concerned, one has to check the growth of populated township and dwellings in the near vicinity of the factory producing or storing hazardous chemicals, biological or radiological. Where it could not be controlled in such locations, where the residential complexes are within the factory, all exit routes should be kept free from all obstacles and in all directions. It's a must, so that sudden evacuation in the direction away from the wind flow can be feasible. Creation of awareness and timely advice during crisis can also help minimizing the casualties and panic. First aid measures and clinical management systems have to be developed at all levels, and medical personnel trained in disaster management are needed to be included in every industry and hospital around the country. Similarly safety engineering has to be made an efficient discipline and an integral part with fail-safe methods. All safety requirements such as temperature control device, fire extinguishing materials and gadgets, safety valves, rupture discs, neutralization provisions, self protective gadgets, have to be tested from time to time, its good stocks are to be kept at hand, and operators trained how to use them.

Periodically, the upper management should check the safety enforcement staff for their preparedness and should also be given training to combat hazards. Instant and improved communication system needs to be installed and made readily available .An improved centralized communication system has to be installed so that instantaneous instructions could be sent to the affected people as well as to bring them to safer places. Meteorological data needs to be obtained and be readily available.

In case of chemical, biological and radiological disasters, apart from the effect on humans, the environment is also affected. Therefore long term follow up and care is required including possible rehabilitation. Adverse effects on livestocks, agricultural materials and ecosystems also have to be controlled in case of such disasters. The national and International expertise is to be sought and mobilized in the control room, and quickly relevant information compiled and used.

With the above perspectives one could visualize that every major industry in the making, which will be storing or using chemicals and hazardous biologicals in large amounts could be considered as disaster prone unless proper preventive measures are undertaken. Petrochemicals, fertilizer industries, synthetic organics and many other chemical industries are thus vulnerable to cause chemical accidents or be the targets of terrorists attack. All atomic energy establishments and the installations where vaccines are prepared and infectious organisms, virus and biological toxins are required to be produced in large enough quantities could be disaster prone or vulnerable for terrorist attack. Wherever there exists a risk of large scale damaging effects on human and animal body, toxicity or immobilizing kind of infections could come under this category. All such organizations, industries or installations and laboratories should be identified and suitable preventive measures taken to avoid major accidents or disasters. Let us all keep it in mind that prevention of hazards is the ultimate aim of any disaster abatement program.

5.8.1 Organizational Set Up: Co-operation and Co-ordination

In the light of the International situation regarding emergency response plans as has been outlined by Bennet et al. (7), it may be of interest to analyze the situations existing in both advanced countries of the world as well as in the developing countries like India. In USA a number of organizations such as NIH/NCI, National Institutes of Environmental Health and safety (NIEHS), National Institutes of Occupational Safety and Health (NIOSH), Center for Disease Control (CDC), EPA (Environmental Protection Agency), FDA (Food and Drug Control Agency) etc. In India, we see organizations such as Bureau of Indian Standards (BIS), Council of Scientific and Industrial Research (CSIR), Indian Council of Medical Research (ICMR), Department of Science and Technology (DST), Department of Biotechnology (DBT), Department of Environment and Forests (DOE), Indian Council of Agricultural Research (ICAR) etc. They have a chain of Research Institutions virtually in every field under their control, and scattered all around the country. Obviously expertise is also available there. Obviously the situations are much better in India than many other developing countries of the World, yet not adequate. The centralized Disaster control plan, regional plan, city based plan, and above all community based plans are lacking. Even though India suffered from a Major Chemical Industry Disaster in Bhopal, its initiatives and preparedness are just satisfactory, and needs to be geared up especially because of the continuous terrorists attack in different parts of the country. The country has the capability but should not sit idle and mobilize its efforts in this direction without any further wastage of time.

The World has just seen how the City of New York and its higher management, improved machineries, extraordinary resources, trained man power, magnificent law and order personnel, and above all the highly trained Doctors and Nurses, Paramilitary forces, and Volunteers had tackled the Disaster situations arising out of the Terrorist attack on the TWIN TOWERS, at the heart of the World Business Centers at Manhattan, New York.

As has been illustrated above, one after another two huge Jumbo Jets hit the Tower No. 1 and 2 within few minutes. Both the Jumbo Jets were with passengers, pilot and crewmembers. It took off from Boston's Logan Airport and crashed into the towers. The inferno created by bursting the fully loaded fuel tanks of the aircraft produced several hundred degrees of temperature, melting the super metal structure, such that the entire floors from the above collapsed and the fire and weight of it brought down the remaining portions of the building to the ground within seconds. Such unprecedented scenarios, which can only be seen in Hollywood Movies, enacted in real before the eyes of the world, killing more than 3500 people, fire fighting personnel, policemen and rescue workers. One of the greatest miseries of Mankind together with one of the rarest sufferings of humanity, filled with cries and despair all around, running in an utmost effort to safe the life in the midst of a huge gulf of clouds of smoke, dusts and debris etc. constituted the scenarios there around the Twin Towers. The cloud was seen from miles around as if a nuclear bomb was thrown on it. Soon it was heard that another plane entered into the Pentagon Building, crushing one side of it, and yet another aircraft crash-landed somewhere in the outskirts of Pennsylvania. The Nation was taken aback. A deep sense of despair was converted into anguish and a desire to take revenge.

Soon almost the whole world came forward to express sympathy, share sorrows and grief, and offer help. For the time being the entire world appeared as one and the feeling of oneness prevailed both within the United States and also in other parts of the world. The world realized that such kind of attacks could be inflicted upon them as well. No body is safe in this troubled world any more. Any body may die anywhere and at any time. One may lose his loved ones in no time and all on a sudden. Husbands, fathers, mothers, wives, sons and daughters who were seen off a few minutes ago in the Airports by their loved ones, were no longer there a few minutes later on that fateful day of Sept.11, 2001. Many book chapters were closed. Many promises were wiped out forever. Many families were totally devastated and Industrial operations suffered bankruptcy. A great jolt came upon the Economy. About 30 Billion dollars were approximated as requirement for payment to the suffering families, industry houses, and airliners. Air travel came down to 50% level or lower. Some airlines had to close down their shutter. The entire Industry suffered great loss everyday. Share markets suffered from some unprecedented and consecutive lows, the Federal Reserve had to cut down the Bank Interest rates. Both small and large investors suffered together. Economic recession fell upon the richest nation of the World, The United States of America. Such is the strength of Terrorists of today and it might get stronger tomorrow. Since we cannot yield in, we cannot surrender, we cannot forget the Democratic freedom we have been enjoying, we have to fight out Terrorism. These people are always under the veil, and in disguise. They normally are with fake identities. It has become our collective responsibility to identify them, keep a close vigilance all around so that our countries can be a safe place to live with.

It is essential that all the citizens of the nation respect law and follow it in strict discipline. Everybody follows safety standards. Similarly national standards and norms and practices for all unit processes and emanations, raw materials, and product safety are to be followed very scrupulously. IT should be mandatory for all to stick to the national standards. Independent bodies should periodically inspect factory premises, and labor institutes and health agencies should check on worker safety and the safety of their health. They have to keep their vigilance on this on a continuous basis so that there is no failure. In developing countries with limited manpower, poverty, corruption etc. do not allow these to be checked properly all the time. Better management procedure with a check and countercheck system can be thought of in those circumstances. It has been seen in the past that in case of fire and explosions, the fire fighting organizations, often aided by defense forces have successfully controlled disaster situations in hundreds of cases. However, in case of sudden disaster all these forces have to be mobilized and their activities coordinated on a war footing. This is where the administration has to step in. For this purpose, under the leadership of the local administration, linking all the factory, local governments, voluntary agencies, police force, civil defense, armed forces and others have to be undertaken. Along with this expertise in technology, science and medicine, especially safety engineering, chemical safety, toxicology, public health, social and preventive medicine, environment and ecology etc. have to be pooled in. For each hazard prone industry, a local set up is to be established. This has to be coordinated at the District level >City level>State level>Hazard Control Board. The hazard control Board has to be equipped with all the expertise mentioned earlier to coordinate and supervise all the activities at various levels. It should be the duty of the Board to identify all the hazard prone sites, industrial or otherwise and also to make lists of those areas, which can be the possible targets of terrorist attack. They should examine their disaster preparedness plans, suggest corrective measures, and draft and implement the emergency-handling program. National Toxicology Program and the hazardous substances control establishments at the national level will set the guidelines, allow interactions between states and administer the system. The various state and federal government agencies could actively participate in this program.

In retrospect, it can be said that the Government of India, primarily CSIR and its constituent laboratories, Industrial Toxicology Research Center (ITRC), Luck now in particular, ICMR and various hospitals under its control all over the country and the State Government of Madhya Pradesh in case of Bhopal Disaster, did a stupendous task during the after math of the Bhopal Disaster.

United States of America and the State Government of New York, especially Governor George Pataki and Mayor Guliani did highly appreciative and commendable job. The setting up of an apex body by every State Government comprising of representatives of various departments, scientists, industrialists, voluntary service organizations, labor leaders and media men is essential. The sooner the better. This body could identify the potential problems and undertake the disaster prevention program.

5.8.2 Suggested Lines of Action at the Local Level

At the local levels, the following lines of actions are suggested.

1. All necessary steps should be taken to minimize the exposure of Workers to those hidden hazards in the chemical, biological and radiological processes. When toxic materials are used in the process it is essential that the workers be given detailed information regarding the materials and due measures are to be taken by them to prevent injury.
2. The working place should be surveyed regularly to get acquainted with the processes, frequency of their operations, raw materials, final products etc. to check any loopholes to prevent any possible accidents.
3. It should be especially checked as to how the flammable materials has been stored, and whether enough of considerations have been given for protection against disaster.
4. Anticipatory actions to assess, abate and avoid chemical, biological and radiological disaster in the premises where they are produced, has to be evolved from the International experiences, as may be available in the literature, but modified to suit the local and national need based on indigenous know-how, facilities and resources available.

Even though the issue involved is more or less similar to those in occupational health risks, and environmental and industrial toxicology of chemicals and biological, of course with a much higher magnitude of amounts and consequences, the basic philosophy can be guided by predictive and preventive toxicology. In view of the past experiences and conceptual research in these areas, the following views are expressed. The line of action should consider all the phases of the program namely, disaster inventory, preparedness, prevention, emergency toxicology and follow up.

5.8.3 Disaster Inventory

In every industrial operation, storage sites or transport agencies, it is essential to make an inventory of items of potential disaster causing abilities, such as explosives, flammables, toxic volatiles, highly toxic chemicals and solvents, harmful microorganism, extracted toxins etc. Apart from the hazardous substances concerned in occupational health and environmental safety, all reactive substances capable of explosion, fire, toxicity or material's damage have to be covered. The amount, details of the processes and standard safety precautions also have to be recorded and made available to monitoring and vigilance agencies of the government. Any chances of mechanical failure or human error also have to be avoided. Similarly run- away reactions, which may allow the unexpected accidental release, have to be anticipated while considering the safety of the processes. Considerable Research and development work in Chemical technology and Health Sciences are needed and so also trained manpower to tackle these problems. A draft proforma for inventory controlling various factories and installations is appended. Periodic scrutiny of all the data is very crucial.

6 Preparedness Plan and Measures Needed to Safeguard the Health of the Population

Appropriate preparedness against any untoward incidents can always help prevent significant loss of life and/or reduce the damage to properties worth millions of dollars. Therefore, any intelligent person(s) would take enough of precautionary measures to minimize the potential adverse effects caused by chemical/biological/radiological disasters. Such preparedness obviously would vary from individual to individual depending on who is involved in what kind of activities during a disaster. Right from persons at the epicenter of the disaster who are the first responders such as, administrative authorities managers, supervisors, care-takers, engineers, electricians, plumbers, security personnel, to the policemen, firefighters, the ambulance drivers and its assistants, nurses, doctors, hospital administrators, civil service authority etc. need to take necessary protective measures and make all other associated arrangements for protection of their own life and that of others. At the city level, the City Governor, The Mayor of the city and their entire service personnel are also required to make plans as to how to averse such a crisis with minimal damages to human life and his properties. The Federal Government and various centrally funded organizations also have to render various help in such a crisis to deal with both the early as well as the later episodes of any of such disasters. Involvement of scientists, microbiologists, radiological experts and specialized experts from environmental control, disease control, waste disposal etc. are also necessary to deal with any of such disasters caused by a potent chemical / biological / radiological agents. In USA, guidance from FDA, EPA, NIOSH, NIH, CDC, National Toxicology Program etc. and in other countries from similar such organizations, will be necessary to handle difficult problems. Such organizations also should make emergency action plan in order to protect them and also to protect others at the national level.

Sometimes it is not enough to use only the indigenous help. Therefore, one may have to seek help from International organizations. Contacts will have to be established with International organizations, such as WHO, IPCS, IRPTC, IAEA, IARC, UN, UNDP, UNEP, FAO and similar such organizations all over the world. Since disaster of any of this kind

(Hiroshima and Nagasaki, Bhopal, Twin Tower) will not spare anybody or differentiate between the White and the Black, Rich and the Poor, Christians or Jews, Muslims or Hindus, and/or the people of any race speaking any language and coming from any part of the world, the tragedy is to be handled at a GLOBAL level. It is to be remembered that anybody, in any part of the world and at any moment may fall victims to such a disaster. Therefore it is essential that a GLOBAL ORDER be established by the United Nations to deal with accidental or Man-made (Terrorist-Orchestrated) disasters. A special fund is needed to be created at the UN level and also locally with each of the Disaster Management Cell to meet all necessary and immediate expenditures before other assistance becomes available. Whenever there is any emergency the first and foremost task is to save the life and property of the people. In the following, we will discuss some specific details for the minimal preparedness necessary for each one at the personal level, who will be involved in dealing with a disaster.

6.1 PREPAREDNESS PLAN AT THE LEVEL OF COMMUNITY HOSPITALS, DOCTORS, NURSES, AND OTHER ANCILLARY STAFF

6.1.1 Emergency Preparedness/Operating Plans in a Community Hospital

For the Emergency preparedness, for any successful preparation of such a plan one has to keep in mind that intelligence is the first, intelligence is the second and intelligence is the third item, which determines the ultimate success of any plan.

For the successful operations or deliberations knowledge occupies the same place. To gather knowledge, correct information is required from authentic sources, since information is the power. One should be careful that the information is coming from dependable sources. Wrong information may complicate the whole issue. Therefore, verification of information from an alternate source is essential as and when necessary. Resource mobilization is yet another very important aspect of providing the requisite type of help (treatment) to the victims and sufferers. Resource distribution, coordination among the different groups, proper supervision and overall management are the key to success of any operations. All these components should be included in an effective operational plan with the hope for the best.

In these days, TV, Radio, Internet, Cell phones, Fax, Telephones etc. are the best source of information. These may be used to obtain information regarding any such incident which may have happened, may be very close to where you are or it may be far from you. After listening to such news one has to find out by himself/herself as to the authenticity of the news. For this purpose newspaper's office, radio stations, local police stations, Fire fighting stations, Police Commissioner's office, Mayor's office, State Governor's office etc. may have to be contacted to find out to what extent the first-hand news is correct, where the incident has actually happened, how did it happen, how many people died and suffered from heavy casualties, was there a fire or not, whether or not houses or buildings got burnt, motor vehicles and buses caught fire or not, how many fire victims might be there etc. It is also necessary to find out information regarding the nature of such an incidence—whether it was a man made or accidental incidence, or due to subversive activities masterminded by the disruptive elements or caused by a Terrorist group. It is very important to find out if it was caused by detonating bombs by a remote control device, or by using some other explosives, toxic chemicals such as pesticides, toxins or toxic solvents, by biologicals such as small pox virus or hepatitis virus or by radiologicals substances such as radium, uranium, cobalt salts etc.

If it is an explosive attack, then the nature of the attack is to be found out. One may like to draw a Scenario to get some more insight into such an event.

Scenario 1. Suppose there was a car parked by the side of a street, either just before a 4-way stop sign or before a four-point traffic crossing, where all cars would come, stop for a while and then cross over. This may be a busy street wherefrom a lot of people walk along the streets for shopping purposes, for coming to or going from their offices, for going to Movie or Theaters, to Restaurants etc.

Scenario 2. Just as a large number of people pass by along the streets and also come up from the stairways downwards, from the metro rail station, the parked car erupts in a big explosion spraying over the crowd flaming debris of all kinds. Several cars get into the fire along with several people. The bodies of several people are thrown in the air, their clothes burning and blood oozing out from different parts of the body. A panicky group of people start running here and there, wherever they could go, some enters into stores wherever they could find the front door of the buildings open, and which have not yet shut their doors. In an effort to go faster to clear off the area the cars start rushing, dashing each other causing more accidents, and blocking the traffic.

Scenario 3. In the mean time the Policemen arrive with their sirens on, ambulances arrive and try to reach the spot, the fire-fighting people rush to the spot to take control of the situation. They start doing their duties. Cries, shouting, sirens, expressions of agonies and sufferings of affected people who got injured make others over-whelmed and speechless.

Scenario 4. The newsmen, photographers, TV cameras arrive to take pictures, as many they can, in an indiscriminate manner, they have no time to wait. The reporters start taking interviews of those who are the eyewitnesses. As the dignitaries arrive, they encircle them for an interview. Hundreds of questions are showered upon them.

Scenario 5. Soon the entire area is cordoned. The entry of any person is not permitted. Only the investigative Government team is permitted to enter there to do their part. Curious people look at the site where it all happened and they slowly disperse. In the mean time, all bodies of victims have been taken away in the ambulance and police vans to do the needful. Disaster management team arrives to clear off the area.

Scenario 6. An assessment of the incident may provide several good information-

— The affected areas will of course depend on the amount of explosives and nature of explosions.

— An immediate assessment reveals that several dozens have died, and about two hundred people got injured.

— Such type of incidents may qualify for a YELLOW ALERT from the emergency point of view.

So a YELLOW ALERT may be sounded.

Scenario 7. As soon as the incident occurs, a huge fire generating large amount of black smoke mushrooming up in the sky, can be seen at the site of the incident, spreading over several miles in the direction of the wind. Several cars down in that direction may be seen catching fire and causing explosions, one after the other, only to increase the extent of damages in life and properties. Unless it can be checked soon, the fire is expected to spread to the jammed parking lot causing havoc.

Scenario 8. Suppose the closest Medical Center is Hospital A, within about 4-5 kilometers. The Hospital A is supposed to have all the necessary facilities including an effective Emergency Management Plan, trained staff, accessories etc. Obviously the load of emergency handling of the victims will be much more In Hospital A than other medical centers, which are at a far-off place. A real life situation in this nearest Medical Center, Hospital A, may be described as follows. The red phone rings and report of an explosion, causing fire, burning man and his properties is received. Information is given that about fifty people have been killed and about 300 injured. There may also be reports that about 100 people are being sent to Hospital A.

In the existing terminology this type of disaster can be termed as a Medical Disaster. A medical disaster is caused when the destructive effects of natural or man made forces overwhelm a community's ability to properly allocate existing resources to cope with the situation. Some inferences can be drawn from some of such incidents, which took place during the past several years, such as:

(*a*) World Trade Center (Twin Tower) Disaster at New York, where >3500 died and > 5000 injured,

(*b*) Bombing of the Oklahoma City Shopping Center killing > 150 and injuring > 900,

(*c*) Toxic Gas Release in the Tokyo Subway, killing > 10 people, and injuring > 5000,

(*d*) Bhopal (India) accidental Toxic Gas Release in a Union Carbide factory, killing >2500 and injuring >10,000.

Although the first three (a-c) were connected with terrorist's activities, the Bhopal Disaster was caused due to an accident in the storage tank of a deadly liquid, methyl isocyanate. However, one can take some lesson from the experiences as to the handling of the after-math of the

Bhopal episode. Use of toxic chemicals or biologicals are in the list of terrorists to cause major insults to humanity.

Let us come back to Hospital A scenario.

The hospital authority has activated the YELLOW ALERT.

The Responsible Medical Officer has been asked to communicate the Yellow alert to suitable implementation groups, who in turn will activate their own teams immediately to be back in action. In a sequence of calls, first the medical central receives the calls, which is then transmitted to Emergency Department (ED) Physician, Nurse in Charge in the Emergency Department, and the Nursing supervisor. The Nurse in Charge of the Emergency department informs the Administrator on Duty (AOD), who activates the YELLOW ALERT. (In a scenario where it is noted that the AOD does not respond within 03 minutes, ED Physician, ED Nurse in charge and Nursing supervisor will have the authority to act together to activate the YELLOW ALERT). These three persons will decide if recommendations are to be given to AOD to call the Emergency Plan into effect.

Once the YELLOW ALERT is received in the Medical Central, the Medical Communicator shall determine the following:

(*a*) Location of MCI,

(*b*) Extent and type of Casualties,

(*c*) Approximate number of fatalities, and

(*d*) Telephone number and appropriate identity of the person(s) who called and gave the information of the disaster.

After the joint recommendation is made to the AOD, the Nursing supervisor will provide the following information to the AOD to decide the extent of help needed to implement the YELLOW ALERT. These include: (*a*) the number and acuity of the patients being treated in the emergency department, (*b*) type of MCI and the number of anticipated casualties, and (*c*) anticipated impact on the emergency department's current operations.

Immediately after the authorization is made to place the YELLOW ALERT into effect, the Nursing Supervisor will notify the Telecommunications console operator to announce YELLOW ALERT via the overhead paging system.

The Emergency department Physician is designated as the Disaster Control Officer (DCO). He/she will decide the staffing pattern of the treatment areas. Those responding to the Emergency department will be given specific assignments by the Nurse in-charge. Person assigned to respond to the Emergency department will report to the core elevator area of the Ground Floor.

AREAS OF OPERATION

↓

Emergency Operations Center

↓

Triage Area

↓

Labor Pool

↓

Primary Treatment | Secondary Treatment | First aid & Non-surgery

DESIGNATED LOCATION

↓

Nursing Office

↓

Emergency Ambulance Entrance
Core Elevator Foyer

↓

ED Core

↓

ED Urgent Area
(ED Non-urgent for Overflow)

↓

Same Day Surgery

↓

Morgue

EMERGENCY DEPARTMENT'S ROLE

↓

The Emergency department will triage all the victims and assign them to the appropriate area

↓

The Emergency Department will coordinate personnel and supplies for the primary and secondary treatment areas as well as the Non-Surgery/ first aid areas

TRIAGE HOSPITAL ARRIVALS

↓

What to expect

↓

Casualty arrival started, but remains mostly uncoordinated

↓

Arrival times vary; for sometimes rush hours CONTINUE; sometimes later the in-flow of casualties becomes lean

↓

"Hospital H" being the closest hospital there is overwhelming pressure on it

↓

Medical attention for the unaffected community continues

It may be mentioned that the word TRIAGE means the sorting of and allocation of treatment to patients and especially battle and disaster victims according to a system of priorities designed to maximize the number of survivors. The TRIAGE system provides the greatest hope and has a psychological impact in the minds of the victims. TRIAGE system has some limitations, such as- it is time consuming, there exists user variability, and its lack of familiarity.

— According to the conventional system MEDTAGS have to be used.
  For all the tubes and bottles (RED/YELLOW/GREEN/BLACK) reagents, drugs etc. All sterile materials have to be properly tagged.

— Stores should be alerted to maintain good stock for emergency items, disposables and drugs.

— The Emergency Room gate should be kept open and cleared off all the parked vehicles by the security personnel and/or otherwise. The entrance areas should be kept clear so that the Ambulances can come to the main gate and they are immediately disposed of. Enough of Volunteers/ service personnel should be kept ready such that the victims are immediately taken to the proper place.

— Hospital emergency areas should be cordoned not to provide entry of unnecessary and curious people jamming the main entrance.

— Sufficient number of telephone connections and computers connected by LAN system with the emergency room computers should be made available immediately to provide information to the relatives and nearest kith and kin of the victims.

— If proper treatment is not available in the particular hospital for any patient, he/she should be referred to a specialized hospital after making sure that the referred hospital possesses the required facilities for treatment.

— For the general public and the press, press bulletins must be released every 10-15 mins. Initially, and then every 30 mins, and later every one hour during the first 12 hours. Later, morning and evening Medical news release should follow.

There is another system called START (Simple triage and rapid transport). It is mostly done in Pre-hospital Mass Casualty Incidents (MCI). Basically it looks at three parameters of the victims-Neurological, Respiratory and Perfusion. The advantage of the START system is that TRIAGE numbers of casualties quickly. The disadvantage being that it is not reliable.

START: NEUROLOGICAL STATUS

↓ Change in Mental Status

↓ Unconscious

↓ Normal Mental Status ↓ Move to next Victim

START: RESPIRATORY STATUS

↓ No respiratory effort

↓ Respirations > 30

↓ Normal ↓ Respirations, move to next Step

START: PERFUSION

↓ Radial pulse absent

↓ Cyanotic

↓ Radial pulse present, Move to the nex step

6.2 MOBILIZATION OF PERSONNEL: IT IS AN IMPORTANT PART OF FUNCTIONING OF ANY EMERGENCY MEDICAL OPERATIONS

6.2.1 Responsibilities of the Disaster Control Officer (Emergency Department Physician on Duty)

- He should be stationed at command post.
- Works with disaster control Nurse (DCN) to control and supervise the ED.
- Maintains contact with EOC (NSG Office).
- Assigns TRIAGE Physician.
  (Trauma incident trauma general surgeon).

- Initiates or designates the contact of other attending physicians as needed.
- Assures adequate coverage of MDs to all treatment areas.

6.2.2 Responsibilities of the Emergency Department Nurse in-Charge

- Maintains normal operations of the ED-Ensure appropriate dispositions of current ED patients.
- Receives initial call from Med central.
- Notifies ED physician on duty and ED leadership staff or nursing supervisor of a possible MCI.
- Takes a current census of the ED.

6.2.3 Responsibilities of the Emergency Department Nurse in-Charge

- When the YELLOW ALERT is activated the following actions are to be taken by the Emergency Department Nurse in-Charge.
- Selects a Disaster Control Nurse (DCN).
- Direct nursing staff to prepare all holding patients for transport to physical therapy.
- Notifies Physical therapy to prepare to receive current ED patients.
- Collaborates with the ED attending to ensure that a TRIAGE MD is assigned.
- Alerts same day surgery staff/leadership that a YELLOW ALERT is being activated and to prepare to become a secondary treatment center

6.2.4 Responsibilities of Disaster Control Nurse (DCN)

- This RN should be the most experienced RN on duty who will work with the DCO.
- Maintain overall function of the incident
- Delegates one RN to act as a labor pool unit leader (LPUL).
- Assigns treatment teams (1 MD and IRN per room
- Assigns appropriate staff to the secondary treatment center.
- Maintains contact with the MED-Central concentrating the number and types of casualties being transported to our facility.
- Distributes radios to he following people. DCN, Disaster Control Officer (DCO), Disaster TRIAGE RN, Labor pool Unit Leader (LPUL) and same day Surgery Charge RN
- Relays patient acuity information from TRIAGE MD RN to the primary treatment teams.
- Serves as the link between the ED and the EOC secondary treatment area, and admitting.
- Relays request for personnel and supplies from charge nurse to the EOC.
- Transmits bed requests to the admitting clerk.

6.2.5 Responsibilities for the Labor Pool Unit Leader (LPUL)

- LPUL should be an RN who is responsible for ensuring that staff is assigned to care for the appropriate patient according to their competency.
- Sets up a staffing post outside the ED adjacent to the CORE elevator.
- Keeps a list of personnel (Medical and Ancillary) responding to the ED and assigns staff to the appropriate area under the direction of the Disaster control nurse (DCN).
- LPUL will assign 2 unit secretaries to assist with personnel accountability. 1st secretary will list incoming personnel and 2nd secretary will list outgoing personnel.

6.2.6 Responsibilities for the Triage Physician

- Positions self in triage reception area. Determines proper routing of patients
- Maintains contact with DCO.
- After triage area is shut down, the triage physician will assist with the treatment of patients in the primary treatment area.

6.2.7 Responsibilities for the Triage Nurse

- Stationed with triage MD to rapidly assess triage patients to appropriate areas.
- Initiates necessary documentation.
- Maintains communication with charge nurse regarding progress and needs for additional triage RNs.
- Remains in the triage area unless otherwise directed by the charge nurse.

In order to specify all items to be used for TRIAGE operations, it may be properly tagged with hospital disaster tags. This will help all others to know that those items are specifically meant for Disaster operations, such that it can be kept and stored separately and accounted for easily.

6.2.8 Responsibilities for Primary Nurse/Physician Treatment Teams

- Assigned to room by the DCN.
- Responsible for evaluation, initiation of treatment, the ordering of all necessary tests and procedures for each patient assigned to that room.
- Will stay with that patient until disposition (in non-critical areas it may be several patients to a team).
- Complete all appropriate documentation.

6.2.9 Responsibilities for Surgical Attending

- Trauma attending responds to the emergency department and consults with the Disaster control Officer (DCO).

- Trauma team responds to primary treatment area for assignment by the trauma attending.
- Delegate to senior resident to recall resident staff(s).
- A senior Resident shall be assigned by the in house trauma attending to the operating room to be in contact with the disaster control officer and TRIAGE Officer in order to keep updated regarding OR space and manpower need.

6.2.10 Responsibilities for Residents Staff

- Surgical house staff responds to the emergency department and consults with the DCO.
- The SICU resident prepares a list of patients capable of being moved should the need arise and reports tally to admitting for inclusion in hospital bed count.
- Remainder of surgical house staff reports to the emergency department. Individual residents responding to treatment areas will be released by DCO as "YELLOW ALERT" resolves.

Let us go back to the spot where the vehicle was parked with the explosive device to have a better understanding about the incident. What one could see on the spot would suggest the nature of injury pattern. These may include fractures, and blunt trauma due to the blast wave effects, ENT trauma from blast, and foreign bodies, Amputation, thermal burns on exposed skin, smoke inhalation causing pulmonary edema, and lacerations and imbedded foreign bodies (shrapnel).

Among various kinds of agents used by the people in subversive activities and/or terrorists activities are explosives and Incendiary devices. In USA alone during 1992-1996 there were > 14,000 incidents, killing > 300 and injuring > 3000. Interestingly, the bomber may be found as one of the victims.

Before a physician gets involved in the treatment episode one should consider the following.

- What type of injuries might be expected from a bombing?
- What hospital departments and resources would be most challenged by a major blast event in your community?
- How would hospital response to this event change if it became known that patients brought to your facility were potentially exposed to chemical, biological or radiological agents disseminated by the blast?
- Special consideration might be required for projectile retrieval. Projectile is any device, instrument or part thereof, which penetrates the body, such as bullets, knife blades, and shrapnel.

- Security upon request will respond and obtain the projectile, secure the item in a valuable envelope, label the envelope and receive a signature from receiving person.
- The Director of the Risks services should release the projectile to the appropriate authorities only by the security operations coordinator or.
- Special hospital consideration should be given considering the gravity of the mass casualty incidents (MCI).

MCI-Disaster planning lesson learned;

- Hospitals provide most of the initial care
- There exist high risks of secondary contamination. In such a case the rescuer becomes the victim.
- Personal protective equipment is required to safeguard the health of all those involved in the patient treatment and management.

If there is a chemical incident the hospital should look into the following:

Normally this type of patients is uncommon in ED, 1 in 3000 patients

- Such type of patients usually involve small number of patients
- Exposure could be any route
- Industrial accidents due to burns are usually due to liquid exposure,
- Suicidal exposures are usually ingestion or inhalation of carbon monoxide gas
- Hospital staff are occasionally exposed
- The risk of staff exposure is related to the severity of the patient's clinical condition.

Immediate steps, which can be taken for the chemical incident, are as follows:

- Isolate the are-Control access to facility; modify HVAC operation.

If appropriate,

- Notify Internal and external resources,
- Identify: Signs and symbols may be crucial to determining class and identity of toxic chemicals
- Protect: Use proper PPE and decontamination to protect staff and facility and assist patients.

6.3 TRIAGE AT THE HOSPITAL

Clinical experience with chemical incidents indicates

(*a*) That patients requiring pre-hospital CPR rarely survive, and

(*b*) Small proportions have life-threatening exposure.

While there is a chemical incident, its proper diagnosis and treatment is extremely essential—it would be based on the following:

- Clinical presentation of the case
- Directed at the evident pathophysiology
- Toxidromic diagnosis may allow use of antidotes for certain exposures
- Selection of toxicological references and algorithms are provided on provided sources.
- Decontamination of the entire area is very essential,
- Since most patients arrive in the hospital without any decontamination, primary goals should be external decontamination to protect care providers and patients,
- Liquid, aerosol or powder exposures must be washed off,
- Vapor contamination is usually in clothing and hair,
- Exchange contaminated clothing for clean, rinsing hair and exposed skin,
- It may be noted that cold water decontamination may be risky.

There could be special problems in chemical incidents faced by the hospital management. Staff exposure could take place from a number of sources in different areas. Initial staff unprotected and exposed when the first contaminated patients present. As a mitigation measure isolate the reception staff from patients. All reception staff must be in adequate PPE if the event is known or suspected. All exposed staff should receive appropriate evaluation, treatment, counseling and follow-up.

A large-scale Incident: Tokyo 1996:

- Liquid SARIN released in several subway cars
- The toxic vapors disseminated gradually in wider areas
- Onset of symptoms appeared among the passengers depending upon the amount and proximity of the vapor
- Subway workers cleaning up the spills were most severely exposed, some fatally

St.Lukes Hospital experience involved the following:

- About 640 patients reported on the first day. Out of that 64 were brought by the ambulance, 35 by the fire/police personnel, 541 by non-EMS transportation (walker, bus, taxi, car)
- 107 patients reported during the next 2-4 days, out of which 5 cases were severe, 2 died (in averaged 8 days in the hospital=1DOA, 1DAA, 1CPA2RA)
- 528 patients were in the mild category (up to 12 hours in the hospital)
- A total of 1410 patients reported by the end of the week

There could be secondary toxic effects:

- Tokyo FD: 135 of 1364 responders with acute symptoms from off-gassing in ambulances
- St.Luke's 110 of 472 hospital staff with symptoms of SARIN toxicity

- Other HAZMAT experiences showed that a University of UTAH study showed that 3 of 24 incidents with clinically significant secondary intoxication.

Current Preparedness:

— State of readiness

— (*a*) Emergency department staff trained in an agent recognition, (*b*) patient management, (*c*) patient decontamination, (*d*) patient transport.

They should be also aware of the supplies and equipment used, such as antidotes (Atropine, 2Pam, Cyanide); antisera, vaccines, antibacterials, antibiotics; KI and KIO3; PPE (level C and level B); decontamination (single or mass) etc.

6.4 RADIOLOGICAL INCIDENTS

6.4.1 Radiation Exposure

It may be noted that the background exposure level is about 150-300mrem/yr.

(*b*) Chest X-ray: 30-90mram

(*c*) CT body scan: 1000-6000 mram

(*d*) 50,000 mram: causes reddening of the skin, transient changes in blood count.

Occupational limits for the radiation workers are:

(*a*) Whole body - 5000 mram/year

(*b*) One year emergency exposure-25, 000 mram.

Most of the hospital employees are not radiation workers, so some of 29CFR.1919.120(q) of USA applies to them.

6.4.2 Detection of Radiation

Radiation intensity can be measured by using the instrument called Geiger counter. This is good for GAMMA and strong BETA radiation. Special probe may be required for detecting ALPHA radiation. Individual dosimeters can be used for measurement of dose of radiation received, it can be rechargeable or badge style. Both the whole body and the extremity can be subjected for measurement using it.

6.4.3 Possibility of Terrorist's Use of Radioactive and Nuclear Material

A terrorist may use

1. A simple radiological device
2. Radioisotopes, medical nuclear waste
3. "Dirty Bombs"—a radiological dispersal device, which is used for dispersal of radioactive substances to contaminate air, water food item. They persist in the environment for a long period of time and continue harming the health of man,

livestock, and other animals. The possibility of its use by the terrorists is higher than the other two types mentioned above.

6.4.4 Diagnosis and Treatment

The PPE required is less cumbersome than for chemical agent protection. Treatment activities can be more efficient in this case.

Conventional treatment for conventional injury by personnel protected against radiation exposure will be primary emergency activity. In these cases treatment of conventional injuries is of highest priority.

6.4.5 Radiation Protection

Keep exposures as low as reasonable achievable. The dose depends on type of radiation, intensity, proximity, exposure time, shielding and PPE.

6.4.6 Protection Principles

Time-one should try to minimize time of exposure in the field of radiation. The farther away you are, the lower the dose. It can be noted that the denser the material of shielding the greater ability to shield particles of radiation. The radiation safety officer can be consulted for guidance. Detailed measures against radiation protection, preparedness, measurement, instruments available, prophylaxis etc. will be discussed elsewhere.

6.4.7 Decontamination

It may be recognized that the radiation materials cannot be deactivated or neutralized. The radioactive materials may remain as dangerous for long periods of time. It can however be contained and isolated. While the question of decontamination is to be addressed one must address both external and internal contamination.

Assurance of decontamination is possible only by surveying for radioactivity on the skin, in respiratory secretions, in GI tract and in urine.

6.4.8 Decontamination at the Hospital

It is seen that most patients arrive at the hospital without any decontamination. It may be noted that used decontamination materials, such as water, towels, soaps etc. are radioactive wastes and so are required to be disposed as per the guidelines. The waste materials should be stored in safe, secure and suitable containers meant for that purposes only. Personnel performing decontamination should have appropriate PPE and personal radiation dosimeter.

6.4.9 Special Problems in Radiological Incidents are Faced Often by the Hospitals

These are due to unsuspected contamination, employee exposure, decontamination, and combined injury. The combined injury could be affected in the form of a surgical risk for patients with trauma and significant acute radiation exposure. It increases 48 hours after the injury. Surgical procedures must be performed early or deferred until recovery (up to months later). Surgical and anesthesia staff must be aware of special consideration in management of trauma radiation exposed patients. It should be kept in mind that open wounds can lead to internal contamination. It may require decontamination. Radioactive foreign bodies must be removed as a routine practice.

6.5 CISM

Such kind of incidents, where hundreds and thousands of patients pour in a hospital within a short period of time, can be very overwhelming for the nurses and doctors. Some of the staff may even develop symptoms of traumatic stress, while many others may be perfectly normal. A CISM team can be established in a hospital. NSG supervisor can activate team for a debriefing or one to one for a defusing.

6.5.1 Preparedness Plan at the Level of An Individual If There is An Accident or Attack?

Should we sit idle and see it happen and become victims of such attack in today's technology primed world? The answer is No. An all round effort is therefore necessary to understand, educate and make every possible efforts to mitigate the deleterious effects of hazardous chemicals or biorganisms released due to the terrorist attack.

The local community hospital or clinic and the practicing physicians will be the first to recognize a bioterrorist attack and initiate a response. Therefore local health care professionals and their facilities must be kept ready for such an event. This has been outlined in detail in the above section.

6.5.2 Duties of Research Organizations

The Research organizations of the country should come forward with programmes for vaccines for immunization purposes, diagnostics to identify rare organism and the Government should store them in sufficient quantities in safe places. The potential toxins are to be identified, and cloned to produce antidotes, such as antibodies (anti-sera), toxin mimics are to be produced having the binding abilities with the receptor molecules (anti-receptor molecules) inhibit the natural binding of toxins on the cell surface receptors, or any such suitable detoxifying agents. Therefore, antibiotics, antibacterial and anti-toxins, and other specific anti-toxicants are to be produced in large enough quantities and stock-plied, at least by those countries which are the potential targets of such type of attacks. World Health Organizations should come forward to develop major expertise with them, so that they could help others in times of their needs.

Perhaps not too many people are yet aware and are concerned about the potential threats of biological weapons. Some are very optimistic that it will never happen. Some keep their fingers crossed, who knows? Some others raise their voice and show their concern and urge everybody to come forward and do something effectively. The response from many is still Luke warm. Many suffer from highest state of anxiety.

It has already been felt at some quarters, that most of us do not know what to do in case of such major disasters, and where to go, who to seek help from, how to get treatments, whether the treatments are at all available, what kind of after-effects are to be seen and how long it will persist etc. Many are therefore advocating that in the college level some course work is essential to learn various aspects of terrorism. In today's world such knowledge is essential at the citizen level such that enough of knowledge is available at the first responder level, if and when such type of disasters are to be fought. A first responder should know the following:

(*a*) Nearest Hospital and their Ambulance Service telephone number

(*b*) The nearest Police station telephone number

(*c*) The nearest fire-fighting station telephone number

(*d*) Telephone numbers of the following personnel of the building or office wherever he/she is placed at a given point of time—care-taker/manager of the building, building maintenance office, elevator maintenance, electrical control and plumbing maintenance office etc.

(*e*) He/she should know the direction of the stairways and/ or other emergency exit points

(*f*) He/she should make handy the telephone number of the nearest Taxi service, in case he/she has to get out of the place or go to the nearest hospital all by himself/herself without waiting for any rescue to arrive. Note if you can walk and see you should immediately go to a hospital/doctor for help. Sometimes waiting in the place of incidence may complicate the situation further. One may invite more troubles than solving anything. No matter how selfish it may sound to be, it is your life and you have to protect it.

For personal preparedness and for all those who are in the household, one may have to procure self protective device containing head gear, goggles, whole body protective clothes, gum boots, portable respirator, face mask etc. It is essential that you give trials beforehand to feel comfortable by wearing it. The elders should help the children. They should also make them aware under what kind of circumstances, there might be a need of wearing them. Special arrangements should be made for those in the household, if any, who may use scratch or wheel chair. In case of any need for evacuation, they are to be evacuated first along with the children.

In every household, some of the emergency medicines are required to be stored. House doctor's suggestions may be taken in this regard. Some life saving anti-dotes against toxic chemicals and toxins may be stored, along with antibacterial, broad-spectrum antibiotics, vaccines, anti-sera etc. Anti-radiation pill i. e. Potassium iodide (KI) and Potassium iodate

(KIO3 may also be stored in the event of any possibility of a radiation-linked disaster. Doctors must be consulted always while going to take any measure in this direction.

Enough of food materials, bottled drinking water, milk and other food items should be stored for a longer duration. One may follow the Military type dried food items, which they stock individually for months of operation in the extremely hazardous areas. It will be discussed later in some detail.

From radiation safety, one may use a special kind of tent set up preferably in the basement of the house to take shelter from radiation in case of an Atomic blast or disaster caused by it. It will be discussed later in some detail.

6.6 PREPAREDNESS AT THE STATE/FEDERAL GOVERNMENT LEVEL

This aspect has been discussed in greater detail in the previous Chapter 5. Here we would like to simply touch upon the area for cohesion in the understanding in the context of the main topic discussed in this chapter. After the episodes of Sept.11, 2001 at the New York City and Washington D.C., the Government of USA, and later the Anthrax and Ricin letter scare, both at the State and Federal level in the United States, vigorous efforts have been made to become extremely cautious to safe-guard its interests both at home and abroad. The Philadelphia Governor was chosen as the Secretary of Home Safety and was given all responsibility for doing everything possible for gearing up the present machinery at all levels, and equipping further the existing machinery to the desired level of operation.

6.6.1 Continuous Monitoring, Vigilance and Intelligence Collection

Continuous monitoring and vigilance of any suspected outfit and or individuals associated with such outfit where hazardous chemicals / biologicals / radiologicals may be manufactured and stored have to be kept. Local people have to be engaged and enough training given such that they can inform the law and order people well ahead of time about any suspicious activities. Visit of suspicious or unknown people in a locality or community have to be noted. Such information should reach the proper authority maintaining vigilance.

6.6.2 Collection of Intelligence Report

While it is very difficult to penetrate into the terrorists' cells to acquire their strategic information to mitigate or prevent an attack, No sophisticated technological arsenals of intelligence can function as the substitute for human intelligence capabilities, it is very much needed to gather information on terrorists.

6.6.3 Collective Approach

A massive, collective, expensive and time-consuming approach is essential to find proper solutions to the whole issue of Terrorism. It has been discussed in the previous Chapter 5 in greater detail. In simple theory, unless democracy is established in those nations and freedom and independence is given in the hands of the people, human rights are upheld, proper education is provided to the people, improved health care and developmental programmes are undertaken, the disparities between the haves and have-nots will continue to increase. These will lead to frustration in the minds of the people, which are bound to be transformed into anger and hatred. The result is—the terrorists will continue to terrorize the people. Terrorism is a social evil. International and collective approach is essential to wipe it out, although it will not be an easy task.

6.6.4 Business Areas are Vulnerable—Needs Special Attention

The World has just seen how the City of New York and its higher management, employment of improved machineries, extraordinary resources, trained man power, magnificent law and order personnel, and above all the highly trained Doctors and Nurses, Paramilitary forces, and Volunteers had tackled the Disaster situations arising out of the Terrorist attack on the TWIN TOWERS, at the heart of the World Business Centers at Manhattan, New York. Preparatory measures are essential to identify all the hazard prone sites, industrial or otherwise and also to make lists of those areas, which can be the possible targets of terrorist attack. They should examine their Disaster preparedness plans, suggest corrective measures, and draft and implement the emergency-handling program. The National Toxicology Program and the hazardous substances control establishments at the national level will set the guidelines, allow interactions between states and administer the system. The various state and federal government agencies could actively participate in this program.

The gigantic circular whirling motion of *Tsunami* at its epicenter before spreading out.

A boy who lost everything is seen after his house has been ruined totally.

The volunteers and security personnel are carrying out dead bodies.

7 Disaster Preparedness: Protection: Safety Devices and Control

7.1 DISASTER PREPAREDNESS, PREVENTION AND CONTROL

Once even a remotest possibility of a disaster is suspected or identified, the next phase is to make adequate preparation for avoiding the disaster. Disaster preparedness consists essentially of safety implementation and organization of suitable machinery to control the situation. For the safety all the precautions suggested for the process as well as for the chemicals and biologicals have to be followed.

If an overhead tank of hazardous chemicals stores large amounts of a chemical, provision for a tall water curtain should be there in case there will be a need of its usage in emergency situations. Storage conditions should be as per the specifications and no chance of mechanical failure should be there. Similarly, substances likely to interact (i.e., oxidants and inflammables) should never be in the near vicinity together. Even if a perfect safety system is installed, maintained and checked for its proper functioning regularly, a set up to face such a situation should be made ready to work on a war-footing. Effective means of fire fighting, neutralization of chemicals, accident relief, first aid etc. should be made handy.

7.2 DISASTER MANAGEMENT AND FORENSIC TOXICOLOGY

Disaster management and forensic toxicology have many things in common. Here everything has to be tackled in a mammoth scale. All information on health effects, their detection, prevention, and cure of individual, toxic substances, and combinations should be combined and made ready in hand. Such information should be constantly updated. Special high-risk groups and sensitized individuals in the work forces and factory neighborhood should be identified and their list prepared. In case of any possible leakage or dispersions of toxic substances these are the people who should be evacuated first. Those who will deal with the health aspect of the exposed victims should be properly trained in toxicological emergencies with information available with them in preventive, predictive and clinical toxicology. Since there is scarcity of institutionally trained personnel, in house training and refresher courses by competent organizations are desirable.

7.3 PREPARATORY MEASURES FOR PROTECTION AND PREVENTION AGAINST HAZARDOUS SUBSTANCES

When we discuss about self-protection, both the protective and preventive measures are considered to be the best ones. For that, is necessary an all round measure to identify, procure, stock and store those materials well in advance. There is nothing to be panicky about it, nor one should lose his/her cool. But one should not sit idle either. Under any circumstances, no body should wait until something happens. It might be too late. When it is a question of life and death, there is no role of any complacency. One should act as early as possible following the guidelines as to what to do.

As a first responder one should always have the emergency kit at his/her disposal, may be in the office or household, and in the car. It is not known nor can it be predicted when the terrorist's would attack and where. These are to be considered as emergency items and those items should be in close proximity to be able to get them when necessary. It should be either in the possession of the individual concerned, say for the fire fighters, policemen, doctors etc. or others should have them in ready access as and when they might need them. Sooner the individual can take the protection by wearing the protective clothes, goggles, boots, head masks, respiratory masks, artificial respirators etc. is better. The longer the time spent to get them after having an exposure or be exposed to continuous exposure before medical care is received, would reflect in the poor prognosis of the patient.

As per the medical advice one should stock at least some anti-dotes against chemical, biological and radiological agents as the first line of defense or to keep the body's defense system active enough to fight out at least the initial insults or injury suffered by the individual or to delay the deleterious effects of the toxic or infectious agents.

Some of the available antitoxic agents, antidotes, anti-sera, antibodies, and other drugs are available in the market. One can take a note of these, and keep oneself abreast of its availability, price etc. In fact, after consulting a Doctor one may buy some of them and keep them in their 'Drug Safety Cabinet' or Refrigerator as the case may be. It should be kept under lock and key and away from the reach of CHILDREN.

7.3.1 Available Drugs, Antibiotics, Antisera, Anti-radiation Pill etc.

The 9/11 horrible incidents on the Twin Tower of the New York City in the United States of America opened the eyes of the world toward the magnitude of disaster that a terrorist attack can cause. People around the globe have become very much concerned about their protection and safety. The question is, are we safe at all? Can we make ourselves safe by any means? Can we minimize our casualties or sufferings? Can we prevent those attacks so as to protect us from the on-slaught of those devastations or disasters? Unfortunately, there are no easy answers to all of them.

7.3.2 Antidotes Against Biological Toxins or Hazardous Organisms or Toxic Chemicals

Some information regarding "Natural antidotes to Biological Toxins" is available in the Internet for the reader to investigate, share, use, or just for the sake of information *per se.* "Eden's Pantry" only brought it for public dissemination. They do not prescribe any medicine or even diagnose it. It is the suggestion of the author also that although naturally occurring anti-dotes would be a better choice to keep the body fit against any infection under the normal circumstances, but when the acute infection occurs, specific drugs, antibiotics, antisera etc. would be more useful. Doctor's guidance is always necessary in this regard.

It appears that besides, prescription drugs, there are naturally occurring medicines which enter into our body almost everyday through our food and drink, fruits and vegetables, plants and herbs etc. Many of those naturally occurring compounds can serve as anti-dotes against toxic agents used in chemical and biological warfare, which could be potential terrorist's weapons as well. Those naturally occurring antidotes or anti-toxicants, anti-oxidants etc. can offer some protection to unvaccinated people or to other exposed people until they can seek proper medical help. It may even save lives on many occasions.

The article (Eden's Pantry) mentioned above said that the chaotic events would make it difficult to obtain appropriate treatment even if it is available. So it suggested that under the normal circumstances we should look forward to those natural antidotes. One should carry these antidotes, since there may not be enough time between the accident or terrorist attack, and the time to walk down or drive to a medical store to buy them. Considering the vast number of people affected in such an attack, and non-availability of that many hospitals, clinics or even doctors to attend to all the victims at a given point of time, the provisions for using proper anti-dotes or specific drugs or anti-toxins etc. should be kept open.

The "Garlic Information Center" in Britain has indicated that the deadly Anthrax is most susceptible to garlic. It has been described in an article published in the March, 2001 issue of the Journal of Nutrition that Garlic is a broad spectrum antibiotic which has the unique ability to block toxin production by various germs. It is interesting to note that before polio vaccine was discovered garlic was used as a prophylactic measure against polio. In one of the tests, garlic was even found to be more potent than conventionally used antibiotics such as, penicillin, ampicillin, doxycycline, streptomycin and cephalexin. Some of these antibiotics are used for the treatment of Anthrax. Garlic was found to be effective against nine strains of E. coli and Staph and other bugs (See Further Reading No.1,10). Garlic capsules that certify their 'allicin' content are preferred and may provide 5-10 milligrams of allicin, which is equivalent to 75-100 units of penicillin.

It is known that the Anthrax organisms can attack and kill the macrophages of the persons it infects. Macrophages are the vitally important cells of the immune system of the body. Besides macrophages provide the first line of defense within our body. It secretes important cytokines and growth factors required for the other cells of the immune system. It also takes part in antigen processing. Therefore, it can be easily realized that loss of macrophages will soon upset the entire immune function, not only directed against Anthrax organism but also against other infectious agents.

Studies have indicated that sulfur-bearing anti-oxidants (alpha-lipoic acid, N-acetyl cysteine, taurine) and Vitamin C, which are known to elevate the levels of glutathione, a natural antioxidant within our own body, counters the toxicity produced by Anthrax (See Further reading no.6). The above sulfur containing antioxidants are available in health food stores and taken in doses ranging 100-500 mg. Vitamin C should not be in acidic form but as buffered alkaline form (as ascorbates) and should be combined with bioflavonoids which prolong Vitamin C's action in the blood circulation. A tablespoon of vitamin C powder can be added to fruit juice before drinking.

Some of the drugs suggested are:

Alacer's powdered vitamin C, Twin lab's Super Ascorbate C powder. Melatonin, a sleep-inducing hormone that has been found to be able to help prevent lethal toxins' effect from anthrax exposure (See Further Reading No.15). At bedtime it can be taken at a dose of 5-20mg. As far its mechanism of action is concerned, it was noted that Melatonin could boost the production of the antioxidants, glutathione during sleep.

One of the ways mustard gas works is its ability to bring about cell death by depleting the levels of glutathione (See Further Reading No.16). Therefore, glutathione is also an antidote of mustard gas poisoning together with all glutathione-producing materials.

It has been stated that all bacteria, fungi and viruses depend on iron as a growth factor (See Further Reading No.4, 12, 13, 22). Iron-chelating drugs and antibiotics (Adriamycin, Vancomycin, others) are effective against pathogenic organisms. The anthrax, small pox, botulinum and plague-causing organism (Yersinia pestis) could be treated with metal-binding chelators. It has been postulated that iron removal retards the growth of plague (See Further Reading No. 13). It was also reported that the biological activity of botulinum toxin depends upon iron, and metal cheaters may be beneficial (See Further Reading No.4) for its treatment.

Phytic acid (IP6) derived from rice bran extract is the most potent naturally occurring iron chelator, and so has strong antioxidant and antibiotic action (See Further Reading No. 22). IP6 has been found to have similar iron chelating properties as desferrioxamine, a drug commonly used to kill germs, tumor cells or to remove undesirable minerals from the body (See Further Reading No. 12). IP6 rice bran extract (2000-4000 mg) has been suggested to be taken in between meals with filtered or bottled water only (no juice).

An antibacterial, antiseptic action of plant oils has been described to be helpful in fighting biological toxins. (See Further Reading No.1). A potent natural antibiotic is oil of Oregano. One literature study showed that Oregano completely inhibited the growth of 25 different bacteria, such as Staphylococcus aureus, Escherichia coli, Yersinia enterocolitica and Pseudomonas aeruginosa. (See Further Reading No. 18).

Oregano has been shown to be effective in eradicating intestinal parasites in humans. (See Further Reading No.18). Wild oregano, which is quite different from the variety on most kitchen spice racks, has over 50 antibacterial compounds. Just one part wild oregano oil in 4000 dilutions sterilizes contaminated water. (London Times, May 8, 2001) Oregano powder from whole leaf oregano is available as OregamaxT capsules (North American Herb & Spice Co.). A spectacular development in natural antibiotic therapy is the manufacture of oregano powder from 100% pure oregano oil, producing one of the most potent antibiotics known. It has recently become available under the trade name OregacinT (North American Herb & Spice Co.). It costs about $1 per pill, but this is a far cry from the $16 per pill for Vancomycin, known as the most potent prescription antibiotic.

Nature also provides nerve gas antitoxins. Nerve gas interrupts the normal transmission of nerve impulses by altering levels of acetylcholine esterase, the enzyme that degrades the neuro-transmitter, acetylcholine. Huperzine A, a derivative of Chinese club moss, has been suggested as a pre-treatment against nerve gases. (See Further Reading No.11). The Walter Reed Army Institute of Research conducted studies, which revealed that huperzine A protects against nerve gas poisoning in a superior manner to physostigmine, a long-standing anti-nerve toxin drug. (See Further Reading No.11).

Huperzine A is available as a food supplement at most health food stores. Suggested dosage is 150 mcg per day. Pretreatment is advised prior to nerve gas exposure.

The threat of biological warfare is real and concern over preparedness of the civilian population and medical professionals is growing rapidly. There is virtually no practical way that vaccines, antibiotics or other treatment can be delivered to a frightened populace in a timely manner during a crisis. The current strategy of having an unprotected citizenry travel to physicians' offices or hospitals to receive prophylactic care or treatment is unfeasible.

The public must be armed with preventive or therapeutic agents in their vehicles, homes, and also in their workplace. Natural antibiotics and antitoxins are well documented in the medical literature, but overlooked by both the health authorities and the people at large. These antidotes are readily available for the public to acquire and use in an emergency.

7.3.3 Radioprotective Agents

Major isotope in nuclear power plant accidents and nuclear bomb explosions

- Radioactive Iodine (Radioiodine) is a major radioisotope constituent of both nuclear power plant accidents and nuclear bomb explosions and can travel hundreds of miles on the winds. Thyroid cancer attributable to Chernobyl *"...has been documented up to 500 km from the accident site."*

- Even very small amounts of inhaled or ingested radioiodine can do grave damage as it will always concentrate, and be retained, in the small space of the thyroid gland. Eventually giving such a large radiation dose to thyroid cells there that abnormalities are likely to result, such as loss of thyroid function, nodules in the thyroid, or thyroid cancer. (Each year 12,000 Americans discover they have thyroid cancer, though from various assorted causes, and about 1000 die from it.)
- Chernobyl has shown, and continues to reveal, that the greatest danger from radioiodine is to the tiny thyroid glands of children. Researchers have found that in certain parts of Belarus, for example, 36.4 per cent of children, who were under the age of four at the time of the accident, can expect to develop thyroid cancer.
- Health experts now estimate that the greatest health concerns affecting the largest number of people from a nuclear accident, or nuclear bomb explosion(s) anywhere in the world, will likely be from the release of radioiodine that is then carried downwind for hundreds of miles. While there will also be many other dangerous radioisotopes released along with radioiodine, if they are inhaled or ingested they are normally dispersed throughout a body and pose less of a risk than if they were to be concentrated into one small specific area of the body, like radioiodine is in the thyroid gland. So, as a plume or cloud of radioactive isotopes disperses with the wind its danger also diminishes, but much less quickly so for radioiodine because whatever little there is that's inhaled will always then be concentrated into that small space of the thyroid gland.
- The *good news* is that taking either Potassium Iodide (KI) or Potassium Iodate (KIO3) before exposure will saturate (fill up) a persons thyroid gland with safe stable iodine to where there is no room for later uptake of radioactive iodine. Once the thyroid is saturated, then any additional iodine (radioactive or stable) that is later inhaled or ingested is quickly eliminated via the kidneys. (See Further Reading No. 9, 14,17, 20, 21, 23, 24)
- The *bad news* is that after Three Mile Island and Chernobyl all available KI and KIO_3 supplies disappeared for months, almost overnight! The KI and KIO_3 market is very thin and current limited inventory will be quickly depleted in any nuclear emergency occurring anywhere in the world. (At www.ki4u.com they expect to be *'out of business* within 24-hours of any nuclear emergency simply because they will be totally sold-out with no illusions of getting re-supplied again any time soon!)
- Potassium Iodide (KI) and/or Potassium Iodate (KIO_3) have already been stockpiled by most developed countries for future nuclear emergencies, they figured it out after Chernobyl, but in the USA they've only just begun. (USA just sold 300,000 doses to

HHS Office of Emergency Preparedness.) However, very limited quantities are available for individual purchase in the USA by the public. (Potassium Iodide (KI) has long been recognized and approved by the FDA for sale for this purpose without a prescription. Unfortunately, it is an over-the-counter (OTC) drug that's to be found on too few counters here in the USA!)

- Two of the KI and KIO3 formulations are currently available on the market today in the USA.
- P.S.- KI or KIO3 would likely not be needed for the so-called "Dirty Bomb" or RDD (Radiological Dispersal Device). Radioactive Iodine is only produced by a fission or fusion weapon detonation or in a Nuclear Power Plant as a byproduct of that process. An RDD simply spreads around existing radioactive material and it's not very likely to have been composed of the relatively short half-life radioactive iodine. We'd more likely see used in an RDD a commercially abundant, and more easily obtained, isotope like Cobalt-60, Cesium-137 or uranium fuel rods, etc.

7.3.3.1 *What is Potassium Iodide (KI)?*

Ans: Potassium Iodide (chemical formula 'KI') is much more familiar to most than they might first expect. It is the ingredient added to your table salt to make it *iodized* salt.

Potassium Iodide (KI) is approximately 76.5% iodine.

For purposes of radiation protection the Nuclear Regulatory Commission (NRC) states in COMSECY-98-016 - FEDERAL REGISTER NOTICE ON POTASSIUM IODIDE:

> *"In 1978, the U.S. Food and Drug Administration found KI "safe and effective" for use in radiological emergencies and approved its over-the-counter sale."*

Most recently (November, 2001) the FDA states in Potassium Iodide as a Thyroid Blocking Agent in Radiation Emergencies:

> "FDA maintains that KI is a safe and effective means by which to prevent radioiodine uptake by the thyroid gland, under certain specified conditions of use, and thereby obviate the risk of thyroid cancer in the event of a radiation emergency."

7.3.3.2 *How Does Potassium Iodide (KI) Pill Provide Anti-Radiation Protection?*

Ans: Going back to June 23, 1966, the New England Journal of Medicine. Vol. 274 on Page 1442 states:

> *"The thyroid gland is especially vulnerable to atomic injury since radioactive isotopes of iodine are a major component of fallout."*

Cresson H. Kearny, the author of Nuclear War Survival Skills, Original Edition Published September, 1979, by Oak Ridge National Laboratory, a Facility of the U.S. Department of Energy (Updated and Expanded 1987 Edition) states:

> *"There is no medicine that will effectively prevent nuclear radiations from damaging the human body cells that they strike.*

However, a salt of the elements potassium and iodine, taken orally even in very small quantities 1/2 hour to 1 day before radioactive iodines are swallowed or inhaled, prevents about 99% of the damage to the thyroid gland that otherwise would result. The thyroid gland readily absorbs both non-radioactive and radioactive iodine, and normally it retains much of this element in either or both forms.

When ordinary, non-radioactive iodine is made available in the blood for absorption by the thyroid gland before any radioactive iodine is made available, the gland will absorb and retain so much that it becomes saturated with non-radioactive iodine. When saturated, the thyroid can absorb only about 1% as much additional iodine, including radioactive forms that later may become available in the blood: then it is said to be blocked. (Excess iodine in the blood is rapidly eliminated by the action of the kidneys.)"

The Nuclear Regulatory Commission (NRC) stated (July 1, 1998) in USE OF POTASSIUM IODIDE IN EMERGENCY RESPONSE :

"Potassium iodide, if taken in time, blocks the thyroid gland s uptake of radioactive iodine and thus could help prevent thyroid cancers and other diseases that might otherwise be caused by exposure to airborne radioactive iodine that could be dispersed in a nuclear accident."

Federal Register. Vol. 43 Friday, December 15, 1978, states in Potassium Iodide as a Thyroid Blocking Agent in a Radiation Emergency:

"Almost complete (greater than 90%) blocking of peak radioactive iodine uptake by the thyroid gland can be obtained by the oral administration of ... iodide..."

National Council on Radiation Protection and Measurements. NCRP Report NO. 55. Protection of the Thyroid Gland in the Event of Releases of Radioiodine. August, 1979, Page 32:

"A major protective action to be considered after a serious accident at a nuclear power facility involving the release of radioiodine is the use of stable iodide as a thyroid blocking agent to prevent thyroid uptake of radioiodines."

The recently updated (1999) World Health Organization (WHO) Guidelines for Iodine Prophylaxis following Nuclear Accidents states:

"Stable iodine administered before, or promptly after, intake of radioactive iodine can block or reduce the accumulation of radioactive iodine in the thyroid."

And, finally, the recently (November, 2001) released FDA document Potassium Iodide as a Thyroid Blocking Agent in Radiation Emergencies states:

"The effectiveness of KI as a specific blocker of thyroid radioiodine uptake is well established (Il in LA, et al., 1972) as is the doses necessary for blocking uptake. As such, it is reasonable to conclude that KI will likewise be effective in reducing the risk of thyroid cancer in individuals or populations at risk for inhalation or ingestion of radioiodines."

7.3.3.3 *Is this the Magic Anti-Radiation Protection Pill?*

Ans: Sorry, but there is no *magic pill* or medicine that will protect you from all radiation sources. In fact, as already stated above.

> *"There is no medicine that will effectively prevent nuclear radiations from damaging the human body cells that they strike."*

Also, the recently (November, 2001) released FDA document Potassium Iodide as a Thyroid Blocking Agent in Radiation Emergencies states:

> *"KI provides protection only for the thyroid from radioiodines. It has no impact on the uptake by the body of other radioactive materials and provides no protection against external irradiation of any kind. FDA emphasizes that the use of KI should be as an adjunct to evacuation (itself not always feasible), sheltering, and control of foodstuffs."*

Potassium Iodide (and Potassium Iodate, KIO3) will provide a very high level of thyroid protection, taken in time, for the specific radio-isotopes of iodine, which is expected by many to cause the majority of health concerns downwind from a nuclear emergency. (And, is the reason most all developed countries have stockpiled it.)

However, there are numerous other, and very dangerous, radioactive noble gases and/or radioactive fallouts that can be associated with nuclear emergencies. You are still exposed to inhale, ingest, or be radiated externally from any number of dangerous non-radioiodine sources.

If you are ever directed to evacuate in a nuclear emergency, do so immediately, regardless of whether you have taken Potassium Iodide (KI) or KIO3, or not.

7.3.3.4 *Radioactive Iodine: Bad News/Good News!*

Ans: The "bad news" first:

Radioactive iodine (predominantly iodine-131) is a major radioisotope constituent in nuclear power plants.

There are 103 currently active commercial nuclear reactors and 39 operating nonpower reactors in the United States. (434 worldwide as of 1998.) Additionally, there are numerous other nuclear processing and storage facilities worldwide with the potential for accidents, too.

The, September 29, 1999, Tokaimura, Japan nuclear accident took place, not in a nuclear reactor power plant, but in an uranium processing plant.

Radioactive iodine-131 gases were confirmed to have been released and were the primary reason for 320,000 Japanese confined to their homes with their windows shut.

Radioactive iodine (predominantly iodine-131) is also a major constituent of detonated nuclear weapons.

Radioactive iodine can not only travel hundreds of miles on the winds, but also still remain health threatening even as other radioisotopes are becoming dispersed and diluted along with it and their likelihood of causing harm diminishes. It is often overlooked that while there will also be many other dangerous radioisotopes released along with radioiodine, if they are inhaled or ingested they are normally dispersed throughout a body and pose less of a risk than if they were to be concentrated into one small specific area of the body, like radioiodine is in the thyroid gland. As a plume or cloud of radioactive isotopes disperses with the wind its danger also diminishes, but always much less quickly so for radioiodine because whatever little there is that's inhaled will always be concentrated into that small space of the thyroid gland.

NUREG-1633 points out an increase in thyroid cancer caused by radioiodine from Chernobyl...

"...was detected in Belarus, Russia, and Ukraine. Notably, this increase, seen in areas more than 150 miles (300 km) from the site, continues to this day and primarily affects children who were 0-14 years old at the time of the accident...the vast majority of the thyroid cancers were diagnosed among those living more than 50 km (31 miles) from the site."

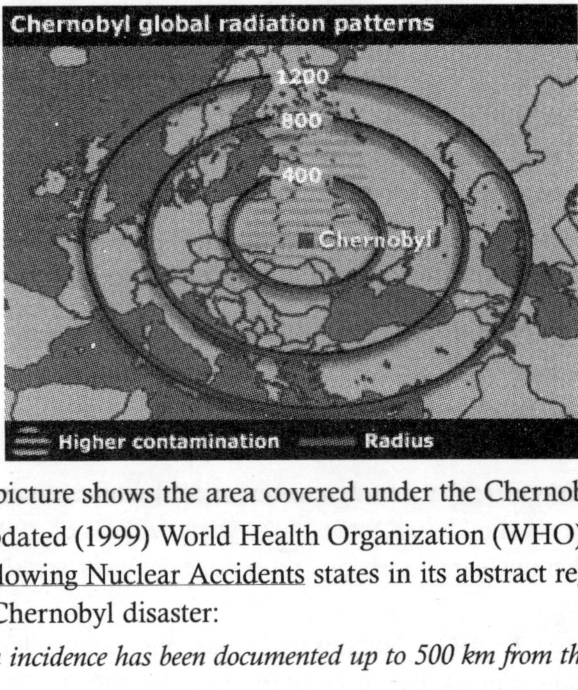

The above picture shows the area covered under the Chernobyl radioactive fall out. The recently updated (1999) World Health Organization (WHO) Guidelines for Iodine Prophylaxis following Nuclear Accidents states in its abstract regarding thyroid cancer caused by the Chernobyl disaster:

"This increase in incidence has been documented up to 500 km from the accident site."

...and therefore...

"...that stockpiling (KI or KIO3) is warranted, when feasible, over much wider areas than normally encompassed by emergency planning zones, and that the opportunity for voluntary purchase be part of national plans."

Many are coming to see now that relying on the current U.S. policy of public safety contingency plans focused on only protecting the populations inside a small "Emergency

Planning Zone" (EPZ) of 5 to 10 miles around U.S. nuclear power plants is "overly optimistic", to put it very mildly.

Undoubtedly, US nuclear power plants are much better designed, operated, and safer than many others elsewhere in the world, and certainly many magnitudes safer than the Chernobyl operation ever was. But, that doesn't mean much anymore when we aren't just concerned with just accidents, but now sabotage or terrorist attacks, too. Without anyone debating here how likely anything is to ever go wrong, it must still be accepted by all that the logic of even having any EPZ's established is to effectively provide for the public safety in that rarest of events if/when anything did go wrong. If that's why we've even bothered with having any EPZ's at all, then shouldn't they be effective ones, if/when it's ever really needed to protect the public downwind? Reality is that the wind just won't know to stop blowing when it comes up against the currently tiny 5-10-50 mile EPZ 'barriers'.

The wind, of course, doesn't respect state boundaries either as our own Nevada atomic bomb testing program in the 1950s and early 1960s made it possible that *"...everyone living in the contiguous 48 states was exposed to low levels of 131 Iodine (radioiodine) for several months following each nuclear bomb test." (Radiation Exposure and Thyroid Cancer - Memorial Sloan-Kettering Cancer Center)* Even more importantly; *"The report also estimates that children aged three to five years probably received doses of radiation three to seven times higher than average during the 90 nuclear tests that were carried out."*

Remember, it's always the children who are at the highest risk of injury from radioactive iodine and eventually developing thyroid cancer from that exposure. Each year, more than 12,000 Americans find out they have thyroid cancer, though from various causes. About 1000 here in the U.S. die from it yearly.

National Cancer Institute Study Estimating Thyroid Doses of I^{131}

Received by Americans From Nevada Atmospheric Nuclear Bomb Tests

The NCI s 'worst case estimate is that fallout from nuclear weapons testing likely generated from 10,000 to 75,000 cases of thyroid cancer!

And, of course, the wind also doesn't respect international boundaries either, nor even continents and oceans, as fallout from a single above ground Chinese nuclear test explosion ("a few hundred kilotons") on December 28, 1966 resulted in the fallout cloud covering most of the United States.

From Cresson H. Kearny's Nuclear War Survival Skills:

"It produced fallout that by January 1, 1967 resulted in the fallout cloud covering most of the United States. This one Chinese explosion produced about 15 million curies of iodine-131- roughly the same amount as the total release of iodine- 131 into the atmosphere from the Chernobyl nuclear power plant disaster."

"Fallout from the approximately 300 kiloton Chinese test explosion shown in Fig. 22 caused milk from cows that fed on pastures near Oak Ridge, Tennessee and elsewhere to be contaminated with radioiodine, although not with enough to be hazardous to health. However, this milk contamination (up to 900 picocuries of radioactive iodine per liter) and the measured dose rates from the gamma rays emitted from fallout particles deposited in different parts of the United States indicate that trans-Pacific fallout from even an overseas nuclear war in which "only" two or three hundred megatons would be exploded could result in tens of thousands of unprepared Americans suffering thyroid injury." (Declassified Fallout Map and full story text in Nuclear War Survival Skills at Trans-Pacific Fallout)

Commenting on the world health effects a nuclear exchange between India and Pakistan would create, for example, Dr. Henry Kendall of the Union of Concerned Scientists said in October of 1999: *"It would be very similar to Chernobyl. But it could be on a substantially larger scale."*

Accordingly, you also have to assess the probable threat from nuclear war, either directed at the U.S. or fallout contamination originating from elsewhere in the world. Russia, China, North Korea, Pakistan, India, Middle East, etc., where any of them are exchanging nuclear blasts with any of their neighbors, could have the prevailing west-to-east trade winds carrying the resultant radioactive fallout to other shores, too.

You'll have to decide whether that's an impossible scenario in your family's lifetime, or not. And, then prepare accordingly.

Radioactive iodine (radioiodine) persists in the environment for a month or more. Most importantly, ingested or inhaled radioactive iodine (radioiodine) persists in the body and concentrates in the thyroid. (Excess iodine in the blood, either radioiodine or stable iodine, is quickly eliminated from the body, but only after the thyroid has become saturated with one or the other type of iodine.) Even very small amounts of radioactive iodine, because it is retained in the small space of the thyroid, eventually will give such a large radiation dose to thyroid cells there that abnormalities are likely to result. These would include loss of thyroid function, nodules in the thyroid, or thyroid cancer. The most likely to see the worst effects, in later life, are the youngest children. (Many of the Chernobyl thyroid cancers appearing in the former Soviet Union among young people today were just children less than five years old at the time of the accident. Experts now contend that as high as 40% of the nodules are cancerous with 5 to 10 percent of the cancers fatal.)

Every year researchers are discovering more from Chernobyl as its legacy continues to reveal itself. According to the World Health Organization, that disaster will cause 50,000 new cases of thyroid cancer among young people living in the areas most affected by the nuclear disaster. Researchers have also found that in certain parts of Belarus, for example, 36.4 per cent of children, who were under the age of four at the time of the accident, can expect to develop thyroid cancer.

For all of the above reasons, health experts estimate that the greatest health concerns affecting the largest number of people from a nuclear accident, or nuclear bomb explosion(s) anywhere in the world, will likely be from the release of radioactive iodine then carried downwind.

However, there really is some Good News amongst all this!

This deadly cancer agent, especially to our children, is easily, cheaply, and effectively blocked!

As mentioned above;

"...a salt of the elements potassium and iodine, taken orally even in very small quantities 1/2 hour to 1 day before radioactive iodines are swallowed or inhaled, prevents about 99% of the damage to the thyroid gland that otherwise would result."

Bottle containing KI
(Potassium Iodide)

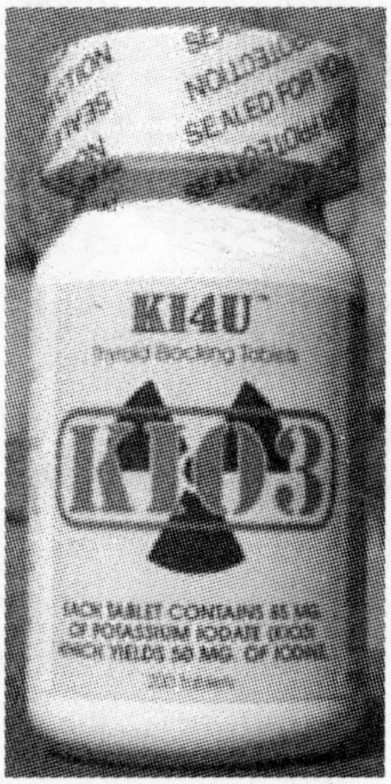

Bottle with KIO_3
(Potassium iodate tabs)

KIO_3 tablets in packaged bottle supplied by KI4U, Ltd

The Nuclear Regulatory Commission (NRC) states in COMSECY-98-016 - FEDERAL REGISTER NOTICE ON POTASSIUM IODIDE:

> *The Chernobyl accident demonstrated that thyroid cancer could indeed be a major result of a large reactor accident. Moreover, although the Food and Drug Administration declared KI "safe and effective" as long ago as 1978, the drug had never been deployed on a large scale until Chernobyl. The experience of Polish health authorities during the accident has provided confirmation that large-scale deployment of KI is safe.*

Additionally, it goes on to say:

> *The revised policy also reflects wide scale change in international practice following the Chernobyl disaster, specifically 1989 World Health Organization recommendations (updated*

in 1995) and 1996 and 1997 International Atomic Energy Agency standards and guidance, which have led to use of KI as a supplementary protective measure in much of Europe, as well as in Canada and Japan.

Also, the newly released (November, 2001) FDA document entitled: Potassium Iodide as a Thyroid Blocking Agent in Radiation Emergencies states:

"Thus, the studies following the Chernobyl accident support the etiologic role of relatively small doses of radioiodine in the dramatic increase in thyroid cancer among exposed children. Furthermore, it appears that the increased risk occurs with a relatively short latency. Finally, the Polish experience supports the use of KI as a safe and effective means by which to protect against thyroid cancer caused by internal thyroid irradiation from inhalation of contaminated air or ingestion of contaminated food and drink when exposure cannot be prevented by evacuation, sheltering, or food and milk control."

What they learned was that children, with their thyroid glands being the most sensitive to radioactive iodine uptake, have today grown up to be the most frequent victims of thyroid cancers there. The children in Russia, the Ukraine and Belarus, where potassium iodide (KI) was not widely distributed, are now experiencing high levels of thyroid cancer. However, in Poland, where over 18 million doses of Potassium Iodide (KI) were administered, and to 97 percent of the children, there has been no similar increase in thyroid cancer. Also, key to Poland's radioiodine protective strategy, was their aggressive interdiction of radioiodine contaminated foodstuffs and milk.

Bottom Line: For all its serious potential for widespread damage to populations (and especially among our youngest), far downwind from the site of a nuclear event, radioiodine health concerns can be largely neutralized by inexpensive thyroid blocking via prompt prophylactic use of potassium iodide (KI). This, in addition to successful evacuation, when indicated, and vigilance that food and milk are not also radioiodine contaminated, has proven itself the best combination strategy.

Some important questions, which are often asked by various people along with their answers, as are prepared by KI4U, Inc are presented below for the knowledge and information of all concerned and in public interests.

7.3.3.5 *Dosage and Safety Regarding Potassium Iodide (KI) Usage?*

Ans: In April of 1982 the Bureau of Radiological Health and Bureau of Drugs, Food and Drug Administration, Department of Health and Human Services released "FINAL RECOMMENDATIONS, Potassium Iodide As A Thyroid-Blocking Agent In A Radiation Emergency: Recommendations On Use".

"Based on the FDA adverse reaction reports and an estimated 48 x 106 [48 million] 300-mg doses of potassium iodide administered each year [in the United States], the NCRP [National Council on Radiation Protection and Measurements] estimated an adverse reaction rate of from 1 in a million to 1 in 10 million doses."

(It should be pointed out that this extremely low adverse reaction rate is for doses over twice as large as the 130-mg prophylactic dose.)

FDA PATIENT INFORMATION USE OF 130-MG SCORED TABLETS OF POTASSIUM IODIDE FOR THYROID BLOCKING

(Potassium Iodide Tablets, U.S.P.)

(Pronounced poe-TASS-e-um EYE-oh-dyed)

(Abbreviated KI)

Take potassium iodide only when public health officials tell you. In a radiation emergency, radioactive iodine could be released into the air. Potassium iodide (a form of iodine) can help protect you.

If you are told to take this medicine, take it one time every 24 hours. Do not take it more often. More will not help you and may increase the risk of side effects. Do not take this drug if you know you are allergic to iodine (see side effects below).

INDICATIONS

THYROID BLOCKING IN A RADIATION EMERGENCY ONLY

DIRECTIONS FOR USE

Use only as directed by State or local public health authorities in the event of a radiation emergency.

DOSE

ADULTS AND CHILDREN ONE YEAR OF AGE OR

OLDER: One (1) tablet once a day. Crush for small children.

BABIES UNDER ONE YEAR OF AGE: One-half (1/2) tablet once a day. Crush first.

DOSAGE: Take for 10 days unless directed otherwise by State or local public health authorities.

Store at controlled room temperature between 15 and 30 C (59 degrees to 86 degrees F). Keep bottle tightly closed and protect from light.

WARNING

PEOPLE ALLERGIC TO IODIDE SHOULD NOT USE POTASSIUM IODIDE. Keep out of the reach of children. In case of overdose or allergic reaction, contact a physician or public health authority.

DESCRIPTION

Each (company trade name) Tablet contains 130 mg. of potassium iodide.

HOW POTASSIUM IODIDE WORKS

Certain forms of iodine help your thyroid gland work right. Most people get the iodine they need from foods like iodized salt or fish. The thyroid can "store" or hold only a certain amount of iodine.

In a radiation emergency, radioactive iodine may be released in the air. This material may be breathed or swallowed. It may enter the thyroid gland and damage it. The damage would probably not show itself for years. Children are most likely to have thyroid damage.

If you take potassium iodide, it will fill up your thyroid gland. This reduces the chance that harmful radioactive iodine will enter the thyroid gland.

WHO SHOULD NOT TAKE POTASSIUM IODIDE

The only people who should not take potassium iodide are people who know they are allergic to iodide. You may take potassium iodide even if you are taking medicines for a thyroid problem (for example, a thyroid hormone or anti-thyroid drug). Pregnant and nursing women and babies and children may also take this drug.

HOW AND WHEN TO TAKE POTASSIUM IODIDE

Potassium iodide should be taken as soon as possible after public health officials tell you. You should take one dose every 24 hours. More will not help you because the thyroid can "hold" only limited amounts of iodine. Larger doses will increase the risk of side effects. You will probably be told not to take the drug for more than 10 days.

SIDE EFFECTS

Usually, side effects of potassium iodide happen when people take higher doses for a long time. You should be careful not to take more than the recommended dose or take it for longer than you are told. Side effects are unlikely because of the low dose and the short time you will be taking the drug.

Possible side effects include skin rashes, swelling of the salivary glands, and "iodism" (metallic taste, burning mouth and throat, sore teeth and gums, symptoms of a head cold, and sometimes stomach upset and diarrhea).

A few people have an allergic reaction with more serious symptoms. These could be fever and joint pains, or swelling of parts of the face and body and at times severe shortness of breath requiring immediate medical attention.

Taking iodide may rarely cause over activity of the thyroid gland, under activity of the thyroid gland, or enlargement of the thyroid gland (goiter).

WHAT TO DO IF SIDE EFFECTS OCCUR

If the side effects are severe or if you have an allergic reaction, stop taking potassium iodide. Then, if possible, call a doctor or public health authority for instructions.

HOW SUPPLIED

Tablets (Potassium Iodide Tablets, U.S.P.):

(). Each white, round, scored tablet contains 130-mg. potassium iodide.

The FDA new (November, 2001) guidance document, that brings it more in-line with the recent World Health Organization recommendations below, is titled; *"Potassium Iodide as a Thyroid Blocking Agent in Radiation Emergencies"*.

It can be seen at <http://www.ki4u.com/fda.htm>. This represents the Food and Drug Administration's current thinking on this topic.

In regards to the differences between the World Health Organization dosing recommendations and these new FDA recommendations:

> *These FDA recommendations differ from those put forward in the World Health Organization (WHO) 1999 guidelines for iodine prophylaxis in two ways. WHO recommends a 130-mg dose of KI for adults and adolescents (over 12 years)? For the sake of logistical simplicity in the dispensing and administration of KI to children, FDA recommends a 65-mg dose as standard for all school-age children while allowing for the adult dose (130 mg, 2 X 65 mg tablets) in adolescents approaching adult size. The other difference lies in the threshold for predicted exposure of those up to 18 years of age and of pregnant or lactating women that should trigger KI prophylaxis. WHO recommends a threshold of 1 cry for these two groups? As stated earlier, FDA has concluded from the Chernobyl data that the most reliable evidence supports a significant increase in the risk of childhood thyroid cancer at exposures of 5 cGy or greater.*

Threshold Thyroid Radioactive Exposures and

Recommended Doses of KI for Different Risk Groups

Predicted Thyroid exposure (cGy)

KI dose (mg)

# of 130 mg tablets

# of 65 mg tablets

Adults over 40 yrs

≥ 500

130

1

2

Adults over 18 through 40 yrs

≥ 10

Pregnant or lactating women

≥ 5

Adoles. over 12 through 18 yrs*

65

1/2

1

Children over 3 through 12 yrs

Over 1 month through 3 years

32

1/4

1/2

Birth through 1 month

16

1/8

1/4

*Adolescents approaching adult size (≥ 70 kg) should receive the full adult dose (130 mg).

The World Health Organization's recent recommendations have a step increase in doses by age (chart below) and also states the potential benefit diminishes with older adults. In fact, if only a limited number of Potassium Iodide (KI) or KIO3 tablets are available, these should always be given to infants, children and young adults first as they are the most vulnerable and also the risk of thyroid cancer fully developing begins to drop off with adults much over 40 years of age.

The World Health Organization (WHO) Guidelines for Iodine Prophylaxis following Nuclear Accidents states:

> *"In general, the potential benefit of iodine prophylaxis will be greater in the young, firstly because the small size of the thyroid means that a higher radiation dose is accumulated per unit intake of radioactive iodine. Secondly, the thyroid of the fetus, neonate and young infant has a higher yearly thyroid cancer risk per unit dose than the thyroid of an adult and, thirdly, the young will have a longer time span for the expression of the increased cancer risk."*

Also, the newly released (November, 2001) FDA document entitled Potassium Iodide as a Thyroid Blocking Agent in Radiation Emergencies <http://www.ki4u.com/fda.htm> determined from the Chernobyl data that:

> *"The risk of thyroid cancer is inversely related to age, and that, especially in young children, it may accrue at very low levels of radioiodine exposure."* and also that *"...adults over 40 need take KI only in the case of a projected large internal radiation dose to the thyroid (>500 cGy) to prevent hypothyroidism."*

Dosing chart from the recently updated 1999 World Health Organization:

Guidelines for Iodine Prophylaxis following Nuclear Accidents

Age Group

Mass of iodine mg

Mass of KI mg

Mass of KIO3 mg

Fraction of 100 mg tablet

Adults and adolescents (over 12 years)

100

130

170

1

Children (3-12 years)

50

65

85

1/2

Infants (1 month to 3 years)

25

32

42

1/4

Neonates (birth to 1 month)

12.5

16

21

1/8

To help make sense of any possible dosing confusion and radiation level thresholds, it should be remembered first that you should not commence dosing until so directed by a doctor or public health officials. Also, the biggest difference in dosage and ages, between the two recommendations, is that WHO suggests an adult dose (130mg KI) for everyone over 12 where the FDA suggests an adult dose for everyone over 18, unless the adolescent weighs 70kg (154 lbs) or more. And, again, the primary reason for this divergence from the WHO recommendations is that, according to the FDA: *For the sake of logistical simplicity in the dispensing and administration of KI to children, FDA recommends a 65-mg dose as standard for all school-age children while allowing for the adult dose (130 mg, 2 X 65 mg tablets) in adolescents approaching adult size.*

At the WHO dosages recommended above, an adverse reaction rate of less than 1 in 10 million children and less than 1 in 1 million adults are expected. However, people allergic to iodine should not use Potassium Iodide. According to the WHO, contraindications for use of potassium iodide are: (1) past or present thyroid disease (e.g., active hyperthyroidism), (2) known iodine hypersensitivity, (3) dermatitis herpetiformis, and (4) hypocomplementaemic vasculitis.

You should also check with your doctor before taking this medication if you have myotonia or hyperkalemia congenita or tuberculosis or kidney disease. See <http://www.mayoclinic.com/findinformation/druginformation/druginvoke.cfm?objectId=0001F9AB-8093-1B79-AB8080AEBC2F0839> for more information.

Pregnant women should consult a physician prior to continuing dosages for more than two days. For pregnant or nursing women, and for cautions to the proper dosing of neonates, also read the appropriate sections here in the newly released (November, 2001) FDA document entitled Potassium Iodide as a Thyroid Blocking Agent in Radiation Emergencies.

The WHO also states, and the FDA concurs, *"Side effects in other parts of the body, such as gastrointestinal effects or hypersensitivity reactions, may occur but are generally mild and can be considered of minor importance."*

Besides contraindications with pre-existing medical conditions, this is also important if you (or they) are taking any regular medications. Especially, though not limited to, Spironolactone (like Aldactone), Triamterene (Dyrenium), Amiloride (Midamor), or medicines for an overactive thyroid, or if you are on medications with any lithium-based or potassium-sparing diuretics.

7.3.3.6 *Is Iodized Salt, Tincture of Iodine, Water Purification Tabs, or other Iodine Sources Effective?*

Ans: Any dietary iodine sources providing for a normal daily sufficient regimen of iodine intake (about 150 micrograms/day in adults) is preferred in that it will then take less stable iodine (and time) to saturate your thyroid in a nuclear emergency and there will be less room there for radioactive iodine before you do. An iodine sufficient diet will also greatly increase the effectiveness of KI or KIO3, but primarily only in the following limited context and not as a substitute for KI or KIO3:

> An iodine sufficient diet is most beneficial, compared to an insufficient iodine diet, when the initial administration of KI had been unavoidably delayed and the KI could only be first taken after exposure to radioiodine.

From the Health Physics Journal, Volume 78 No. 6, June 2000, "EFFECTS OF TIME OF ADMINISTRATION AND DIETARY IODINE LEVELS ON POTASSIUM IODIDE (KI) BLOCKADE OF THYROID IRRADIATION BY 131-I FROM RADIOACTIVE FALLOUT" Pat B. Zanzonico and David V. Becker (Read abstract by searching title at Health Physics Journal):

> *"The 131-I thyroid absorbed dose is two-fold greater with insufficient levels of dietary iodine, 2,900 cGy/37 MBq, than with sufficient levels of dietary iodine, 1,500 cGy/37 MBq. When KI is administered 48 h or less before 131-I intake, the thyroid-absorbed doses (in cGy/37*

MBq) are comparably low with both sufficient and insufficient dietary iodine levels. When KI is administered after 131-I intake, however, the protective effect of KI is less and decreases more rapidly with insufficient than with sufficient dietary iodine. For example, KI administration 2 and 8 h after 131-I intake yields protective effects of 80 and 40%, respectively, with iodine-sufficient diets, but only 65 and 15% with iodine-deficient diets."

From the Salt Institue:

"U.S. salt producers use potassium iodide at a level of 0.006% to 0.01% KI."

According to Morton® Salt:

"Each 1/4 teaspoon serving of Morton® Iodized Salt (1.5 gram weight) contains 130 MICROGRAMS of Potassium Iodide."

Thus, to achieve an intake of 130 MILLIGRAMS of Potassium Iodide (what one KI adult dose tablet contains) would require ingesting 250 teaspoons or over 5 cups of iodized salt per day! Don't even think about it! (Morton Lite Salt® Mixture comes in lower yet, at only 90 MICROGRAMS of Potassium Iodide per 1/4 teaspoon!)

Sea Salt is an even worse 'option'. Iodine per Kilogram of sea salt is about 3 mg. You'd be looking at over 33 kilograms of Sea Salt a day! Hardly an option!

A 6-ounce portion of ocean fish only contains about 500 MICROGRAMS of iodine. Some specific seafoods, portion size and their iodine content in MICROGRAMS: Mackerel 150g 255 mcg, Mussels 150g 180 mcg, Cod 150g 165 mcg, Kipper 150g 107 mcg, Whiting 150g 100 mcg, Fish fingers 75g 75 mcg, Scampi 150g 62 mcg, Herring 150g 48 mcg, Prawns 150g 42 mcg, Sardines, canned in oil 150g 35 mcg, Trout 150g 24 mcg, Tuna 150g 21 mcg. Well, you can do the math here! More fish per day than most eat in a year!

Kelp Tablets...hardly. Solgar® Kelp Tablets, for example, contain only 225 MICROGRAMS of iodine! (Fortunately, it is also available in a 1000 tablet bottle, unfortunately though, you'd need to be swallowing 442 of them per day and not wander too far from a bathroom!)

Medicines contain Potassium Iodide: Potassium iodide (KI) is an old drug used as an expectorant in the treatment of asthma, bronchitis and emphysema. It is used to treat coughs with phlegm, feeling of fullness in the chest or pressure in the face/sinuses. Potassium iodide helps loosen phlegm (mucus) and thin bronchial secretions to drain bronchial tubes and make coughs more productive. It increases secretions in the respiratory tract in approximately 30 min. Today it is mainly used to treat an overactive thyroid and, of course, to protect the thyroid gland from the effects of radiation from inhaled or swallowed radioactive iodine. Potassium iodide also has anti-infective properties and is sometimes used to treat certain skin conditions caused by fungus, like toenail fungus.

PIMA (Fleming & Company) and SSKI (Upsher-Smith Laboratories, Inc.) are both available in tablets or liquid, but only with a prescription. Another, that used to be a non-prescription cough and expectorant medicine available over-the-counter (OTC) is Pediacof Cough made by Sterling Health, a Division of Miles, Inc. Common 5 ml dose contains Chlorpheniramine 0.75 mg, Codeine 5 mg, Phenylephrine 2.5 mg, Potassium Iodide 75 mg.

Also, FYI, Potassium Iodide can be found in some livestock preparations, too, such as Equi-Tussin, which is a liquid expectorant and aromatic oil supplement for horses. It contains 125 mg of Potassium Iodide per fluid ounce, but it also contains Molasses, Mentholated Syrup of White Pine, Eucalyptus Oil, Peppermint Oil, Glyceryl Guiacolate and Ammonium Chloride and is obviously formulated for horses, not people. You might want to keep this in mind, though, for protecting your livestock and pets.

Regarding ingesting (drinking/swallowing) iodine, iodine tablets (widely sold for water purification), tincture of iodine, or Povidone-iodine solutions (like the Betadine® brand solution): Department of Energy (Updated and Expanded 1987 Edition) states on page 115:

Elemental (free) iodine is poisonous, except in the very small amounts in water disinfected with iodine tablets or a few drops of tincture of iodine. Furthermore, elemental iodine supplied by iodine tablets and released by tincture of iodine dropped into water is not effective as a blocking agent to prevent thyroid damage. If you do not have any potassium iodide, DO NOT TAKE IODINE TABLETS OR TINCTURE OF IODINE.

Iodine is normally used in doses of 8 PPM to treat clear water for a 10-minute contact time. The effectiveness and safety of this dose has been shown in numerous studies. As far back as 1953 in the study "Test of chronic toxicity of iodine as related to the purification of water". U.S. Armed Forces medical journal, 1953, 4:725-728 Morgan DP, Karpen RJ. It was shown that:

"No adverse health effects were reported in men who drank water providing iodide at doses of 0.17-0.27 mg/kg of body weight per day for 26 weeks"

That works out to a reported safe ingestion of elemental iodine via treated water of between 14 and 22 mg per day for a 180 lb adult. To attempt to achieve a thyroid-blocking dose of nearly 100 mg of iodine (the iodine content of a 130 mg KI tablet) would thus require exceeding that proven safe level by a factor of at least four to seven times for an 180 lb adult. And, this would be with potentially poisonous elemental free iodine that is also claimed above by Cresson H. Kearny to be *"...not effective as a blocking agent to prevent thyroid damage."*

Additionally, USP tincture of iodine contains 2% iodine and 2.4% sodium iodide dissolved in 50% ethyl alcohol and according to the National Academy of Sciences in Drinking Water and Health. Vol. 3. Washington, DC, National Academy Press, 1980.

Doses of 30-250 ml of tincture of iodine (about 16-130 mg of total iodine per kg of body weight) have been reported to be fatal.

The small typical one ounce bottle of tincture of iodine contains about two tablespoons or approximately 30 ml of fluid. (The larger pint bottles contain 473 ml.) To a small child, ingesting the small 1 ounce bottle, even if well diluted to make it palatable, could prove fatal.

Everyone needs to understand that all 'tincture of iodine' bottles are clearly marked "POISON" for a very good reason. Ingesting elemental free iodine, such as 'tincture of iodine', in quantities sufficient to attempt thyroid blocking in a nuclear emergency is not a safe, nor an effective, alternative.

Finally, if someone does attempt thyroid-blocking for themselves or their children by ingesting iodine, iodine water purification tablets, tincture of iodine, or Povidone-iodine solutions (like the Betadine® brand solution), and we are strongly advising against it, they can look forward to:

- shock (potentially fatal lowering of blood pressure)
- extreme thirst
- metallic taste
- sore teeth, gums and mouth
- severe headache
- fever
- no urine output (kidney failure)
- corrosive effects on the gastrointestinal tract
- esophageal stricture, asphyxiation (swelling of the throat, esophagus)
- vomiting
- diarrhea
- abdominal pain with internal damage
- delirium
- stupor

Then, be prepared to call the Poison Control center for further guidance. DO NOT INDUCE VOMITING. Give milk, cornstarch, or flour by mouth (15 gm in 500 ml, or just over a pint of water). Continue to give milk every 15 minutes.

And, at the Emergency Room expect some or all of the following procedures to be performed: Gastric lavage (depending on the extent of esophageal injury), establish and maintain airway, be given milk every 15 minutes, and treatment for the symptoms.

7.3.3.7 *Is the Government Ready with Emergency Stocks of Potassium Iodide (KI)?*

Ans: No," The American Thyroid Association through its Public Health Committee has strongly recommended the stockpiling of KI for prophylaxis in the event of a nuclear reactor accident. Unfortunately, the Nuclear Regulatory Commission has not accepted this recommendation."

Even the latest (November, 2001) FDA document entitled Potassium Iodide as a Thyroid Blocking Agent in Radiation Emergencies states:

"As time is of the essence in optimal prophylaxis with KI, timely administration to the public is a critical consideration in planning the emergency response to a radiation accident and requires a ready supply of KI." and *"FDA also emphasizes that emergency response plans and any systems for ensuring availability of KI to the public should recognize the critical importance of KI administration in advance of exposure to radioiodine."*

U.S. Lacks Stockpile of Special Drug

Anti-Radiation Doses Goal Unmet Since '79

By Justin Gillis

Washington Post Staff Writer

Monday, December 31, 2001; Page A01

"A generation ago, as a nuclear disaster unfolded in central Pennsylvania and 140,000 people fled the area, pharmaceutical executives were rousted from bed in the middle of the night by a plea for help.

At the federal government's request, they cranked up a production line in Illinois at 3 a.m., and hours later, thousands of bottles of potassium iodide, an anti-radiation drug, were secretly rushed to Harrisburg by military jet. Ultimately the nuclear reactor at Three Mile Island was brought under control and the drug was not needed, but it was a close call. When it was over, policymakers in Washington vowed to stockpile the drug, saying they would not be caught short again.

It never happened".

7.3.3.8 *Will Potassium Iodide (KI) Flush Radioactive Iodine Out of the Thyroid Gland?*

Ans: The question might better be: If you don't have any Potassium Iodide (KI) and rely on the government to acquire and distribute KI, and after some delay, you do eventually get Potassium Iodide (KI) for your family, but it's now hours or days into the nuclear radiation emergency, will Potassium Iodide (KI) still help?

Yes and No.

Yes, but only to the degree your thyroid is still less than 100% saturated with either form of iodine (radioactive or stable). Then the Potassium Iodide (KI) will safely fill up the balance so your thyroid will not have room for later additional uptake of radioactive iodine.

But, No, Potassium Iodide (KI) can't flush out radioactive iodine that's already there before taking KI.

Therefore, KI or KIO3 should be taken before Nuclear emergency starts, as a prophylactic measure.

The following information is also given in the INTERNET by KI4U, Inc., Gonzales, Texas for the benefit of all concerned about a large number of FAQs available addressing individual items on various aspects of Radiation, its exposure, measurements , protection and treatments. Those information are presented here in public interest. The author is very grateful to the authorities of KI4U, Inc.

ki4u.com, not K14U or Kl4U, but rather www.ki4u.com

KI4U, INC advertisements for their products, its benefits, availability, information regarding the placement of orders are presented in the following

MRE's FAQ

Military-Style Meals Ready to Eat

In-depth info on additional preparation topics can be found at the...

Potassium Iodide Anti-Radiation Pill FAQ

Nukalert™ Key-Chain Attachable Rad Monitor & Alarm!

Civil Defense Rad Detection Survey Meters, Geiger Counters and Dosimeters FAQ

Nuclear Blast & Fallout Shelters FAQ with free plans, books & ready made shelter sources!

Chemical (Nerve Gases) & Biological Detector FAQ & sources!

Emergency Water Filters & Purification FAQ

First-Time Customers, You Can Check Out KI4U, Inc.

NOTE (6/1/03): Below you will find information on MRE's and our two versions offered here; individual single serving MRE Entree's and the larger MRE Tray Packs that each contain 9-18 servings. Industry wise now, with the recent military demands, MRE's are getting much harder to find and you'll see that some of our 38 different MRE varieties below are, for the first time, sold out.

Depending on your anticipated family food requirements, there are still available additional emergency food alternatives, at this time. These other long-term storage food options require some preparation, but are a great deal cheaper than MRE's, thus extending the number of weeks and months you could afford to prepare for. Many families will utilize a mix of different food sources (MRE's, dried, bulk) to add variety and economy to their family food storage strategy.

Here at KI4U we have arranged special pricing from the two leaders in non-MRE food storage (I have personally bought from them both for my own family needs for years) and invite you to check them both out, too. With either of these two following companies, if you find their products appropriate to your needs, we can secure for you a 5% discount when you first contact us here at webmaster@ki4u.com before placing your order with them.

Ready Reserve Foods: Since 1972, the leader in nitrogen packed long-storage food units of 3 days to 3 months to 3 years!

...and...

Wheat Montana: Economical quality source, straight from the farm, for wheat, grains, beans, etc. Many selections available in strong 45# Pails sealed with oxygen absorbers for long-term storage requirements.

Remember, contact us first here at webmaster@ki4u.com, before ordering, and we'll secure for you an additional 5% discount with either of the above two outfits.

Now, before we go onto the MRE's, a quick word about *water*...

If you ever have to make use of your emergency food stock, odds are you could also have some problems with water, too. Clean water, free of dangerous pathogens and chemical contamination, is more essential than food. Most everyone can go without food for a week, or even two, and survive the unpleasant experience, but just a couple or three days without safe water can become life-threatening for all. And, risking the use of an unknown water source could be even worse.

Alternative sources of clean, safe water either stored and/or filtering equipment acquired, is too often overlooked because of our being accustomed to abundant clean waters at the turn of a tap. But, if the electricity that pumps the water is interrupted or water sources are contaminated, we'll all see very quickly how especially dependent we truly are on clean water. Bottled water will disappear off the store shelves quicker than most can even begin to imagine! The majority, after that, will then spend many hours of each day standing in long lines awaiting the rumored water truck coming to their neighborhood next. It need not be so for your family...

Bottom Line: Be sure to have also secured alternative water storage and/or water filtration equipment. We also invite you to explore the inexpensive, and our family proven in Venezuela for four months filtering muddy hillside runoffs, KI4U Combo Water Filter here that can also be ordered below, too.

Now, onto the MRE's...

Background & Shelf Life...

SOPAKCO's Tray Packs and single Entree meals utilize many of the same menu items packaged for the U.S. fighting forces. (MRE Tray Packs with individual entree meal MRE pictured above). SOPAKCO is the major MRE supplier to the Department of Defense with about 45% of that market.

7.4 WHAT IS AN "MRE"?

MRE's (which are pronounced as separate letters M,R,E's) are ready-to-eat meal kits. The name MRE comes from their military description Meals, Ready-to-Eat. Your SOPAKCO MRE's contain many of the same components found in the meal bags of the U.S. fighting forces. Developed for soldiers in combat conditions, these meals are already cooked and moist. No finding water, boiling water or waiting for re-hydration. Great tasting, long shelf life and always in high demand and short supply whenever disaster strikes.

THE FLEXIBLE CAN The flexible aluminum retort pouches used in MRE pouched food products are composed of multiple laminations of aluminum foil and plastic film. Rugged durability, extended shelf life and ease of stowing have earned the MRE pouch a well-deserved nickname "the flexible can".

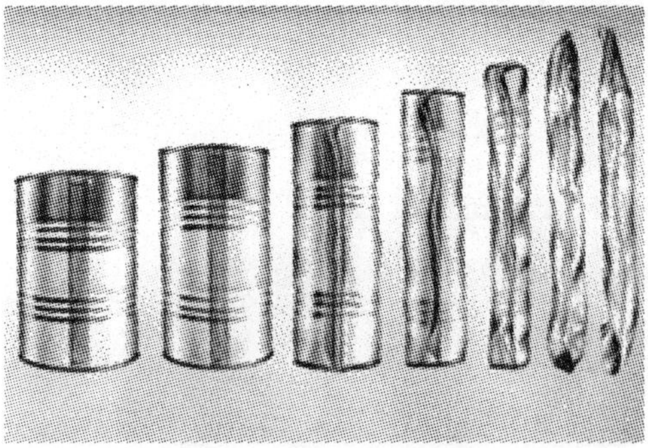

7.4.1 Are SOPAKCO MRE's Dehydrated or Freeze Dried?

No. Dehydrated or freeze dried foods typically require that water be added in order to be prepared and eaten. Your SOPAKCO MRE main courses are "ready to eat", and do not require you to add water to the contents.

7.4.2 Can I Eat the Products Cold?

Yes. The main entrees (such as Beef Stew, Chili with Macaroni or similar items) do not require additional cooking prior to being eaten. All products may be eaten cold, directly from the pouch. Heating of the products is considered optional, although most people do prefer to warm their food when possible.

7.4.3 How Do I Warm My Food?

MRE pouches may be warmed in many ways. Although the pouch is a reasonably sturdy and durable container, it can be damaged if too high of a temperature is applied. DO NOT apply a direct flame to the pouch. DO NOT use any high temperature heating process that could harm the pouch or cause injury or damage to your skin. Instead, the following methods are suggested methods of "gently warming" your food

1. The unopened pouch may be placed in a pan of warm water for 5-10 minutes. Do not use hot water, which may burn the user if spilled.
2. Lay the pouch in direct sunlight, allowing it to warm;
3. The unopened pouch may be placed inside your shirt, allowing your body temperature to help warm the food inside;
4. The unopened pouch may be laid on a warm surface, to absorb the heat from the warm object;
5. The pouch may be opened and the food placed into a pan for heating.
6. MRE pouches may also be heated using Water-Activated Flameless MRE Heaters. SOPAKCO does not make these heaters. Please speak with your retailer about the possible availability of these items.

7.4.4 Why are the Packages in Plain Brown or Green Colors?

Most items in your SOPAKCO MRE's are packed in standard military packaging. The brown and green colors are selected to help the products have low visibility.

7.4.5 How Long will these Products Last?

SOPAKCO Packaging uses an estimated shelf life figure of "5 years, plus or minus" for its MRE-type pouched food products. Actual shelf life may vary from this estimate. A key factor effecting actual shelf life is the temperature of the storage environment. Storage at temperatures higher than 85F (85 degrees Fahrenheit) may shorten the shelf life of MRE-type food products. On the other hand, lowering the storage temperature will help extend the products' shelf life. This effect is common to most processed food products.

The shelf life figures given below for MRE's are based on studies conducted by the U.S. Army's NATIC Research Laboratories. This study was conducted by NATIC without participation of the MRE manufacturers. As such, SOPAKCO Packaging cannot verify the test procedures used by the NATIC labs, nor do we adopt these shelf life figures as a guarantee of any sort. The data is useful, though, as a general indication of the effects of storage temperatures on the shelf life of MRE-type food products.

Temperature (Fahrenheit)	*Storage Life in Months*
100°	22
90°	55
85°	60
80°	76
75°	88
70°	100
60°	130 +

The above storage data and time periods were based on "acceptable taste" measures, which is a subjective standard that may vary among each individual. Test participants were asked to indicate which products they were presented would be rated to still be of "acceptable taste". Responses were noted, and average values were calculated to yield the data above.

The above data does not indicate the maximum useful life of MRE food products. The NATIC study noted that nutritional value and product safety value of the products often extended far beyond these time points.

Again, SOPAKCO Packaging in no way adopts the NATIC shelf life figures as any form of express or implied guarantee of the actual shelf life of its MRE food products. This information is provided as a general indication of the effects of storage temperature on MRE-type packaged foods.

Will these products work for camping trips?

Absolutely! The ready-to-eat convenience of SOPAKCO MRE's make them ideally suited for use while camping, hunting, fishing and hiking.

Would it make sense for me to store MRE's as a source of food for my family or employees in the event of a natural disaster or other emergency?

It makes very good sense. Many individuals, companies and other organizations purchase and store our MRE's as emergency food supplies in the event of earthquakes, hurricanes, tornadoes, ice storms or other emergency situations.

The Need for Emergency Reserve Food Storage...

7.5 ALERT ON FOOD TERROR ATTACKS

Reuters - February 1, 2003

GENEVA - The World Health Organization warned yesterday that terrorists could try to contaminate food with chemical, biological or radioactive agents and urged states to tighten their defenses. The U.N. agency called on its 192 member governments and on industry to boost surveillance and emergency response measures to minimize the risk. In a report, "Terrorist Threats to Food Guidance for Establishing and Strengthening Prevention and Response Systems," WHO said that developing countries with poor food safety controls were the most vulnerable to attack.

7.6 EXPERTS WARN ON FOOD SUPPLY THREAT

09/19/2002 - Updated 0436 PM EDT

WASHINGTON (AP) - The United States is poorly prepared for a bio-terrorism attack on farm animals, crops and the food supply, a panel of scientists concluded Thursday. It blamed this situation on a communications gap between intelligence agencies and among agriculture officials, farm groups and universities. The Agriculture Department commissioned the report by the National Academy of Sciences but - fearing that it would be used as a manual for terrorists - fought its release until discussions of specific threats were excised. The panel of 12 scientists which wrote the report concluded that the nation is more prepared for an accidental outbreak of potentially catastrophic diseases such as foot-and-mouth among cattle than one triggered by terrorists.

The academy's National Research Council said that while working on its analysis, "Countering Agricultural Bioterrorism," questions arose over what scientific information about terrorism should and shouldn't be made public. But when the National Academies met with the department and the Office of Homeland Security, "the government did not assert that the report contained classified information," the council wrote.

Scientists also had reservations about the report, said William E. Coalglazier, executive officer for the National Academy of Sciences, an independent research group chartered by Congress to guide the government on scientific matters.

"Clearly the academy does not want to provide a road map for terrorists," Coalglazier said. Because the council used some classified documents for the assessment, the National Academies decided to remove information from a section that described specific case studies, Coalglazier said. Only government officials can access those excluded details.

"The guidance that we were sort of using in our heads was if there was specific information that perhaps could be used to harm the public, then we would exclude it," Coalglazier said. Although the classified information was excluded, the analysis concluded that the United States has a lot of work to do to ensure farms and communities are protected from bio-terrorism.

Scientists and farm groups became worried the United States wouldn't be able to contain an outbreak when foot-and-mouth disease infected livestock herds in Britain last year. Although the disease doesn't harm humans, an outbreak can disrupt the economy and cost millions of dollars to control and eradicate.

The terrorist attacks and appearance of anthrax-laden letters in 2001 added to concerns that diseases like mad cow disease could be used as weapons to poison food supplies, harm people, and sink the economy. The scientists pointed out several problems, but were particularly critical of gaps in communication between agricultural and intelligence officials, farm groups, and universities - all of which have a role in helping farmers and the public to cope with food and farm security threats.

The council recommended that the government immediately

- Increase its efforts to understand plant and animal diseases and how they spread.
- Establish a network of laboratories that would respond, detect and diagnose diseases.
- Form a nationwide system to manage and collect bio-terrorism information.

Although a bio-terrorist attack seems unlikely, "it's not a matter of 'if.' It's a matter of 'when'," said R. James Cook, a committee member from Washington State University. "What's important to keep in mind, though, is that while there may be a very low probability now, what about in 20 years?"

7.7 LOCAL FOOD COMPANIES HEED FBI WARNING

Food Industry Urged To Increase Security

KSBW-TV, April 3, 2003

SALINAS, Calif. — The FBI is warning that it would not be difficult to contaminate the nation's food supply and is urging the food industry to increase security. It's a move that could have a major impact on Central Coast companies.

It's not easy to get past the white doors into the Smucker's processing plant in Salinas.

Smucker's has always worried that someone could poison or contaminate the jams and jellies they process. They won't say if employees go through background checks, but they do check everyone who visits the site.

"We can't really get into too much, but that is one of the items that we focus on. We look at everyone who comes on the property ... even a truck driver," plant manager Jeff Pasquino-Greco said.

Tanimura and Antle wouldn't discuss specifics either, but told Action News they have also added security after the FBI's warning, focusing in part on their water supply used to wash and freeze produce.

Even dairy farms are told to look out for anthrax and foot and mouth disease, which could wipe out their herds. Officials say terrorists are looking for targets that will hurt the U.S. ecomony, and the Office of Emergency Services knows the country's food supply is vulnerable.

"If they can get an economic impact and cause mass panic and terror in the process then they've achieved their goals, and that's one of the reasons why the USDA has stepped up their security efforts," Monterey County OES spokesman Harry Robins said.

OES and all the companies Action News spoke with said they are working with Food and Drug Administration and the United State Department of Agriculture to follow security requirements.

And, on top of all that...

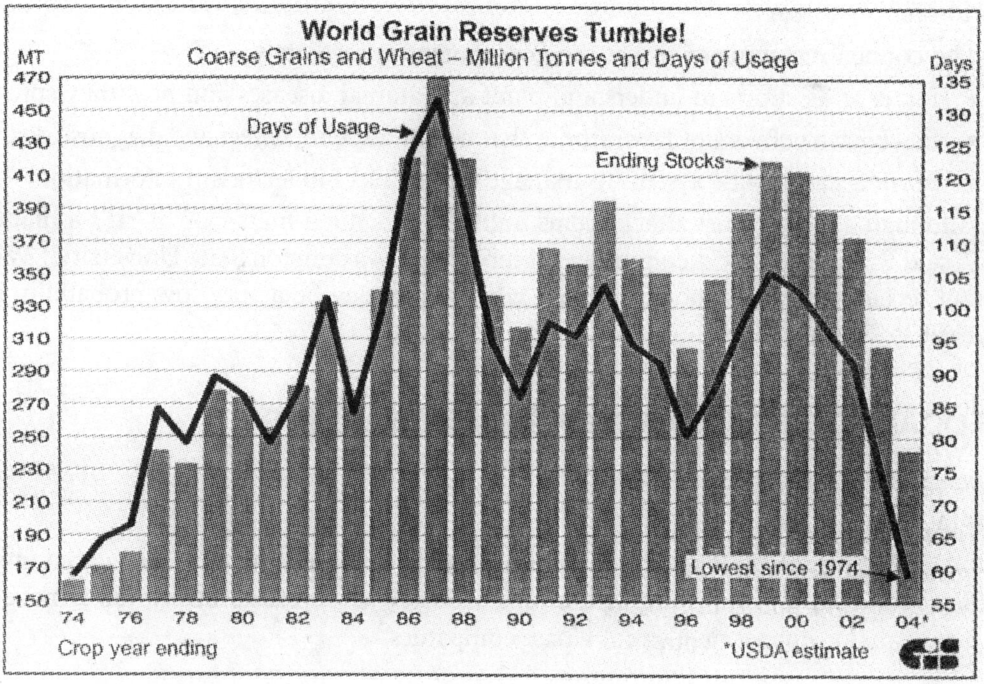

I personally find it very fascinating that while, till this day, nobody can say for sure what caused the widespread Blackout's last month, the federal government came out within an hour of it happening and proclaimed that it was NOT terrorism! How could they possibly know what it wasn't, when they still don't know what it was!

Terror attack on grid would collapse U.S.

By SHAUN WATERMAN, UPI Homeland and National Security Editor

WASHINGTON, Sept. 4 (UPI) — Government scientific advisers and officials painted a grim picture Thursday of the consequences of a terror attack on the nation's power grid, saying that any outage that lasted longer than a couple of days would reduce urban centers to chaos and collapse the economy.

"With power out beyond a day or two, both food and water supplies would soon fail. Transportation systems would be at a standstill ... natural gas pressure would decline and some would lose gas altogether — not good in the winter time ... Communications would be spotty or non-existent. ... All in all, our cities would not be very nice places to be... Martial law would likely follow," Paul H. Gilbert of the National Research Council told a congressional panel.

Lawmakers on the House Homeland Security Committee were trying to see what lessons about the nation's security could be drawn from the massive Aug. 14 power outage, which left 50 million people in the United States and Canada without electricity for more than 24 hrs—in some cases—up to three days.

But Gilbert said that recovery from an outage caused by a deliberate attack could "take weeks or months rather than hours or days."

Such frightening scenarios are not the product of a nightmarish imagination. Gilbert's analysis was based on the work of a high-level brains trust within the National Academies. Nearly 200 scientists, experts and officials worked for six months on the report he cited as the basis for his assessment.

Nor is such an attack beyond the realm of reality. Larry A. Mefford, counter-terror chief of the FBI, told the panel that, "Al-Qaida and other terrorist groups are known to have considered energy facilities ... as possible targets."

While cautioning that there was "no specific, credible intelligence about threats" to the nation's power infrastructure, he said that methods of attack could range from blowing up pylons or power stations to sophisticated cyber attacks on the automated computer-run elements of the grid.

"That would depend on their infrastructure in this country and the extent of their knowledge of the grid," he told United Press International, adding that a successful assault is "a lot easier than we wish it were."

John McCarthy, director of the Critical Infrastructure Protection Project at George Mason University, described how a student of his — using information in the public domain — had created a comprehensive map of the nation's entire fiber optic cable network as part of his Ph.D. dissertation.

The document so alarmed officials — one described it as "a road map for terrorists" — that they wanted to classify it. His student was "very, very smart," said McCarthy, but his work could be replicated for the power grid. "I am convinced there are equally smart people looking at our infrastructure who don't have our best interests at heart."

Some lawmakers were impatient that — nearly two years after the terror attacks of Sept. 11, 2001, and six months after it had been established — the Department for Homeland Security had not yet completed one of its primary tasks — a comprehensive survey of the nation's critical infrastructure and its vulnerabilities. "We understand they're working on that," Mefford said.

Rep. Christopher Cox, R-Calif., pointed out that without a comprehensive assessment of the nation's weak spots, it was hard to know where the country needed defending.

"In the absence of that it seems you would have a very difficult time knowing where our priorities should be and where we should spend our limited dollars."

Gilbert said that the August outage could have lasted much longer, and pointed out that it exposed the weakness of the "fragile" power grid, which had "little reserve within which to handle power or load fluctuations."

9/11 seemed pretty improbable, too, ...before it happened!

But, the neatest thing about investing in, and storing some, emergency food for your family is that if nothing bad does happen to you and yours in the years ahead, like floods, blizzards, tornadoes, hurricanes, earthquakes, etc. you can always just simply eat them! So, it need never be a wasted investment! No family insurance policy guarantees a better return than that! Nor, is anything more essential or basic to your family survival than plentiful and wholesome food!

BTW, I eat these MRE's for lunch probably every 2nd or 3rd day here and 8 out of the 11 are great to my taste, and the others are fair. (Of course, get hungry enough, and they will all taste great, too!) Also, check out our inexpensive Sampler Pack detailed below with the 6 different flavors (4 of each for a total of 24 MRE Entrees) and see how you and your family like them, too.

Shane Connor (USA)

"What We Have Available...

I discovered in the fall 2001 that a church member was the Comptroller for the major MRE manufacturer to the Department of Defense and had been talking to him ever since ('pestering' he'd say) about letting me buy truckloads of freshly manufactured MRE Entrees for re-sale to the public. (These main meal Entrees, usually meat and 8 ounces each, come 72 retort Entree pouches to a case and are the main course of the full MRE meal.)

Negotiations on price/quantity were completed in April, 2002 and the first MRE cases arrived that same month. Additional truckloads since then have us stocked up now with about 100,000 Entree's of the different menus listed below. They all new, recent manufacture, and we turn our stock quickly. Most of it was produced within the last year, and the 'oldest' we have here was produced in the latter half of 2001. (That's both very 'fresh' and unusual amongst MRE's normally offered for sale to the public that are more often surplus or stock rotation that can be many years old.) These are the primary main meal Entree, not the more expensive full meal pack with the side dishes, crackers, napkins, spoons, etc. (Note: We just recently also added MRE Tray Packs, too. Details below in the new Update section.)

We offer the MRE Entree's by the case only. Each case of 72 Entree Retort Pouches will contain all of the same menu MRE. (While we can not break or offer mixed cases, we did put together a 'Sampler Pack' detailed down below.) The available Entree menu flavors and current inventory as of this morning (Thursday, 9:35 AM CST, 1/1/2004) is as follows:

- COUNTRY CAPTAIN CHICKEN (MRE) - 32 cases
- BEEF ENCHILADA (MRE) - 66 cases
- MEAT LOAF (MRE) - 54 cases
- BEEF W/MUSHROOM (MRE) - (OS - SOLD OUT)
- BEEF IN TERIYAKI SAUCE (MRE) - 8 cases
- GRILLED CHICKEN BREAST PATTY (MRE) - 158 cases
- JAMAICAN PORK CHOP (MRE) - 122 cases
- TURKEY BREAST IN GRAVY W/POT.(MRE) - (OS - SOLD OUT)
- CHICKEN CAVATELLI (MRE) (OS - SOLD OUT)
- BLACK BEAN & RICE BURRITO (MRE) - (OS - SOLD OUT)
- BEEF PATTY, GRILLED (MRE) (OS - SOLD OUT)
- BEEF FRANKFURTERS (MRE) (OS - SOLD OUT)

(OS) means Out-of-Stock, do not order it, re-supply here is very unlikely.

The Sampler Pack consists of four of each of the above six different available menus, 24 MRE Entree's total, and is available on the order form below. This is a great way to personally sample all the flavors before getting cases of 72 of all one menu flavor.

BTW, the Sampler Pack, for a limited time, is only half-price. *IF* you are also buying at least $100 of our other products offered over there at the same time. (Anti-Radiation tablets, NukAlert™, rad meters, chem detection, nuke books & CD's, etc.). But, there is a limit of only one Sampler Pack per customer at that introductory reduced price over there. However, below, there is no restriction, and you can order as many as needed at the regular price.

Most outfits are selling these cases of 72 MRE Entree's for well over $100, some much more, and not a few of them are out-of-stock, too. We are finding it much harder, and much more expensive, to replenish our inventory now that the military has doubled their normal yearly demands and they have all the manufacturers running at overtime just to keep up. We fully expect, as we run out of some of our selections here, that we will not be able to replace that inventory and offer them again, perhaps for a very long time.

We are able to sell them for *$100 per case* of 72 Entree pouches and shipping will be the same per case, regardless of the weight within the same shipping zone. (Most cases are 46 - 48 lbs, though three are under 30 lbs, so we averaged out the shipping cost per case for our UPS chart below.) Checking some zip codes at the farthest points from us here in Texas works out to less than $29 per case for shipping. Closer points were under $10 per case. (I can only ship these here within the Continental USA, though, so no Alaska, Hawaii or foreign sales, unfortunately.) Check your UPS shipping charges per case with your zip code from the rate chart.

We can also do pallet loads via cheaper truck freight, too, if anyone has a group needing at least 36 cases for a full pallet.

Besides shipping costs, it's very important also, when shopping MRE prices, to know how old the MRE's offered are, if at all possible. Many of the dates on MRE's offered for sale, that we've seen elsewhere, were measured in multiple years, not months. Most of ours were produced within the last year, the 'oldest' stock here being some from the latter half of 2001. (That's why it was so hard to talk my comptroller friend into letting me have them direct at all, their current production is normally slated for the military exclusively!)

BTW, Inventory will be updated daily below on the order form, too, and all orders received before 3 PM CST will ship via UPS that same day.

I know this is a really good deal, especially with them being current production, and invite spreading the word to friends and family, for as long as they last!

Best Regards,

Shane Connor,

UPDATE

"We now are also stocking and offering the MRE Trays! " Connor says.

These MRE tray packs are ideally suited to feeding larger groups and families. Each tray contains 9-18 servings in a 10" × 12 1/2" × 2" tray. The trays are built to be stacked, making them ideal for food storage closets, cupboards, pantries, and tight spaces. And when you are ready to eat, you can even warm your food right in the tray. Great for Scouts and camping trips, as well as emergency use! These MRE entrees taste best when eaten within five years. Trays sold here by the case.

Each tray pack case comes with four (4) same-menu MRE trays.

Tray Packs - for large groups

Tray Packs are large, shelf-stable cans designed for foodservice and other mass feeding applications. Each case contains 4 Tray Packs of 6 LB 10 ounce net weight per tray.

Some Tray Pack menu items feed 9 people per Tray (please see chart below). Since each case contains 4 Trays, a case will feed 4 × 9 people = 36 people per case.

Some Tray Pack menu items feed 18 people per Tray (please see below). Since each case contains 4 Trays, a case will feed 4 × 18 people = 72 people per case.

Tray Packs are designed to fit 2 units side-by-side in a standard steam tray opening. The Tray Packs serve as the heating and serving containers. The Tray Pack containers are thrown away after use, saving you from having to clean the normal pots and pans used in food service applications.

There are many ways to heat Tray Packs. Although Tray Packs were designed to fit into a standard steam tray unit, they may be heated in many other ways

<UL

1. Place the unopened tray in warm water for 20-30 minutes,
2. Puncture the lid and slowly heat in the oven,
3. Remove the lid and slowly heat over a stove or campfire,
4. Leave tray pack in direct sunlight to absorb warmth, or
5. Remove the contents and heat by your method of choice.

SOPAKCO® Tray Packs

Complete list of menu items below this chart...

Pork Ribs in BBQ

Beef Patties in Broth

Chicken Breasts in Gravy

Ham Slices

Pork & Beans

Servings per Tray

9 servings of

2 rib sections each

18 servings of

1 patty each

9 servings of

2 breast portions each

18 servings of

3 slices each

18 servings of

2/3 cup each

Servings per Case (4 Trays per Case)

9 servings

× 4 = 36

18 servings

× 4 = 72

9 servings

× 4 = 36

18 servings

× 4 = 72

18 servings

× 4 = 72

Gross weight per case

38 lbs

38 lbs

38 lbs

38 lbs

38 lbs

Cubic feet per case

0.83 ft3

0.83 ft3

0.83 ft3

0.83 ft3

0.83 ft3

Cases per pallet

48

48

48

48

48

Pallet weight

1,874 lbs

1,874 lbs

1,874 lbs

1,874 lbs

1,874 lbs

Available MRE *Tray Pack* Menu flavors and current inventory,
as of this morning (Thursday, 9:35 AM CST, 1/1/2004), below.
Each case contains four (4) of the same menu flavor Tray Packs.

- CHICKEN BREAST MEAT IN GRAVY (9 servings each 2 Ck Brst half, 4oz gravy) (OS - SOLD OUT)
- HAM SLICES IN BRINE (18 servings each 3 slices of Ham) (OS - SOLD OUT)
- BEEF PATTIES IN BROTH (18 servings each 1 patty) (OS - SOLD OUT)
- TURKEY SLICES W/ GRAVY (18 servings each 2 slices of Turkey) (OS - SOLD OUT)

- PORK RIBS, BONELESS IN BBQ (9 servings each 2 rib sections) - 8 cases
- CORNED BEEF HASH (18 servings each 2/3 cup) - 820 cases
- BEEF STEW (9 servings each 1 1/4 cup) - 125 cases
- BEEF CHUNKS/NOODLES/SCE (9 servings each 1 1/4 cup) - 145 cases
- CHICKEN W/ VEGS IN TERIYAKI (18 servings each 2/3 cup) (OS - SOLD OUT)
- SPAGHETTI W/ MEATBALLS (9 servings each 2/3 cup w/ 4 meatballs) (OS - SOLD OUT)
- MEATBALLS/BROWN GRAVY (9 servings each 2/3 cup w/ 4 meatballs) (OS - SOLD OUT)
- PASTA & ITLN SSGE LNKS/TOM SAUCE (9 servings each 1 1/4 cup w/2 sausage) - 12 cases
- LASAGNA W/ MEAT SAUCE (9 servings each cut 3" X 3") - 20 cases
- OMELET W/ BACON & CHEESE (18 servings each 2/3 cup) - 12 cases
- OMELET W/SMOKED SGE & POT. (18 servings each 2/3 cup) - 10 cases
- SCRMBL EGGS W COLORING (18 servings each 2/3 cup) - 65 cases
- POTATOES,SWEET,GLAZED (18 servings each 2/3 cup) - 870 cases
- RICE ORIENTAL (18 servings each 2/3 cup) - 820 cases
- POTATOES W/ BACON PCS/SAUCE (18 servings each 2/3 cup) - 23 cases
- BEANS W/ RICE & BACON (18 servings each 2/3 cup) - 10 cases
- APPLE DESSERT (18 servings each 2/3 cup) - 510 cases
- BLUEBERRY DESERT (18 servings each 3/4 cup) - 379 cases
- POTATOES, MASHED W/ BRN GVY (18 servings each 2/3 cup) (OS - SOLD OUT)
- PORK & BEANS (18 servings each 2/3 cup) (OS - SOLD OUT)
- POTATOES/DICED W IN SAUCE (18 servings each 2/3 cup) - 332 cases
- RICE WHITE (18 servings each 2/3 cup) - 1,480 cases

(OS) means Out-of-Stock, please do not order it, we most likely won't be getting more.

Cost per tray above is $16.00, with a minimum of one case which contains four of the same menu trays. We can not split/mix cases, each case will contain four of the same menu. Total cost per each case of four trays then is $64.00.

ORDER TRAY PACKS & MRE ENTREES BELOW

Shipping MRE Entree Cases AND/OR Tray Pack Cases ...

#1 - Determine UPS shipping cost per case of MRE Entree's or MRE Tray's from the first three numbers of your zip code here...

YOUR ZIP	Shipping
004-005	$24.31
006-007	—
008 - 009	—
010-043	$24.31
044	$28.77
045	$24.31
046-048	$28.77
049-089	$24.31
090-099	—
100-139	$24.31
140-147	$20.06
148-149	$24.31
150-179	$20.06
180-194	$24.31
195-199	$20.06
200-241	$20.06
242	$15.89
243-286	$20.06
287-293	$15.89
294-295	$20.06
296	$15.89
297	$20.06
298-299	$15.89
300-328	$15.89
329-334	$20.06
335-339	$15.89
340 - 341-347	$15.89
349	$20.06
350-364	$15.89
365-366	$13.26

YOUR ZIP	Shipping
367-368	$15.89
369	$13.26
370-374	$15.89
375	$13.26
376-379	$15.89
380-381	$13.26
382-385	$15.89
386-397	$13.26
399	$15.89
400-427	$15.89
430-449	$20.06
450-454	$15.89
455-458	$20.06
459-466	$15.89
467-468	$20.06
469-479	$15.89
480-499	$20.06
500-528	$15.89
530-534	$20.06
535-538	$15.89
539-545	$20.06
546	$15.89
547-558	$20.06
559-561	$15.89
562-567	$20.06
570-573	$15.89
574	$20.06
575	$15.89
576	$20.06
577	$15.89
580-594	$20.06
595	$24.31

YOUR ZIP	Shipping
596-597	$20.06
598-599	$24.31
600-638	$15.89
639	$13.26
640-646	$15.89
647-648	$13.26
649-653	$15.89

654-658	$13.26
660-666	$15.89
667-668	$13.26
669	$15.89
670-676	$13.26
677	$15.89
678-679	$13.26
680-693	$15.89
700-705	$13.26
706	$11.82
707-709	$13.26
710-711	$11.82
712-732	$13.26
733	$9.86
734-735	$11.82
736-746	$13.26
747	$11.82
748-749	$13.26
750-757	$11.82
758	$9.86
759-764	$11.82
765-775	$9.86
776-777	$11.82
778-782	$9.86
783-785	$11.82

YOUR ZIP	**Shipping**
786-789	$9.86
790-791	$13.26
792	$11.82
793-794	$13.26
795-797	$11.82
798-799	$13.26
800-820	$15.89
821	$20.06
822-823	$15.89
824-825	$20.06
826	$15.89
827-828	$20.06
829-830	$15.89
831-834	$20.06
835	$24.31
836-837	$20.06
838	$24.31
840-844	$20.06
845	$15.89
846	$20.06
847-874	$15.89
875-885	$13.26
889-898	$20.06
900-938	$20.06
939-960	$24.31
961	$20.06
962-966	—
967-968	—
969	—
970-978	$24.31
979	$20.06
980-994	$24.31
995-999	—

Order directly at KI4U by phone, mail or e-mail. You ll need to use PayPal for all credit card orders after completing and submitting your order form above.

MAILING ADDRESS

KI4U, Inc., 212 Oil Patch Lane, Gonzales, TX 78629

Radiation protection devices of KI4U, Inc. has been written up in the... *Washington Post* (4/13/03) & (3/16/03), *NYTimes* (6/13/02), *USAToday* (6/11/02) & (7/11/02), *SF Chronicle* (6/23/02), *Wall Street Journal* (3/14/03) & (10/5/01), *IEEE Spectrum* Mag (9/01), *Newsday* (11/24/01). And, our products featured on CNN, FOX, CBS and in TIME Magazine!

7.8 WHAT IS THE PURPOSE OF THIS FAQ? SHANNE CANNOR STATUS

Ans: Hi, my name is Shanne Connor and the author of the *Potassium Iodide Anti-Radiation Pill FAQ* at **ki4u.com** and the *Civil Defense Radiation Detection Survey Meters, Geiger Counters & Dosimeters FAQ* at **RadMeters4U.com**. (History of KI4U, Inc. here.)

Since the launching of the KI4U FAQ in 1999 and now also with the RadMeters4U FAQ site launched early in 2001, we've had a steady stream of inquiries and requests for info on nuclear blast and fallout shelters. We've always linked to numerous shelter resources, amongst them Bruce Beach's extensive Ark II site, and also host at our sites the entire 280 page *Nuclear War Survival Skills* book and some FEMA books free on-line, too.

The next logical step, with this growing public interest, is this FAQ web site where we've brought together under one roof all of these resources, and many more, while answering the most Frequently Asked Questions about nuclear sheltering.

As with researching potassium iodide and its use in nuclear emergencies for the ki4u.com FAQ and then later the radiation meters for the RadMeters4U.com FAQ site, we found much fiction, misinformation, and critical omissions overwhelming the few solid facts. What we've discovered, and share below, from the pioneers, engineers and todays leaders of nuclear shelter building, will both dispell the myths and show the practical steps you can take to protect your family.

It is not an overstatement that what has been distilled down and presented here will actually save the lives of many families who study the realities of nuclear explosions, accidents and radiation and then take from it the appropriate measures readily available to protect themselves from it. Nuclear war, accidents, terrorism and radioactive fallout are all much more survivable when you know exactly what you are up against and how to properly defend yourself and your family from its effects. It not only can be done, but even with very limited resources you can raise your families odds of surviving 100 fold simply by reading, learning and applying what's presented here below. And, for most, that's all the edge they'll need!

7.9 WHO NEEDS NUCLEAR PROTECTION SHELTERING STRATEGIES?

Ans: The reasons for learning about and formulating a family nuclear response strategy are as varied as are peoples concerns for the future and the safety of their loved ones in this ever changing world. The following all-inclusive list would require different responses (sheltering or evacuation) depending on the particular nature and location of the threat and your ability and preparations to respond to it.

7.9.1 The specific causes of potential life-threatening nuclear radiation emergencies include...

- Nuclear power plant accidents here or abroad (Three Mile Island, Chernobyl)
- Nuclear materials processing plant accidents (Tokaimura, Japan)
- Nuclear waste (radioactive waste from hospitals, spent fuel and radioactive waste from nuclear power plants, radioactive contaminated materials, etc.) storage or processing facilities mishaps
- Nuclear waste transport truck or train accidents
- Accidents involving non-waste, but normal daily nuclear materials transport (trucks, planes, trains, couriers). One out every 50 HazMat shipments contain radioactive materials. Approximately three million packages of radioactive material are shipped in the United States each year.
- Improper storage of radioactive materials (non-waste) at any point during their normal material life cycle. (Power plants, Medical, Industrial, Academic, etc.)
- Lost or stolen radioactive sources (Over the last 50 years, incidents of lost and stolen *licensed* radioactive devices occur at the rate of once every other day. See *Lost and Stolen Nuclear Materials in the United States* and *NRC Documents Revealing Thousands of Radioactive Source Are Missing.*)
- Nuclear terrorism here via...
  - An attack on, or sabotage of, a nuclear power plant. (See *Sabotage and Terrorism of Nuclear Power Plants*)

- Or, a real terrorist atomic bomb detonated here (See *Do terrorists really have nukes here?*)
- Or, much more likely, conventional explosives used to disperse radioactive materials (dirty bomb) to effectively contaminate an area and much within in it. (See *Do terrorists really have nukes here?*)
- Or, food or water supplies could be contaminated with radioactive materials.
- Or, a strong radioactive source could be placed in a location adjacent to where large numbers of the public would file past. They could be unknowingly and dangerously exposed to it, such as at a subway que, sports arena or stadium, etc.

- Limited nuclear war overseas with the fallout carried here (USA) by the wind (See *Trans-Pacific Fallout* for threat here if any of the 'players' went nuclear in the Mid-East, or Pakistan, India, Korea, China, Russia, etc.)
- Nuclear War involving a direct attack upon the USA. (Think that's highly unlikely in your life-time? See *Nuclear War Unthinkable? Russian & Chinese Preparations Today! and The Final Phase*)

While only a few of the potential nuclear threats above would entail blast damage, all would involve possible radiation exposure and a few with actual radioactive fallout that the wind had then carried far from the original scene of the incident.

Many variables will determine the nature of the nuclear threat and the level of protection needed at varying distances from ground zero.

For instance, for atomic bombs, whether it was a ground burst or air burst will determine whether there is significant fallout or not. Also, the explosive yield of the bomb, which is typically measured in kilotons (KT) or megatons (MT) of an equivalent quantity of TNT, will determine its blast circumference damage area. (A one-megaton bomb is 1000 times more powerful than a one-kiloton bomb.) Another effect is the thermal pulse or heat flash that can burn exposed people and ignite combustible materials. These *direct effects*, the blast wave and thermal pulse, are examined first below here. Then, following that, the radiation effects, both the initial radiation and fallout radiation are detailed.

Bottom Line: Exploring and developing your nuclear response strategies in this day and age is cheap family insurance and, like major medical insurance, we can also hope & pray never to have to use it! Also, like any real insurance, it'll be near impossible to quickly figure it all out and implement it after the fact! *Knowledge is King* here while a false embrace of nuclear myths could be downright deadly.

7.10WHAT ARE THE NUCLEAR BLAST AND THERMAL PULSE EFFECTS?

Ans: Half of all the energy released by nuclear explosions is in the form of blast and shock and about 35% is in the form of heat. The following four drawings show what level of blast damage (at different psi overpressure) and fire ignition from the thermal pulse might be expected for different strength nuclear explosions (both ground and air bursts) at different distances from ground zero. Take note of the damage range distances from GZ - ground zero. (Courtesy of *Nuclear Attack Environment Handbook*, FEMA - August, 1990)

Atomic explosion

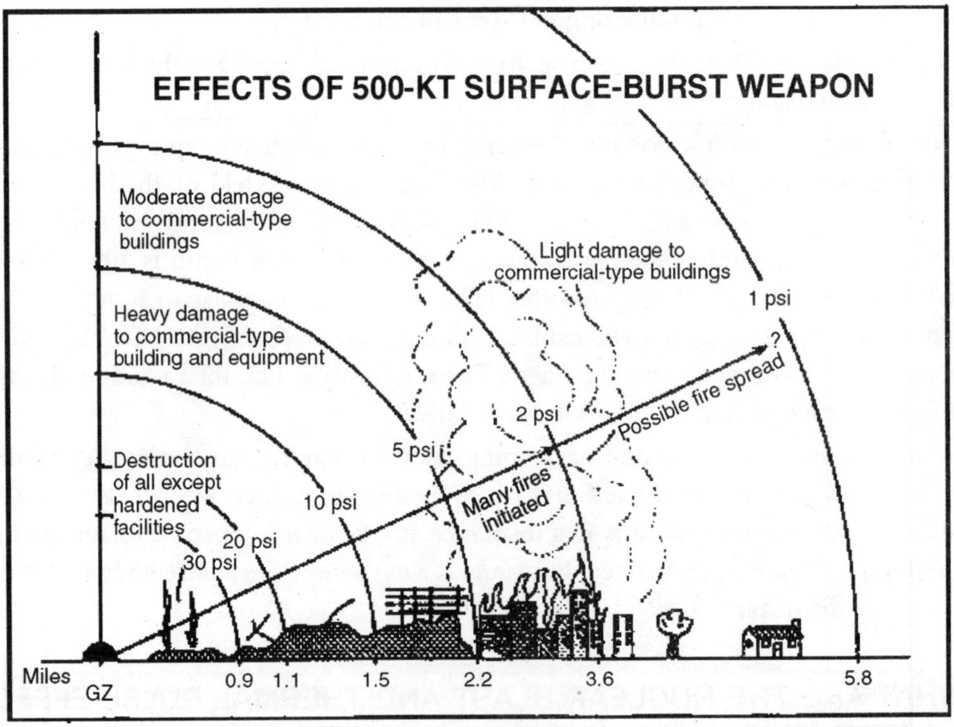

Fig. 7(a) Effects of 500 KT surface-burst atomic weapon.

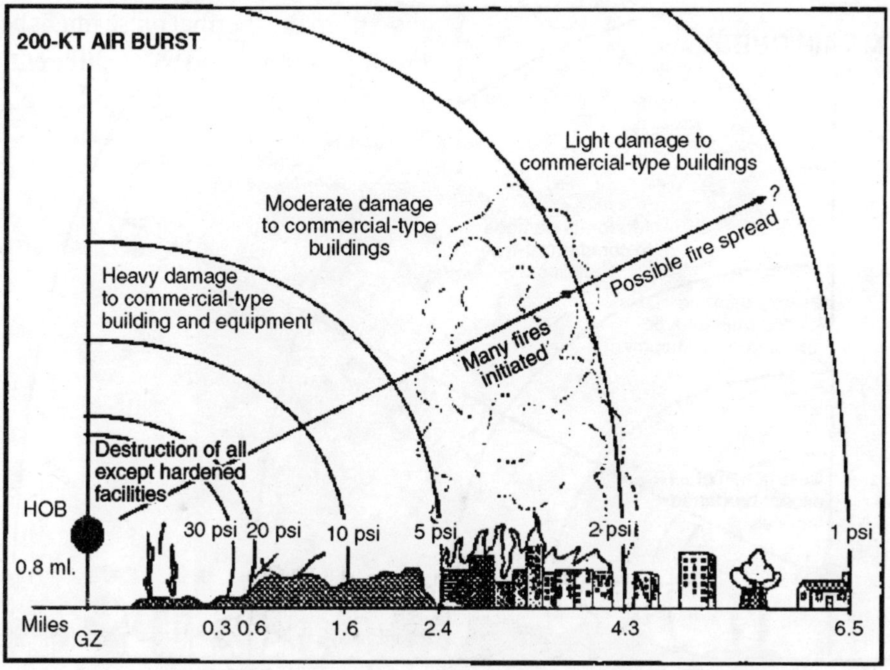

Fig. 7(b) Effect of 200-KT air burst atomic weapon

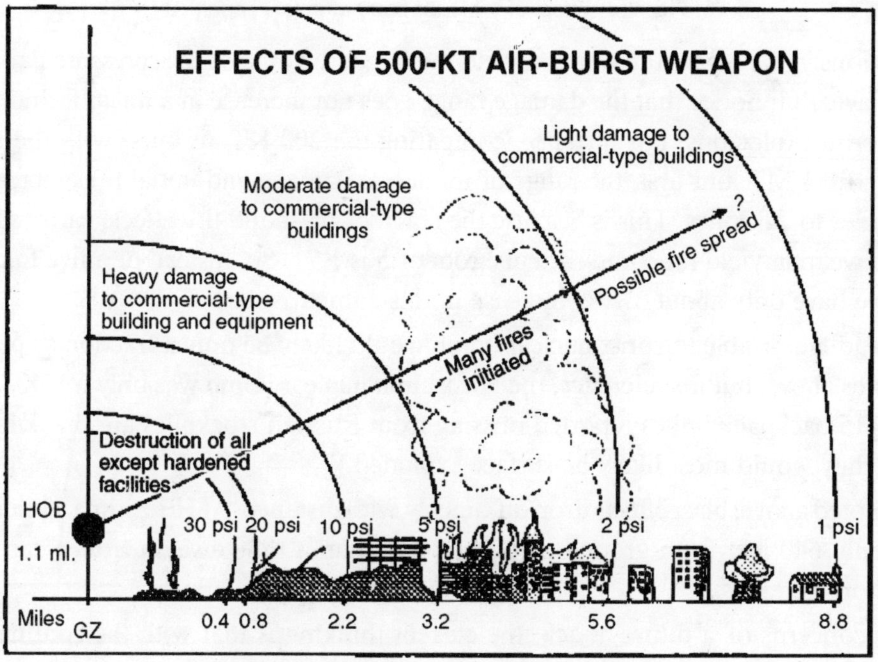

Fig. 7(c) Effect of 500-KT air burst atomic weapon

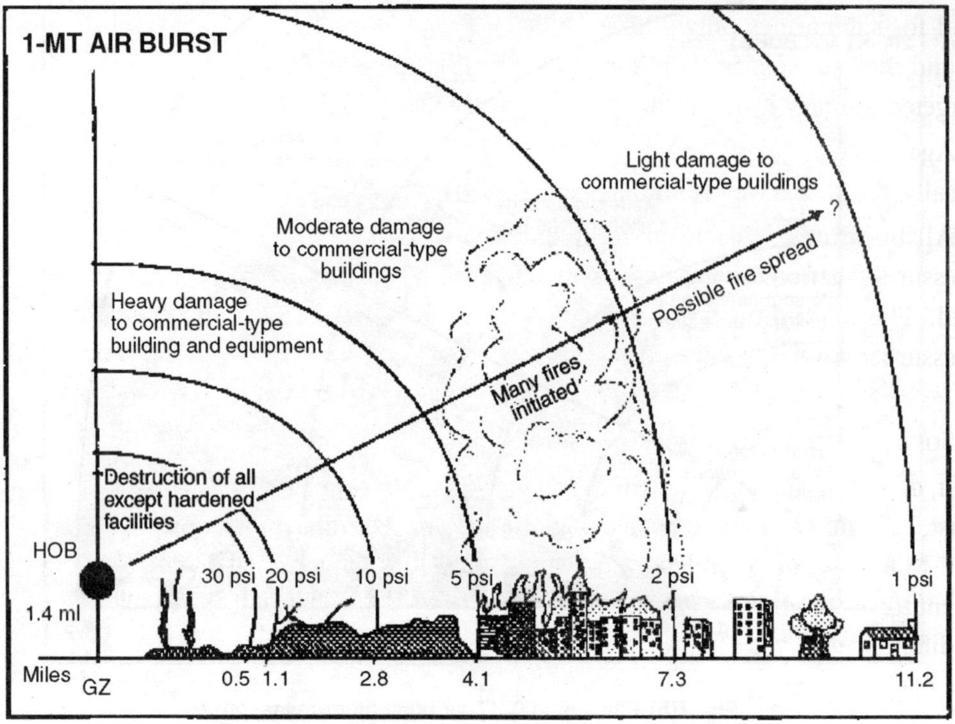

Fig. 7(d) Effect of 1 MT air burst atomic weapon

Obviously, the bigger the weapon yield the larger the area of overpressure damage from the blast wave. But, notice that the damage range does not increase in a linear fashion with the more powerful explosions. For instance, comparing the 200 KT air burst with the five times more powerful 1 MT air burst, the range of moderate damage and initial fires increased from only 4.3 miles to 7.3 miles. This is because the reach of blast and fire effects varies as the cube root of the weapon yield ratio and the cube root of 5 is 1.71. So, instead of a five-fold increase or 500% we have only about a 70% increase in this comparison.

A readily portable terrorist nuclear bomb would likely be only a fraction as powerful as the examples above, but for reference, the Hiroshima nuclear bomb was only a 15KT air burst. (The RA-115 backpack nukes reported missing from Russian stockpiles are one kiloton yield each, and they would most likely be surface exploded.)

As noted above, blast effects drop off quickly with distance. At Hiroshima a brick building survived only 640 feet from ground zero. And less than a mile away a trolley car remained intact and on its tracks.

For concerns of a future attack, the current thinking is that with the continuing trend towards more accurate MIRV'ed (multiple, independently targetable, re-entry vehicles) nuclear weapons, they are now mostly smaller than in the past, averaging on the order of 500 KT or less and for submarines only 200 KT. Of course, there are now more warheads per missile (4-10) and they are substantially more accurate than during the height of the cold war. Also, any targeted military installations can expect to receive multiple hits.

Again, we are exploring here only the initial direct effects of a nuclear explosion, and specifically, the shock wave and blast effect. (Thermal Pulse effects will be covered below.)

All buildings will suffer light damage from the shock wave at even 1 psi peak overpressure—shattered windows, doors damaged or blown off hinges and interior partitions cracked. The maximum wind velocity would be only about 35 miles per hour. As the overpressure increases, so does the blast wind—exceeding hurricane velocities above about 2 psi.

So, how much blast or overpressure is too much to survive?

It, of course, depends on where you are when it comes charging through, but from a 500 KT blast, 2.2 miles away, it'll be arriving about 8 seconds after the detonation flash. (An even larger 1 MT blast, but 5 miles away, would give you about 20 seconds.) Like surviving an imminent tornado, utilizing those essential seconds after the initial flash to *'duck & cover* could be the difference between life & death for many. Both the overpressure in the blast shock wave and the blast wind are important causes of casualties and damage.

Peak Overpressure (psl)	*Wind Velocity (mph)*	*Wind Duration For 500-KT Burst (sec)*
1	35	4.4
2	70	3.9
5	165	3.2
10	295	2.8
20	500	2.7
30	670	1.6

For the man-in-the-open example above, that's 2.2 miles from the detonation of a 500 KT air burst where the shock wave would arrive about 8 seconds after the detonation flash, this sharp body slap would produce a 10-psi overpressure over his body that might perforate his eardrums. Additionally, though, he would experience a blast of wind of about 295 mph for about three seconds that would launch him careening into a probably fatal impact and he would also likely suffer injuries from flying missile fragments of glass and debris. See the following chart from *A. Longinow* People Survivability in a Direct Effects Environment and Related Topics:

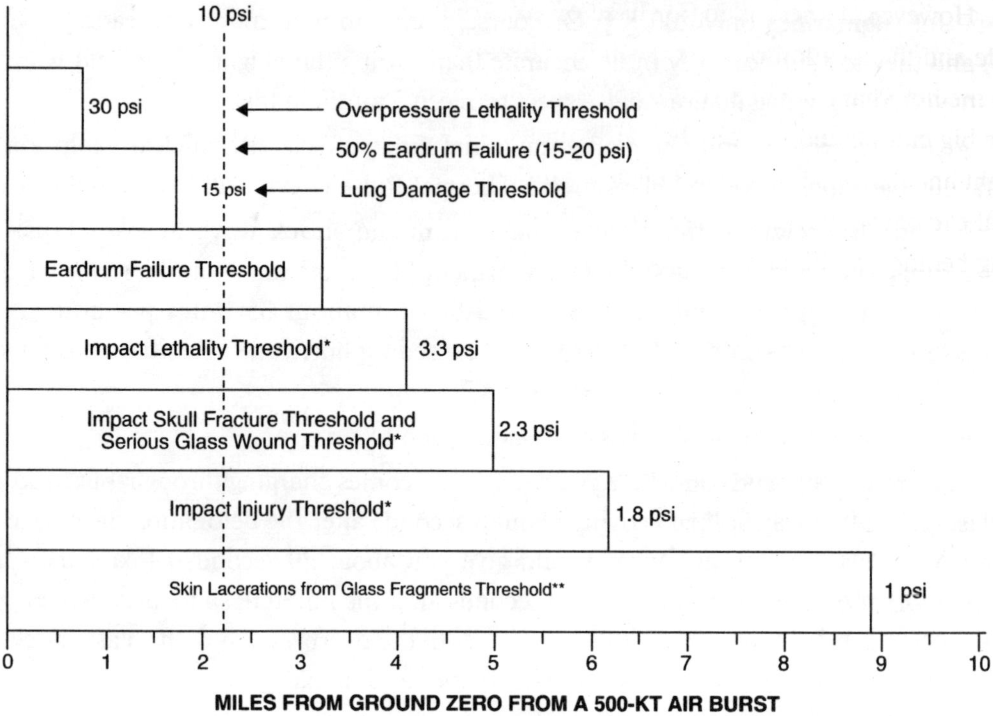

* *For impact injury or death to occur at stated overpressure, the body must be thrown at least 10 feet before impact. Otherwise, a higher overpressure is required to achieve necessary velocity.*

** *Glass fragments must also travel at least 10 feet.*

Again, though, as in a tornado, prompt protective actions can make a great difference in ones survivability. For example, it requires about eight times the blast wind force to move a person who is lying down compared to a standing person. Diving into a ditch, depression, basement or anywhere else normally thought of for tornado protection will improve your odds greatly. You are also much less a target for glass shards and debris missiles. This simple change in vulnerability, but of this magnitude, can save many lives.

Regarding the *Thermal Pulse* that accompanies the *thousand suns brighter flash*, that represents 35% of the energy expended in a nuclear explosion, burns caused by this heat energy of the fireball can produce the most far reaching consequence of the immediate weapons effects. For our example above of the man-in-the-open, 2.2 miles from a 500 KT air detonation, fatal blast injuries would have served in most cases to put him out of his misery. The thermal pulse, travelling at the speed of light, would have already delivered lethal burns and his clothing would have burnt into fire if truly exposed in the open. In fact, about 50% of those fully exposed to the fireball anywhere in the 2 psi or greater range would eventually die from the severity of their burns.

However, if there is fog or haze or any kind of opaque material or structure between people and the location of the fireball the effects of the thermal pulse can be greatly reduced. With medium haze it can be cut by 50% and with heavy fog down to even just 10%. So, smog in the big cities could actually be partly protective for once. Also, while it arrives at the speed of light and delivers most of it's energy within the first second, the larger the bomb the longer it'll take to deliver its full compliment of thermal energy, perhaps even several seconds. Quickly diving behind anything creating a shadow could be lifesaving.

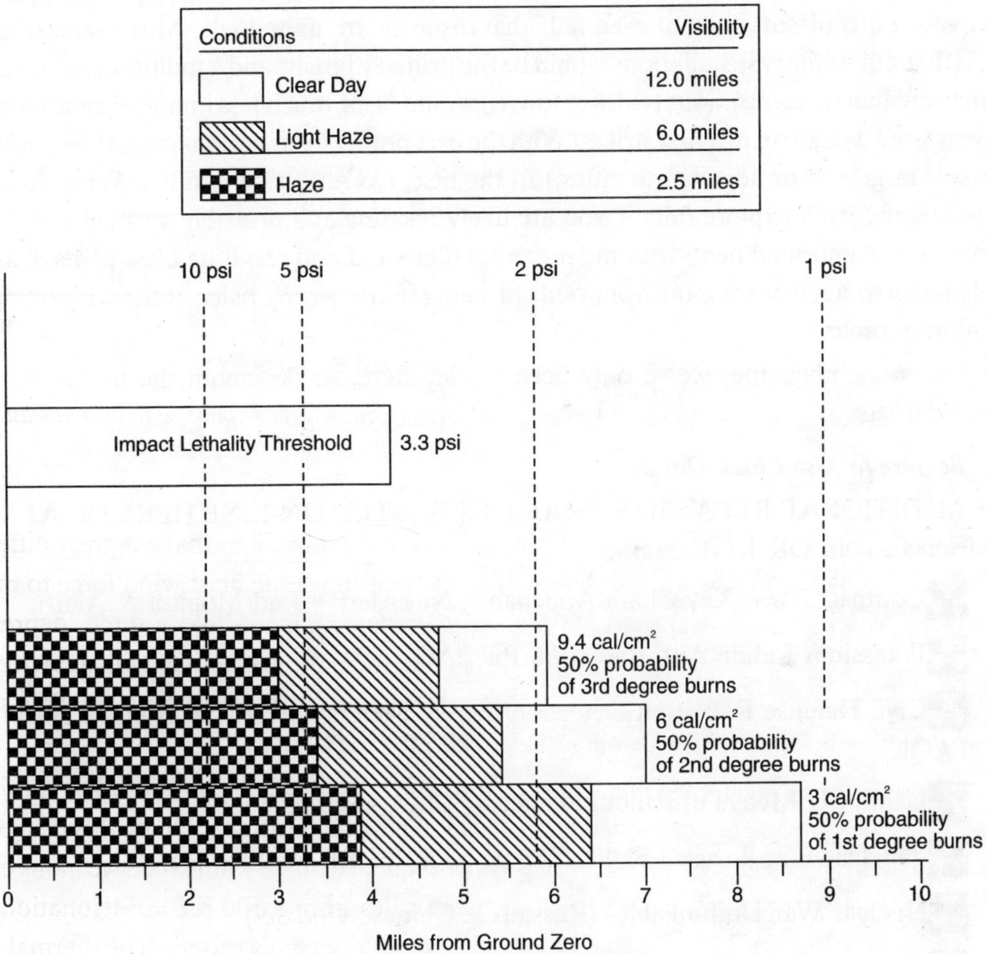

BURN INJURIES IN THE OPEN
(500 KT, HOB = 1.1 Miles)

In most places however, besides fog, smog, haze or clouds, there are buildings, trees, hills and other objects that would also block and reduce some portion of the thermal pulse. In fact, the more densely built up an area is then the less likely the inhabitants would be exposed to suffer the full impact of the thermal pulse. Of course, though, they may still have to deal with the resultant fires created by the thermal pulse and from any blast damage.

Bottom Line: The majority of Americans, even in a full-scale all-out nuclear war, would survive the initial blast and thermal effects of nuclear explosions. Even with a large 1 MT explosion and being as few as 8-10 miles away from ground zero, you would likely find that you had survived the initial thermal, blast and shock wave. With any kind of prompt protective action your odds of surviving at even half that distance are quite high. Also, increasing your odds, is that our military installations would be the primary targets and a multitude of thousands of purely civilian concentrations (cities & towns) would be of much less importance strategically to have wasted a nuke on in a first strike. (With the exception of our nations capital and militarily important targets in or adjacent to cities.) In the next Q&A section entitled: What Areas are Likely Targets? we'll explore fully if you are likely residing at a probable 'ground zero'. Also, it needs to be mentioned here, with the much smaller yield and resulting blast damage area of a likely terrorist nuclear weapon, your odds of being in the wrong place at the wrong time are even more remote.

But, remember, too, we've only been talking here, so far, about the initial blast and thermal damage...

Be Sure to Also Check Out...

ADDITIONAL RELATED RESOURCES HOSTED ON-LINE HERE OR AT SITES RadMeters4U.com OR KI4U.com...

- Compact 24/7, Key-Chain Attachable, NukAlert™ Rad Monitor & Alarm
- Potassium Iodide Anti-Radiation Pill FAQ
- Civil Defense Radiation Detection Survey Meters, Geiger Counters & Dosimeters FAQ!
- Using CD Meters in Fallout Shelters (FEMA - 120 pg book)
- 'Nuclear War Survival Skills' (280 pg book) FREE On-Line Here!
- Nuclear War Unthinkable? (Russian & Chinese Update!)
- FEMA Nuclear Weapon Target Maps For Each State!
- Trans-Pacific Fallout (Don't be caught off-guard by these ill winds!)
- 'You Will Survive Doomsday' (A myth-busting eye-opener!)

- '11 Steps to Nuclear War Survival' (Canada Emergency Measures Organization)
- Sabotage and Terrorism of Nuclear Power Plants
- Lost and Stolen Nuclear Materials in the United States

Comments or Suggestions for additional resources to add here:

webmaster@ki4u.com

KI4U, Inc.
212 Oil Patch Lane
Gonzales, Texas, 78629
(830) 672-8734

---

8 Safety Agents/Devices Required for Protection

8.1 PROTECTION FROM CHEMICAL AND BIOLOGICAL AGENTS CAUSING DISASTERS DUE TO ACCIDENTS/TERRORIST ATTACK/WARFARE

The above material has been adapted from an article authored by Jack Sawicki; MS.He is the Occupational and Health Officer at the GEOMET, Technologies, LLC, Germantown, MD, USA. The author is an expert on chemical and biological field operations. He develops and tests personal protective equipment. Information were also drawn from the September 1999 issue of Surgical services management, published by the Association of periOperative Registered Nurses (AORN). For subscription one may contact AORN **at http://www.aorn.org/ssm/**

In view of the growing possibility of terrorist attack in different parts of the world, many people are suffering from acute mental stress, fear and anxiety. One of the major concerns in their mind is the concern of safety. How to protect oneself from the brunt of the attack is the major question troubling their minds. Most of the people do not know what kind of preventive and protective measures they should take, where those devices are available and how to procure them.

Recent terrorist activities in different parts of the world have raised a number of very pertinent questions about how the ordinary citizens of the nation can protect themselves against chemical/biological/radiological weapons of mass destruction. While some of the Government agencies (e.g., firefighters) are already trained to work in atmospheres that pose imminent danger to life and property, this is not the case for health care professionals working in hospital emergency departments. The current training and personal protective equipment provided to the health care workers is simply not adequate to protect emergency department staff members from chemical/biologicalradiological agents. The victims who got exposed and are brought to the hospitals for treatment carry these. From their clothes and body it spreads inside the internal environment of the hospital to which the Doctors, Nurses and other hospital staff get exposed, apart from their direct exposures. Therefore, there is a need to first of all know what those gadgets are and wherefrom it can be obtained.

8.2 CHEMICAL AND BIOLOGICAL AGENTS FOR POTENTIAL USE BY THE TERRORISTS OR IN WARFARE

Any poisonous or extremely hazardous substance can be a terrorist's weapon. But some of those agents are developed specifically for the purpose of their use by the terrorists or as warfare agents to cause maximum damage. It makes them more difficult to handle than even the most toxic materials.

In a comparison of the relative toxicity of agents (Table 1), Sarin is several orders of magnitude more toxic than commonly encountered industrial chemicals. Additionally, Sarin and other organophosphate chemical warfare agents are acetylcholinesterase inhibitors (e.g., Soman, Tabun, V-agents) and thus, are cumulative poisons. These are neurotoxic. Extended respiratory exposure to even very low concentrations of these agents, such as might occur in a clinical setting where large numbers of contaminated victims may be present, can result in toxic effects to the doctors, nurses and others. While the data in Table 1 are for respiratory exposure, chemical warfare agents also are extremely toxic via skin exposure and direct contact with the liquid chemical, such as might be found on shoes, on clothing, or in decontaminated effluent.

Defining biological warfare agents, or biological weapons for the terrorists, is difficult because the organisms and toxins involved are naturally occurring. Some of those most likely to be used as weapons are listed in Table 2. There is a lack of effective treatments for highly infectious biological warfare agents having high mortality. After symptoms occur (e.g., smallpox) providing effective protection becomes even more critical than for chemical warfare nerve agents, with which symptoms occur quickly and effective antidotes are more readily available.

Table 1: Relative Toxicity of Poisonous Chemicals

Compound	*8-hour AEL/TWA (mg/m^3)*	*Immediately dangerous to life and health (mg/m3)*
Chlorine	3.0	30
Cyanogen chloride	0.6	Not determined
Phosgene	0.4	8
Mustard gas	0.003	Carcinogen
Sarin	0.0001	0.2

Table 2: Properties of Probable Biological Warfare Agents

Agent	*Type*	*Untreated mortality*	*Relative infectivity/dose*	*Incubation period*	*Treatment*
Anthrax	Bacteria	99%	Moderate 1000+ spores	1-4 days	Antibiotics*
Viral Equine Encephalitis (VEE)	Virus	1%	High 25 viruses	2-5 days	Symptomatic
Plague	Bacteria	99%	High 10 organisms	2-3 days	Antibiotics
Q fever	Rickettsia	1%	High 1 organism	2-10 days	Antibiotics
Smallpox	Virus	30%	High	7-14 days	Vaccine*
Tuleremia	Bacteria	30%	High 25 organisms	2-4 days	Antibiotics
Hemorrhagic fevers (ebola, lassa, marburg, hanta)	Virus	50-90%	High	2-7 days	Symptomatic

* Not effective after symptoms develop.

8.3 PERSONAL PROTECTIVE EQUIPMENT

Personal protective equipment for clinically hazardous materials and its applications, including chemical, biological, radiological agents of mass destruction, has been suggested by a number of agencies. They had also discussed about the regulations over the years.1 it cannot be clearly ascertained how these regulations relate to chemical and biological warfare protection, and are subject to considerable debate. The range of protection could be from nearly complete protection to almost no protection. For example, a multi-laminate film, liquid-protective, gas-tight, positive pressure, completely encapsulating suit worn over a positive pressure requiring self-contained breathing apparatus, meets regulations and provides protection from all chemical and biological warfare threats. Using these systems in a clinical setting, however, is nearly impossible because of cost, time needed to wear it and ergonomic factors. Because of this, less effective personal protective equipment must be considered. Of course depending on the gravity of the situation, one should apply one's mind as to which one should serve the purpose.

In USA and in other advanced countries of the world, the common medical personal protective equipment used for standard precautions usually consists of nonwoven or woven fabric suits or aprons, safety glasses, N-95 particulate respirators, and latex surgical gloves.

These items, however, are not adequate for emergency chemical, biological, radiological weapons of mass destruction for a number of reasons.

- Liquids and viruses readily penetrate through uncoated clothing and masks, especially under pressure (e.g., kneeling, leaning against objects).
- Chemicals readily permeate almost all coated or laminated "breathable" clothing.
- Latex surgical gloves are ineffective against chemicals because of permeation and against viruses because of penetration.
- Safety glasses do not protect against liquid splash, and medical shields do not stop chemical vapors or chemical or biological warfare aerosols.
- The N-95 respirators allow significant penetration through the filter (i.e., 5%) and around the mask (i.e., 10%).
- Typical interfaces between clothing, gloves, masks, and glasses do not protect against intrusion, including that of decontamination liquids.

It is almost certain that a terrorist attack with either chemical / biological /radiological agents would result in significant casualties among the health care workers, if only normal personal protective equipment is used. Because of these factors, a compromise between protection equipment that meets all regulations and commonly used protection equipment is required.

Users of the equipment, infection control staff members, industrial hygiene staff members, administrators, and manufacturers need to use a systems approach to ensure that respirators, clothing, work practices, monitoring, decontamination facilities, ventilation, and other engineering controls are considered together. Less expensive and restrictive personal protective equipment must meet safe limits. It is critical that ventilation in areas where personal protective equipment is worn is sufficient so that the airborne concentration of toxic and dangerous materials (e.g., sarin) does not exceed levels for which the protection afforded is adequate.

8.3.1 Respiratory Protection

Respirators used by most civilian workers must be approved by a National Laboratory, which has been assigned that responsibility by the Government. As for example, the same responsibility is on the National Institute for Occupational Safety and Health (NIOSH) of NIH at North Carolina. This agency approves respirators under various categories. While NIOSH regulations are mandatory and provide some selection guidance and quality assurance relevant to chemical and biological warfare protection, additional selection information must be obtained from respirator manufacturers. Additionally, respirators must be properly fitted to ensure adequate protection.

There are a number of factors to consider when selecting appropriate respirators for chemical and biological warfare protection (3). Typical N-95 respirators are ineffective for chemical warfare agents because they provide no absorbent capability. The number of contaminant particles required for infection and the degree of mask leakage strongly suggest that N-95 masks are not acceptable for protection against biological warfare agents. Health care workers wearing N-95 respirators who are exposed to an agent (e.g., plague) for which 10 aerosol particulates are judged sufficient to cause infection will be compromised quickly. Though the protection of a positive pressure demand self-contained breathing or a supplied airline escape breathing apparatus-which allows a maximum leakage of 0.001% and typically performs several orders of magnitude better-certainly would be nice to have, they usually are unsuitable for use in the medical setting because of their weight, bulk, limited duration, and cost.

For chemical and biological warfare agent protection, the US Department of Defense currently relies on the M-40 and MCU/2-P gas masks. These masks are sophisticated full-face respirators and are equipped with a NATO C2A1 filter canister. The C2A1 contains a 99.97% effective particulate filter and non-toxic activated/impregnated charcoal that is optimized for absorption of a wide range of organic and inorganic materials. Department of Defense masks are engineered to fit a wide range of people. While these masks probably are adequate for almost any conceivable chemical or biological warfare scenario likely to be encountered in a clinical setting, they have some drawbacks. The most significant is that the mask canister and exhaust valves have high breathing resistance, which precludes the respirator from receiving NIOSH approval. For most civilians to use the masks, a variance from the relevant regulatory agency, such as the state Occupational Safety and Health Agency (OSHA) office, must be obtained. While the federal OSHA has done this for civilian employees of the US Army, to my knowledge, variances for other employees (e.g., firefighters) have been issued in only one state.

While commercial NIOSH-approved full-face respirators similar to the Department of Defense masks are available, NIOSH only approves them to provide a maximum leakage of 2%, even if the respirator is capable of better performance. Also, while commercial P-100/ organic vapor/acid gas canisters or cartridges may provide adequate filtration against chemical warfare and other toxic agents in concentrations likely to be encountered in a clinical setting, most manufacturers do not have available data to substantiate this. Several US respirator manufacturers, however, currently are seeking NIOSH approval for full-face respirators that are derived from military gas mask designs and that meet US regulations. An important feature of military masks and many civilian designs is a speech-transmitting device that allows easier communication, which is critical in a medical setting.

It also is critical that manufacturers provide supporting data that their masks provide leakage resistance similar to military masks on a wide range of test subjects. Manufacturers of NIOSH-approved respirators will have this information, though they may not wish to share it. If the manufacturer will not provide this information, do not buy the respirator. Manufacturers also should provide data about the protection their NIOSH-approved cartridges afford against chemical warfare agents. In my opinion, such commercial masks are the most likely candidates for providing effective protection for clinical chemical and biological warfare applications.

Even more effective are systems that use the same type of mask combined with a 115-liters per minute (LPM) powered air purifying respirator (PAPR) blower. In these systems, a battery powered fan forces air through the filter into the mask. This approach minimizes breathing resistance and increases comfort and protection. If properly designed, these masks can decrease the risk of inward leakage. These systems are more costly, however, and also can reduce the service life of canisters because significantly more air is used than is used at the average 40-LPM breathing rate.

Problems exist with all mask type respirators, including

- Users must be clean shaven;
- Special lens inserts must be provided for glasses; and
- To provide adequate protection, users must have yearly quantitative fit tests.

Realistically, these conditions may not be possible in many health care settings where temporary or part-time personnel commonly are used. For this reason, respirators that do not have these limitations are desirable. Two alternatives are available that can reduce these problems, but they have their own limitations.

The first alternative is a PAPR with a loose-fitting hood. This respirator must have a minimum 170-LPM blower, typically a separate belt-mounted unit that is equipped with two or three canisters and powered by a battery pack. Previously, most PAPRs were for industrial use and had rechargeable NiCad batteries. Now units specifically designed for emergency applications are available. They typically are equipped with long-term, storage-capable lithium batteries, although some use alkaline D-cell batteries. These PAPR units allow users to wear glasses and have beards and do not require quantitative fit testing. Another advantage of these systems is that a standard surgical mask, which is designed to filter exhaled air, can be worn under the hood. Maximum leakage for these designs is defined by NIOSH regulations to be only 4%, although they can be more protective.[3]

Powered air purifying respirator hood systems for chemical and biological warfare applications that are available overseas provide greater protection, but they are not approved in the United States. In these systems, a tight neck seal is provided at the bottom of a hood, and a blower, typically 115 to 130 LPM, provides filtered air into the body of the hood. Several foreign and domestic manufacturers are experimenting with similar designs, in which airflow is boosted, to 170 LPM to meet US requirements for PAPR hoods. These units meet NIOSH regulations, and the protection offered is as effective as a close-fitting mask with the same airflow. Except for costs, these are the most likely candidates for use by non-full-time personnel in health care settings.

The most effective full-face PAPR units are computer-controlled, breath-responsive systems that maintain a positive pressure even at peak breathing flows, which can be 500 LPM or more. They do not needlessly use up filter life. These units do not provide the constant flow required by NIOSH regulations, so they currently are not certified in the United States. Hopefully, NIOSH will recognize the situation and use advanced testing techniques like those used for self-contained breathing apparatuses to approve these systems in the future. Though these units are costly, they offer the best protective solution.

8.3.2 Protective Clothing

There is a variety of protective clothing available for people working in situations in which they might encounter chemical or biological warfare agents. These clothing types include

- Protective suits,
- Gloves,
- Boots, and
- Hoods.

Protective Suits. The first thing purchasers of protective clothing usually ask for is test data determining barrier performance. When comparing barrier performance, a number of points should be kept in mind regarding the test parameters used, including

- Contamination density, which can range from five grams per square meter to more than 100 grams per square meter;
- Cell configuration (e.g., open or closed top);
- Breakthrough endpoint-typically 4: g/cm^2 for HD (i.e., mustard gas);
- Airflow; and
- Test duration or mission length.

Any durable impermeable fabric that can be manufactured reliably without pinholes should be an adequate barrier against biological warfare agents, but there are tests that can confirm barrier performance. It should be noted that seam test data is as important as data for the basic fabric, and test cells used for seam testing must be large enough to challenge the edges of the sealing tape.

Though many fabrics may have potential applications in clinical chemical and biological warfare protection and barrier performance information is important, many users often ignore the durability of the material and the construction techniques used to manufacture suits. Because of this, very lightweight materials (e.g., Tyvek-based fabrics) may be suitable for in-hospital use, but probably are inadequate for field use (e.g., by emergency medical technicians, firefighters, hazardous materials personnel).

Medical protective clothing typically consists of coveralls, which can be made with front or rear closures or as simple closure-less “”sack suits”. Very few commercial closures can resist either chemical splash or a spray with a decontamination solution, and those that can are more complex and expensive. An expensive suit closure with a double or triple storm flap of non-wicking materials with sealed seams usually is required to pass a simple spray test.

Several attempts to improvise closures with duct tape or other such materials failed, especially when the tape is applied to a person wearing a real suit in a real-world emergency situation. For this reason, the sack suit design probably is preferred. A similar situation exists for cuffs. Several manufacturers have simple, inexpensive cuff designs that provide a positive seal between the glove and the suit and are more effective than tape.

Expect to pay at least $50 to $100 for a suit, depending on durability. Suits costing less than this should be examined very carefully for design suitability and quality assurance.

Gloves. While surgical gloves are adequate as undergloves to provide secondary protection, they are not suitable as outer gloves because of permeation and penetration protection and durability issues. Standard chemical and biological warfare gloves that meet military specifications are between 25 mm and 35 mm thick and do not provide sufficient dexterity for some medical applications. Thinner gloves (i.e., 14 mm, 7 mm) also are available, and they provide much better dexterity. The 7-mm glove should be adequate for in-hospital use, while the 14-mm glove is preferred for field applications. Most chemical and biological gloves are made of butyl rubber and should not be exposed to solvents or oils, though chloroprene/butyl gloves are available that provide broader resistance. Gloves of this type are available from several sources and cost between $20 and $40.

Boots. There are two ways to provide foot protection. The primary chemical barrier should be booties attached to the suit. These may be sized so that they fit over stocking feet or over shoes (e.g., sneakers, safety shoes). If worn over stocking feet, the over-boots selected should be fairly heavy duty and, for field use, should have an impact resistant toe and a puncture resistant sole. Boots of this type will range between $25 and $50. If shoes are worn, the over-boots can be of lighter construction and should cost less than $25. In no case should suit booties be worn as an outer layer.

Hoods. The clothing item most often overlooked is the chemical splash hood, which is essential to cover the head when a full-face respirator is worn with a sack suit. It also covers that gap that exists when the mask is worn with a zip-front coverall. Hoods usually come in two types. The most common hood type is the butyl-coated nylon military style hood, which usually is provided with the respirator and fitted closely around the lens with elastic. The other type of hood is the suit hood, which is purchased from the suit manufacturer and made of the same material. It is designed to provide a universal fit with any mask. This usually is accomplished by using a clear vinyl window to completely cover the respirator. While the first choice generally provides greater visibility, the universal hood provides more positive splash protection. Both types of hoods can increase the overall resistance of the entire personal protective equipment system to intrusion by vapor and aerosol because they trap some of the user's exhaled air, providing an additional buffer area.

8.3.3 System Integration

There are several rules that should be applied when evaluating the effectiveness of personal protective equipment. When the system is completely donned and the user goes through the full range of motion, no skin should be exposed. This seems obvious, but many times large gaps are obvious, especially around the neck and face. The solution is to go back to the suppliers for personal protective equipment that is better designed for the application. Users should never just slap on duct or surgical tape.

If the system passes the first test, it should be sprayed with a squeeze bottle of soapy water that has food coloring added. The food coloring helps distinguish the water from perspiration, and leaks can be identified. Leaks are particularly common at the cuffs and closures. Again, tape should not be relied upon unless the system is designed so that it can be applied correctly all the time. I gave up on using tape to attach gloves to suits because I noticed that 30 minutes after my partner and I carefully taped our 25-mm butyl gloves to our elastic-cuffed coveralls and entered a contaminated area, perspiration was dripping right through the "chemical barrier" onto the ground. Obviously, if sweat could get out, contaminated liquid could get in.

A key issue in suit design is how to safely remove it after decontamination. In many cases, decontamination will not be completely effective, and serious exposures can result if the mask is removed before the suit or if the suit is touched while it is being taken off. For this reason, it is important to wear a second pair of lightweight synthetic gloves (e.g., nitrile surgical gloves) under the outer gloves. It also is important to consider removal when selecting a suit design. It is important that the last item to be taken off is the respiratory protection so that the wearer is protected from any residual contamination on the suit. With some suits, the wearer must take the mask off and don another one or even try to hold his breath for an extended period while taking off the suit.

8.4 SUMMARY

Providing adequate protection against chemical and biological warfare applications for health care personnel is not an impossible task, but it cannot be done by picking up a catalog and ordering what is on sale. Samples of each of the items to be purchased must be obtained, and they must be looked at as a complete system. If personal protective equipment commonly available is not adequate, vendors should be contacted directly with specific questions and requirements. It is becoming more common for large vendors to have arrangements with knowledgeable personnel who can answer chemical warfare and biological warfare related inquires, and it is the responsibility of the health care facility to know all the facts before equipping staff members with personal protective equipment (Further Reading 3, 10).

For more information on personal protective equipment the users may contact:

Jack C. Sawicki, Director, Business Development
GEOMET Technologies, LLC
20251 Century Blvd.
Germantown, MD 20874
301-428-9898 (V); 301-428-9482 (F)
Email: jsawicki@geomet.com

9 Disaster Cum Emergency Handling Procedures/ Preparedness

9.1 SAFETY IMPLEMENTATION

Once even a remotest possibility of a disaster is suspected or identified, the next phase is to make adequate preparation for avoiding the disaster. Disaster preparedness consists essentially of safety implementation and organization of suitable machinery to control the situation. For the safety all the precautions suggested for the process as well as for the chemicals and biologicals have to be followed.

If an overhead tank of hazardous chemicals stores large amounts of a chemical provision for a tall water curtain should be there in case of its usage in emergency situations. Storage conditions should be as per the specifications and no chance of mechanical failure should be there. Similarly substances likely to interact (i.e., oxidants and inflammables) should never be in the vicinity together. Even if a perfect safety system is installed and maintained and checked for its proper functioning regularly, a set up to face such a situation should be made ready to work on a war footing. Effective means of fire fighting, neutralization of chemicals, accident relief, first aid, evacuation, and medical management should be available there. The whole machinery should be aptly coordinated and all manpower adequately trained. Such team should be able to do the needful immediately whenever a disaster strikes anywhere. Depending on the nature and magnitude, external assistance also has to be brought in. In disaster preparedness, preventive aspects also are very important. All protective gears, appliances, and facilities should be made ready. During the operations, all risk factors and proper procedure for containment of the toxic substances, their washings, its temporary and long term storage and disposal methods etc. are to be given appropriate attention. At a shortest notice all these should be made available. Similarly considerable attention has to be given to any possible deleterious effect of any change in temperature, pressure, humidity etc., and runway reactions. The occupational health team and the medical emergency team should immediately identify the condition, give first aid, and symptomatic treatments until proper and appropriate treatments can be provided. Methods for early diagnosis have to be developed, where not available, and made available. Antidotes for chemical and biological toxicities should also be made available at shortest notice. The perfect disaster preparedness should also have all physical support for mobilizing all resources at shortest notice to control the situations. In an excellent treatise Katz (55) had described the importance of disaster prevention in plant operations.

9.2 EMERGENCY TOXICOLOGY

Disaster management and forensic toxicology have many things in common. Here everything has to be tackled in a mammoth scale. All information on health effects, their detection, prevention, and cure of individual, toxic substances, and combinations should be combined and made ready in hand. Such information should be constantly updated. Special high-risk groups and sensitized individuals in the work forces and factory neighborhood should be identified and their list prepared. In case of any possible leakage or dispersions of toxic substances these are the people who should be evacuated first. Those who will deal with the health aspect of the exposed victims should be properly trained in toxicological emergencies with information available with them in preventive, predictive and clinical toxicology. Since there is scarcity of institutionally trained personnel, in house training and refresher courses by competent organizations are desirable.

Apart from human health, the safety of domestic animals, vegetation and wild life have to be given adequate attention and all necessary arrangement for their protection have to be made. The affected organisms and animals may serve as specimens for in depth study for the development of knowledge and guidelines for the management of human problems too. Accumulation of toxicants in food chains could be a major outcome of chemical disaster. Biological monitoring of chemicals and environmental monitoring of water, air etc. should continue to understand the extent of such contamination, for taking all possible measures.

9.3 DISASTER FOLLOW UP

The most immediate necessity in disaster abatement is the evacuation of all persons, other than those who are equipped for disaster control operations. All persons should be evacuated to safety, away from the directions of the wind current towards which the Toxic chemicals, gases, lethal dusts containing deadly organisms, toxins, lethal pesticides, acids etc. is blowing and sometimes a toxic cloud might be seen floating and moving in a direction where it was projected, dispersed etc. Immediate precautions like wet towels, or respirators have to be undertaken. Proper awareness has to be created for chemical and biological safety precautions and psychological counseling to avoid panic is desirable. The factory and civic personnel could do the needful in an orderly manner free from confusions and obstacles. The safety engineers could do the needful to restore normalcy while the health personnel could attend to the sufferers. If required the site should be sealed off, cordoned and all movements of people and vehicles should be temporarily withdrawn, until it is brought back to safe conditions.

Environmental decontamination measures have to be undertaken, by chemical, photochemical or biological approaches as needed, taking care of the fact that too much dilution and dispersal may lead to severe consequences elsewhere. Contaminated food items should be destroyed. In case of suspected genotoxic agents, as with TCDD in Seveso and Methyl isocyanate in Bhopal, all affected humans, animals and plant species have to be examined and proper actions taken. It is better than exposed animals and plants are exterminated to avoid food chain risk.

After a disaster has struck somewhere and immediately all measures have been taken, still one cannot be complacent. Long-term follow up studies on the conditions of the survivors, and any deterioration of health or susceptibility to long term effects including cancer, genotoxicity, reproductive toxicity and psychobehavioral effects etc., have also to be followed. Socioeconomic, physical and mental rehabilitation is also desirable. Such studies are needed on farm animals and vegetation as well.

9.4 DISASTER RISK MANAGEMENT

There are a large number of approaches, including mathematical models and computerized facilities for assessing disaster proneness and risks (26,60,63,75). If all possible data are available and facilities are also existent, any good procedure can be adopted for this purpose. But not all the facilities are available equally well everywhere. Till such capabilities are built, a sample system is suggested as under:

Disaster risk index (D1) can be broadly classified into 4 categories - material (A), affected people (P), and natural resources (N). Therefore, the Risk appraised multiplied by Total consequences: 1. Health hazard (H) 2.Fire hazard (F), 3. Reactivity ®, and 4. Environmental/ Ecological risks (E). Similarly the magnitude and consequences can be graded in terms of the amount of the material (A), affected people (P), and natural resources (N). Thus multiplying the total consequences anticipated and the total consequences- can calculate the potential disaster impact

I (Impact) — (H+F+R+E) (A+P+N), The risk is to be anticipated and controlled by disaster preparedness and industrial safety condition (S), on behalf of the management and disaster coping capacity of the entire community and the entire administration machinery (M)

Thus the actual magnitude will be

$$I/S+M$$

i.e. $$\frac{(H+F+R+E)(A+P+N)}{(S+M)}$$

This could serve in rating the chances of hazards in each storage, manufacturing, transport facility of the factory. Each of the categories can be graded for each chemical in a 1-4 scale, as done in International practice. For example, health hazards can be rated based on guidelines by EPA, NIOSH, ILO etc., based on TLV/MAC values, ambient air quality standards and documented toxicology literature (91,54). Similarly the National Fire Protection Agency guidelines will be useful for grading the fire risks. Chemical reactivity (air, water temperature, environmental conditions, materials, and corrosiveness) chances and nature of runaway reactions, all together can be assessed and different chemicals rated in the scale 1-4 by experts in the area Environmental Toxicology. Data including effects on Farm animals, vegetation, crops, wild life and ecosystems, acute short term, low dose long term, genotoxic effects, environmental persistence, residue accumulates, can set the criterion for grading potential Environmental Impact (E)

In Environmental Impact Assessment the views of Tonhill (106), Cairns (13) and Amson (2) will be useful. This can also be graded for all the concerned chemicals. In fact, once the inventory of chemicals, which are potentially disaster-prone, is worked out, a standard National Research or regulatory Agency should be able to grade them properly. They will provide also data regarding the toxicity, prevention and treatment for each one of those chemicals as has been done to evaluate the national permissible level of chemicals in the work environment. Raj (84) and Mitchell (74) describe the data for ammonia and Chlorine, the most serious ones.

The values for A (amount of substance) can be graded in terms of amount in tones maximum stored at any one time and has to be arbitrarily made like 0-10, 10-100, 100-1000, and so on. Similarly the affected people (in plant and neighboring human settlements) have to be graded in terms of numbers, 100-1000, 1000-10,000 and so on. The grades for loss (N) is to be done with the same principles as used for assessing the damage by natural disasters like floods and accidents for loss of life, disability, destruction of nationals resources and agriculture.

Safety preparedness in the part of the factory management is to be graded by the expert panel on the basis of their records of safety engineering, accident record, occupational health, environmental pollution, trained man power, resources, fire and explosion containment capacity and medical facilities. The index of community preparedness judged in terms of actual situation, is to be made by the district administration and related government departments. An annexed document (Annexure III) of community preparedness may be useful for it.

If a substance has the highest rating in all the cases, the total impact will be $(4 + 4 + 4)$ $(4 + 4 + 4) = 144$ and Minimum of $(1 + 1 = 1)$ $(1 + 1 + 1) = 9$. The preparedness indices will have minimum and maximum of $(1 + 1) + 2$ and $(4 + 4) = 8$.So the disaster risk rating can vary from 9/8 to 144/2 i.e. from 1 to 72. In this range of 1 to 72, one could visualize that materials below 18 may not be disaster prone, the factory being able to control any situation. Rating of 118-36 is moderately disaster prone, the factory being able to control and reduce the existing problems to minimize the effects. If the index is above 48, all our efforts to reduce it including modified process or even closure of the process may be considered.

The above exercise has to be done for each hazardous substance, whether raw materials, immediate products or wastes separately. If there is combination of more than one substance in terms of biological effects or fire, the risk factors are taken as additive. So the Di of a Combination will be

$$\text{Di Total } \frac{\text{Di}_1 + \text{Di}_2 + \text{Di}_3 + \ldots\ldots}{\text{No. of Chemicals}}$$

Provided none of the individual values exceed 36. Also only actual disaster prone chemicals should be included in this and individual values below 18 should not be included. Whether any interacted substance or the combination exceeds 36, it has to be taken seriously. The value of 24 is suggested instead of 36 for combination to make allowance for combined effects. The above proposition has to be discussed and changes made accordingly when new information and capabilities are available.

9.5 ROLE OF ESTABLISHED RESEARCH AND TRAINING INSTITUTIONS IN THE COUNTRY

Every country of the world has established certain number of research Institutions within their country to train manpower in various areas of science and technology. In some cases it is very extensive, in some other it is moderate and in some other cases it is not quite satisfactory.

In general, the developed nations of the world has sufficient number of such institutions, which are capable to handle any kind of eventualities. USA, Britain, Russia, Germany, France, Japan, China and India have adequate number of such competent Institutions, and trained manpower, but their overall capabilities may vary in terms of resource mobilization, stockpiling of large amount of medicines and vaccines etc. What is required is the International coöperation in case of any such disaster, small or large in magnitude.

In today's world no body can or should sit idle when humanity suffers. Every hand, strong or feeble, should stretch forward with some kind of help. Every eyes shed tears. Every mind gets troubled. Such a unique example has been witnessed by the world during the recent TWIN TOWER DISASTER on September 11, 2001 at lower Manhattan of the New York City. The International community, both friends and foe, showed an unprecedented response of sympathy and togetherness together. Help started pouring in. The RED CROSS collected so much of funds that they were thinking that certain percentages should be kept separated and spent for other charitable purposes. It almost became a scandal, but for the timely intervention of the concerned authorities.

In USA, research organizations such as NIH and its cluster of Institutions, NIEHS, NIOSH, National Toxicology Program, EPA, FDA, CDC, more than 200 University research departments, large number of Industrial Pharmaceutical Research Departments, Defense

Research Departments etc. where extremely good capabilities and facilities exist. But still what perhaps is still desired is coordination among these Institutions. Demarcation of the responsibilities of each one is needed, especially when there is a chemical or biological disaster engulfed the nation. When there is chaos, very systematic and well-coordinated operations are required under one supreme command. When the decision making process gets delayed, thousand may die in between. Every second is important. Everybody everywhere has to be very alert, prompt and ready to work on a WAR-FOOTING.

Countries like India have built quite a large capability in Research and Development areas, having a large number of Institutions all around the country under the supervision and administrative control of a number of central agencies. These are- CSIR (Council of Scientific and Industrial Research), ICMR (Indian Council of Medical Research), ICAR (Indian Council of Agricultural Research), DST (Department of Science and technology), DBT (Department of Biotechnology), BARC (Bhabha Atomic Research Center), and DRDO (Defense Research and development organizations. Apart from these there are Ministry of Health, Ministry of Non-conventional Sources of Energy, Space Research Organization, more than 240 University Research Departments, Indian Institute of Technology, a large number of Industrial and Pharmaceutical Research Institutions etc. But again, in a relatively large country like India, a well-coordinated program for Disaster Control is vitally necessary. Stockpiling of drugs and vaccines are also necessary to control any such eventualities. It should be kept in mind that two of the worst victims of terrorist's attack were in the USA and INDIA. They should not only exchange their knowledge and technologies, but also share each other's resources to tackle such problems together. A joint treaty in this regard would help each other.

The existing organizations should maintain a large data base on toxic chemicals, its chemical and physical properties, reaction potential, toxicity dose and nature of such toxicity, how to detoxify them, how to treat the exposed victims-first aid and long term treatments etc. Detailed disposal methods should also be made available so that finally the materials can be disposed off without causing much of a harm to the environment. The database should be continuously updated. Any change should be made based on recommendations from experts attending a workshop organized by the Central Disaster Managemen+ Agency (CDMA) from time to time. International experts should be invited to obtain the benefits from their experiences. CDMA should be connected on line with the state Agencies, and the State Capital to their representative organizations.

9.6 ANTICIPATORY ACTION

If the past experiences are followed scrupulously, some similar type of hazards can be avoided once it strikes again. Even the spillage can be successfully cleaned up, greatly reducing the after effects. Thus lessons from the past, with appropriate corrections and changes of course, should always be helpful to avoid similar such accidents to happen once again with the same substance, technology and conditions. However, in most cases when a chemical or biological disaster strikes for the first time, everyone is caught unprepared. To save such situation, anticipatory planning and actions are vital.

9.7 CANVEY REPORT

One of the major efforts in this direction, which may be consulted as guidelines for all future approaches, is the Canvey Report (17). Let us examine the report.

When an additional refinery was to be established in a highly industrialized area of the city, around Canvey Essex, UK, an expert committee was established in 1976. The committee was assigned the task to investigate the potential risks to public from serious accidents, which may occur at existing and proposed industries. A large number of Health and safety Executives, with the expertise of over 30 persons, and a cost of 400,000 pounds completed the study in over two years time. They were given the following terms of references- to look into the overall risks towards health and safety arising from manufacturing, storage, handling, processing, transportation and use, including loading and unloading. Their lines of investigations were:

1. Identification of potential hazards including its sites and the magnitude,
2. Compilation of hazards and toxićity data,
3. Identify possible ways of causing community hazard,
4. Identify possible routes of failures - operator level, mechanical errors, fatigue of plant, corrosion, control defect, impurities in raw materials, explosions etc., and
5. Quantification of the probability of failures and their consequences.

Specific industrial aspects such as potential impact of each type of disaster, the evacuation of people, evacuation schedule, environmental dynamics of the chemicals, their ideal storage and transport conditions were also investigated. Quantitative strategy for risk assessment had to be designed.

The industrial risks were defined as the probability of general danger and social risks as a combination of amounts and consequences. Toxicological data, chemical nature, fire and explosion chances were linked with fault-free approach and past experiences and knowledge were used in extrapolations. Considerable thought was given in the design of the investigation, so that realistic predictions can be made within reasonable confidence limits. Similarly the great care with which any possible uncertainties in the experimental design were anticipated and amended accordingly is an objective lesson for all risk assessments. Another interesting aspect is the thought given into specific risk assessment, accounting for all other causes like natural calamity, traffic death etc. and extrapolating the condition for the consequences of a particular chemical or biological event only.

The major accident-prone area was also identified by the commission, as release of ammonia during transport, collision of ships, explosion of fire. As remedial measures a reliable quick acting water spray system was designed for reducing impact of ammonia spill. Other improvements to reduce accidents and minimize effects were suggested for risks like pressure vessel rupture, and leakage of HF, liquid natural gas, petroleum and ammonium nitrate. Chances as remote as the railroad accidents along with a petrol tank car explosion nearby, causing explosion of ammonium nitrate storage or a missile attack were also assessed.

After the assessment of potential hazard from the then existing and proposed industries, suggestions were made to reduce the identified additional risks. The remedies were firstly by improvement of plant equipment of methods of operations. For example containment walls around storage sites to prevent spreading and, evaporation and fire were put in many places. Speed limit restrictions were imposed for cargo ships to reduce collision. Secondly, improvements arising from further assessments periodically were suggested. Under this category, consequences of interaction between different hazardous situations were visualized and remedial measures implemented. Also, improvement of safety conditions and codes of practice were suggested. Additional facilities for sudden evacuation were advocated in units.

The executive summary of the report is followed by the several investigative reports of the team on specific issues. The detailed discussion on the quantification of the "risk", both industrial and societal, and identification of causes of failure are very informative in disaster preparedness. It is suggested that if a previous explosion with "*a*" ton of chemical affected an area of R meters with "*b*" ton of chemicals, area of $((b/a)^{1/3}$ R meters. TNT equivalence correlation was also developed to assess the practical impact of different explosives.

Possible quantitative pattern of disposal, distribution and hazard of accidental toxic gas emission also received a critical discussion in this report. During a massive leakage of ammonia, the gas often does not rise high as expected from its density of only about 50% of the air. The reason is that the mixed cloud of cold ammonia and air, is heavier than pure ammonia at NTP air, In the case of HF, the polymerized molecules will be heavier than air. The possible sequence of events likely to occur, during release of ammonia from pressurized or refrigerated storage facility under various conditions, has been described. This is also very valuable information. Correlation is also given for calculating the magnitude of effects of the accident based on toxicity data, amount of spillage, conditions of spillage, climatic factors etc. Other types of explosions, of hazards like fire; projectiles from explosions, structural failures are also subjected to quantitative conceptual studies. Another silent feature of this document is the principle developed for risk assessment. On the basis of the detailed study the Canvey Report suggested measures to be implemented in the island to reduce any accidental release and accompanying disaster episodes.

A lot of very valuable information has also been appended with the report. For example, a quantitative assessment of factors leading to reduce the hazards from air borne toxic clouds describes the influence of population density, weather, rate of release, escape routine and shelter. Remaining doors with closed air vents, could be a safety measure, especially in case of rapid releases of ammonia, chlorine etc. From theoretical considerations and experiences from past ammonia spills, the dispersal of ammonia, its environmental fates and consequences and after accidents involving pressurized and refrigerated storage are elaborated. In the case of gases denser than clean air, hazards can be anticipated from the mathematical models suggested. Depending on tons of ammonia, weather and wind speed, the size of cloud and its movement is modeled. These models are very useful for disaster management in all ammonia storage sites; linking these models with toxicity and population data, graphical calculations are possible on the extent of hazard.

9.8 COORDINATED APPROACH ON SAFETY AND OCCUPATIONAL HEALTH

The Bhopal gas disaster (December 2-3,1984) has raised the need for enforcing effectively safety and occupational health measures in all chemical industries, not only in India but also elsewhere in the World. Each incident of this kind is an eye opener. We learn from each other and one another. Our mistakes of the past become a boon of the future. No body wants to see and experience such a disastrous situation as much as was seen recently during the TWIN TOWER Disaster on September 11, 2001 in New York. But long-term human sufferings were much more in case of Bhopal disaster than that in Twin Tower disaster. Exposed Pregnant women gave birth to deformed babies, premature childbirth, babies with mental aberrations. And other disorders were very common. Since the poor communities, who live in shanties were exposed in a major way, they were the worst victims. Because of poverty their immune competence was naturally weak, it became further depressed as a result of their exposure to the toxic methyl isocyanate gases. Chromosomal nicks and breaks were larger in the exposed victims than their normal unexposed counterparts.

It has been learnt from all these experiences of the past that a coordinated approach to tackle the problem of safety and occupational health in the hazardous industries is desired. Such an approach should envisage specific action to be taken by the Federal Government, State Government and Union Territories, industrial establishments, employers and Trade Union organizations. Such a scheme should be developed by each of the organizations and implemented. Some of the rationale needed for the formulation of such a scheme is given below and in the additional information given in the appendices of this volume.

At the state level, expert panels on Hazardous Chemical and biological Industries or laboratories should be formed. They should review from time to time the existing safety measures followed in those establishments. They should also identify if any additional measures are necessary for safety and control of accidents in these industries or laboratories recommended by the respective Government departments looking after such things, such as the Directorate General of Factory Advisory service and Labor Institutes (DG FASLI) or similar such bodies. The State Government may revise its rules and regulations prescribed in the model rules and schedules as updated by the DG FASLI with respect to dangerous manufacturing processes. State of the art situation in the particular field, based on national and International experiences should be prepared to serve as guidelines, which should be adopted and followed by well-trained and experienced persons. Safety officers have to be identified by their functions and responsibilities. These are necessary for enforcement of safety conditions and standards in the industry. Periodic training of safety personnel for the industry should be always encouraged. A list of accident vulnerable spots has to be prepared and an effective system of monitoring of safety provisions has to be developed in each State.

9.9 SAFETY MONITORING SYSTEM

A safety monitoring system is to be made for each establishment. For monitoring, the implementation of safety measures data will have to be collected according to the hazardous industries identified, known dangers associated with them, safety measures followed and any improvements in the previous corrections suggested on the then existing safety measures. A high-powered committee at the state level should from time to time review the progress of implementation of control of hazards. To facilitate this, it may also be essential to strengthen the present system of factory inspectorate and the system of inspection should be streamlined. The labor organizations should always be taken into confidence, which should always be kept in mind.

9.10 WHOSE RESPONSIBILITY?

It is obligatory for the employers to take all necessary steps to provide total safety and control system in the hazardous industries as per norms suggested by the respective Governments. Therefore, it should be capable of ensuring protection against occupational diseases to the workers and control of any danger to the population in the neighborhood because of environmental pollution. Both acute and chronic toxic hazards on the one hand during the normal operation, and unforeseen accidental exposure on the other, have to be taken into consideration. For this safety and health accident reduction action plan has to be developed for each industry and other such installations to establish total safety control system in respect of Chemical and Biological Industries. This should be based on corporate policy on safety and hazard control system. The employers should supply statutory information on the risks involved in the processes used in the industry and in the availability of engineering and control measures for safety and accident prevention incorporated and implemented in the industry. As mentioned above, Worker's participation in the safety program through Safety Committees will be beneficial. While the management has the primary responsibility for the safety and health of workers, the implementation of the safety system will greatly depend on the extent of cooperation from and participation of workers. The workers' organizations could greatly help in identifying potential risks, vulnerable sites, defective systems, and in creating awareness. They can objectively help in the organization of safety system and contribute towards accident containment, control and follow up.

9.11 EXPERIENCES FROM SOME MAJOR CHEMICAL ACCIDENTS OF THE WORLD

9.11.1 Sevesso Dioxin Episodes

A chemical epidemic had been observed for the first time in densely populated area of about1800 hours on a Sunday afternoon, on Jul y 10, 1976.

The cause was an accidental release of a chemical cloud containing 2, 3, 7, 8-tetrachlorodibenzo-p-dioxin (TCDD) and 2, 4, 5, trichlorophenol (TCP) into the atmosphere of the GivaudanLa Roche ICMESA, plant in Sevesso north of Milan, Italy. The discharge originated from a reactor being used for synthesizing 2, 4, and 5-TCP by alkaline hydrolysis of 1, 2, 4, 5 -tetrachlorobenzene.

The fact that a bursting disc ruptured could only be accounted for by some abnormal rise in temperature in the reactor, which was normally controlled at a maximum temperature of 180C. It is known that when sodium trichlorophenate, is heated above 180C, the highly toxic compound, TCDD, starts to form. The amount of course varies according to the temperature excess and the time for which it is maintained (53). The abnormal rise in temperature was probably due to the exothermic reactions in mixtures of ethylene glycol and caustic soda (70). An aftermath of the accident and its immediate effect on the local communities has been described by Hay (51), DiDomenico (31), Pocchiari et al., (81).

The wind driven settling of the cloud produced a hazardous chemical, TCDD, highly toxic (95), teratogenic (99), mutagenic (97), chloracnegenic (22) and possibly carcinogenic compound stable in biological systems, to present a threat to life and environment. Leaves of plants near the ICMESA plant, courtyard animals and birds were seriously affected, many dying within a few days of the accidents. Considerable toxicological data on TCDD left no doubt that it was a very potent poison (95, 58, 67), especially to animals. Its toxicity against Guinea pig is cited as around 0.6 ug/kg. As a result of previous accident or industrial exposures in the manufacturing industry of 2, 4, 5-TCP, effects on humans were also experienced. No fatal cases have been reported in humans, at least within 2 years of the exposure. But minute quantities are capable, when absorbed through skin, of causing chloracne, inflammation of the eyelids, and loss of hair. These features have been chiefly responsible for the medical problems in Sevesso. The portion of the population most affected by the incident consisted of children among whom there was an increased frequency of chloracne, though mostly mild. Dermal lesions among human beings who had been exposed to the toxic alkaline cloud began to appear (81). Many animals however, died due to the heavily contaminated vegetation and soil.

It is known that chloracne patients can show an increase in serum triglyceride and cholesterol (78) and also that the skin surface lipids of such patients contain increased proportion of cholesterol, squalene and wax esters (27). Since the latter two compounds are known to induce comedo formation in experimental animals, it is possible that a disturbance in lipid metabolism in the cells of sebaceous follicles is responsible for the dermal toxicity of TCDD. It is also a potent inducer of delta-aminolevulinic acid synthetase (ALAS, the initial and rate limiting enzyme of heam synthesis) and aryl hydrocarbon hydroxylase. The ability of various halogenated dibenzo-p-dioxin congeners to induce ALAS and AHH correlates closely with their lethal teratogenic and acnegenic potency, as judged by the available toxicological data (95). There was some evidence of subclinical neurological damage as well as cases of clinically detectable polyneuropathy in adults, based on the screening in about 700 individuals.

9.12 DECONTAMINATION

TCDD is chemically very inert, reacting neither with acids nor with bases. It is also very resistant to bacterial degradation (65). TCDD is also stable up to a temperature of 800C. All these factors made decontamination of the affected areas very difficult.

Samples of vegetation, soil and mixtures of the two and wipe tests from suitable surfaces were collected in the immediate aftermath of the release at Sevesso. Rapid establishment of local analytical facilities, were commissioned in an emergency program which included examining pathological samples from dead animals collected from affected areas and samples of soil, vegetation, swabs from wipe tests of building surfaces and samples of drinking water collected from a wide variety of sites in the communes considered to be affected by the release. The results indicated high levels of TCDD contamination on vegetation foliage taken from trees especially in the path of the cloud. There was a low incidence and level of contamination inside buildings, since at the time of the accident, factories, schools, workshops, and public premises were closed. There was an absence of evidence of well water or water supply contamination, not only by TCDD but also by 2,4,5-TCDD-sodium salt, which is far more water-soluble than TCDD. This shows there was little penetration in depth of contamination in the soil.

The analytical results of the first emergency phase of sampling of animal mortalities and dermatological symptoms in population comprised the evidence on which the health authorities first defined the boundaries of the controlled zones. Once the health authorities had adopted tolerance levels for the interior samples of buildings and for the ground in their precincts, a systematic sampling program covering all educational premises both within and close to the periphery of a buffer zone (areas considered to be unaffected by TCDD contamination) was initiated.

Most of the premises were visited more than once and within 6 months of the accident's occurrence. Samples of all kinds were collected and analyzed for TCDD contamination by the gas chromatography-mass spectrometry method, already numbered in thousands. It was a remarkable achievement that a high standard of reliability was maintained.

Using modeling techniques and computer predicted programs, a theoretical distribution and deposition of TCDD on the grounds. This provided a useful reference picture against which the analytical results from the sampling program could be compared.

The distance of the rise of the vapor cloud above the point of emission was the first requirement in the analytical study. Taking into account the vast pipe internal diameter, discharge height above ground and the bursting disc rupture pressure of ethylene glycol exit velocity was calculated.

Plume trajectories were plotted by the estimation of vertical rise followed by the horizontal displacement. Rates of deposition were calculated by using published data deemed most appropriate and allowing the progressive depletion of the particulate burden of the cloud as it traveled downwind.

The studies outlined above were continued and refined when more detailed information began trickling in. The wind speed and direction traces from the nearest anemograph station (Carate Brianza) were analyzed to give 1min. average values of wind direction and speed over the period of the incident and analysis surveying, which resulted in a more precise and final mapping of zones A & B. Zone A extended some 2.2 Km south-east from the factory and covered 1108 hectres. Contamination by TCDD at smaller concentrations than in Zone A led to the initial definition of Zone B, 269.4 ha in all. The first phase of this study was over by 1976 end.

Definition of criteria for contamination level was the most controversial problem confronted by the Italian authorities, since any quantitative data on the amounts of TCDD absorbed or ingested by individuals to correlate with observed clinical symptoms was not available. Therefore, the tolerance levels and definition of contaminated areas were used as the criteria for assessing the effectiveness of decontamination. On this basis, the Medicoepidemiological Commission assessed the risk of oral ingestion of TCDD and its absorption through the skin as a result of incidental contact with contaminated soil, surfaces, objects etc., inside or adjacent to houses, public buildings and work places. On the basis of toxicity data for animals (95), a tolerance limit of about 5ug/m^2 for soil was indicated. For indoor areas such as schools the probability of contact would obviously be greater than with the soil surface in the open. A lower tolerance limit of 0.1ug/m^2 proposed by the commission with an additional safety factor of 500 for interior surfaces.

From the thermal behavior of TCDD an incinerator was designed for total destruction of contaminated materials, excepting soil. However, this method was not adopted due to divergences in opinion about the desirability and practicability of any large-scale incineration. Apart from incineration, photolysis was the only other known practicable method for the decomposition of TCDD. Although microbiological degradation did contribute to the destruction of TCDD in the soil, this would have been a matter for long-term observations since TCDD had a half-life of 1 year.

All operations within the boundary of the Zone "A" had to be carried out under strictest control of access and with minimum protection of personnel. Procedures were modeled on those adopted in "hot" areas of nuclear installations. At the "filter stations", contaminated materials could be transferred from small in-field trailers to large trucks for conveyance to main stockpiles.

As a criterion of physical removal of soil, it was decided that in open fields a level below 15ug/m^2 would not be disturbed but fenced. Above that level, the top 10 cm was scraped off and removed to the stockpile areas, Decontamination of the furthermost areas of Zone "A" was achieved by a combination of high intensity vacuum cleaning followed by washing with high pressure water jets. The carcasses of small farmyard animals were kept in strong caustic soda solution, transported to the ICMESA works and then buried under earth to give 1m. of cover.

By late 1977 most of the people evacuated from the farthermost areas of Zone " A" were able to return to their houses. In March 1978, the Department of Dermatology of the University of Milan, concluding that the incidence of chloracne in the TCDD- contaminated areas had decreased issued a report. It also stated that the condition of previously affected patients was improving and the number of skin cases in those areas was getting closer to those found in pollution-free areas. These developments have been reassuring enough to justify the decontamination efforts carried out. The Sevesso clean up is an object lesson in all decontamination of large-scale spills of highly toxic, non-radioactive recalcitrant and organic substances.

9.13 ENVIRONMENTAL MANAGEMENT OF SOME OF THE TRANSPORT DISASTERS

Chemical and biological accidents during transportation have been observed from time to time. It could be due to human error, mechanical failures, hitting by another car, collision with rail bogies etc. Of course Terrorist attack on this type of transport vehicles cannot be any more ruled out. No matter how it happens, casualties would be parallel, destruction of life and property will be similar. To tackle such problems are also identical. In the Emergency Response Guide Book (64), aspects of chemical accidents during transportation have been discussed. Apart from the precautions to be taken, first aid to be adopted, information needed for management of health hazards, fire explosion risks, and spill leak containment are given. Procedure for isolating zone of spill and evacuation are also discussed. The chemical hazards have been classified into 09 Classes:

1. Explosive solids

2. Explosive gases
3. Flammable liquids
4. Flammable solids
5. Oxidizers
6. Poisons
7. Pathogens
8. Radioactve material
9. Corrosive chemicals,

and miscellaneous substances as per the U. N. Classification System are further classified in terms of risks and emergency response schedule. This is a very useful monograph for all chemical emergencies. Information on the right approach for environmental clean up after transportation accidents, comes from the performance of Williams and Works Environmental data Inc. (82).

In 1978, a goods train derailment in Michigan Country side led to spillage of 15,000 Gallons of Ethylene Oxide. Due to low temperature, phenol solidified. Liquefied Vinylidene Chloride percolated into the soil. Scraping of 5000 cubic yards of soil, removed most of phenol, while vinylidene chloride spread over 17 acres of land reaching up to 300 mg/l in well water. Seven purge wells to capture contaminated ground water were treated, with six 20,000 pounds of activated charcoal absorbers in two aerated ponds at a flow rate of 700 Gallons per minute. In order to avoid eutrophication, phosphorous free carbon had to be developed. In 15 months over 95% of the spill was removed in such a way that the effluent discharge from clean up was within permissible limit. Spray irrigation and microbial degradation removed the remainder. Throughout the process, environmental monitoring safety discussion and toxicological studies were conducted. The whole procedure, even though very expensive, was a remarkable success, leading to the ACE6 conception Award for Engineering Excellence in 1982. The experience gained in such efforts along with detailed understanding of the toxicology, chemistry and technology of the spill will help in all clean up operations.

The major proportion of tonnage of total toxic relcases recorded refers to chlorine (98). In November 1979, a freight train was derailed in Mississauga, Ontario, Canada (12). Out of thee 24 derailed tank cars, one caused all the trouble; this was loaded with 90 tons of chlorine. A massive chlorine leak occurred since it spreads relatively rapidly. Depending on the size of the leak (2-1/2 ft. diameter leak) and the atmospheric conditions, chlorine could cover an area of 1-2 Km^2 in 4 mins. Evacuation began within minutes after the accident, and in 24 hours nearly 2,50,000 people had been removed from the area of 117Km^2. Fire had spread quickly through the wreckage, which burnt out in a period of over 48 hours and had involved three BLEVE-type explosions. No harm was caused even after some 70 tones of chlorine had escaped in the first few minutes of the accident. This could be due to tremendous convectional up draught caused by the heat of the propane fires (11 tank cars contained propane). Thus the chlorine was carried high into the atmosphere where it got diluted and dispersed safely.

The Chlorine Emergency Plan (CHLOREP) team, which had arrived at the accident site, had now to remove the remaining chlorine in the tank car. A patch on the hole of the car was applied and by vacuum process, the chlorine tank car was finally emptied and rendered innocuous. Thus by the ninth day all the evacuees could return.

A tragic disaster occurred in Bhopal on the night intervening 2nd and 3rd December 1984 due to leakage of methyl isocynante (MIC) gas from Union Carbide factory. The accident is reported to have resulted from the pressure built up in one of the 40-ton capacity tank storing MIC, used for producing pesticides.

The ammonia smell on March 12, 1985 near a Fertilizer factory in Bombay, India was attributed to emissions from a factory. There was a leakage of chlorine gas from 2 old cylinders on October 15,1985 at 11 a.m. in another factory of the same state. Due to this leakage 31 persons were affected. They were discharged after the first aid. In another chlorine gas leakage episode, one person died and some 200 were affected.

Two out of a consignment of 156 drums continuing Hexa-chlorocyclopentadiene (HCCT_, while being transported from Bombay, India to Cochin, India was found to be leaking. This affected about 42 children travelling in a Bus in India.

Oleum gas leakage from Sreeram factory at New Delhi, India creating a huge cloud overhead in the sky scared the entire capital city of India. People fleeing in a rush caused severe road jam and panic in the minds of the people.

There are many such incidents, which occurred in different parts of the world. No matter how it was caused, handling of those episodes, its clean up etc. has had a lot in common. Some of them were discussed here to give an example as to how to deal with such disasters.

10 Social Aspects of Chemical/ Biological/Radiological Disasters: Awareness Program, Psychological Counselling, Spiritual Guidance and Rehabilitation Arrangement

10.1 AWARENESS PROGRAM

Cardinal services to create awareness regarding chemical, biological and radiation disaster preparedness, its containment and follow up are being rendered by the Pioneering Institution in the field in every country of the world. In USA, the Disaster Research Center, The Ohio State University, Columbus, Ohio, USA has such responsibility. The Federal Bureau of Investigation (FBI) is designated as the lead Agency for operational response to a terrorist incident. Obviously there will be many partners in the response to such a crime, including the Federal Emergency Management Agency (FEMA), but the FBI will direct the operation. It is very important to note that a terrorist's attack may not always be confined to people or buildings, but it may be directed toward agricultural animals, plants, food items, drinking water sources and aerial environment.

In 1979 Quarantelli et al. has conducted detailed studies on the disaster probability of a country and has described the rationale for disaster preparedness. The actual steps to be taken in each situation may be modified according to the local context. However, the general guidelines set in are helpful in all community disaster preparedness planning (45).

Fawcett (36) after a critical appraisal of the historically changing pattern on acute chemical hazards pointed out that the lack of adequate control rather than the chemical itself caused the disaster. In a conceptual treatment of threat to community by potential disasters Helms (52) pointed out that the chemical spills, chemical explosion, sudden chemical releases are the significant probabilities making them serious threat to the society. Models designed to anticipate community effects are also useful in disaster planning.

Tierney (105) developed a model to analyze the organizational and community preparedness for acute chemical emergencies. She suggested that the awareness of a need for preparedness could be materialized into a functional program only with the support of proper social factors. Gabor (40) advocated a mutual aid system by different agencies to combat such emergencies. Population size, topography, previous disaster exposures, objective chemical vulnerability, perceived chemical vulnerability, financial capacity and emergency resource availability have major roles in community disaster plan. In any disaster containment program, the socio-behavioral patterns of the particular community affected also have to be taken into consideration (44,45). Whittaker (109) suggested that a comprehensive emergency plan for the management of dangerous chemicals and biologicals have to be prepared by every industry. The above articles can be of immense help in developing and maintaining a community plan for chemical disaster prevention and containment and the principles are employed in developing the suggestions offered in this document.

10.2 DISASTER MEDICAL ORGANIZATION

A number of authors have given a considerable importance on Disaster medical organization (62,90,89). The Pergamon Press considering the importance of the subject published even a Journal on "Journal of Disaster Studies and Practice". Da Boer and Baille (30) have elaborately covered this aspect in their treaties on Disaster Medical Organization. Legal aspects, emergency community medicine, disaster plan for municipalities, railways, airports, civil, defense and other crash teams, Red Cross, and disaster hospital organization are elegantly covered. The chapters on evaluation of casualties, responsibilities of surgeons, and anaesthetists and physicians, ambulance facilities are of special importance and relevance in disaster medicine. Williams's paper (114) on disaster organization and chemical works is of special interest in this context. The three types of unexpected events like unusual occurences, disasters, and calamity are differentiated. The strategy for preventing and controlling all the three types are also outlined. This book on the whole is highly useful in disaster preparedness program by medical agencies.

It should be kept in mind that the medical treatment or counselling is to be considered as the first priority. Many people will be panic-driven, engrossed in a deep shock or anxiety. Particularly those who have experienced injuries, minor or fatal, and also many of those who have simply witnessed the disaster to cause to happen before their eyes, a deep sense of shock permeates all through their minds. They all need direct treatment and/or counselling by Doctors or Clergymen. Individuals or close relatives whose family members may have died or suffered injuries may also require counseling by neurologists, medical experts or clergymen depending on their needs and situations. The Doctors will have to assess their needs and accordingly arrange for the appropriate type of treatments or counselling.

The Doctors should also have contact with the appropriate Governmental and Private Rehabilitation organization to arrange for the appropriate type of Rehabilitation for the close family members of the victims.

10.3 CLEAN UP OPERATIONS AFTER HAZARDOUS SPILLS—ENVIRONMENTAL PROTECTION

It is a huge task, somewhat risky and has to be performed as quickly as possible without contaminating the environment. Every measure has to be taken to conserve the Environment and preserve the ecological species as far as practicable. Considerable information is available in the context of a few chemical disasters where few exhaustive clean up and reclamation have been done and long term effects were avoided. In an interesting case, after 265 gallons of PCB was spilled into a river in Seattle while transporting a transformer, EPA organized the clean up (114). Massive efforts in monitoring, dredging, chemical treatment, collection, safe storage, and disposal at a cost of almost half a million dollars resulted in complete success of the operation. The development of efficient mobile units for containment of spills was a major advancement (104). Other systems for clean up to be sued are described by Brugger and Wilder (10). A universal gelling agent developed by Baier et al., (5)-offer promise in containing a wide variety of toxic spills. Floating mass transfer of agents has also been tried for containment of hazardous materials (29). Stover and Metry (102) have outlined the approach needed for handling emergencies in hazardous waste management facilities. The system for efficient management of hazardous waste can be triggered to meet the challenge of immediate clean up after major spills also. Contingency plan and trained manpower and facilities for containment of hazardous materials have to be made adequately available. This system could immediately respond to emergency situations. The first step is the assessment of the disaster. This involves (*i*) identification of character and composition and amount of discharge, (*ii*) an appraisal of the extent of discharge, expected direction and rate of travel, (*iii*) the degree of hazard or imminent hazard and what action could be taken to mitigate damage, (*iv*) preventive steps in halting other processes to avoid further complications, (*v*) what corrective measures may be necessary both at the facility and in the local community. The first step in containment is to try to restrict the movement of the spilled hazardous materials. The rest of the action can be decided on the nature of the hazard, generally following the U.S. Dept. of Transport (1976) guidelines. The schedule for evacuating potentially prone population worked out for nitric acid in terms of size of spills and wind conditions, is very useful in disaster planning. Similar schedules and mathematical models have to be worked out in every countries of the world.

The field implemented measures (94), technology (39), and biological (3) and chemical (33) methods for clean up have been compiled in the authoritative handbook on hazardous chemical spills by Bannet et al., (7). The description of a few cases of spill responses in the past including methods for containment and treatment (94) is of immense use. In view of time, journey, manpower and material, it will be better to achieve clean up as early as possible in confined areas rather than after large scale environmental release. The technological aspects of active charcoal as a clean up agent are described and design for portable units given. Freestone and Brugger (39) have described the modus operandi in all the stages of disaster clean up, namely prevention of further spills, pre-response planning, clean-up safety, analytical aspects, confinement, containment, concentration, and separation and ultimate disposal, protocols are also given for restoration of damaged area and testing long term safety. Similar schedule can be worked out for each chemical and biological causing disaster.

10.4 A PROTOCOL FOR DISASTER PREPAREDNESS/MANAGEMENT IN HAZARDOUS CONDITIONS

The best kind of preparedness will provide the best kind of management after the incidents take place. This is very much true in case of Disaster Management. Based on international literature citing past incidences, a program suitable for hazardous industry management is being outlined as follows. A similar programme can be adopted in other establishments with some modifications here and there with respect to the designations, actual needs and response necessary, may be in somewhat small scale.

A. Every organization should prepare a detailed scale maps showing-

1. The entire unit, ancillary facilities, residential areas etc.
2. Sites of pressure vessels, fire risks areas, storage facilities, in red color,
3. Plan diagrams of the process,
4. Fire fighting, first aid facilities and points,
5. Neighboring communities likely to be affected, roads, routes of evacuation etc.,
6. Meteorological data collection areas showing wind direction, rate charts,
7. Nearby hospitals, rescue shelters, voluntary agencies,
8. Nearby law and order authorities, appropriate government departments.
9. Telephone numbers, Fax numbers and e.mail addresses of all key personnel at all levels.

10.4.1 Educational Cum Consciousness Arousing Program

1. Appropriate slogans, pamphlets, posters etc. are required to be used for educating people,
2. Safety instructions are to be given at sites by organizing mock drills from time to time like that of fire drills,
3. Different types of personal protective devices are to be shown. It is to be demonstrated as to how they are worn and places where they are kept,
4. First aid and fire fighting equipment are to be made available closeby and their use should be learnt by some persons in each operational areas,
5. Periodic in house refresher courses, rehearsals, mock exercises should be practised and recorded.

10.4.2 Safety Organization

A typical set up is presented in the chart (Appendix IV). It may need modifications in different places according to the needs and extent of operations etc. Modifications may look into the matter of nature of risks involved, resource availability etc. It is very important that the expertise, strength and experiences should be adequate to meet any crisis.

10.4.3 Disaster Anticipation

An inventory of all hazardous processes, chemicals, biologicals and radiologicals' facilities etc. should be anticipated. For this inventory control, a proforma is to be used. This is given in Table-1 (p-299). For each of the major chemicals, biologicals used in large amounts at a time, this information has to be made available.

10.4.4 Toxicological Know-how About the Adverse Effects

International know-how on the long-term and short-term effects of single and repeated exposures on various forms of life should be available for each type of hazardous materials. A format is available in Table 2 (p-230). All the information required for diagnosis, first aid, follow-up as well as disaster containment and clean up are to be included.

10.4.5 Interaction with Other Agencies

The emergency unit should keep constant liaison with their counterparts in local administration. Periodic brain storming sessions will be useful in evolving effective strategies for disaster control and prevention. At each major industry, a disaster control program has to be developed by this procedure. Such a streamlined and well-rehearsed set up, adequately equipped to function fully immediately after a disaster can greatly help in reducing hazardous accident risks.

10.4.6 Emergency Handling Procedure

Emergency in a plant can be defined from the safety viewpoint as that of a situation, which is likely to endanger the personnel working in that area, but which can be, combated internally (i.e., a bad gas leak and/or a local fire break out).

A model plan of action during accidents involving chemicals and biologicals is given below. This is based on several such programs for fire and explosions and Toxic chemicals available in literature. Each establishment should prepare such a protocol for each of the major item used, made or stored by it.

10.5 A STEP BY STEP ACTION PLAN TO DEAL WITH A HAZARDOUS GAS LEAK: (AMMONIA, CHLORINE, ETC.,)

(*a*) At the first instance the concerned shift engineer will take necessary action to reduce the risk by isolating the equipment or by stopping the leak as the case may be.

(*b*) If the situation does not improve, the shift engineer will ask the personnel present there in the area to evacuate the premises at once.

(*c*) He will immediately post an operator in the phone booth to pass on information to the higher authorities in the order stated below:

1. Fire services over the telephone
2. First aid, telephone
3. Security supervisor
4. The concerned plant superintendent
5. Superintendent (fire and safety)

The above operator will remain at the phone booth to receive and transmit messages until "**ALL CLEAR**" is declared.

1. In the mean time the shift Engineer will lead operators equipped with suitable respiratory protection apparatus, and other proper safety appliances, like PVC suits, hand gloves etc., to take necessary action.
2. The Plant Superintendent on his arrival will assume the overall responsibility of the situation and direct further action as needed.

   The superintendent will ensure that no one is left behind as a casualty (by roll call)

   (*a*) The superintendent will contact the fire and safety and medical departments and ensure their prompt attention.

   (*b*) The plant superintendent will contact Production manager and apprise him of the situation.

   (*c*) The plant shift fire supervisor on his arrival will take such action as may be necessary to prevent an outbreak of fire or deal with an outbreak if it has occurred.

   (*d*) If the hazard is likely to endanger the safe working of the adjacent plant, the information will be passed on immediately by the plant superintendent

   (*e*) Once the hazard is reduced to safe limits the plant superintendent will declare "**ALL CLEAR**"

Table 1 : Format for Monitoring the Use of Hazardous Substances

Name	***Unit/ Name, Address***
Name of the chemical, biological formula	Amount processed per day
Physical properties	Amount stored
B. P.; M.P.; F. P.: Autoignition, process details temp. R. D., R.V.D.;V.P.	
Solubility, relative molecular mass, etc.	In-plant facilities
Chemical properties Reactivity, air, water, etc., run away reactions etc.,	Medical facilities
Other characteristics	Disaster preparedness

(Contd...)

(Contd...)

Occupational risk	Organization
	Trained manpower
Environmental risks Toxicology	Governmental facilities
Hazards/symptoms	Local voluntary organization
First aid/treatment medical follow up	Storage condition
Preventive precautions	Transport
Spillage containment	Packing and labeling
Neutralization	Any specific information
Environmental persistence	
Sensitization risks	
High-risk groups	

Table 2 : Criteria for Risk Assessment of Hazardous Substances

1. Commercial/ chemical/biological or other names

   CAS NO.
2. Molecular formula/Genera or species of the organism, its light and electron micrograph, PCR data
3. Sources/production
4. Uses
5. Physical /chemical and biological properties

   A. (*i*) State, color, odor, shape

   (*ii*) Mol. Wt., Pictures (light and electron micrograph) PCR data

   (*iii*) B.P.; M.P.; F.P.; Vapour pressure, vapour

   Density/density/explosive limits /autoignition temp.

   B. Solubility

   (*a*) Reactions with other chemicals, biologicals, internal organs
6. Routes of absorption/entry

   (*i*) Inhalation

   (*ii*) Ingestion

   (*iii*) Skin absorption
7. Physiological response

   (*i*) Toxicity (LD50)

   (*ii*) Acute effects

   (*iii*) Chronic effects

(Contd...)

8. Excretion/elimination
   (*i*) Exhaled air
   (*ii*) Urine (*a*) free contaminants
   (*b*) Live organisms
   (*c*) Metabolites
   (*i*) Sweat
   (*ii*) Feces
9. Test indicating exposure
   (*a*) Hematological estimations
   (*i*) TLC
   (*ii*) DLC
   (*iii*) Hb
   (*iv*) MHb
   (*b*) Free contaminants in urine/blood
   (*c*) Metabolites
   (*d*) Enzyme estimation
   (*e*) Pulmonary functions
   FEV1/FEV2, VC, RV
   (*f*) Exhaled air analysis
   (*g*) Sputum, nail/hair/sweat
10. Threshold limit values
    (*a*) Ambient
    (*b*) Biological thresholds
11. Methods for detection/determination
    A. Physical
    B. Chemical or
    C. Biological
12. Health protection and control measures
    (*i*) Pre-employment medical examination
    (*ii*) Personal hygiene
    (*iii*) House keeping
    (*iv*) Protective equipment
    (*v*) Substitution by less toxic material or processes
    (*vi*) Ventilation
    (*vii*) Local exhaust
    (*viii*) Education
    (*ix*) Maintenance
    (*x*) Wet methods/Engineering methods

(Contd...)

13. Emergency measures and first aids
    (*i*) Remove victim to uncontaminated areas
    (*ii*) Artificial respiration, if needed
    (*iii*) Administration of oxygen
    (*iv*) Antidotes
    (*v*) Eye fountains and showers, chemical burns of eyes should be washed with sufficient water followed by weak solution of sodium bicarbonate after which medical help should be sought
15. Precautions in storage and handling
16. Precaution against fire and explosion hazard
17. Waste disposal
18. Legal and other information
19. Any past record in literature as hazards, accident

10.6 DISASTER HANDLING PROCEDURE

1. The disaster can be classified as a " Dangerous Occurrence" which may involve men and/or materials inside a factory or an establishment, for example:
   (*a*) Burning of a container holding steam, liquid, or gas under pressure
   (*b*) Fire causing damage
   (*c*) Explosion causing damage
   (*d*) Collapse or failure of an apparatus, structure of a building
   (*e*) Collision at shunting yard, railway crossing, accidents on the road
   (*f*) Bombing or warfare.
2. The course of actions to be taken during these occurrences is stated as the "Emergency Procedure".
3. If the situation cannot be tackled with the internal resources as under "Emergency Procedure", the situation has to be dealt with as under "Major Crisis".
4. The responsibility of deciding the gravity of the situation rests with the Shift Engineer or person in-charge who will be actually present at site.
5. The factory requires that all dangerous occurrences must be reported promptly to the Inspector of Factories. Superintendent (Fire and Safety will report the occurrences in the prescribed format to the next higher authorities.
6. Details of accident and dangerous occurrence procedure have been circulated separately.

10.7 MAJOR CRISIS HANDLING PROCEDURE

The "Major Crisis" is a serious accident or occurrence which the factory personnel or the establishment personnel cannot control by themselves and which endangers not only the personnel of the factory or establishment, but also those who live in the surroundings, neighbors, highway traffic, as for example:

(*a*) Serious ammonia spills or tank rupture

(*b*) Major fires

The purpose of this procedure is to have a plan of action that can be studied, practised and put into effect immediately without delay, to prevent injury and hazards to the personnel, equipment and surrounding community during the crisis. This procedure is based on international experiences; procedures and the systems employed in various major factories or establishments in different countries.

The responsibility of determining the degree of the crisis will fall on the senior personnel at the site. During the non-general shift hours and holidays, the shift engineer will be responsible for making this determination, activating the crisis procedure and carrying out these duties until more senior personnel and experts arrive at the site.

10.7.1 An Example of Ammonia Leakage Disaster Handling Procedure

10.7.1.1 *General*

Since ammonia is an item stored in large quantities in various units in the country, this has been taken as the model for elaborating the disaster-handling schedule. The views expressed here are based on the protocols used in many units in India. We are thankful to them for the information.

The possibility of ammonia spills under adverse conditions like mechanical failure of equipment, thunder storms, operational difficulties, accidents, fire, explosions, and bomb blasts during hostility with the neighboring countries or terrorists attack can not be ruled out.

So it becomes necessary to formulate an emergency plan and put it into action if such situation arises. However, simplicity and clarity to be the key to any effective emergency plan.

10.7.1.2 *Objective*

This emergency plan has been worked out with the following objectives-

(*a*) To deal with the spills or heavy leakage in the early stages before it becomes disastrous.

(*b*) To take immediate corrective action for repairs and maintenance of the ammonia handling facilities by hastening the return to normalcy.

(*c*) To save the lives of plant personnel, limit property damage and cut production losses.

(*d*) To save the lives of local inhabitants and carry out evacuation operations from down wind localities if leakage or spill becomes too heavy.

(*e*) To acquire police and fire service help from local community if situation tends to become out of control of the plant personnel. By wireless messages, telegrams, telephones, satellite phone services, Fax, e.mail etc. more elaborate support may be sought, if needed.

(*f*) To train the concerned personnel regarding specific safety measures required to meet such emergency, specially cleaning personnel and other employees staying in the surrounding areas.

10.7.1.3 *Health Hazards*

The following health hazards are posted when spillage occurs and atmosphere is heavily contaminated with ammonia gas: (Table 3 on p. 235)

(*a*) At low concentration in air, ammonia vapor irritates the eyes, nose and throat.

(*b*) Inhalation of high concentration of ammonia produces a sensational suffocation quickly, causes burning off respiratory tract and may even result in death.

(*c*) Liquid anhydrous ammonia causes severe burns on contact with the skin, while its effect on being swallowed would be to cause severe corrosive action in the mouth, throat and stomach.

(*d*) Severe eye damage can be caused by exposure period associated with specific ammonia vapor concentration.

Table 3 : Toxicity of Ammonia

Vapor Concentration (ppm / V / V)	*General Effects*	*Exposure Period*
25	Odor detectable by most persons	maximum for 8 hours working period
100	No adverse effects for an average man	Deliberate exposure for longer period not permitted
400	Immediate nose and throat irritation	No serious effect up to ½ to 1 hr.
700	Immediate eye irritation	No serious effect up to ½ to 1hr.
1700	Convulsive coughing, severe, eye Nose and throat irritation	Could be fatal after ½ hour
2000-5000	—do—	—do—
5000-10000	Rapid respiratory spasm	fatal within minutes

10.7.1.4 *Fire Hazard*

Anhydrous ammonia forms flammable mixture with air within the limits of 16-25% by volume. The presence of oil or other flammable materials increase the fire hazard.

(*a*) Contact of ammonia with other chemicals notably mercury, chlorine, iodine, bromine, calcium, silver oxide or hypochlorites can form explosive compounds.

(*b*) The explosive limit of ammonia in oxygen is 15-79% by volume.

10.7.1.5 *Safety Precautions Against Fire and Spills*

High vaporization rate from a liquid ammonia source and a gas escape from a pressure source are more likely to create a fire hazard than vaporization from a cold pool of liquid anhydrous ammonia. A large pool of anhydrous ammonia may be considered to constitute a negligible fire hazard.

(*i*) Ammonia vapor can however, be ignited from a vigorously boiling pool. Flames above cold pool of ammonia do not radiate enough heat to maintain the vaporization ate for continuous burning.

(*ii*) Small fires of ammonia can be extinguished with the help of carbon dioxide or dry chemical powder extinguishers.

(*iii*) Ammonia fire should not be fought with water but allowed to burn out.

(*iv*) Foam for blanketing the spilled ammonia to be made available.

10.7.2 Toxic Discharge

Ammonia is a toxic gas, which can be detected because of its pungent odor.

(*i*) *Ammonia spills.* When ammonia escapes, it may do so as a gas, liquid or combination of both. This is a colorless gas lighter than air and adequate ventilation is the first best method of avoiding accumulation. Gaseous discharges are best dealt with by allowing them to be dispersed in the atmosphere at height although it may be necessary to evacuate personnel several hundred yards down wind of the discharge, should a massive escape occurs.

(*ii*) *Minor spills.* Minor spills should be diluted by flooding or immediate application of copious quantities of water and washed away down the drain.

(*iii*) *Major spills.* Water should not be used on major spills of liquid ammonia. The application of water will cause boiling and burning AND INCREASE THE VAPORISATION rates thereby aggravating the toxic hazard.

If the quantity is comparatively small and once the ground has become locally frozen, it forms an effective isolating barrier strong convection current will beset up since ammonia gas is lighter than air, and further evaporation will continue. The heat of vaporization will be drawn from the liquid thereby reducing the temperature of the pool. The vapor air mixture produced during this stage will tend to rise, air turbulence will, however, probably cause the atmosphere to be contaminated from considerable distance down wind.

10.7.3 Personal Protection

The degree of protection required must be related to the potential hazards of the job. Personal protection is treated as injury prevention while working under adverse conditions and should be restored to only when other measures fail.

(*i*) *Eye protection.* Goggles are worn while entering liquid storage area where leaks may occur.

(*ii*) *Head protection.* Hard hats are worn even though there is no danger from falling material.

(*iii*) *Foot protection.* Boots give complete foot protection against liquid ammonia. Trousers should be worn outside the boots.

(*iv*) *Hand protection.* PVC or rubber hand gloves give protection against ammonia. Sleeves should be kept outside the gloves.

(*v*) *Full body protection.* Depending upon the degree of hazard and nature of exposure, PVC combination suit comprising of full sleeves coat, trousers and hand gloves gives complete body protection. This can be supplemented with respiratory protective equipment.

(*vi*) *Respiratory protection.* Exposure to ammonia may occur during the routine cleaning of tanks, decontamination of area after spillage or due to failure of the equipment. The following types of safety equipment is used, however, the correct method of use and proper maintenance is a must to ensure greater safety:

(*a*) **Ammonia gas masks.** The mask gives protection up to three percent ammonia concentration in the environment. These are not suitable in oxygen deficient atmosphere.

(*b*) **Plus pressure suit for air fed face mask.** These masks are connected with the plant air supply line and keep the wearer under positive air pressure. The air supply should be free from oil or water vapors. However, the mobility of the wearer is restricted because of limited length of the airline hose.

(*c*) **Air blower mask.** These are used in the tanks and confined spaces when atmosphere from where the air is blown, is free from contaminants. The use of man hoisting safety bolt and deployment of two persons for the operation of the air blower is essential to ensure safety. Rescuer should also be ready to meet an eventuality.

(*d*) **Self-contained Breathing Apparatus.** This set allows the wearer to carry a supply of normal air cylinder on his back and does not restrict his mobility. These are used when grave situation arises. However the air cylinder imposes the limitation, which is to be replaced after every half an hour.

10.7.4 Plan for Dealing with Major Spills

A major leakage of ammonia will cause immediate contamination of the surrounding atmosphere and contamination will spread rapidly down wind of the incident. Speed is therefore essential to make the emergency known to all concerned.

Shift Engineer (Officiates) who possesses the first hand knowledge of the situation will work as Shift manager (Emergency). If however, an accident escalated beyond the capability of fire crew and plant operators he should have the authority to request the activation of the Emergency Central Control and take the following action:

10.7.4.1 *Shift Emergency Manager (Shift Engineer-Officiates)*

He will take the following actions immediately

(*i*) Call shift fire supervisor.

(*ii*) Inform Shift Security Supervisor-he can communicate to all the Plant's Shift Engineers.

(*iii*) Shift Engineer.

(*iv*) Inform Shift Engineer (maintenance).

(*v*) See the wind direction and direct emergency operations with the help of operation and fire crew available at site accordingly.

(*vi*) He should inform immediately the General manager and joint general manager (O) after Superintendent (Officiates) taking action (*i*) to (*v*) as stated being a major leakage.

10.7.4.2 *Shift Fire Supervisor*

He will report at the scene of emergency immediately and take the following steps:

(*i*) Put all the safety appliances in service).

(*ii*) Work under the directions of Shift Emergency Manager (SE Officiates).

10.7.4.3 *Shift Security Supervisor*

On receiving emergency call, he will do the following:

(*i*) Send available security guards immediately to assist Shift Fire Supervisor.

(*ii*) Inform Nurses and inform Medical Officers.

(*iii*) Inform Safety supervisor.

(*iv*) Inform superintendent (fire and safety).

(*v*) Call fire service.

(*vi*) Inform concerned superintendent.

(*vii*) Inform superintendent (Stores).

(*viii*) Inform all managers or next Sr. Officer of the Department.

(*ix*) Inform manager (Personnel and Administration).

(*x*) Deploy Security guards to control panic.

10.7.4.4 *Superintendent (Fire and Safety)*

On reaching at the scene, he will take the following actions:

(*i*) To put into service all safety gears available in stores.

(*ii*) To reinforce the shift fire crew.

(*iii*) To supervise the control and rescue operation as directed by the emergency central control.

10.7.4.5 *Superintendent (Officiates)*

On reaching at sight, he will assess the gravity of the situation and do the following:

(*i*) To take charge from Shift Emergency Manager and direct emergency operation till the formation of Emergency Central Control.

(*ii*) Inform Manager (Utilities).

(*iii*) Inform Manager (Production).

(*iv*) Inform Manager (Maintenance).

(*v*) Inform Manager (Technical).

(*vi*) Inform Jt. General Manager (Operation).

(*vii*) Inform General Manager.

10.7.4.6 *Security Officer*

On receiving information and reaching at the spot, he will take the following actions:

(*i*) To control traffic and allow only authorized employees to enter.

(*ii*) To inform the Factory Medical Officer for reporting in Plant First Aid Post.

(*iii*) To send out contractors and casual labor.

(*iv*) To pool up departmental transport with the help of Manager (P & A) and keep vehicles ready for use.

(*v*) To reinforce security force.

10.7.4.7 *Senior Nurse/Compounder*

(*i*) They will prepare for emergency.

(*ii*) Rush ambulance to the scene of accident.

(*iii*) inform the medical officer immediately.

10.7.4.8 *Medical Officer*

On reaching the site, he will go directly to the first aid post and take the following actions:

(*i*) He will keep necessary first aid medicines and artificial respiration equipment ready.

(*ii*) Inform local Doctors to be ready for attending serious injury and gas poisoning cases.

(*iii*) Inform all major hospitals authority for the treatment of serious cases on an emergency basis, if any.

10.7.4.9 *Task Fire Fighting Force*

On receiving information from shift manager and section incharge, task fire fighting force on duty will do the following:

(*i*) They will proceed to the scene of occurrence and report to Shift Fire Supervisor.

(*ii*) They will note that wind direction and work along with the fire crew as per the direction of the Shift Fire Supervisor after taking full precautions for their own safety.

10.7.4.10 *Fire Brigade*

On reaching the site, they will take the following actions:

(*i*) Report to Shift Emergency Manager or Emergency Central Command.

(*ii*) Appraise themselves about the hazards, wind direction, and personal protective appliances.

(*iii*) Work in close cooperation with the shift fire crew, as per the direction of the Emergency Central Command.

10.7.4.11 *Emergency Central Command*

(*i*) On receiving information and reaching at the spot, Emergency Central Command will be formed under the authority of the General Manager. This will be constituted with the following officers:

(*a*) Jt. General Manager

(*b*) Manager (production)

(*c*) Manager (Utilities)

(*d*) Manager (Maintenance)

(*e*) Manager (Personnel and Administration)

(*f*) Superintendent (Stores)

(*g*) Senior Police Official (after reaching at site)

(*h*) Medical Officer

(*i*) Rehabilitation Officer

10.7.5 The Emergency Central Command

After it is formed at site will assume the following responsibility from Shift Manager Emergency and take following action:

(*i*) To direct emergency control and rescue operations.

(*ii*) To sound emergency siren situated at Time Office Fire and Safety at high and low pitch to announce plant emergency.

(*iii*) Inform the local Police Officials and district administration as the need may be.

(*iv*) To ensure assistance from fire service.

(*v*) To call maintenance crew for arranging immediate repairs and maintenance of equipment, if necessary.

(*vi*) To arrange for medical treatment of the injured persons, if any nearby.

(*vii*) To arrange to notify families of any personnel that are injured.

(*viii*) To maintain the supply line like food, water, and other material needed for supporting control and rescue crew.

(*ix*) To keep in touch with the state police authority and see that evacuation work, if necessary, is being done satisfactorily.

(*x*) To inform the Factory Inspector.

(*xi*) To sound all clear siren when emergency or crisis is over.

(*xii*) No statement or comments about the crisis will be made to any one outside the plant except by the General Manager who will arrange for the press release or report to the higher company officials or members of the Board, as per the policy of the company or the establishment.

10.7.5.1 *Action by the District Administration and Police*

On receiving the message, the local police should dispatch a police car to central command. The police officers will collect safety appliances on arrival and do the following:

(*i*) To inform the communication line between the Central Command and local or head quarters Police throughout the duration of the crisis.

(*ii*) If warning of house holders is necessary, public roads are to be closed, the police officers will advise their local as well as headquarters, indicating the need or otherwise for reinforcement.

(*iii*) They will assist in getting safety appliances, if need be, from other agencies through their official influence.

(*iv*) They will take necessary steps to inform the public in the affected areas about the situation, evacuate the persons to safer place and provide medical aid.

10.7.5.2 *First Aid*

After severe exposure to ammonia gas or liquid it is important to move the patient from the contaminated area promptly. Speed is very essential.

(*i*) *Contact with the skin or the mucous membrane.* Flashing with large quantities of water should be continued for at least 15 minutes. Contaminated clothing should be removed immediately. No ointment should be applied to the skin or the mucous membrane burns during the 24 hours period following the injury without doctor's advice. Subsequent treatment is the same as for thermal burns.

(*ii*) *Contact with the eyes.* Eyes should be irrigated with copious quantity of water or with eyewash bottle (2.1% borax and 2.1% of boric acid). The irrigation should be continued for 15 minutes after keeping the eyelids open to remove the last traces of ammonia from all the tissues of eyes. No ointment should be applied without doctor's advice.

(*iii*) *Taken internally (Swallowing).* Give plenty of water if the patient is conscious and able. Do not induce vomiting if patient is in shock, extreme pain or unconscious. If vomiting begins, keep the patient's face downwards, head lower than hips, as this prevents vomiting entering the lungs and causing further injury.

(*iv*) *Inhalation.* Exposed persons should be removed to fresh air immediately. No treatment is required for low concentration except this. Severe exposure to high concentration requires oxygen administration by an authorized person or a doctor. If breathing has stopped, apply an effective method of artificial respiration. The patient should be kept comfortably warm but not too hot and should be kept at rest.

10.8 REMEMBER: THE RIGHT AID IS THE BEST AID. THE WRONG AID CAN DO MORE HARM THAN GOOD.

10.8.1 Counselling

Whenever a disaster strikes, no matter whether it is chemical/biological or radiological by nature and whether it is caused by an accident or due to a terrorist attack, hundreds and thousands of people die, thousands become injured, several thousands of family members and friends becomes mentally affected. Some get emotionally upset and speechless; some others cry out loudly. Some of them suffer from a deep anxiety in their minds. The eyewitnesses suffer from a terrible shock. The pain and agony of the people who have lost their dearest ones linger many months and years later in their minds. Thousands of families get shattered, particularly those who have lost their only earning members or the company they worked for got totally ruined in the devastation.

All these people need psychological counseling and or spiritual counselling depending on the particular case. While the hospitals have such facilities in general, the religious people from various religious Institutions of the locality should extend their hands for counselling purposes. The counselling should be provided up until the time they become normal and take part in their day-to-day routine work.

10.8.2 Rehabilitation

The surviving victims and their families need rehabilitation of different kinds. Families where an earning member died or has become incapacitated due to the disaster should be appropriately rehabilitated- by proving jobs to the eligible members of the family, a one-time compensation package, taking educational responsibilities of the children of the victims by the state etc. The rehabilitation should be quick and must not wait for an indefinite period of time. At the initial level food, medicine and other day-to-day needs have to be provided in the family of majority of the victims until such time that they are properly rehabilitated. Aids and help coming from various countries of the world have to be properly stored and then distributed among the needy people. Apart from the Government's own endeavors, voluntary and philanthropic organizations must come forward for this humanitarian cause. In disastrous situation help from anybody and everybody are required, including volunteers and those who know how to provide first-aid to the injured. You cannot wait with a suffering victim who needs immediate help. Take them to the nearest hospital. Give a little of your valuable time and energy to save the needy.

11 *Tsunami*—Earthquakes, Volcanic Eruptions, Typhoons, Tornadoes, Cyclones, High Tides, Flood and Similar Such Natural Disasters

Until the devastating *Tsunami* trust upon the coastal regions of eleven countries in two continents of South East Asia in the night of December 26, 2004, not too many people knew about the word, *Trunami.* This horrifying 'wave giant' killed several thousands of people, displacing many more, and wounding many others whose count will never be known. The devastation caused by this *Tsunami* are unprecedented in the history of all *Tsunami*s. The world had never seen such a *Tsunami*-related catastrophe caused by any natural disaster. It surpassed all previous *Tsunami*'s in terms of its magnitude of destruction and vastness of miseries it inflicted upon the people and his environment.

The UN organization had pledged a $ 4 billion aid package for the estimated 5 million people who got affected in 11 countries of the world and needed relief and immediate rehabilitation. The worldwide toll is approximately 1,55,000, of which in Indonesia alone the number has been about 1,01,318, Sri Lanka 30,615, India about 10,000. Among the most affected areas in India were—Tamilnadu (7941), Andaman and Nicober Islands (1196), Pondicherry (583), Kerala (170), and Andhra Pradesh (105). In a mammoth rehabilitation effort, a total of 6,42,297 people from the coastal areas were shifted to safer places, and 3,82,586 people were still in 630 relief camps spread across Tamil Nadu, Andaman and Nicober Islands, Kerala, Pondicherry, and Andhra Pradesh. About 5689 people were reported still missing from various parts of India.

11.1 WHAT IS A *TSUNAMI* ?

A *Tsunami* often referred to as a "tidal wave", which appears to be a wave train, or series of waves, generated in a large body of water by an impulsive disturbance (caused by an Earthquake of submarine landslides) that vertically displaces the water column.

11.2 HOW DOES A *TSUNAMI* FORMED?

Earthquakes that occur on the seafloor or in coastal areas usually cause tsunamis. The energy generated by the earthquake is transmitted through the water. In deep oceans the energy in these sea waves can travel unnoticed because the wave height may be only twelve inches. When this energy reaches the shallow waters of coastlines, bays, or harbors, it forces the water into a giant wave. Some *Tsunamis* may reach heights of 100 feet or more.

Besides the above cause submarine landslides, which often accompany large earthquakes, can also disturb the water as sediment and rock slump down-slope and are redistributed across the sea floor. When these large amounts of dirt, mud, or sand slide into the ocean, it often generates an uplift the water bodies causing a *Tsunami.*

On the night of December 26, 2004, the *Tsunami* which struck the ocean floor near the Indonesian island, Sumatra, was caused by a massive Earthquake (about 9 in the Richter scale). It took about 2-3 hours to reach the coastlines of countries in the region, such as India, Sri Lanka, Indonesia, Sumatra, Malaysia, Thailand etc. While Indonesian island Sumatra was virtually devastated, the Maldives, Andaman and Nicober Islands of India, and the coastal regions of Kerala, Tamilnadu, Orissa, Karnataka, and Andhra Pradesh were severely affected. Somalia in Africa got affected too.

The world got stunned and horrified by seeing the effect of *Tsunami*, which affected more than 15,00,000 people in the entire South East Asiatic region. The result of a massive earthquake (9.0 in the Richter scale) originated in the sea close to Sumatra island, resulted into very high and powerful coastal waves (about 100 feet high), which is characteristic of a *Tsunami.* The giant waves burst upon the coastal regions washing away hundreds and thousands of people and converted a huge number of small hunts, wooden constructions, cars, livestock, etc. into nothing but debris. Even "pucca" buildings, roads, railway tracks, concrete bridges, trees, electrical connections etc. were considerably damaged and levelled off. Such type of devastation was never seen before.

11.3 PAST *TSUNAMI*

The United States of America has had the information about several submarine landslides causing *Tsunami* along the country's west coast in Palos Verdes Peninsula, California, Santa Barbara Channel, Washington, Commencement Bay, Alaska, and Port Valdez, Resurrection Bay etc. Using multi-beam bathymetric imagery and acoustic reflectors landslide deposits could be identified. It can detect either predate or postdate landslide events. Three landslides had resulted *Tsunami* post-1750 AD. High-resolution sub-bottom reflection profiles may allow us to estimate the dimensions of the failed masses. Unfortunately, data in the Indian Ocean areas are lacking. High resolution, very sensitive equipments are essential for this purpose.

11.4 GLOBAL CHANGE, CLIMATE CHANGE—NATURE'S FURYS

Nature's fury was converted into a *Tsunami* with such magnitude and power appears, which appears to be warning to all of us. Continuous insults and injuries, which are being inflicted upon 'Mother Nature' by various types of man-made activities, resulted in significant Global atmospheric change. As has been predicted that by the year 2025, the earth could be an average 2 degree Celcius warmer than it was in 1750. It might have serious repercussions world wide, not only in the Arctic regions alone but also in different parts of the world. Already the consequences of global warming phenomena are being felt in different parts of the globe.

A small region in Africa, Lesotho, altered suddenly in 2003 experiencing severe storms and untimely frost, which destroyed their crops. The World Meteorological Organization (WMO) announced in a report in the same year that a pre-monsoon heat wave in India that killed 1400 people, 562 Tornadoes that hit USA in May 2003 killing 40 people, were related to Global warming phenomena. In 1998, there were 63 weather related disasters far more than the average of 21.78 per year in the year 1080s, meaning thereby more human causualties and significantly more economic losses. It has been reported that in 1980s, the world's property insurers lost an average of US $2 billion annually to extreme weather conditions.

It is the nature's own design that it has to react and adjust to maintain equilibrium in one way or another. *Tsunami* is perhaps one of such "nature's adjustments". Whenever mother nature may have to adjust and readjust, a lot of casualties and sufferings come down on the common man and woman, children and the elderly, both rich and poor alike. The devastations set in an unimaginable proportions. The casualties are usually very high. The loss is tremendous, in terms of millions of dollars.

The recent *Tsunami* has already earned the name as being notorious in that it caused severe destruction unseen in recent times. It has surpassed all previous natural disasters, such as Gujarat earthquakes, earthquakes in China etc.

11.5 CAN *TSUNAMI* BE PREDICTED?

A great controversy has arisen as to whether or not *Tsunami* can be predicted or not. Such a question has surfaced because of the failure of the Indian Meteorological Department to transmit any early warning signal, although *Tsunami* hit the coastal areas of India almost about three hours later than when it originated in its epicenter. Such failures have been explained as due to (1) insensitive equipments, (2) failure to distinguish between *Tsunami* related earthquake and other earthquakes, (3) failure to detect any mid-sea turbulence, (4) mistakes of being a signatory to the International Treaty of several *Tsunami* countries of the world which share their information and resources with each other to deal with a *Tsunami* and its after effects, and 5) of cource human error, carelessness, neglect and indifference to the job responsibility of all those people who are supposed to deal with such kind of work and activities.

Principles of Physical Geology states strong submarine earthquake cause *Tsunami*. The major feature associated with it is that giant sea waves usually thrust upon the coastal regions. The displacement of water caused due to sudden large-scale changes of the level of the sea floor e.g. by fault movements responsible for the earthquake or by submarine slumping set off by the earthquake. In recent years, strong earthquakes, of the order of >8 in the Richter scale were invariably followed by a *Tsunami*.

The seismographs all over the world immediately record earthquakes. After the triangulation, the epicenter can be identified. Once the epicenter is located on the sea floor and if the earthquake is of very high magnitude, one can expect a *Tsunami*. The approximate arrival time of the giant wave in the coastal areas of the world can well be calculated. One can calculate it by the distance from the epicenter, and the depth of water above the sea. Thus India got about three hours time after the earthquake hit the sea floor causing the recent *Tsunami*.

11.6 REHABILITATION

Severe damages are caused by a *Tsunami* on man and his environment, bringing in a lot of miseries to the people.

The wave of destruction left millions homeless. Many Philanthropic organizations have come forward with help and support of different kinds; some are focusing on supporting the identified children, women, families of *Tsunami* victims to enable them region their lost livelihood.

A fisherman, being old, was at home and did not go to catch fish. At the time *Tsunami* struck, he was away from home; when he returned, he found everything grounded. His house was leveled off. His entire family was swept away. He needed desperate help. Many women lost their husbands and children, and children lost their parents. They are now homeless, penniless. They have no clothes to wear, no food to eat, and no place to go and sleep. All drinking water sources got contaminated. There are severe shortages of drinking water food and garments. It is feared that soon epidemics might start.

The Government of India showed unprecedented coordination leadership and efforts to deal with this natural disaster-related after effects. They immediately put in place, its army, navy and air forces personnel for sending all kinds of supplies, and also to manage its distribution, providing medical help to the people, establishing camps, transporting people from odd places where they were found stranded, coordinating with other voluntary organizations and individual volunteers who came forward with their support and to engage themselves in this gigantic humanitarian efforts etc. The Government of India also sent its team of experts, doctors etc. with food, drinking water, clothes, medicines etc. in other countries also, such as Indonesia, Sri Lanka, Maldives, Thailand etc. to join others in the relief and rehabilitation work.

World response was spontaneous. Reporters, writers, politicians, religious groups, Industrialists, film personalities, sportsmen from India and abroad came forward with their help. School college students donated their pocket money, workers gave one day's salary. In fact every man and woman came forward to donate whatever he or she could.

Led by UN Secretary General world leaders pledged a $ 4.0 billion rehabilitation package. WHO, IMF, Work Bank and similar such organizations also came forward with their help to stand by the surviving members of the victim's families. Almost the entire world jumped upon this massive cause. For the time being, it looked like we are living in one world and we have only one identity—we are citizens of the same mother Earth.

Humanitarian help is a major thing in all kinds of disaster management, no matter whether it is caused by human mistake, or orchestrated by a terrorists, due to a war or by natural disasters, such as Earthquakes, *Tsunami*, Tornadoes, Typhoons, Hurricanes, Floods, Fires etc. The nature of sufferings to the common man is more or less the same. Its magnitude obviously may be different in different cases. Therefore, an appropriate Disaster Preparedness Programme associated with an appropriate Disaster Management Programme is essential and is to be installed in every disaster prone sites, which may be considered to be vulnerable. This help in the mitigation of casualties limiting the number of victims and saving millions of dollars.

11.7 PREPAREDNESS PLAN AND PREVENTIVE MEASURES

One can take several preventive measures to avoid massive damages caused by natural disasters and similar such episodes:

1. India and other coastal nations should immediately establish a National Institute for Disaster Management and Rehabilitation to train people with adequate knowledge in an effort to develop various preparedness plan, management plan, mitigation and rehabilitation plan pertaining to various types of disaster—disaster caused by accidents (chemical, biological and radiological), by terrorist's attack, various natural disasters caused by *Tsunami*, Typhoons, Tornadoes, Hurricanes, Cyclones, Tidal waves, Flood etc. It would promote public education and awareness as well as community participation in disaster prevention and mitigation. It would also develop and promote national and regional human and institutional capacity, transfer of knowledge and know-how, technology in building and managing a regional early warning system and disaster management through international cooperation and partnership.

2. Scientists and Engineers, Meteorologists, Geoligists should be engaged indigenous research to develop very sensitive measurement systems (1) for early warning, (2) to measure

the strength of the ocean bed earthquakes, (3) its transmittance velocity and direction, (4) to calculate the possible height of the wave it might generate when it hits various coastal regions, and (5) devices for accurate calculation of time when a *Tsunami* would hit the coastal areas of various countries in the region. Such information would help in the early evacuation of people from the vulnerable areas.

3. A national flood hazard mitigation should be launched and equiped with all equipments, gadgets, drugs and vaccines, tents and other rehabilitation materials in stock. It should coordinate the various relief efforts and keep close touch with International organizations to seek help and cooperation if there is need be. When other countries are affected, it should carry out the emergency operations extending help for relief, rehabilitation and reconstruction activities. World financial organization may be contacted for financial help for the viability and sustainability of various programmes. It should promote and encourage private sector participation for rehabilitation and reconstruction. A regional mechanism for disaster prevention and mitigation programme is to be established with the participation of all coastal countries. An effective regional early warning system for the *Tsunami* in Indian Ocean, Atlantic Ocean and South East Asia has to be established.

4. There has to be a National Flood Insurance programme. It should be launched immediately and made available for all the people living in flood prone coastal areas. This will reduce the costs for relief and rehabilitation, which otherwise comes heavily upon the Government in most cases.

5. Laws should be enacted for the natural disaster prone areas to establish appropriate type of construction norms. Such special type of contruction should only be permitted so that it can withstand wave and wind pressure, earthquake movements etc. Weak constructions should not be permitted in coastal areas. All *Pucca* constructions must abide by those rules and regulations. Today such knowledge is available in the civil and mechanical engineering areas.

6. Until such time that is not possible for any nation to make all those available through indigenous efforts, each of the vulnerable nation must be a signatory to those International Treaty meant for exchange of all kinds of supports in *Tsunami* related matters including early warning, disaster control, rehabilitation etc.

Close cooperation with USA and Japan, which is ahead of others in terms of its scientific knowledge and technology in this regard, is essential.

7. Each country has to develop a Disaster Preparedness Plan and also a Disaster Management Plan and put it in place, in every district, towns, city and state.

8. There has to be a Central command at the State level with its head quarters at the Central (Federal) level, with its components going down-stream up to district and community level.

9. During the peace-time they may be engaged in various developmental activities of the Government.

10. Mock drill should be performed to ensure that everything is intact; equipments are in place in functional order. Central Audit should perform their duties to ensure that materials are not improperly utilized, smuggled out or are simply lost, simply for improper storage.

11. They should have a list of all voluntary and philianthropic organizations, NGOs, charitable trusts, religious organizations so that they can be contacted if there is a need.

12. At every level people at command, should know wherefrom orders would flow down; their telephone, fax, e-mails, and cell phone numbers should be available, as also other vital numbers of the nearest police stations, numbers of DMs office and his residence, fire fighting stations, hospitals, doctors, local councilors, MLAs and MPs.

13. Kacha shanties with bamboo structures, tin shades, wooden plies etc. should be removed at a comfortable distance from the coastal areas. The poor people residing there should be rehabilitated at a safe distance in an appropriate manner.

14. A disaster management fund is to be created at the Central and State level and financial provisions made in the Annual Budget. Apart from Prime Minister's Relief Fund and Chief Minister's Relief Fund, such a fund has become a necessity.

15. Enough of stores, such as food, water, medicines and various medical accessories, vaccines, clothes, tents, boats, helicopters etc. are to be kept stored for tackling such kind of disasters without losing any time and energy. Losing time is a crime in such circumstances.

India has set an example to deal with and properly managing the aftermath of the recent *Tsunami* victims, which took a toll of about 10,012 people, while about 5624 were not traceable and several millions became homeless. They were provided with food, drinking water, medication, clothes etc. immediately by engaging the Army, Navy and Air Force personnel. A major rehabilitation plan had been put in force together with a huge financial package. This unilateral approach to provide relief and rehabilitation to the affected *Tsunami* victims and their families is a unique example in history of management of disaster victims. It would help others to learn from India in this regard.

12 Concluding Remarks

Today's world is facing a new challenge. The challenge of survival against chemical/biological/radiological accidents or disaster caused by terrorist's attack. It is no longer a conjecture. It has become a reality. Therefore, it is of utmost importance that we make ourselves aware first about the terrorism per se, their nature of functions, who becomes the terrorists, their psyche, and their choices of weapons etc. so that an adequate preventive and protective efforts can be made at all levels. This is the reason why at the beginning of this volume this aspect has been discussed. Thereafter, discussions were held regarding the preparedness plan at all levels, in order for keeping oneself abreast of the various needs in case one has to face an emergency. In the subsequent chapters an elaborate discussions were held regarding the diagnosis, identification and various available treatment procedures for the victims. The author made tremendous search in the literature to find out available information regarding various gadgets to safeguard oneself against the exposure to hazardous chemicals, biologicals and radiologicals. The detection device, drugs for prophylaxis, stored uncontaminated foods available commercially are described for storage for the emergency. It has also been discussed that there is a need for providing psychological and religious counseling to the victims, members of the family of victims and very often the eyewitnesses. Also no one should forget that the victims and their families need proper rehabilitation. Apart from the Government, the Philanthropic and Charitable organizations have a major role to play in this area.

It must be kept in mind that accidents happen when safety ends. If there are lapses in the preventive and precautionary measures, the casualties will be definitely more as and when one has to face an accident or terrorist attack using chemical/biological/radiological agents. Personal safety always depends upon the knowledge of personal protection per se, protective device or agents, its source of availability, to make arrangement for possessing them, and keeping them within easy access. One should also know how to use or wear them properly. Constantly improving safety conditions and developing disaster preparedness can reduce the chances and impact of chemical, biological and radiological disasters reduced to a minimum. In fact, Disaster's handling is no individual's job. It requires collective actions, with of course the major participation of the Government Agencies. Development of suitable machinery, Disaster

Control Groups and specific Disaster Management plans, to deal with critical situations will further scale down the calamities. Since prevention is better than cure, anticipatory actions for disaster control in hazardous chemical, biological and atomic energy establishments are necessary.

Predictive and preventive toxicology has a major role in this. The following recommendations are offered for anticipatory action to avoid chemical or biological accidents or attacks and their after effects.

1. Every major industry making, using, storing or transporting flammable, explosive or toxic chemicals/ biologicals/radiologicals in large amounts should have an effective, well planned, streamlined disaster control program with all requisite facilities and trained manpower.
2. The city/district/state administration with the help of proper governmental expertise (medical, labor, factory inspectorate etc.) should have a disaster control program.
3. Inventory of potential disaster sites in each unit and each town is required to be made and constant vigil should be sounded at state and central level.
4. Institutional facilities and training should be organized for disaster containment, management, clean up and rehabilitation.
5. Disaster medicine should be developed as a discipline to implement action plan and monitoring system.
6. Role of predictive and preventive toxicology in disaster management should be effectively realized. It should be put to use through the existing R & D Institutions. Say for example, in a country like USA, Institutions like NIH, NIEHS, NIOSH, OSHA, National Toxicology Program, CDC etc. and many other Institutions can be utilized for providing necessary back-up information as may be required for providing data on diagnosis, and treatment. In India, Institutions like ITRC, Lucknow for Toxicology, NIOH, Ahmedabad for Occupational Health, NICED, Calcutta for dealing with enteric diseases, Virus Research Laboratory at Pune, India to deal with Virus infection, Center for Communicable and Infectious Diseases, New Delhi for dealing with infectious disease control, NEERI, Nagpur, India for Environmental Engineering, the entire group of CSIR and ICMR Laboratories, Medical Colleges and Hospitals can be engaged to take part in respective areas of its expertise to provide an effective control. Similar such Institutes in other countries and or their smaller counterparts can serve the same purpose.
7. Disaster preparedness planning at the central and state level should be a priority area and appropriate institutions and agencies should be created for that purpose.
8. Creation of awareness and development and compilation of know-how and its release to users, for all aspects of disaster containment, should be done by appropriate agencies.

9. In areas where indigenous capabilities are limited such as dispersion of pollutants and atmospheric chemistry, technology (conventional and genetic) for clean up and development of simple diagnostic and curative methods, considerable amount of research and development work may be necessary. In this regard, collaborative approach with International agencies such as WHO, NIH and CDC of USA, BIBRA of England, IAEA of UN at Vienna and similar such agencies of the world is necessary.
   (*a*) Brain storming sessions among all sectors (industries, government, local administration, labor, society, and scientists) in each location will help in identifying problems involving collective programs and in testing and improving safety measures.
   (*b*) The principles involved in disaster preparedness, as outlined in this treatise, should be put to use by all concerned with industrial health and safety.
   (*c*) Well-equipped mobile laboratories for providing necessary help during the disaster, to provide relief, containment of the hazardous substances, and evacuation, follow up should be organized in each of the major industrial belts with high density of industries. In India, heavily industrialized cities and states are-Ahmedabad, Gujrat, Bombay, Kolkata, Gaziabad, Faridabad, New Delhi, Kanpur, UP, Haryana, Punjab, Bangalore, Hyderabad, Chennai, Cochin, Tatanagar, Jamshedpur, Asansole, Haldia and Durgapur. By rail and road, the teams could reach any unit in the vicinity also. In other countries, detailed plans are to be made.
   (*d*) Transport of hazardous chemicals or biologicals by rail or road has to be regulated, taking into account possible accidents and their effects. It should be kept in mind that good judgement comes from experience. Constant improvement of the processes and safety precautions, through the process of learning from research and development can insure the safety of mankind against any chemical disaster.

Appendix I

EMERGENCY RESPONSE SYSTEM

WHO-IPCS (1981) Guidelines for Emergency Response Systems to Chemical Accidents

Note: The same can be adopted for dealing with bioterrorism and terrorism using radiological agents also, with some changes here and there.

A. Types of Emergencies

(*i*) Disaster explosion in a plant handling toxic substances.

(*ii*) Accidents in storage facilities for large amounts.

(*iii*) Accidents during transport.

(*iv*) Large-scale contamination of food, water and environment by chemicals, biologicals and radiological substances.

(*v*) Improper waste management.

B. Criteria for Emergency Planning

(*i*) Level of accident (operator, community, country and international).

(*ii*) Type of operation (probability of accidents).

(*iii*) Character of accident (poison, fire, explosion).

(*iv*) Characteristics of chemical or biological toxicity (immediate, short term, long term, environmental persistence).

(*v*) Local condition.

(*vi*) Probable consequences.

C. Systemic Approach to Establishment of Emergency Response System

(*i*) Investigation of vulnerable points, processes and activities.

(*ii*) Estimation of possible chemical spills or dispersion of biological agents.

(*iii*) Knowledge of toxicity or infectivity.

(*iv*) Knowledge of protective and remedial measures.

(*v*) Designation of responsibilities.

(*vi*) Preparation of plan of action.

(*vii*) Establishment of liaison with external authorities.

(*viii*) Resource mobilization for handling the emergency.

(*ix*) Communications.

D. Structure and Elements of Emergency Response System

(*i*) Alert system.

(*ii*) Evaluation and classification of accidents.

(*iii*) Activation of response system.

(*iv*) Provision of information to the higher ups (fire fighting, police, health, transport, care administration etc.).

(*v*) Channeling of external help.

(*vi*) Quick implementation of predictive and remedial measures.

(*vii*) Continuous monitoring of past accident situation, adoption of strategies,

(*viii*) Maintenance of communication levels.

(*ix*) Preparation of plan for rehabilitation.

(*x*) Past accident analysis and evaluation of response activities.

(*xi*) Reporting.

Appendix II

EVALUATION OF PUBLIC HEALTH HAZARDS ASSOCIATED WITH CHEMICAL ACCIDENTS. WHO (CF. SILANO, 1981)

Similar procedure can be utilized for evaluation of public health hazards caused by biological and radiological agents.

A. Statistics of Previous Major Chemical Disasters

Table 4 : Release of Chlorine

Location	*Date D/M/Y*	*Area/site*	*Source of leakage*	*Quantity released, tons/Number of fatalities*
Baton rouge, Lousiana	10/12/76	Rural	Rail	90/0
Brandsville, Pennsylvania	28/4/63	Rural	Rail tanker	8/0
Cornwall, Ontario	30/12/62	Urban/Rural	Rail tanker	28/0
La barre, Louisiana	31/1/61	Urban/rural	Railway tanker	27/0
Lake Charles Louisiana	10/3/56	Factory	Connecting pipe work	3/0
Mobile Alabama	12/7/64	Factory	Pipeline	Unknown/1
Walsum Germany	4/4/52	Factory	Storage tank	15/7
Zarnesti Rumania	24/12/39	Factory	Storage tank	26/60
St.Auban France	13/12/26	Factory	Storage tank	24/19
Rauma Finland	5/11/47	Factory	Storage tank	30/1
Mojdolen Norway	24/1/40	Factory	Rail Tanker	7/3

Table 5 : Release of Ammonia

Location	*Date D/M/Y*	*Area/site*	*Source of leakage*	*Quantity released, tons/Number of fatalities*
Potchefstroom S. Africa	13/7/73	Urban	Storage tank	38/18
Crete, Nebraska	18/2/69	Urban	Rail tanker	90/9
Houston, Texas	11/5/76	Urban	Road Tanker	19/6
Lievin, France	21/8/68	Urban	Road Tanker	19/6
Landskrona, Sweden	16/1/76	Port	Ship storage Connection	180/2

Table 6 : Sudden Releases of Flammable Gases or Vapor

Location	*Date D/M/Y*	*Area/ site*	*Source of leakage*	*Nature of incident/ material*	*Quantity (tones) involved*		*Number before/ after Fatalities*
Bhopal, India	2-3/12/84	Urban	Storage tank	Explosion/ MIC	40	~ 1	2,500 people, livestock, properties
Climax, Texas, USA	29/6/74	Rural	Rail Tanker	Explosion/ Vinyl Chloride	>100	100	0
Decatur, Illinois, USA	19/7/74	Urban	Rail Tanker	Explosion, Fire/ Isobutane	69	10	7
Austin	22/2/73	Rural	pipe line	Fire/NGL	530	80-100	6
Flixborough	1/6/74	Factory	Chemical Reactor	Explosion/ Cyclohexane	> 40	40	28
Ludwigshafen Germany	28/7/48	Factory Tanker	Rail dimethyl	Explosion/	30	30	207
Meldrim, USA Georgia	28/6/59	Rural	Rail minethyl	Fire/LPG	36	18	23
New Berlin, NY,USA	25/7/62	Urban	Road Tanker	Fire/LPG	13	13	10

(Contd...)

Beek Holland	7/11/75	Refinery	Reactor	Explosion/ propopylene	5.5	5.5	14
Los Angeles Calif./USA	18/1/43	Rural	Road Tanker	Fire/ butane	8	8	5
Longview Texas, USA	25/2/71	Factory	½ diam. pipe line	Explosion/ ethylene	0	5	4
Cleveland, Ohio, USA	20/10/44	Urban	Bulk Storage	Fire and Explosions LNG	>2000	128-136	
San Carlos, Spain	11/7/78	Holiday camp	Road Tanker	Fire/ Propylene	>221	>150	
Amsterdam, Holland	10/8/71	Factory		Explosion/ Butadiene	>45	8	
Lake Charles, Luisiana USA	8/8/67	Refinery	Storage sphere connec-tion	Explosion/ isobutane	40	7	
Natchitoches Louisiana, USA	4/2/65	Urban	Pipeline	Explosion/ Methane	17	21	
Antywerp, Belgium	10/2/75	Factory	Com-pressor pipe	Explosion/ Ethylene	4	6	
Umm Said Qater	3/4/77	Refinery	Storage Tank	Explosion & Fire/NGL	—	6	
Devers Texas, USA	12/5/75	Rural	Pipeline	Explosion/ NGL	800	4	
Hearne Texas, USA	14/5/72	Rural	Pipeline	Explosion, Fire/Crude oil	1000	1	
Petal City, Missisippi, Several USA	25/8/74	Storage	plant	Underground Explosion/ Storage cavernbutane (LPG)	100	0	

A close look to the above figures (Table 4, 5 and 6) reveal that both in rural and urban areas accidents took place, but apparently the number of fatalities are somewhat more in the urban areas than in the rural surroundings. This could be due to the population density in the urban areas. Thus from the hazard point of view, such type of industries should not be allowed to be established in urban environment.

Other information resulting out of these historical data point out to the fact that majority of accidents were caused due to explosions and fire, and from volatile organic liquids. Gradual increase in vapor pressure in the storage tanks, improper checking at periodic intervals either to seal leaks in an appropriate manner or to install proper safety checks etc. may have caused sudden explosions and fire during these accidents. The major casualties were seen in the Bhopal Disaster in India in the year 1984. A detailed discussion on the Bhopal Disaster are given in an appropriate place in the book.

The historical data also provides information regarding the most vulnerable areas of accidents, such as storage tanks, pipeline, road/rail tanker, reactors, refineries etc. These places should be under HIGH ALERT situation. All types of safeguards should be installed around these areas to protect them from both accidents and/or terrorist attacks.

Table 7

Locations	*Date D/M/Y*	*Area/ site*	*Circumstances*	*Material involved*	*Tons*	*No. of fatalities*
Oppaau, Germany	21/9/21		Store Exploded	Ammonium Nitrate	4000	561
Texas City Texas, USA	16-18/4/47	Docks	Two ships blew up	Ammonium Nitrate	~ 4000	550
Brest, France	28/4/47	Docks	Ship blew up	Ammonium Nitrate	2500	21
Doc Run, New York	17/5/62	Factory	Storage tank blew up, aerial explosions followed	Ethylene oxide	35	1
Antwerp, Belgium	4/6/64	Factory	Reflux vessel Blew up, aerial Explosions followed	Ethylene oxide	1	1

From the above data (Table 7) it reveals that ammonium nitrate and ethylene oxides are yet another two extremely sensitive organic chemicals, which may lead to explosions, causing major casualties.

B. Responsibilities of People Concerned with Individual Accidents or Terrorist Attacks

(*a*) Responsibilities of industry/establishment (Operator/Director Disaster Control) in the control of accidents or terrorist attacks,

(*i*) The Operator/Director should develop a contingency plan and ensure that it is compatible with that of the local community;

(*ii*) They should have their own emergency services, or make such arrangements with the local community to use theirs;

(*iii*) They should cooperate and collaborate with different authorities, providing all the information for an effective, coordinated contingency plan;

(*iv*) They should conduct hazard survey from time to time, indicating all the risks and possible remedial measures which are required, and ensure that these are done appropriately and in proper time;

(*v*) They should share information with other plants in the same locality;

(*vi*) They should provide mutual assistance by providing equipment and trained personnel, particularly in case of major accidents or attacks resulting in a crisis, and access to centers of expertise;

(*vii*) They should follow international labeling and handling procedures;

(*viii*) They should provide public authorities with all toxicological, medical, and other relevant information.

C. Responsibilities of the Local, Regional, and National Governments in the Control of Accidents or Terrorist Attacks:

(*i*) The Government should require all chemical biological/radiological (using or producing) industries to undertake a "major hazard analysis" and submit it to the Government for approval;

(*ii*) They should require all chemical industries to prepare and submit for approval a contingency plan; this requirement, as well as the former one, should apply to all premises where potentially hazardous chemicals and biologicals are prepared, handled or stored;

(*iii*) They should prepare their own plan for coordinating the many agencies and levels of Government involved in responding to an accident or a terrorist attack; it is particularly important that a national contingency plan be developed, adopted and tested before it needs to be exercised;

(*iv*) They should mobilize, identify and maintain lists of experts advice at all levels, including the lower and even the highest levels;

(*v*) They should maintain information at the local level on all potentially toxic chemicals in or transported through that area; it is important that at least sufficient information be readily available to deal with any emergency that might arise;

(*vi*) They should give careful consideration to prohibiting transportation of all certain potentially toxic chemicals on certain routes through certain jurisdictions; this can restrict the area at risk and under emergency response more manageable;

(*vii*) They should engage negotiations with neighboring countries where chemical and biological plants are close to national boundaries;

(*viii*) They should engage in negotiations with the surrounding countries where chemical plants are close to the national boundaries, so that any contingency plan involving a transboundary effect be complete and approved *a priori*;

(*ix*) They should consult with unions, conservation groups, and professional and learned societies in the development of laws and regulations concerning chemical biological and radiological products;

(*x*) They should ask all the industries , which have been involved in an accident, to submit detailed report and indicate as to how to improve upon the methodology to avert such accidents;

(*xi*) They should involve industrial experts in analyzing accident reports to improve safety for the future.

D. Responsibilities for the Scientists in the Control of Accidents or Terrorist Attack

Scientists who are required to give expert assistance in a chemical or biological radiological disaster should:

(*i*) Provide information for contingency planning in advance;

(*ii*) In an emergency, be able to provide soon, reliable information under stress, so that it can be understood and acted upon by layman, such as firemen and police;

(*iii*) Know, and be known to, scientists and experts in other countries so that they can exchange information rapidly, in an inter-personal information network;

(*iv*) Be available at, or to, data banks and information centers in order to interpret the data of the accident; this availability should be on 24-hour basis;

(*v*) Include social and economic scientists, as well as national, environmental and medical representatives;

(*vi*) Maintain an up-to date roster of national experts and have one of them identified as an international contact in case help is needed in another country;

(*vii*) Form an international committee of such contact persons to meet from time to time to exchange experiences, and to evaluate control actions taken in cases of major emergencies;

(*viii*) Be able to be effective under pressure, and wearing protective equipment; such equipment, in the possession of those scientists expected to play such a role, should be routinely tested and maintained;

(*ix*) Assist in proposing short term emergency exposure tolerable limits for various risk populations to permit evacuation decisions to be taken as appropriate; premature evacuation decisions can have just as high social costs as late decisions;

(*x*) Take part in the evaluation of accident records for the purpose of preventing or mitigating future accidents;

(*xi*) Help to plan pre-agreed detoxification and rehabilitation procedure.

E. Questionnaire for Data Collection on Potential Risks in Stationary Installations

1. (*i*) Name and location of enterprise

   (*ii*) Sector

   (*iii*) Category (food, chemical, microbiological etc.)

   (*iv*) Kinds of goods (used, stored, produced, marketed)
2. personnel and working condition
3. Dimensions (area, layout,set plan with details)
4. Past records
5. Health Services (first aid, transportation, medical care system, hospital facilities)
6. Chemical biological/radiological agents (raw materials, intermediate products, solvents, primary products, secondary products, run away reaction products etc.). For each chemical following information are required:

   (*i*) Name of the chemical biologial/radiological.

   (*ii*) Quantity (maximum retained and utilized or produced per day).

   (*iii*) Calculated risks (fire explosion, toxicity and any other).
7. Description of the process (production, scheme, cycle, regulatory precaution etc.)
8. Emanations, effluents and solid wastes

   (*i*) Substances emanated, amounts (*a*) normal working (*b*) abnormal cases

   (*ii*) Frequency

   (*iii*) Method of treatment and (*iv*) disposal.
9. Security and safety system, description, monitoring, vigilance, precautions.
10. Health indications

    (*i*) Occupational health

    (*ii*) Industrial toxicology

    (*iii*) Environmental hygiene

    (*iv*) Ecological impact

Fire and explosion hazards.

F. Protocol for Acquisition of Data for Retrospective Study of Accidents or Terrorist Attack

1. Source of production

   (*i*) Raw materials, fuels, products, energy, electricity

   (*ii*) Transportation (vehicles, pipelines, cranes)

(*iii*) Services

(*iv*) Storage (all types)

(*v*) Disposal processes (waste management, treatment, recycling, burning, dumping).

2. Apparent cause

Collision, derailment, crash, overflow, leak, discharge, gasket joint of valve failure, mixture of chemicals, terrorist attack, bombing missile attack etc.

3. Apparent reason

Intent, error, vandalism, negligence, natural calamity, fire explosion, power failure, machine failure, physical damage, terrorist intent, warfare

4. Site and area affected
5. Amount of chemical released
6. Properties of chemical released

(*i*) Explosives, gases, radioactive substances, oxidizers, inflammables, corrosive substances.

(*ii*) Toxic substances (Chronic, acute poisons, irritants, allergens, mutagens, carcinogens, teratogens, pathogens, recalcitrant substances, ecological poisons etc.)

7. Dynamics of chemical release (self evident), non-evident or unknown)
8. Main routes of human exposure (air, water, soil, food, contact)
9. Human health impact data

(*i*) Mortality (number of casualties, post-mortem data)

(*ii*) Morbidity (age wise distribution, acute illness, chronic illness).

9. Environmental, social, and economical impact

(*i*) Damage to soil microflora and productivity

(*ii*) Damage to vegetation crops

(*iii*) Damage to livestock, wild life

(*iv*) Damage to aquatic flora and fauna

(*v*) Environmental contamination

(*vi*) Residual level risks

(*vii*) Social and economic disruption

(*ix*) Duration of effects

(*x*) Total economic loss.

10. Environmental rehabilitation methods (evacuations, contaminant, removal, treatment, chemical and biological disposal, recycling, dumping, rehabilitation of affected people)
11. Level of resources management for emergency response or rehabilitation.

Appendix III

COMMUNITY PREPAREDNESS/CAPABILITY FOR SUDDEN EMERGENCIES INVOLVING HAZARDOUS MATERIALS

(Based on Tierney, 1982)

A. Definition

Disaster preparedness refers to all documents, activities, formal or informal agreements and social arrangements which over the short and long-term are intended to reduce the probability of disaster and/or the severity of the community disruption occasioned by its occurrence.

B. Some Examples

(*i*) Meetings to share knowledge on disaster planning

(*ii*) Holding disaster drills, rehearsals, simulations

(*iii*) Developing techniques for training, information transfer, hazard assessment, containment.

(*iv*) Mutual aid agreements

(*v*) Awareness education

(*vi*) Drawing up community disaster preparedness organization.

Responsibilities

Local industry—In-plant safety, adherence to hygiene standards, resources and information

Local government and public safety organizations—Coordination of various activities, liaison with various agencies, external help, evacuation supervision, expertise.

Civil defense—Volunteer free essential services, transport of man and material.

Fire department—Fire protection, rescue

Law enforcement—Controlling the situation

Private relief organizations—First aid, evacuation, rehabilitation, supply of essential items, nursing

Hospital and medical services—First aid, antidotes, follow up

Voluntary agencies/local residents—Support to all the above, contribution of service, material and knowhow

Media—Actual awareness creation, precautions to be taken, to avoid unwanted panic.

Community Checklist of Resources and Disaster Preparedness Activities

1. Community disaster plan.
2. Role, persons, addresses, and activities of fire, police, civil defense, hospitals, industries etc., in the plan.
3. Specific emergency responses and persons responsible in the society, e.g. warning, evacuation, rescue, first aid etc.
4. Safety system in factory
5. Local safety enforcement mechanism of Government
6. Drills, training, facilities and resources for the disaster preparedness program
7. Inventory of material—human and informational sources.
8. Liaison with other agencies
9. Assessment of specific risks and development of containment methods.

Appendix IV

TYPICAL ORGANIZATION FOR DISASTER PREPAREDNESS

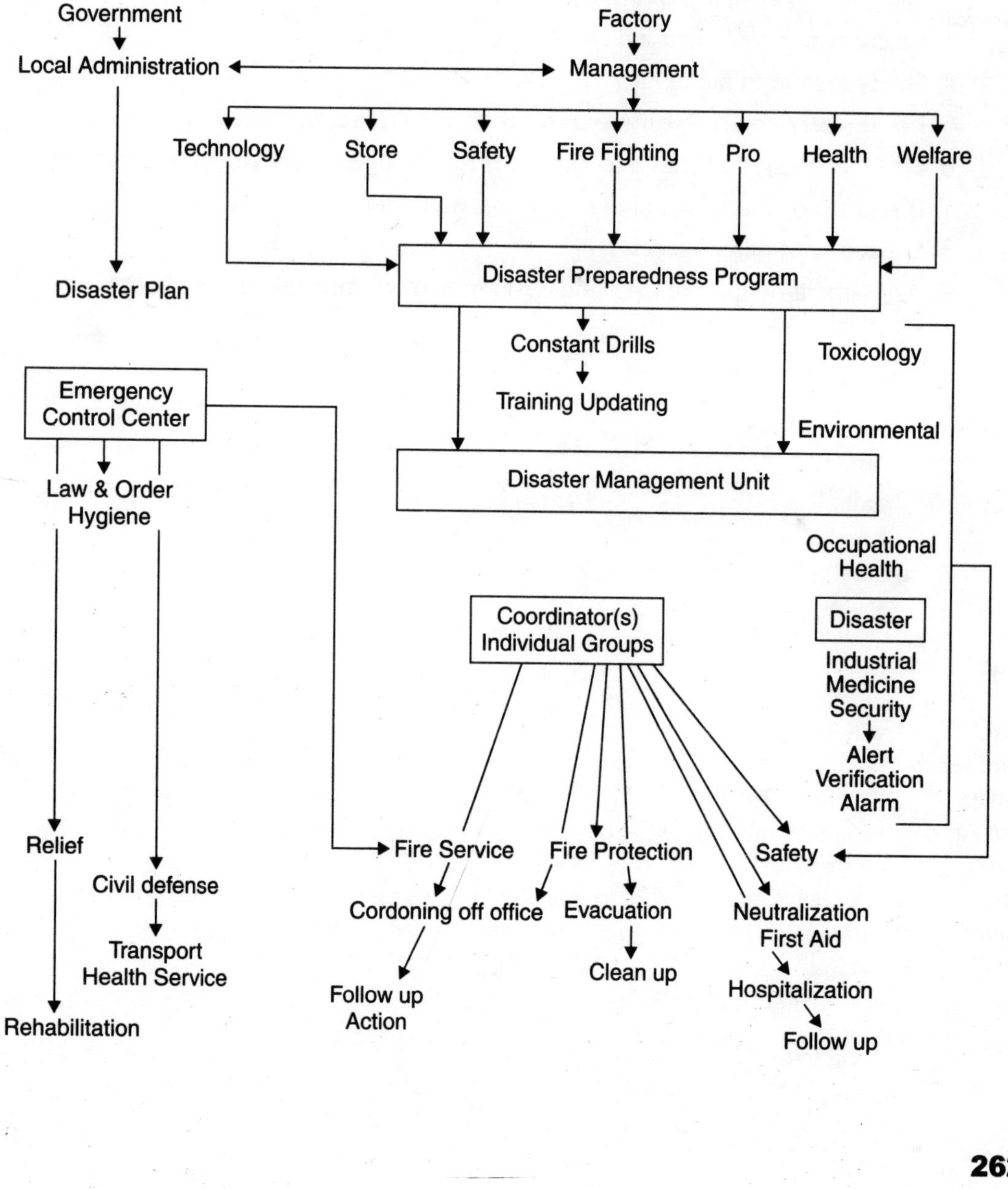

Appendix V

DISASTER MANAGEMENT INFORMATION ON SOME MAJOR AND COMMON HAZARDOUS CHEMICALS

Source: Handling Chemical Safety, Dutch Association, Safety Experts (Sax, 1982)

Chemical	*Toxicity/Hazards*	*Prevention*	*First Aid treatment*	*Spillage Containment Storage*
1	*2*	*3*	*4*	*5*
Acetic acid MAC 10ppm with pungent smell	Flammable, could form explosive mixtures with air above 40C. Highly reactive, attacks metal producing hydrogen. Inhalation : Pungent, Sore throat, breathing trouble, edema. Eye: Corrosion, blurred vision. Skin: Corrosive. Ingestion: Spasm, nausea diarrhea, serious fatal cases.	No flames, sparks, ventilation needed, resporatory protection (self contained protective face sheild)	Fire fighting, alcohol resistant foam, water, CO_2, NO powder fresh air, half up-right position, doctor, hospital with excess water.	Collect liquid in sealable containers, wash remainder rest with rinsing large amount of water. No splashing. Fire-proof storage, away from oxidants. Never pour acid into water. Acrylonitrile
(Vinyl Chloride), MAC 4 ppm, vapor heavier than air, travels along ground.	Flammable could form explosive mix. with air Inhalation: Breathing difficulty, dizziness, irritant, metabolic inhibitation, corrosive to skin, eyes, somethimes much after contact, serious cases unconsciousness, death.	No open flames sparks, closed systems, ventilation, strict hygiene, breathing protection protective gloves, clothing.	Fire fighting powder foam, CO_2, keep drums cool by water spray. Rinse with water, fresh air, rest, on inhalation call doctor, hospital.	Evacuate, consult experts, collect liquid in sealable containers or inert adsorbent, neutralization with chlorine, bleaching liquor.

(Contd...)

1	*2*	*3*	*4*	*5*
Ammonia MAC 25ppm, lighter than air	Combustible, explosive mixture with water. Highly reactive with acids, oxidants, halogens corrosive to eye, skin, lungs. Inhalation causes breathing trouble, edema. Rapid evaporation of liquid causes frost bite.	No open flames, closed system ventilation. Cold insulated gloves, protective clothing face shield, eye protection and resporatory protection.	Close leakage extinguish with powder, CO_2. Keep temp. cool. Rinse with plenty of water, Doctor.	Needs experts, evacuate danger area never play water jet on liquid. Water curtain for gas cloud, walled area for confinement store fire-proof away from acids, halogen under pressure or liquid.
Benzene MAC value 10 ppm, heavier than air.	Flammable, travels along ground with distant, ignition can cause static electricity. Do not use compressed air strongly reactive, explodes in air inhalation: Headache, nausea, dizziness, unconsciousness, systemic toxicity, hemopoietic effect.	No open flames, sparks, closed system ventilation respiratory protection, gloves, protective clothing face shield, eye protection.	Fire fighting powder, foam, CO_2, keep drum cool by water spray, fesh air, artificial resporation, rinse contaminated clothing, with water, doctor, hospital.	Collect liquid in sealable container. Adsorption sand remove (additional respiratory protection needed) Unbreakable packaging or container. Fire proof storage in cold.
Bromine MAC 0.10 ppm reddish brown fumes, pungent odor.	Not combustible but reactive. Inhalation: Sore throat, respiratory difficulty, dizziness corrosive to eyes and skin. Ingestion: Highly toxic, spasm, irritant.	Ventilation, respiratory protection protective gloves, clothes face shield, eye protection.	Keep temp. cool fresh air, half-upright position rest, doctor hospital. Rinse contaminated clothes ith planety of water.	Evacuate danger area, call experts, collect and seal materials, wash away, neutralize with lime water. Cool, dry, ventilation along floor in storage.

(Contd...)

1	2	3	4	5
Chlorine MAC 1.0 ppm, greenish yellow pungent gas, heavier than air.	Not combustible highly reactive, fire rish with hydrogen, ammonia reacts with moisture. Inhalation: Pungency sore throat, trouble in breaking, corrosive to eye or skin, causes delayed lung edema.	Respiratory protection, stable gloves, face shield, protective clothing.	Keep cylinder cool, fresh air, rest, half up-right position doctor. Remove contaiminated clothes. Rinse with plenty of water, cortico-steroids.	Evacuate danger area, neutralize with alkali (dilute) wash away with water. Combat gas with water curtain. Cool, dry storage. Do not apply water spray on leaking cylinder.
Hydrochloric acid, MAC 5 ppm (ceiling) fuming liquid.	Not combustible inhalation pungent, cough, shortness of breath. Corrosive to eye, skin. Lung edema, abdominal pain, highly reactive.	Ventilation Resp. protection, gloves, protective clothing face sheild, eye protection.	Fresh air, rest half up-right position, remove contaminated clothes, wash with water, doctor, corticosteroids.	Collect and seal material, precipitate fumes with water spray neutralize and wash with water. Keep away from bases, oxidants, unbreakable container.
Nitric acid MAC 2 ppm	Not combustible highly reactive, oxidizing, may cause explosion. Inhalation: Pungency, cough, labored breathing corrosive to eye, skin and G.I. tract, NO_2 is a systemic toxic oxidant.	Ventilation resp. protection gloves, goggles, face sheilds, protective clothing.	Keep drums cool with water, fresh air, rest, half up-right position, hospital, remove contaminated clothes, rinse with lot of water.	Collect, seal, remove adsorb on inert subs. Wash off with water. Store away from combustible and reducing subs., dark and cool ventilation, Inbreakable containers.
Oleum (H_2SO_4) MAC 1 ppm, Pungent odor	Not combustible reactive, may cause explosion. Inhalation: Pungent breathing problem, corrosive to eye, skin, G.I. Tract, dehydration, generates heat.	Ventilation, exhaust, resp. protection, gloves, face shield, protective clothing.	No direct contact with water. Amyl nitrate, half up-right position, hospital.	Evacuate the danger area. call expert. Collect samples in proper container. Cordon off to minimum spreadings (soil) combat gas cloud with water curtain store away.

(Contd...)

1	2	3	4	5
Phosgene MAC 0.02 ppm	Not combustible highly reactive, severe respiratory poisoning. edema. Corrosive to skin, eye, edema aggravates with time and exertion.	Keep cylinder cool, ventilation, gloves, goggles, face shield, respirators.	Fresh air, half upright position hospital, corticosteroid spary.	Evacuate the danger area, ventilation. Avoid heat (330 C) and water which decompose it into toxic gases store away from oxidants, ammonia, and cool.

CLEAN UP TECHNOLOGY

Various Treatment Systems that could be Used for Clean Up

Technique	*Useful in the case of*
Carbon adsorption	Chlorinated hydrocarbons, organic phosphates,nitiles,volatile organics
pH adjustment	Ammonia, nitriles, organics
Air stripping	Ammonia, nitriles, organics
Precipitation	Latex
Neutralization	Chlorine, caustics, ammonia,acids and bases, depending on nature of chemicals
Biological	Chlorinated hydrocarbons, organic phosphates
Destruction	White phosphorous
Dilution	Chlorine, acid, alkali
Mixing	Chlorine, acid, alkali
Land spraying	Organophosphate, acid, alkali, volatiles

The sequence is to be decided by the nature of the substance, e.g., for chlorine, the correct order is neutralization, mixing dilution, and land spraying, while it is pH, air striping, dilution and land spraying for ammonia. The technical details and the development of mobile units for clean-up are also given by Smith (1981).

Appendix VI

PREPAREDNESS OF A CONTINGENCY PLAN AT THE OPERATOR LEVEL

Flow Chart for the Preparation of a Contingency Plan at the Operator Level

Stage	*Activity*	*Assisted by*
1	*2*	*3*
Planning Process	Assignment of responsibilities for contingency planning and for Implementation of emergency Response system	Decision of Management
	Assessment of the risk	Provision of expert advice
	Drafting of Emergency Response System	Provision of expert advice
	— Alert Procedure	Management and community
	— Monitoring and Evaluating Situation	Provision of external help Environmental Services Expert Laboratories Data bank
Elements Of Emergency Response System to be Considered	— Decision making Process on alerting of Emergency Response System	Verification by Experts (Additional) Approval by management
	— Utilization of own resources And provision of external help	Establishment of cooperation with community authorities Fire brigade Ambulance Health Services & Hospitals, Police Military or Civil Defense Services

(Contd...)

1	2	3
		Ensuring provision of Extl. Help Personnel Equipment Material
	— Implementation of protective and Remedial actions	Provision of the expert Advice
	— Preparation for plans for reclamative and rehabilitative actions	Provision of expert advice Guidelines from community
	— Analysis of the accident and evaluation of the response activities	appraisal by experts, External approval and management and community
	— Preparation of the final report of the Accident	
Approval and Testing system	Approval of Emergency Response System Implementation of Emergency Response System	External appraisal by experts, management and local community. Approval of management And local community
	Periodical testing of the system	Comments from Management from local Point of higher level (Community) and from expert services. Advice and help from the Management Focal point management Community

Appendix VII

PREPAREDNESS OF A CONTINGENCY PLAN AT COMMUNITY LEVEL

Flow Chart

Phase	*Activity*	*Assisted by*
1	*2*	*3*
Planning	Assignment of responsibility For contingency planning and For implementation of Emergency Response System	Decision of relevant Authorities
	Inventory of Vulnerable points	Contingency plan of operators
	Assessment of Risks	
	Drafting of Emergency Response System	Expert advice
Elements of Emergency Response System to be Considered	— Alert Procedure	
	— Links to communication	Expert advice confirmation By focal point of higher level
	— Decision making Procedure	
		Inventory and standard procedure for use of internal resources
	— Utilization of internal resources — And provision of external help	Ensuring provision of additional external help
	— Implementation of protective And remedial actions	Expert advice
	— Preparation of plans for	Expert advice

(Contd...)

1	*2*	*3*
	— Reclamation and rehabilitation	Inventory of resources
	— Analysis of accidents and evaluation of response activities	External appraisal by Experts and higher level
	— Preparation of the final report Of the accident	Focal point approval
Approval and testing of system	Approval and implementation of emergency response system	External appraisal by Experts and focal point of higher level
		Approval of higher Authority and higher focal point
	Periodical testing of the system	Comments from relevant Authority and higher focal point Information to operators

Appendix VIII

ELEVEN POINT PLAN FOR SURVIVAL

Canada Emergency Measures Organization
Department of National Defence

Blueprint for Survival No. 4

(Printed here in public interest)

- **"Make this your handbook for emergencies.**
- **Keep it in a handy place so that you and your family can refer to it quickly should any emergency threaten.**
- **Keep other emergency advice such as first aid and artificial respiration instructions, antidotes for poison, emergency telephone numbers, in the same place."**

INTRODUCTION

The Canadian Government has joined other peace-minded nations in doing everything possible to reduce world tensions, to assist in the settlement of international disputes by peaceful means and to achieve disarmament with such controls as are necessary to preserve the security of all nations. However, the awesome threat of a major nuclear war involving North America remains a factor in plans for the defence of Canada.

The nature and scale of a possible nuclear attack on North America, and the extent to which Canada would be involved in such an attack, cannot be predicted with accuracy. Our major centres would be at some risk of deliberate attack, random explosions could occur, and there would be the certainty of the danger from widespread, radioactive fallout over most of the Country, the blue print started.

Governments at all levels have made, and are continuing to make, preparations which will reduce the number of casualties, safeguard survivors and contribute to the capacity of this nation to survive and recover from such a tragedy. The purpose of this booklet is to assist individuals and families in making personal survival plans and preparations to guard themselves against the potential dangers of nuclear war the blue print started.

Many of the precautions which are recommended will serve a double purpose in that they will save lives in peacetime disasters such as flood, tornado, fire, hurricane, blizzard, ice storm or earthquake. Attention has been directed to this important feature throughout the various steps.

All Canadians are urged to read "11 Steps to Survival" with care to act on the advice it contains and to keep it handy for emergencies the blue print started.

The Queen's Printer
Ottawa, 1969
Cat. No. Id 83-1/4

THE ELEVEN STEPS TO SURVIVAL

Governments and communities at all levels are planning for the survival of our Nation in the event of a nuclear war. But the survival of individuals also will depend upon the preparation that each person makes. Persons ready to take the right action before and following an attack will increase their chances of survival.

This pamphlet describes what YOU can do before and following a nuclear attack. You can greatly increase your family's and your own protection by taking the Eleven Steps to Survival:

- **Step 1:** Know the effects of nuclear explosions.
- **Step 2:** Know the facts about radioactive fallout.
- **Step 3:** Know the warning signal and have a battery-powered radio.
- **Step 4:** Know how to take shelter.
- **Step 5:** Have fourteen days emergency supplies.
- **Step 6:** Know how to prevent and fight fires.
- **Step 7:** Know first aid and home nursing.
- **Step 8:** Know emergency cleanliness.
- **Step 9:** Know how to get rid of radioactive dust.
- **Step 10:** Know your municipal plans.
- **Step 11:** Have a plan for your family and yourself.

Step 1: Know the Effects of Nuclear Explosions

A nuclear explosion releases vast amounts of energy in three forms:

1. Light and heat
2. Blast
3. Radiation

The amount of energy released depends upon the size and design of the weapon. A wide range of weapons and delivery systems are available to an aggressor and we have no way of knowing what size of explosions might take place in Canada. For illustration purposes, we describe in this pamphlet the effects of a 5-megaton H-bomb equal to the explosive force of five million tons of TNT. Such a bomb could substantially damage the largest Canadian city.

The effects depend upon whether the weapon is exploded high in the air, or on, or near the ground. An air burst usually produces more fire and blast-damage than a ground burst which results in a big crater and more radioactive fallout. The effects described below are approximate for a 5-megaton explosion and can only be approximate since effects depend upon a number of conditions such as weather, terrain, etc.

Light and Heat

A blaze of light brighter than the sun is produced by a nuclear explosion. It lasts for about 15 seconds. Temporary blindness and eye injury can result from the glare if eyes are not shielded.

The heat rays from the explosion travel at the speed of light or about 186,000 miles per second. It can start fires up to 20 miles away. Many fires are caused when the heat pulse comes through a window to set fire to curtains, paper, clothing and furniture. The heat flash also can set fire to the outside of wooden buildings.

The following are some examples of the predictable effects on unprotected skin of the heat flash of a 5-megaton weapon exploded on a clear day:

1 Skin is badly burned up to 15 miles from the explosion.
2 Skin is blistered up to 18 miles from the explosion.
3 Sunburn types of burns up to 23 miles from the explosion.

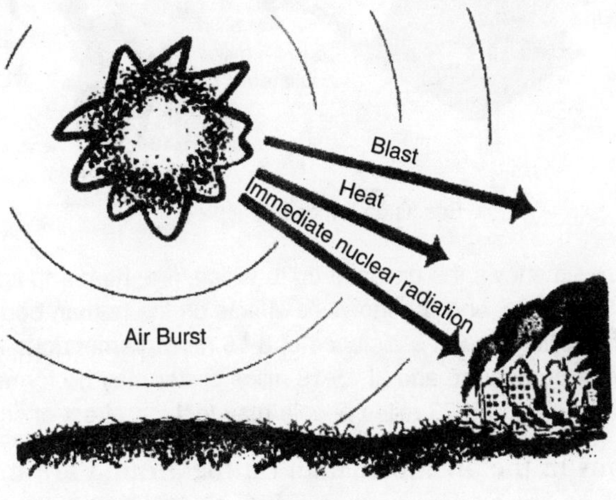

Fig. A

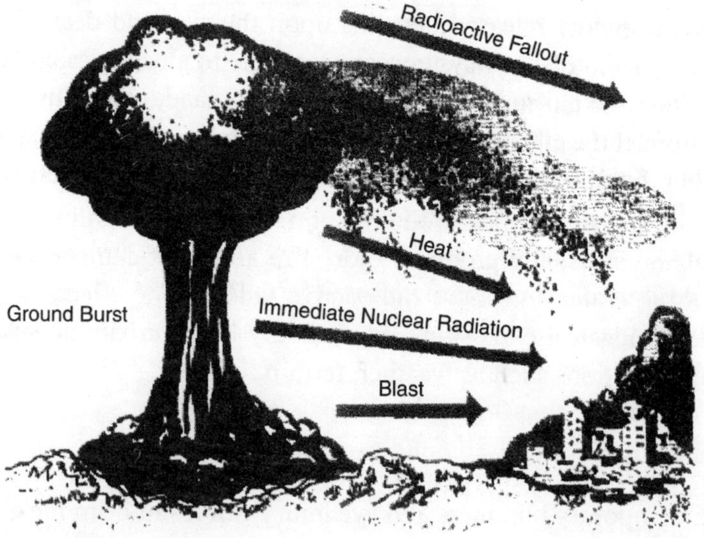

Fig. A-1 : Picture shows the extensive areas covered under Blast, heat and radiation, (*a*) when the blast is in the air, (*b*) when the blast is on the ground. Of course the areas covered will always depend on the amount of explosives, and the nature of the atomic device used.

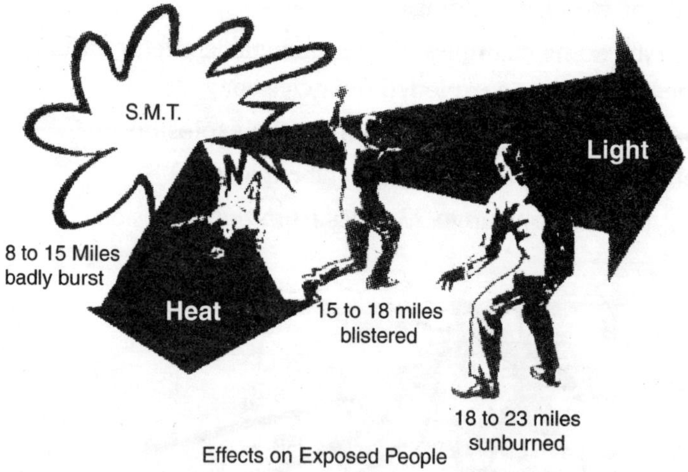

Fig. A-2 : Picture (*a*) shows the distance up to which, fire, heat and light may be seed after an atomic explosion, and (*b*) shows its effects on the human body. Up to 5 miles fire may grip the entire area at a distance of 8-15 miles tremendous amount of heat may cause severe body burn, and at 15-18 miles blister may be formed on the body, and beyond 18 and 23 miles people may feel the effect of sunburn.

Nuclear explosions in the air rather than on the ground are more likely to produce a greater number of serious burns through the heat flash. Clothing will give some protection. A shield between you and the light will give protection against burns from the heat flash.

Blast

The blast wave travels more slowly than the heat flash. Several seconds may pass after you have seen the light or felt the heat before the blast wave reaches you, depending on the distance you are from the explosion. It is like the time between seeing the flash of lightning and hearing the sound of thunder. For example, at ten miles from the centre of an explosion, it would take about 35 seconds for the blast wave to reach you. If caught in the open during a nuclear explosion, this time can be used to find some protection from the blast wave.

You might be injured by being thrown about by the blast; therefore, keep low. The greatest danger is from flying glass, bricks and other debris. The blast from a 5-megaton explosion could injure people as far away as 15 miles.

The kinds of damage that the blast can do to buildings are:

- Complete destruction of all buildings three miles from the centre of the explosion.
- Damage beyond repair to buildings three to five miles distant. They would have to be torn down.
- Major repairs required to buildings five to 10 miles distant before they could be occupied.
- Light to moderate damage to buildings 10 to 15 miles distant. They could be occupied during repairs.

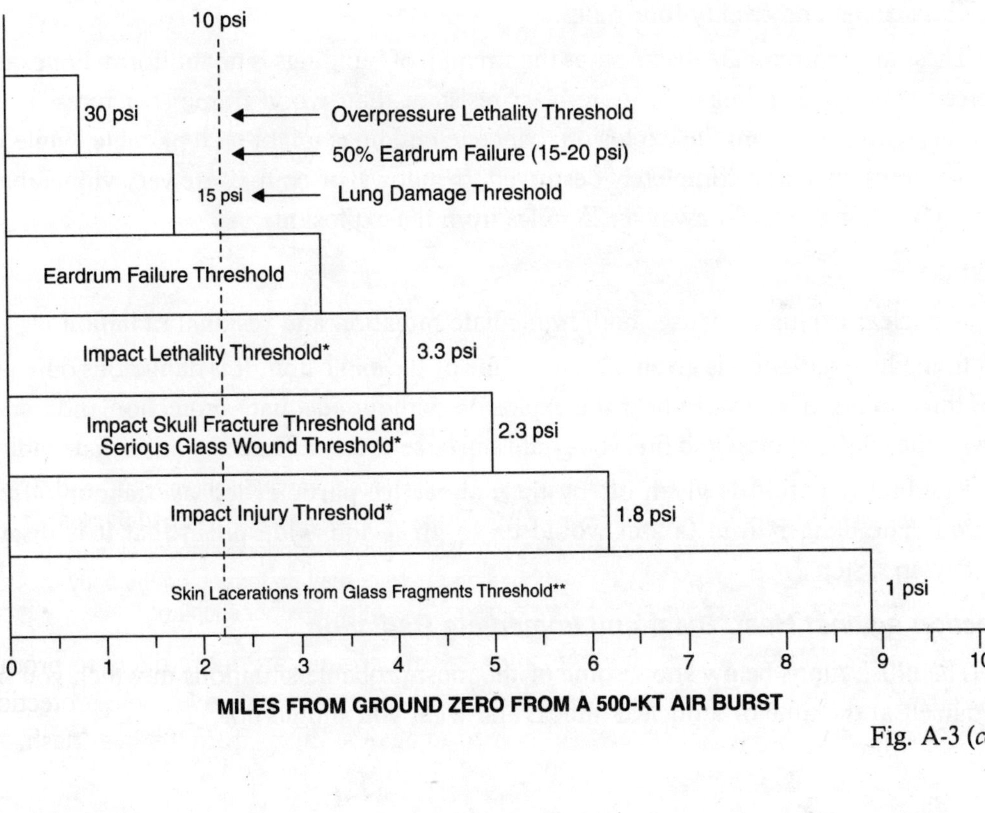

Fig. A-3 (*contd...*)

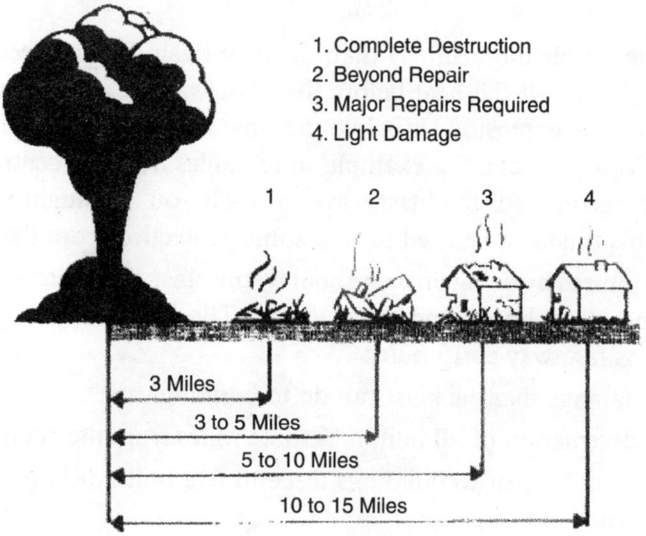

Fig. A-3. A pictorial demonstration of nature of devastations caused by an atomic explosion in extended areas around the center of explosion. A 20-megaton bomb may extend its damage up to 25 miles.

A 20-megaton bomb increases the approximate ranges of damage described above to five, eight, sixteen and twenty-four miles.

These are approximate distances as the strength of buildings is not uniform. For example, reinforced concrete buildings are more blast resistant than wood frame structures. In some areas four miles away from the explosion, concrete buildings might be repairable, while wood frame buildings would be completely destroyed. Windows, of course, are very vulnerable and are apt to be blown in as far away as 25 miles from the explosion.

Radiation

A nuclear explosion causes both immediate radiation and residual radiation.

Immediate radiation is given off at the time of the explosion. It is dangerous only within two or three miles. If you were near the explosion without adequate protection and managed to survive the effects of blast and fire, you could still be seriously affected by immediate radiation.

Residual radiation is given off by the radioactive particles left as "fallout" after the explosion. The danger from fallout would be so great and widespread that it is discussed separately, in >Step 2.

Protection against Heat, Blast and Immediate Radiation

The illustrations below show some of the most probable situations in which you might find yourself at the time of a nuclear attack, and what you should do:

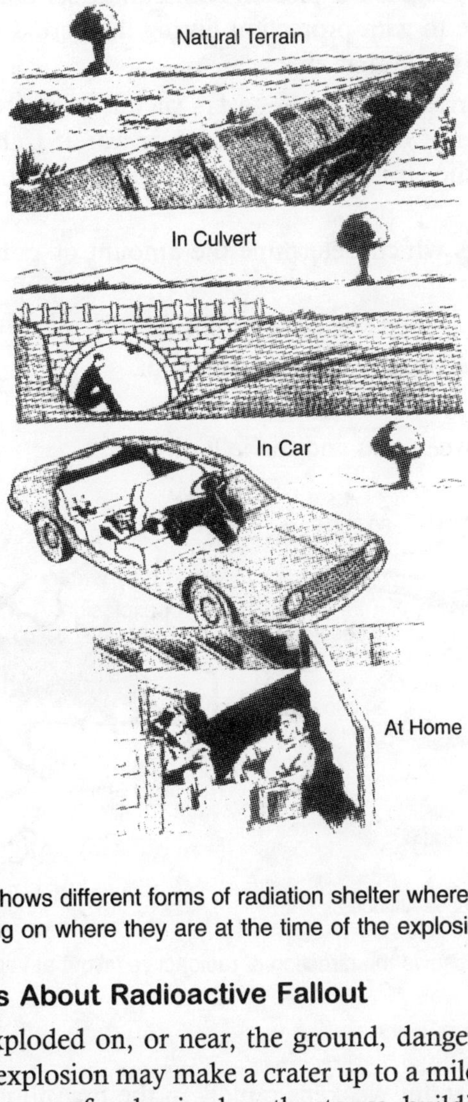

Fig. A-4. Picture shows different forms of radiation shelter where one could take their shelters, depending on where they are at the time of the explosion.

Step 2: Know the Facts About Radioactive Fallout

If a nuclear weapon is exploded on, or near, the ground, danger from radioactive fallout is greatest. The force of the explosion may make a crater up to a mile wide and to a depth of one hundred feet. Millions of tons of pulverized earth, stones, buildings and other materials are drawn up into the fireball and become radioactive. Some of the heavier particles spill out around the point of explosion. The rest are sucked up into the mushroom cloud.

This radioactive material is then carried by winds until it settles to earth. This is called "Fallout". Under some circumstances you may see the fallout; under others you may not.

The radioactivity it gives off cannot be seen. You can't feel it. You can't smell it.

But fallout doesn't come out of the sky like a gas and seep into everything. It can best be described as a fine to coarse sand carried by the winds. Because the wind direction varies at different heights above the ground, it is not possible to judge from the ground where the fallout will settle. It can settle in irregular patterns hundreds of miles from the explosion.

The fallout from a 5-megaton explosion could affect seriously an area of 7,000 square miles. If nothing were done to gain protection during the period of high radioactivity, there would be a grave danger to life in that area.

Because fallout is carried so far and covers such a large area, it could be the greatest danger to the largest number of Canadians in a nuclear war. If Canada was not hit by nuclear bombs, those exploding in the United States close to our border could result in serious fallout in many parts of Canada.

There are four things which determine the amount of radiation reaching your body from fallout:

1. The time that has passed since the explosion.
2. The length of time you are exposed to fallout.
3. The distance you are from the fallout.
4. The shielding between you and the fallout.

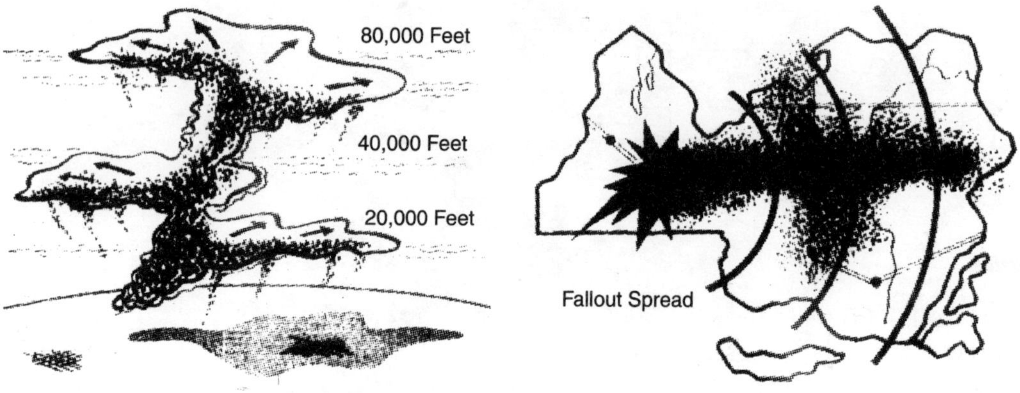

(a) Direction of Fallout at Various Altitudes (b)

Fig. A-5. (*a*) Picture shows the direction of radioactive fallout at various altitudes, and (*b*) fallout spread.

Time

The radioactivity in fallout weakens rapidly in the first hours after an explosion. This weakening is called "decay". After seven hours, fallout has lost about 90% of the strength it had one hour after the explosion. After two days it has lost 99%; in two weeks 99.9% of its strength is gone. Nevertheless, if the radiation at the beginning were high enough, the remaining 0.1% could be dangerous.

Radiation must be measured by special instruments handled by people trained to use them. But, if you stay in a shelter during the first days following an explosion, you escape the strongest radiation. *You should stay in the shelter until radiation has been measured and you have been told aver the radio that it is safe to come out.*

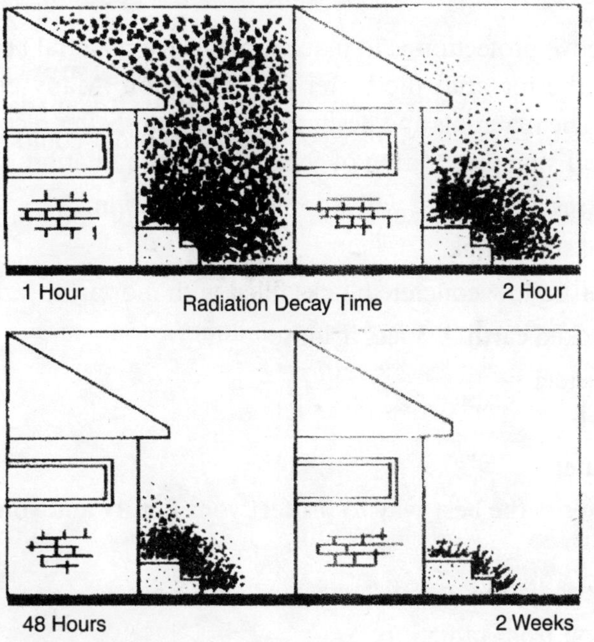

Fig. A-6

Distance

The strength of radiation reaching your body is reduced the farther you are from the fallout. Here are some illustrations of the safest place to be when you are in various kinds of buildings.

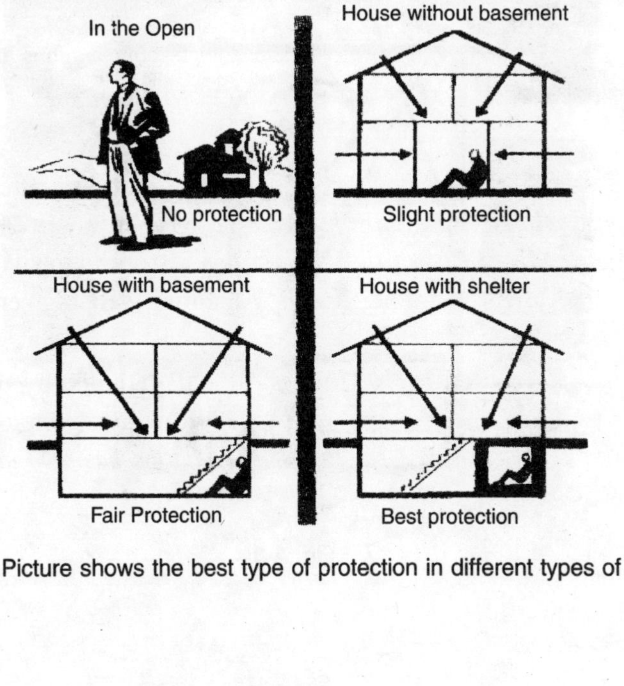

Fig. A-7. Picture shows the best type of protection in different types of houses.

Shielding

The most effective protection is to place some heavy material between yourself and the fallout. The heavier the material the better the protection. Many common materials give excellent protection. The materials and design of the fallout shelter recommended in **Blueprint for Survival No. 1** will stop penetration of 99% of outside radiation.

These thicknesses of material will stop 99% of radiation:

- 16 inches of solid brick
- 16 inches of hollow concrete blocks filled with mortar or sand
- 2 feet of packed earth Ä 3 feet if loose
- 5 inches of steel
- 3 inches of lead
- 3 feet of water

A fallout shelter is the best way to protect your family and yourself against radiation because:

- It keeps the radiation at a distance.
- It shields you from radiation.
- The time spent there is the period when radiation is most intense.

By providing your family and yourself with a fallout shelter, you are unlikely to suffer serious effects from radioactive fallout.

Fig. A-8

Personal Danger from Fallout

Radioactive particles in contact with your skin for a few hours may produce burns. Follow Step 9 to prevent this danger.

Radioactive particles swallowed in food or water might be harmful. Follow Step 9 to prevent this danger.

Radioactivity from an area of fallout may produce illness in the unprotected individual after a few days. Follow Step 4 to prevent this danger.

Radiation illness develops slowly. It cannot be spread to other people. Except for temporary nausea shortly after exposure, evidence of serious effects from radiation may only appear after an interval of from a few days to three weeks. A combination of loss of hair, loss of appetite, increasing paleness, weakness, diarrhoea, sore throat, bleeding gums and easy bruising indicate that the individual requires medical attention. *Nausea and vomiting may be caused by fright, worry, food poisoning, pregnancy and other common conditions.*

Step 3: Know the Warning Signal and have a Battery-Powered Radio

All Canadian communities where there is a likely need are provided, or will be provided, with sirens. Other areas should have warning arrangements based on local systems such as telephones, horns, bells or factory whistles.

Warning devices are only attention-getters. Dependent on the size of your municipality, the sirens, bells, telephones, etc., will sound the Attack Warning.

There is one type of siren warning signal in Canada:

The ATTACK WARNING Signal

The ATTACK WARNING Signal: A wailing (undulating) tone on the sirens of three to five minutes duration or short blasts on horns or other devices repeated as necessary means:

- An attack on North America has been detected;
- Warning of fallout.

WHEN YOU HEAR THE WARNING SIGNAL, YOU SHOULD TAKE PROTECTIVE ACTION AND LISTEN TO THE RADIO FOR INSTRUCTIONS

A Radio is Essential

When the Attack Warning sounds, you must take protective action. Take a battery-powered radio with you. Broadcast advice and instruction may help to save your life. If you don't have a portable radio, turn up the volume of your house radio so that it can be heard in your shelter. If away from home you are forced to take emergency shelter and are near a radio-equipped vehicle, turn up the volume and open all the vehicle's doors or windows.

The Canadian Emergency Broadcasting System, a network of all Canadian radio and television stations which will be formed when a nuclear attack on Canada has been detected, will tell you when and how to take emergency protective action against possible attack and shelter against fallout if an attack occurs.

Fig. A-9

Before Attack

If sirens or warning systems signal impending attack, regardless of where you are or what you are doing, you must take the best available cover against the blast, heat and light effects of nuclear explosions.

Emergency broadcast instructions will include the following advice:

- If you are at home go to the basement or strongest part of your house or building which offers the best protection. If material is handy, improvise blast protection. See Step 4.
- Take your battery radio with you, or turn up the house radio so that you can hear it while under cover.
- Stay away from windows.
- Lie down and protect yourself from flying glass and falling debris.
- Shield your eyes from the flash of an explosion.
- If you are away from home take protective cover immediately.
- If you are travelling, stop and take protective cover immediately, or if you are only a few minutes from a safe destination, proceed and take protective cover immediately.
- Listen to your radio for further instructions.

After Attack

If sirens or warning systems sound following nuclear attacks, the warning may mean another attack or that radioactive fallout is approaching your area. **You will be advised over the radio.** If the advice concerns fallout, you must take cover against the fallout effects. (See Step 4).

Radio broadcasts will identify areas which will be affected by the fallout and give instructions and advice. These might include:

- Location of nuclear explosions causing local fallout.
- Information about the parts of the country to be affected by fallout.
- Length of time before fallout is likely to reach specific communities or areas.
- Ways to increase fallout protection.
- Supplies to take to your fallout shelter.
- Whether it is safer to stay in your community or area, or to go to other areas.
- Advice as to which areas are free of danger.
- Advice on when to leave shelters and for how long as danger from radioactive contamination diminishes.
- Requests for help in rescue operations, such as rescue, firefighting and medical assistance.
- Advice on conservation of food, water and fuel.
- How to keep warm when power is off and the weather is cold.

Don't Use The Telephone

When the sirens sound don't use the telephone. Listen to a radio or television for information. In the event of an Attack Warning telephone lines will be required for official use.

Step 4: Know How to Take Shelter

It is important to provide your family and yourself with a shelter. But what kind of shelter? This is a decision you must make yourself after studying the problem.

Study your shelter requirements in the same way that you would study accident or fire insurance. Decide upon the degree of protection you want for your family and yourself. Shelter is your insurance against something you hope will not happen, but if it does, will give you protection.

Shelters of the type commonly used in Europe during the Second World War would not provide protection against the blast of a nuclear explosion. They were designed to withstand short shock pressures lasting something like 1/100th of a second. Shelters designed to withstand the pressures created by a nuclear explosion must be able to stand up to pressures lasting as long as 6 seconds. In addition, they must be capable of giving the occupants protection against fires outside the shelter as well as against radiation.

The fallout shelter is designed to give protection against radioactive fallout only. Because most people in Canada probably would not be affected by the blast and heat effects of nuclear explosions, protection against fallout is all that is required by them.

The type of shelter for good protection depends upon the distance it will be from the explosion. Unfortunately, it is not possible to know this in advance. That is why each individual must make his own decision when selecting the type of shelter he wishes to have.

Blueprint for Survival No. 1 gives details of a fallout shelter for the home in which you now live. If you rent the home, the decision to construct a shelter must be taken jointly with your landlord.

Blueprint for Survival No. 2 gives details of a fallout shelter for the new home you may be planning to build.

Blueprint for Survival No. 6 gives details of blast shelters which may be built outside the home.

These pamphlets are available from your local Emergency Measures or Civil Defence Organization (Canada).

Improvised Protection Against Blast

One of the simplest ways to improvise some anti-blast protection is to build a lean-to (bed springs or boards) against a work bench or heavy table, preferably in the basement, and pile mattresses on it and at the ends. If the material is readily available it could be built in a matter of minutes after the ATTACK WARNING is sounded and could protect you from loose bricks, flying glass, etc.

If you are in the open and there is a ditch or culvert within easy, quick reach, lie face down in it and cover your face with your arms. Make sure this shelter is not too close to buildings which could collapse into it.

"After" the blast and heat of the explosion, you would have to find other protection against fallout which will come down later. (Don't forget your battery-powered radio).

None of these improvisations is as good as a properly equipped blast shelter, but any single one of them could mean the difference between life and death.

Improvised Protection Against Fallout

You may not have a fallout shelter when warning of approaching fallout is broadcast. Here are some tips on how to increase your protection in a basement. The amount of protection you can build will depend on how much time you have available until fallout arrives.

- You can improvise a small emergency shelter by using furniture, doors, dressers, work-bench and other materials.

- Select a corner of your basement, if possible, away from windows, in which to build your shelter. Remove inside house doors from hinges to use as a shelter roof over supports. Supports for the improvised roof can be cabinets, chests of drawers, workbench, or anything which will bear a heavy load. Use the house doors as a roof surface to provide a base for the heavy material you will have to place on it. Bricks, concrete blocks, sand-filled drawers or boxes, books or other dense items on the roof will help reduce radiation penetration. Around the sides and front of your shelter build walls of dense materials to provide vertical shielding. A small cabinet or dirt-filled box as may be used as a crawl-in entrance which can be closed behind you.

Fig. A-10. Store your basement with all necessary food drink and other daily necessities at least for 15 days following a nuclear explosion, since you may not be able to go out because of fear of radiation exposure.

- Remember, the heavier or more dense the material around you, the greater the protection.
- Block basement windows with earth, bricks, concrete blocks, books or even bundles of newspaper. In winter, use packed snow.
- On the floor above the corner of the wall, you select as your shelter area, pile any heavy objects you may have available, such as furniture, trunks filled with clothes, dirt-filled boxes, books, newspapers, or earth from outside.
- Outside, against above ground walls of the basement around your shelter area heap earth, sand, bricks, concrete blocks or packed snow.

If your home has no basement or crawl space, build your emergency shelter in that part of the house (centre hall or clothes closet) farthest away from outside walls and the roof. Build it as described for houses with basements. On the floor immediately above your shelter area, and against surrounding walls, pile up furniture, trunks, dressers, dirtfilled boxes or other heavy material which will reduce radio-active penetration into your emergency shelter.

Step 5: Have 14 Days Emergency Supplies

Nuclear attacks on centres of production, and fallout conditions, may curtail the distribution of available food stocks for several days or even weeks following these attacks. Persons who had taken shelter against fallout might be advised to stay in their shelters for as long as 14 days. Those who had chosen to evacuate larger cities would be dependent largely on the resources available in reception towns. Because of these possibilities, it is recommended that every person should have emergency supplies. These supplies should include food, water, battery-powered radio, first aid kit, and where necessary, medical supplies as recommended in Step 7. Heavy clothing would be necessary in winter. Extra changes of clothing should be considered particularly stockings and underclothing.

For those who may choose to evacuate major centres, supplies must be selected carefully because of space limitation in the family car. Supplies should be packaged beforehand so that they can quickly be put into the car. See the pamphlet "Your Emergency Pack" available from your local Emergency Measures or Civil Defence Organization.

Many of the recommended items are already in your home.

Whether you choose to evacuate or take shelter locally, you should have a road map with you. You could then relate the information about areas under fallout, which you would hear about on the radio, to your actual location. Toys, games, books for your children would help to occupy their time if they had to remain in shelter from fallout. Your battery-powered radio will keep you in contact with the outside world.

The following is a suggested list of items from which your two weeks' supplies should be developed to be in your shelter or handy to it.

Equipment

- Beds (bunks or folding)
- Bedding
- Toilet
- Polyethylene bags for toilet
- Table (folding or other)
- Stools (folding)
- Cups and plates (disposable)
- Knives, forks, spoons
- Can opener
- Cooking utensils
- Kerosene cooker *(Do **not** use a pressurized stove in the confines of your shelter.)*
- Kerosene lamp
- Kerosene (sufficient for 14 days)
- Candles
- Safety matches
- Hand basin
- Calendar
- Paper towels
- Garbage can (two if no waste water runoff is possible)
- Garbage bags
- Shovel
- Broom
- Battery radio and spare batteries
- Electric lamp and spare bulbs
- Clock
- Flashlight and spare batteries
- Fire extinguisher
- Hand tools
- Pocket knife
- Axe
- String
- Light rope

Recreational

- Books
- Paper
- Pencils
- Playing cards
- Chess, checkers, other games
- Crosswords, other puzzles
- Knitting, sewing, etc.
- Hobby materials
- Plasticine

Toiletries

- Soap
- Toothpaste
- Toothbrushes
- Detergent
- Nail brush
- Razor, blades and soap
- Women's basic cosmetics
- Tissues (face and toilet)
- Face cloth
- Towels
- Brush and comb

Clothing and Personal Items

Coveralls, rubber boots, rubber gloves for adults. To be used in venturing outside even after instructions have been given that this is safe for short periods.

- Bedding (blankets preferable)
- Warm sweaters and socks
- Change of underclothing and socks
- Personal hygiene items for women
- Baby clothes
- Baby feeding equipment
- Disposable diapers (two-week supply)
- Legal papers
- Plastic sheeting

Medical

(See Step 7)

Food

These are suggested items and amounts for each adult for 14 days in shelter. Check off the items as you stock them in the shelter and mark the purchase date on them. Food stored for emergency use should be used and replaced at least once a year.

- Milk: 14 cans (6-oz) or 6 cans (15-oz) evaporated milk or 1-lb dried skim milk
- Vegetables: 6 cans (15 or 20-oz) - beans, peas, tomatoes, corn
- Fruits: 6 cans (15 or 20-oz) Ä peaches, pears, apple sauce
- Juices: 6 cans (20-oz) Ä apple, grapefruit, lemon, orange and tomato
- Cereals: 14 individual packages (sealed in wax bags inside or outside)
- Biscuits:
  - 2 packages of crackers (1-lb. each)
  - 2 packages of cookies or graham wafers
- Main Dish Items:
  - 2 cans meat (12-oz) - corned beef, luncheon meats
  - 2 cans beef and gravy
  - 2 cans baked beans (15 or 20-oz)
  - 2 jars cheese
  - 2 cans fish (8-oz)
- Canned and Dehydrated Soups: 2 cans (10-oz) - bean, pea, tomato, vegetable

Other Foods

- 1 large jar or can honey, syrup, jam or marmalade
- 2 lbs. hard candy
- 1 jar or can peanut butter
- 1 package tea bags or instant tea
- 1 jar sugar
- 1 jar instant coffee
- Salt and pepper
- Instant chocolate powder
- Chewing gum

Special Requirements for Children

- For each infant include 14 cans evaporated milk (15 oz) and infant food for 14 days.
- For each child up to 3 years, include 8 extra cans of milk.

- Decrease amounts of other foods according to appetite.
- Food for older children can be the same as for adults; adjust amounts according to appetite.

Water

- Requirements: 7-14 gallons for each adult member of family; more for younger children (some water may be replaced by canned beverages).
- Containers: Store in well-cleaned, covered containers such as large thermos jugs, new fuel cans, large bottles, or plastic containers.
- Change: Change stored water at least once a month.

Step 6: Know How To Prevent And Fight Fires

Misinformation about the fire danger from nuclear explosions is widespread and common. For example, some persons believe that the fire-ball would completely incinerate a city. This is not true.

The heat from the fire-ball lasts about 15 seconds and would create fires which are no different from the fires you see in peacetime. They can be put out with water and extinguishers, and if each survivor were able to put out a small fire quickly, mass fires would not take place.

The heat flash from the fire-ball entering through windows and doors could set fire to curtains, clothes, furniture and paper. Other fires could break out in attics, in backyard trash, on wooden shingles and on the outside of houses built of wood particularly if they are unpainted or weathered.

Knowing how to prevent and fight fires at home and at work reduces the number of peacetime fires. The same knowledge will also reduce the number of fires caused by a nuclear explosion.

But how can you fight fires in the presence of fallout? From 5 to 15 miles from the centre of the explosion, there will be many survivors. Fallout will not start coming down for about 30 minutes. During this half hour, survivors should inspect their houses and put out all the small fires they can. They must not rely on the fire department to extinguish these fires.

You should have in your home and place of work, fire extinguishers, or in an emergency, create a water supply for fire fighting in pails, bathtubs, washtubs, etc. Don't rely on being able to use the established water supply system.

Even those who live in areas not attacked may find their fire departments will have to fight major fires elsewhere. Every householder should learn how to carry out fire prevention and know how to fight small fires. It may prove of value in peacetime!

Your local fire authorities are always anxious to advise you on how to fight fires. Attend any emergency fire fighting classes held in your area.

Here are some tips for an emergency:

- Prepare for emergency by preventing accumulations of trash and rubbish in and around the home. This would include dry leaves and grass, lumber, boxes, cardboard cartons, old unused furniture, bales of newspapers, etc. Keep waste and garbage in covered containers.
- The shaking and twisting of buildings and homes due to blast waves in wartime or earthquakes and explosions in peacetime, may break utility inlets at the point they enter the structure. This may allow gas or fuel oil to flow into basements creating a severe hazard. Do not smoke, strike a match, or a lighter, to light your way into a darkened basement. Gas or oil vapours may be present and a violent explosion and fire may result.
- To lessen the danger of fires and explosions follow local instructions about shutting off utility services when the ATTACK WARNING sounds.
- If you have a coal-burning furnace, or a wood-stove, extinguish it or at least be sure to close all fuel and draft doors.
- Close curtains shutters or venetian blinds on all windows and remove furniture from window areas.

TO FIGHT AN ORDINARY FIRE

- **Take away its fuel.** Get the burning material out of your home.
- **Take away its air.** Smother it with a blanket, wet if possible, or a rug.
- **Cool it** with water, earth, sand or fire extinguisher.

GAS, OIL, ELECTRICAL FIRES REQUIRE SPECIAL METHODS

- **Gas fire:** Make sure the gas is shut off and then try to extinguish anything still burning.
- **Oil fires:** Make sure the supply is shut off then smother the fire with earth, sand, rugs or other heavy materialsÄDon't use water.
- **Electrical fires:** Make sure the electricity is shut off then put out the fire. Don't use water if the power is still on.

PROMPT ACTION TO PUT OUT SMALL FIRES IMMEDIATELY FOLLOWING A NUCLEAR ATTACK WILL SAVE LIVES

Step 7: Know First Aid And Home Nursing

The acquisition of First Aid and Home Nursing skills prepares individuals to serve effectively in a national emergency. If such an emergency occurs, the care of many thousands of injured or seriously ill persons becomes a tremendous task for the organized health services. Doctors and nurses may not be readily available to assist you. Thus the importance of First Aid and Home Nursing skills takes on a new dimension. The survival of the injured or sick members of your family may become your responsibility.

The main objectives of training individuals in first aid and home nursing are:

1. To preserve life
2. To minimize the effects of injury or illness
3. To relieve suffering or distress
4. To provide continuing care and assist in rehabilitation.

Therefore you must:

- Know and practice life-saving first aid.
- Know and practice simple home nursing measures.

First Aid Supplies

A simple first aid box kept in your shelter or in your evacuation kit should contain:

- 1 bottle mild antiseptic solution (use to clean cuts)
- 5 yards 2-inch gauze bandage
- 2 triangular bandages (use for slings)
- 12 4" x 4" sterile pads (use to cover cuts, wounds and burns)
- 12 assorted individual adhesive dressins (use for minor cuts)
- 2 large dressing pads (shell dressing type) 8" x 8" (Available at minimal cost from St. John Ambulance Association)
- 5 yards 1/2 inch adhesive tape
- 9 assorted safety pins
- 1 small bottle toothache drops (for temporary treatment of toothache)
- 1 tube of petroleum jelly
- 1 small bottle aspirin tablets
- 1 thermometer
- 1 small scissors (blunt ended)
- 1 medicine glass
- 1 pair tweezers
- 4 oz baking soda and 8 oz table salt (make a drinking solution by adding 1 tsp salt and 1/2 tsp baking soda to 1 qt. of water)
- 1 First Aid Manual (St. John Ambulance Association)

- 1 Home Nursing Textbook (St. John Ambulance Association and/or Canadian Red Cross Society)
- 1 packet paper tissues

NOTE: individuals requiring special medication such as insulin should maintain at least 100-days supplies.

First Aid Hints

General Rules:

- Keep calm.
- Keep the injured person lying down in a comfortable position, his head level with his body until you determine whether his injuries are serious.
- Examine for stoppage of breathing, serious bleeding or broken bones. These must be treated immediately before any attempt is made to move the injured person. Do not be hurried into this unless you are in a situation of extreme danger.
- Keep him comfortably warm with blankets or other coverings, under and above the patient.
- Never attempt to give a semi-conscious or unconscious person anything to drink.

Unconsciousness:

An unconscious patient lying on his back may be strangled by his own tongue which will tend to fall back and obstruct the airway. All unconscious persons should be placed lying half over on their faces, (three-quarter-prone position).

If the patient is breathing quietly and easily and his lips are pink and have no froth on them, breathing is not obstructed.

If the patient is breathing noisily and with difficulty, if his lips are blue and frothing, or if his chest is sucked inwards when he breathes in, his airway is obstructed and needs immediate attention.

Keep the airway clear by:

Placing the casualty on his back; supporting his shoulders on a pad of any suitable material available; tilting the head back with one hand on the forehead, the other lifting the neck.

If his breathing stops you can breathe for the patient by blowing air into his lungs. Take a deep breath. Pinch the casualty's nostrils. Place mouth to mouth tightly. Blow into the casualty's lungs strongly enough to cause his chest to rise. The cycle should be repeated every 3 to 5 seconds for an adult and a little more frequently for a child. Blow more gently for a child or a baby, but strongly enough to make the chest rise.

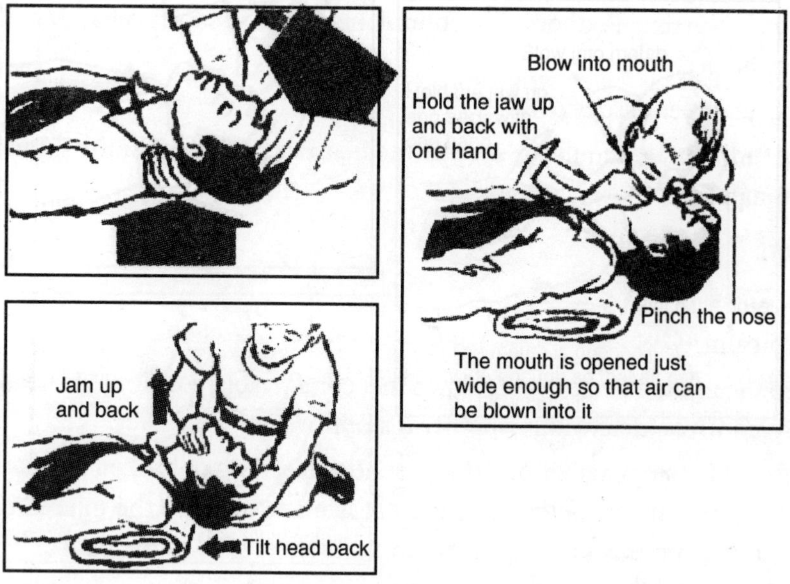

Fig. A-11

Wounds:

You Must:

- Stop bleeding (haemorrhage)
- Keep out germs (infection)

Cover the wound with a clean dressing to keep out dirt and germs. Bandage it on firmly to stop the bleeding. If a wound is bleeding profusely, hold it firmly with your hand until you can secure an emergency dressing. Any thick pad of clean, soft, compressible material large enough to cover the wound will make a good dressing. Clean handkerchiefs, towels, sanitary pads, tissue handkerchiefs or sheets make good emergency dressings.

Burns:

Cover the burned area with large, thick, dry dressing and bandage it on firmly.

Encourage the casualty to drink plenty of fluids. A solution of salt and soda is useful to give to casualties with burns and to those who have suffered from serious bleeding.

Broken bones (fractures):

If a limb is very painful and cannot be used, appears to be bent in the wrong place or the casualty says he heard or felt the bone snap, it is likely that a bone is broken.

Sharp ends of a broken bone may damage important structures such as blood vessels and nerves. A broken limb should be steadied and supported to prevent movement of the broken ends before attempting to move the patient.

If a person's back or neck is so severely injured that he is afraid to move because of pain, or cannot move or feel his limbs, you should assume that he has a broken back. He should be moved on a hard, firm stretcher taking great care not to "jack-knife" him by picking up his feet and shoulders. Improvised stretchers can be made from a door, wide board, window shutter, etc. Fill in the natural hollows of the track and neck with padding and support the head on both sides to prevent movement.

DO NOT

- Put strong antiseptics into a wound.
- Use a tourniquet.
- Remove clothing which is stuck to a burn.
- Break any blisters or apply creams or grease to a large burn.
- Give anything by mouth to a semi-conscious patient, or to a patient with internal abdominal wounds.

HOME NURSING HINTS

Before medical or nursing help becomes available you may also encounter infant care problems. emotional problems and persons suffering from radiation sickness. What to observe, and what to do for these latter cases, is outlined below.

Infant Care

Breast feeding is preferable but, if not possible, then a formula using powdered or evaporated milk should be prepared under clean conditions.

If vomiting or diarrhoea occurs infants and children become dehydrated very quickly. To avoid this happening give frequent sips of boiled water.

If a rash or fever develops, keep others away from the sick child.

Emotional Problems

Persons who become emotionally disturbed following a disaster should be treated calmly but firmly. They should be kept in small groups, preferably with persons whom they know and encouraged to "talk out" their problem. If they are not otherwise injured they should be given something to do. It may be necessary to enlist the aid of one other calm person to help subdue the overexcited patient. If a stunned or dazed reaction persists over 6 to 8 hours this should be reported to a doctor or nurse immediately one becomes available.

Radiation Sickness

The signs and symptoms of this illness are described in Step 2.

Treatment includes rest, the provision of whatever nutritional food and drink is available and personal encouragement to get well. Swab the mouth gently with mild, warm salt and water if it becomes sore. As these patients are susceptible to infection, keep wounds clean and covered with a sterile dressing. Separate these patients from persons with colds, rash or fever.

Improvised Equipment

The following suggestions may help you care for your patient when proper equipment is not available.

- Bed: A couch, mattress or any well padded, firm surface; if too low raise on bricks, boxes or wooden blocks.
- Bedding Protection: Old crib pads cut into a convenient size and placed over a waterproof sheeting; or several layers of newspaper and heavy brown paper covered with old soft cotton. (Never use thin plastic if patient is a child.)
- Backrest: A straight-backed chair turned upside down at head of bed and securely tied to bed; a triangular bolster or cushions from a chair or chesterfield.
- Bed Cradle: A light wooden box or firm cardboard carton approximately 10 x 12 x 24 inches, with two sides removed; or a hoop sawn in half and the two pieces joined together in the centre.
- Pressure Pads: Soft cushion or foam or sponge rubber pads will protect heels, elbows, back of head or any other body pressure point.
- Bedpan or Urinal: For bedpan use a padded dish or pan; for urinal any wide-necked bottle or jar.
- Hot Water Bottle: A heated brick wrapped in several layers of newspaper.

START TRAINING NOW!

One Person in Every Family should be Trained in First Aid and/or Home Nurshing

Courses in these skills are available in most municipalities from your local St. John Ambulance Association or Canadian Red Cross Society.

REGISTER NOW!

Step 8: Know Emergency Cleanliness

Your limited supply of water will have to be rationed and used only for essential purposes. If you have enough warning time before the arrival of fallout, fill your bathtub, all available buckets and pans with water. And remember that there is an emergency supply in your hot water tank. (Don't forget this if in peacetime your water supply has been temporarily disrupted).

The problems of garbage and human waste disposal can be solved even if fallout keeps you in the shelter. Put all your garbage in tightly covered garbage pails. After using your emergency toilet, you should tie human waste in waterproof plastic (polyethylene) bags and place them in the garbage pail. Store a 14-day supply of the plastic bags. After the second day in the shelter, you may risk leaving it for a few minutes for essential tasks. Therefore, when your garbage container is filled, move it out of the shelter.

Keep a soft broom in the shelter for tidying it up.

Remember, personal cleanliness in crowded shelter conditions is important to you and your family.

Fig. A-12. Figure shows various types of storage containers for their ultimate disposal.

If your area is free of fallout but is without sewage services, bury human waste and garbage in the ground. Dig the pit deep enough so that the waste will be covered by at least two feet of earth.

Step 9: Know How To Get Rid Of Radioactive Dust

In Step 2, fallout was described as "sand". To remove the danger, remove the sand. If you suspect that your clothes have fallout on them, remove your outer clothing before you come inside your home and leave it outside. Don't shake these clothes inside the house or shelter. You would only scatter the fallout grit and create unnecessary danger to others. If you have water, wash thoroughly, particularly exposed skin and hair. But do not scrub your skin as this might rub in the radioactive particles.

Exposure to fallout does not make you radioactive.

Even if you are stricken with radiation sickness, *this sickness cannot be passed on to others.*

Fallout on your clothing or body would expose you and those close to you to radiation. If you suspect you have been exposed to fallout, you will not be a danger to others if you carefully get rid of your outer clothing outside the shelter and wash.

Food and Water

Since most of your food will be in tightly covered containers (cans, bottles, plastic, boxes), it will all be safe to eat or drink if you dust the containers. Food, if it is unspoiled and free of grit or dust, may be eaten during the emergency period.

Be sure to wash fruit and vegetables and peel carefully.

Water will be safe if it is in covered containers, or if it has come from covered wells, or from undamaged water systems.

Step 10: Know Your Municipal Plan

It is important that your local municipality have a plan for a war emergency. And it is just as important that you know that plan.

Over the past several years, provincial and municipal governments, with the assistance of federal authorities, have been steadily developing plans for the protection of the population and the continuity of essential government services in wartime. Most municipalities in Canada have emergency plans to deal with both peacetime disasters and a nuclear attack situation. These include the details of how welfare, health, police, public utilities, fire and other emergency services will operate.

Some larger communities have developed plans to assist in the evacuation of those who would choose to leave before an attack or who might have to be evacuated as survivors or casualties following an attack. These plans include traffic arrangements to reception centres and medical facilities in nearby communities.

It would be unwise to try and prepare your own family survival plan without first checking to see how it fits in with municipal plans. This would be true whether you plan to go to a safer area before attack or remain at home. It is particularly important that you know and understand the arrangements to instruct the public about staying in shelter and coming out of shelter when it is safe. Fallout is a health hazard which will require countermeasures for personal and family protection including assessment of radiation and advice and instructions to those in shelter.

There must be close understanding and cooperation between the public and municipal authorities responsible for their protection.

Find out about your municipal emergency plans now and keep well informed about them as they are further developed.

Step 11: Have A Plan For Your Family And Yourself

If you know what is contained in the first nine steps, and you know your municipal plan for a war emergency, you should now make your personal and family survival plan. The success of your plan will depend on how many of the suggested recommendations you carry out. Your chances of survival increase as you carry out each recommendation.

Thinking about the problems with which you would be faced should nuclear attack be launched against North America is the first important step. Blast, light, heat and radioactive fallout are the problems. A workable survival plan will include all of the preparations you can make in advance to meet those problems.

In making that plan, there are certain things you must know:

When to take protective action

When the sirens or other warning devices sound and your local broadcast station confirms that an attack on North America has been detected it means that you must take protective action immediately. Would you and your family

- Recognize the Attack Warning signal ?
- Turn on the radio or television and listen for instructions?

Where to take shelter

Deciding where you will take initial protective action and where you and your family will seek shelter from fallout are two basic points which you must consider in making your survival plan. Can you answer the following questions about seeking immediate protection and shelter:

- Have you decided where you will take shelter if you're not at home when the Attack Warning sounds?
- Will you try to get home?
- Will your family know what to do if you are not at home?
- Is there a shelter plan for your children at school?
- Do you want them to try to get home?
- Does everybody in your family know your survival plan?

In thinking about what you will do or where you would go, you might consider leaving your home to find shelter elsewhere. Before you decide to plan on evacuation, consider the following questions:

- Will protection there be better than in your home?
- Are there sufficient supplies there?
- Can you carry emergency supplies for 14 days?
- Do you know how to get there quickly?

How to take shelter

If you don't have a fallout shelter built in your home, study the guide given in Step 4. It shows how you can improvise emergency home protection. Bearing in mind that density and distance between you and the fallout is necessary, try to estimate if there is enough material and furniture to build an emergency shelter in your basement or the central part of your house.

- Can you move it to where it will be needed quickly?
- Will you have the help you require?

Based on the lists of emergency supplies suggested in Steps 5, 6, 7 and 8, try to answer the following questions:

- Do you have them at home?
- Can you collect and move them to the shelter area quickly?
- Does your emergency cooker, lamp, flashlight, radio work?
- Have you containers for water, garbage, hygiene?
- DO YOU HAVE A BATTERY RADIO AND SPARE BATTERIES?

There are many other points which you and your family must resolve for a workable survival plan. This booklet provides most of the essential information on which to base your plans. Read the Steps again, and, as you review each Step, try to answer the questions which apply to your surroundings, your home, your family. Here are a few more which may help:

- Do I know the recommended fire precautions?
- Does anyone in my family know how to fight small fires?
- Can an emergency supply of water be obtained quickly - for fire fighting? for personal use?
- Are first aid supplies and special medicines readily available?
- Does anyone in my family know how to render fist aid?
- Can materials for personal hygiene and cleanliness be gathered near the shelter area quickly?
- Do I know what I must do about radioactive dust?
- Do I know the emergency plans of my municipality - for public shelters? for planned evacuation routes? for schools, hospitals, welfare centres? other special instructions?

REMEMBER! YOU MUST PLAN FOR:

- **Protective Action when Warned of Attack and**
- **Provision of Shelter against the Effects of Fallout**

On the basis of what you've read and the questions and answers you've thought about, you should now make your survival plan and start making whatever arrangements you can. BUT MAKE SURE THAT ALL MEMBERS OF YOUR FAMILY KNOW YOUR PLAN AND WHAT TO DO WHEN THE TIME COMES.

The best way to arrive at a workable plan which will be remembered by your family is to practice it. If you plan on building an emergency shelter, try it now to find out if you have enough material, how much help you'll need, if your proposed area is large enough, and how long it will take to build. Locate and practice moving essential supplies, water, clothing, bedding, etc. Practice the essential things you would have to do.

If you plan to move to what you consider a safer location, make a practice run to make sure you know the quickest and safest route, that protection is available when you get there, and that you can carry all the supplies you think you'll need.

A GOOD SURVIVAL PLAN IS A PLAN WHICH YOU KNOW YOU CAN CARRY OUT

Write Down the Important Parts of Your Plan

List for quick reference the important things to be done in the event of warning. As examples, note when and where all members of your family will take shelter at all times; where essential items of food, shelter and other supplies will be obtained; how shelter will be improvised; what windows must be blocked; if you plan on going to what you consider a safer area, details of the route and supplies you will need at your destination".

References

1. Agres, T. *Biosecurity Gets Needed Attention*. The Scientist, 15(22), November 12, 2001.
2. Amson, J. E. *Economic Effects*. In : Bennet *et al.*,(eds.) *Hazardous Materials Spills Handbook.* McGraw Hill Book Co. 4.13-4.39. (1982)
3. Armstrong, N.E. *Biological Measures.* In : Bennet *et al.*,(eds.) *Hazardous Materials Spills Handbook.* McGraw Hill Co. 9.40-9.49. (1982).
4. Auerbach, P. S. and Gheer, E.C. *Management of Wilderness and Environmental Emergencies.* Macmillan Publishing, New York. (1983).
5. Baier, R. E. , Michalovich, J. G. Depalma, U. A. and Pilie, R. J. *Universal Gelling Agent for the Control of Hazardous Liquid Spills.* J. Hazardous Materials, 1, 21-23, (1975).
6. Barnett, D. J. E*mergency Planning and the Environmental Health Officers*. Proc. of the Environ. Health Off. Association, Bournmouth (1980).
7. Barnett, G. F., Feates, F. S. and Wilder, I. *Spill Clean Up.* In *: Hazardous Materials Spills Handbook*. McGraw Hill Book Co., New York, Chapter 9, (1982).
8. Bretherick, L. *Handbook of Reactive Chemical Hazards* (92nd Ed.) Butterworth, London (1979).
9. Brown, P., Berger, G. J. and Desta, J. J. *Handling Chemicals Safety.* Dutch Association of Safety Experts, Dutch Chemical Industry Association and Dutch Safety Institute (1980).
10. Brugger, J. E. and Wilder, I. A. Review of the USEPA's Research Programme on the *Prevention and Control of Hazardous Material Spills*. J. Hazardous Materials, 1, 3-11, (1975).
11. Buckley, J. L. and Weiner, S. A. *Hazardous Materials Spill* EPA(1978).
12. Burton, I. *Case Study. What Happened at Mississauga*. Report of a train derailment in Canada involving liquid chlorine. Health aspect of chemical safety. Interim document (1), Planning Emergency Response Systems for Chemical Accidents, WHO, Copenhagen (1981).
13. Cairns, J. Environmental Effects, In: Bennet *et al.*, (ed.) *Hazardous Materials Spills Handbook.* McGraw Hill Book Co. 4.13-4.21 (1982).
14. Cairns, J. and Buikema, A. L. *Restoration of Habitats Impacted by Oil Spills*, Butterworth, London (1984).
15. Cairson, P. A. *Hazardous Materials,* 3, 149 (1979).
16. Caltaheri, F., Cavallaro, A. and Galli, G. Dioxin : S.P. Medical and Scientific Books, New York (1978).

17. Canvey, *An Investigation of Potential Hazards from Operations in the Canvey Island, Thurrock Area*. Health and Safety Executive, HMSO, London (1978).
18. Carson, P. A. and Mumford, C. J. *An Analysis of Incidents Involving Major Hazards in the Chemical Industry*. J. of Hazardous Material, 3,149-165 (1979).
19. Challis, E. J. *Management of Major Hazard Plant*. J. Hazardous Substances, 3, 49-60 (1979).
20. CISHC.(Chemical Industry Safety and Health). *Recommended Procedures for Handling Major Emergencies*. Council of Chemical Industries Association, London (1980).
21. Comer, P. J. *The Dispersion of Large-scale Accidental Release such as Sevesso*, Paper presented to the Royal Meteorological Discussion Meeting, London June 15, (1977).
22. Courtney, K. D. and Moore, J. A. *Teratology Studies with 2,4,5-Trochlorophenoxyacetic Acid and 2,3,7,8-Tetrachlorodibenzo-p-dioxin*.Toxicol.Appl. Pharmacol.20, 396, (1971).
23. Cralley, L. J. and Cralley, L. V. *Industrial Hygiene Aspect of Plant Operator.* Vol. I. MacMillan, London (1984a).
24. Cralley, L. J. and Cralley, L. V. *Industrial Hygiene Aspect of Plant Operator.* Vol. II. MacMillan, London, (1984b).
25. Crane, P. *The American Thyroid Association has been Pleading since 1989 for a More Enlightened Policy on KI. U.S.* Nuclear Regulatory Commission, September 13 (1999).
26. Cumberland, R. J. and Hebden, M. D. *A Scheme for Recognizing Chemicals and their Hazards in an Emergency.* J. Hazardous Materials, 1,65-81 (1975).
27. Cunliffe, W. J. *et al.*, *Acta Dermatovener,* Stockholm 55, 211 (1975).
28. Datta, K. K., Gupta, G. S., Mishra, A., Joshi, A., Tandon, G. S. and Ray, P. K. *Inhalation Toxicity Studies of Methyl Isocyanate (MIC) in Rats:* Part I- *Pulmonary Pathology and Genotoxicity Evaluation.* Ind J Exp Biol 26(3), 177-82 (1988).
29. Dawson, G. E. *Treatment of Hazardous Materials Spills in Flowing Streams with Floating Mass Transfer Agents*. J. Hazardous Materials, 1 65-81 (1975).
30. De Boer J., and Baillie, T. W.(Eds.) *Disaster Medical Organizations*, Pergamon Press, 1979.
31. Didomenico, A., Silano, V., Viviano, G. and Zappolni, G. *Accidental Release of 2, 3, 7, 8-Tetrachlorodibenzo p-dioxin (TCDD) at Sevesso, Italy* : II TCDD distribution in the Soil Surface Layer. Ecotoxicol. Environ. Safety, 4, 298-320 (1980).
32. Dwivedi, P. D., Mishra, A., Gupta, G. S., Datta, K. K., Das, S. N. and Ray, P. K. *Inhalation Toxicity Studies on Methyl Isocyanate (MIC) in Rats : Part IV-Immunological Response of Rats One Week after Exposure : Effect on Body and Organ Weights, Phagocytic and DTH Response.* Ind J Exp Biol 26 (3), 191-4 (1988).
33. Eckenfelder, W. W. *Chemical and Physical Measures*. In: Bennet *et al.*, (eds.) *Hazardous Materials Spills Handbook*; McGraw Hill Book Co., 9.50-9.58 (1962).
34. Emery, T.F. *All Bacteria, Fungi and Viruses Depend on Iron as a Growth Factor. In"Iron and Your Health*", CRC Press, 1(1991.

35. European federation of Chemical Engineering (EFCE). *The Assessment and Control of Major Hazards*. Publication 42 (1985).

36. Fawcett, H. H. *The Changing Nature of Acute Chemical Hazards. A Historical Perspective.* J. Hazardous Materials, 4, 313-319 (1981).

37. Fawsett, H. H. *Hazardous and Toxic Materials Safe Handling and Disposal*. Wiley Interscience, New York (1984).

38. Fawsett, H. H. and Wood, W. S. *Safety and Accident Prevention in Chemical Operations* (2nd Ed). John Wiley and Sons, New York, (1982).

39. Freestone, F. J. and Brugger, J. E. *Technology Development*. In: Bennet *et al.*,(eds.) *Hazardous Materials Spills Handbook*, McGraw Hill Book Co. 9.24-9.39 (1982).

40. Gabor, T. *Mutual Aid Systems in the United States for Chemical Emergencies.* J. Hazardous Substances. 4, 343-356 (1981).

41. Gillis,J. *Anti-Radiation Doses Goal Unmet Since 79.* Washington Post, Staff Writer, Page A01, Monday, December 31 (2001).

42. Gloss, D. S. and Wardle, M. G. *Introduction to Safety Engineering*. John Wiley and Sons, New York (1983).

43. Goldfrank, L. R. *Toxicological Emergencies*, Appleton Century Crafts, New York, 1982.

44. Gray, J. *Characteristic Patterns and Variations on Community Response to Acute Chemical Emergencies.* J. Hazardous Materials, 4, 357-365 (1982).

45. Gray, J. and Quarantelli, E. L. An editorial to the special issue : *Social Aspects of Acute Chemical Emergencies.* J. Hazardous Materials, 4, 309-312 (1981).

46. Gupta, B. N., Rastogi, S. K., Chandra, H., Mathur, A. K. Mathur, N., Mahendra, P. N., Pangtey, P. N., Kumar, S., Kumar, P., Seth, R. K., Dwivedi, R. S. and Ray, P. K. *Effect of Exposure to Toxic Gas on the Population of Bhopal. Part I- Epidemiological, Clinical, Radiological and Behavioral Studies*. In J Exp Biol 26(3), 149-160 (1988).

47. Gupta, G.S., Bajpai, R., Kaw, J. L., Datta, K. K. and Ray, P. K. *Modulation of Biochemical and Cytological Profile of Bronchoalveolar Lavage Constituents in Rats following Split Dose Multiple Inhalation Exposure to Methyl Isocyanate.* Hum. Exp. Toxicol.12(3), 253-7 (1993).

48. Gupta, G. S., Kaw, J. L., Naqvi, S. H., Dixit, R. and Ray, P. K. *Inhalation Toxicity of Methyl Isocyanate : Biochemical and Cytological Profile of Bronchoalveolar Ascites Fluid in Rats.* J Appl Toxicol 11(3), 157-60 (1991).

49. Gupta G. S., Jaffery, F. N., Datta, K. K., Viswanathan, P. N., Misra, A. and Ray, P. K. *Inhalation Toxicity Studies on Methyl Isocyanate(MIC) in Rats. Part II-Biochemical Studies on Hemolysates, Lactate Dehydrogenase, Isoenzymes and Lipid Peroxidation.* Ind J Exp Biol 26(3), 183-6 (1988).

50. Hausman, F. C. and Timmerman, P. *Guide to Emergency Planning and Responsibilities in Criteria Emergencies and Risk Research*. University of Toronto (1980).

51. Hay, A. W. M. *Toxic Cloud Over Sevesso*; Nature 262, 636 (1976).

52. Helms, J. *Threat Perceptions in Cute Chemical Disaster.* J. Hazardous Materials 4, 321-329 (1981).

53. IARC. Monographs. *The Evaluation of the Carcinogenic Risk of Chemicals to Man.* 15, 54 (1977).

54. IRPTC (International Register of Potentially Toxic Chemicals) *MAC and Tentative Safe Exposure Levels of Harmful Substances in the Environmental Media.* UNEP (1978).

55. Katz, W. B. *Plant Operations.* In Bennet *et al.*,(eds.) *Hazardous Materials Spills Handbook*, McGraw Hill Book Co., 6.20-6.24 (1982).

56. Kearny, C. H. *Nuclear War Survival Skills*, Original Edition Published September, 1979, by Oak Ridge National Laboratory, a Facility of the U.S. Department of Energy (Updated and Expanded Edition) page 115 (1987).

57. Kearney, P. C., Isensee, A. R., Helling, C. S., Woolston, E. A. and Plimmer, J. R. *Environmental Significance of Chlorodioxins.* In : E. H. Blair (Ed.) *Chlorodioxins: Origin and Fate.* Am Chem Soc, Washington, pp 105-11 (1973).

58. Khera, K. S. and Ruddick, J. A. *Poly (Chloro) Benzene-p-dioxins: Perinatal Effects and the Dominant Lethal Testing in Wister Rats.* In, E. H. Blair (ed.) *Chlorodioxin: Origin and Fate.* Amer Chem Soc , Washington, pp.70-84 (1973).

59. Kling, A. L., *Action Station and Disaster Planning.* In *: Safety and Accident Prevention in Chemical Operation* (Editor H. H. Fawcett and W. S. Wood), Interscience, New York, 556 (1965).

60. Lakey, R. J. *The 1973 Marine Pollution Convention, Impact on Ships Transporting Hazardous Materials.* J. Hazardous Materials, I, 113-28(1975).

61. Laws, E. A. *Radioactivity.* In *: Aquatic Pollution.* John Wiley and Sons, New York, 404-73 (1981).

62. Manning, W. J. *Disaster Technology and Biogeography.* Pergamon Press (1975).

63. Marshall, V. *Assessment of Hazard and Risk.* In : Bennet *et al.*, (Eds). *Hazardous Materials Spills Handbook*: Mcgraw Hill Book Co., 5.1-5.23 (1982).

64. MTB (Materials Transportation Bureau). *Emergency Response Guidebook.* U. S. Dept. of Transportation. A. H. D. T.,Washington (1984).

65. Matsumura, F. and Benzet, H.J. *Studies on the Bioaccumulation and Microbial Degradation of 2, 3, 7, 8-tetrachlorobenzo-p-dioxin.* Env Hlth Sci Res Triangle, N.C (1973).

66. Matthiaschk, G. *Survey about Toxicological Data of 2, 3, 7, 8 tetrachlorobenzo-p-dioxin (TCDD).* In: F. Cattabeni, A. Cavallero, and G. Galli (Eds.) *Dioxin.* In : F. Cattabeni, A. Cavellero and G. Gdioin : *Toxicological and Chemical Aspects*: Spectrum Publications, Inc. New York, pp.123-136 (1978).

67. Mcconnell, E. E. and Moore, J. A. *The Toxicopathology of TCDD.* In :F. Cattabeni, A Cavellero and G. Galli, (eds) *Dioxin Toxicological and Chemical Aspects*: Spectrum Publications Inc. N.Y. pp.137-42 (1978).

68. Meidle, J. H. *Explosive and Toxic Hazardous Materials*. Glencoe Press, Beverly Hills, California (1970).

69. Meyer, E. *Chemistry of Hazardous Materials*. Prentice Hall (1977).

70. Milnes, M. H. *Formation of 2, 3, 7, 8 Tetrachlorbenzodioxin by Thermal Decomposition of Sodium 2, 3, 5 Trichlorophenate*. Nature 232, 395 (1971).

71. Misra, U. K., Nag, D., Nath, P., Khan, W. A., Gupta, B. N.and Ray, P. K. *A Clinical Study of Toxic Pas Poisoning in Bhopal, India.* Ind J Exp Biol 26(3), 201-4 (1988).

72. Mishra,.A., Gupta, G.S., Kumar, V. S., Datta, K. K. and Ray, P. K. *Inhalation Toxicity Studies on Methyl Isocyanate (MIC) in Rats. Part III- Studies on Biotransformation Enzymes.* Indian J Exp Biol 26(3), 187-90 (1988).

73. Mishra, A., Dwivedi, P. D., Verma, A. S., Mishra, J., Sinha, M., Datta, K. K. and Ray, P. K. *Modulation of Microsomal Membrane Associated Detoxification Enzymes Activity by Methyl Isocyanate (MIC) Exposure*. Bull Environ Contam Toxicol 47(5), 675-81 (1991).

74. Mitchell, R. L. *Chlorine*, In : Bennet *et al.*(eds) *Hazardous Materials Spills Handbook*. McGraw Hill Book Co., 10.52-10.64 (1982).

75. Morrissette, M. D. *Hazard Evaluation of Chemicals for Bulk Shipment*. J. Hazardous Materials 3, 33-48 (1979).

76. Morgan D.P. and Karpen R. J. *Test of Chronic Toxicity of Iodine as Related to the Purification of Water*. U.S. Armed Forces Medical Journal, 4:725-728 (1953).

77. Negy, J. and Verakis, H. C. *Development and Control of Dust Explosions*. Marcel Dekker (1983).

78. Oliver, R. M. *Toxic Effects of 2, 3, 7, 8-tetrachlorodibenzene 1, 4-dioxin in Laboratory Workers.* Brit J Ind Med 32, 49 (1975).

79. Piper, W. N., Rose, J. Q. and Schering, P. T. *Excretion and Tissue Distribution of 2, 3, 7, 8-tetrachloroxibenzo-p-dioxin in the Rat*. In : E. H. Blair (ed.) *Chlorodioxin Origin and Fate.* Am Chem Soc Washington, pp. 85-91 (1973).

80. Pipitone, D. A. *Safe Storage of Laboratory Chemicals.* Wiley Interscience, New York (1984).

81. Pochiari, F., Didomenico, A., Silano, V. and Zapponi, G. *Accidental Release of TCDD at Sevesso : Assessment of Environmental Contamination and of Effectiveness of Decontamination Treatments.* In: The Proceedings of the Sixth International Codata Conference. B. Dreyfus.(Ed) pp. 31-37(1979).

82. Posthuma, A. R., Kraus, J. G. and Rutherford, J. A. *Cleanup of a Vinylidene Chloride and Phenol Spill*. In : *Management of Toxic and Hazardous Wastes*. H. G. Bhatt, R. K. Sykes and T. L. Sweeney, Levis Publishers, Inc. Chelsea, 297-306 (1985).

83. Quarentelli, E. L., Lawrence, C., Tierney, K. and Johnson. *Initial Findings from a Study of Socio-behavioural Presentations and Planning for Acute Chemical Disasters.* J Hazardous Materials 3, 77-90 (1979).

84. Raj, P. *Ammonia.* In : Bennet *et al.* (Eds) *Hazardous Materials Spills Handbook.* McgrawHill Book Co 10.34-10.51 (1982).

85. Rastogi, S. K. Gupta, B. N., Husain, T., Kumar, A., Chandra, S. and Ray, P. K. *Effect of Exposure to Toxic Gas on the Population of Bhopal. Part II- Respiratory impairment.* Ind J Exp Biol 26(3), 161-4 (1988).

86. Rayl A. J. S., *Reflections from the Nobel Conference* XXXVII 15(22), November 12 (2001).

87. Ridley, J. R. *Safety at Works,* Butterworths (1983).

88. *Robbens Committee Report Great Britain*: Department of Employment, HMSO, London(1972).

89. Rutherford, W. H. *Disaster Procedures.* Brit Med J 1, 443 (1975).

90. Savage, P. E. A. *Disasters,* Hospital, I. C. Easton (ed.). The international J of Disasters Studies and Practice, Pergamon Press (1977).

91. Sax, N. I. *Dangerous Properties of Industrial Materials* (VIth ed.). Van Nostrand and Reinhold (1984).

92. Saxena A. K., Singh, K. P., Nagle, S. L., Gupta, B. N., Ray, P. K., Srivastava, R. K. Tewari, S. P., Singh, R. *Effect of Exposure to Toxic Gas on the Population of Bhopal:* Part IV- *Immunological and Chromosomal Studies.* Ind J Exp Biol 26(3), 173-6 (1988).

93. Saxena, A. K., Singh, K. P., Datta, K. K., Gupta, G. S., Nagle, S. L., Mishra, A., Zaidi, S. L., and Ray, P. K. *Inhalation Toxicity Studies on Methyl Isocyanate (MIC) in Rats* : Part V- *Immunologic Response of Rats Two Weeks After Exposure : Phagocytic Response, Endotoxin Susceptibility, Local Lung Immunity, Mitogenic and DTH Response.* Ind J Exp Biol 26(3), 195-200 (1988).

94. Scholtz, R. C. *Field Implemented Measures.* In : Bennet *et al.,* (eds). *Hazardous Materials Spills Handbook.* McGraw Hill Book Co.9.2-9.23 (1982).

95. Schwetz, B. A., Morris, J. M., Sparschu, G. L., Rowe, V. K. and Gehring, P. J. *Toxicology of Chlorinated Dibenzo-p- dioxin.* In : E. H. Blair (Ed.) *Chlorodioxin Origin and Fate.* Amer Chem Soc Washington. pp 55-69 (1973).

96. Schwetz, B. A., Morris, J. M., Spaschu, G. L., Rowe, V. K., Gehring, P.J., Emerson, J. L. and Gerbig, C. G. *Toxicology of Chlorinated Dibenzo-p-dioxin.* Environ Health Perspec 5, 87 (1973).

97. Seiler, J. F. *A Survey on the Mutagenicity of Various Pesticides.* Experiencia 29, 622 (1973).##

98. Silano, V. *Evaluation of Public Health Hazards Associated with Chemical Accidents.* Pan Amer center for Human Ecology and Health, WHO, Mexico (1984).

99. Sparschu, G. L.Dunn, F. L. and Rowe, V. K. *Study of the Teratogenicity of 2,3,7,8-Tetrachlorodibenzo- p - dioxin in the Rat.* Food Cosmetic Toxicol 9, 405 (1971).

100. Srivastava, R. C., Gupta, B. N., Athar, M., Behari, J. R., Dwivedi, R. S., Hasan, S. K., Bharti, R. S., Singh, A., Misra, M. and Ray, P. K. *Effect of Exposure to Toxic Gas on the Population of Bhopal:* Part III- *Assessment of Toxic Manifestations in Humans- Hematological and Biochemical Studies*. Ind J Exp Boil 26(3), 165-72 (1988).

101. Stehl, R. H., Papenfuss, R. R., Bredeweg, R. A. and Roberts , R. W. *Stability of Pentachlorophenol and Chlorinated Dioxins to Sunlight Heat and Combustion*. In : E. H. Blair (ed.) *Chlorodioxins: Origin and Fate*. Am Chem Soc Washington, pp. 119-125 (1973).

102. Stover, E. L. and Metry, A. A. *Handling Emergencies in Hazardous Waste Management Facilities.* In : *Toxic and Hazardous Waste Disposal Vol. 4. New and Promising Ultimate Disposal Options*. R. H. Rojasek (ed.). Ann Arbor Science Publisher Inc., Ann Arbor, Michigan,29-48 (1980).

103. Suskind, B. R. International *Agency for Res. Cancer Meeting*, Lyon,January, 1978.

104. Tenzer, R., Boro, B., Mathox, W. and Brugger, J. E. *Characteristics of the Mobile Field Use System for the Detoxification Incineration of Residuals from Oil and Hazardous Materials Spill Clean Up Operations*. J Hazardous Materials 3, 61-75 (1979).

105. Tierney, K. J. *Community and Organizational Awareness of and Preparedness for Acute Chemical Emergencies.* J Hazardous Materials 4, 331-42 (1981).

106. Touhill, C. T. Municipal facilities. In : Bennet et al., (ed.) *Hazardous Materials Spill Handbook*. McGraw Hill Book Co 4.1-4.20 (1982).

107. USDOT (U. S. Department of Transportation) Hazardous Materials . *Emergencies Action Guide*, National Highway Traffic Safety Administration (1976).

108. Walters, D. B. *Safe Handling of Chemical Carcinogens, Mutagens, Teratogens and Highly Toxic Substances*. Vol.1, Arbor Science, Ann Arbor, Michigan (1980).

109. Whittaker, H. *State Perspectives on Hazardous Materials Management*. J Hazardous Materials 4, 367-72 (1981).

110. WHO-IPCS : *Emergency Response to Chemical Accidents. Health Aspects of Chemical Safety,* WHO regional Office. Europe, Copenhagen, IPCS Interim Document 1, (1981).

111. WHO, IPCS : *Rehabilitations following Accidents Involving Toxic and Potentially Toxic and Hazardous Chemicals*. WHO(IPCS) (1985).

112. Wielmann, J. C. *PCB Transformer Spill*, Seattle, Washington J Hazardous Materials, 1, 361-72 (1975).

113. Wilson, J.F. *Biological Terrorism*. The Scientist, 15(22): November 12 (2001).

114. Williams H. J. *Disaster Organization and Chemical Works*. De Boer and Baile, (ed). *Disasters Medical Organization*. Pergamon Press, p. 41-45 (1980).

115. Wilson, E. A *Selected Bibliography and Guide to Sources of Information, Planning for and Response to Chemical Emergencies.* J Hazardous Materials 4, 373-94 (1981).

116. Wilson, J. F. *New Targets in the Battle against Anthrax*, The scientist, 15(22), November 12 (2001).

117. Wipf, H. K., Homeberger, E., Newner, N. Schenker, F. *Field Trials on Photo Degradation of TCDD on Vegetation after Spraying with Vegetable Oil.* In : *Dioxin, Toxicological and Chemical Aspects*. pp. 201-217 (1978).

118. Young, A. L., Thalken, C. E., Arnold, E. L., Cupello, J. M. and Cockerham, L. G.USAFATR-18. U. S. Airforce Academy Colorado Springs, Colorado, October (1976).

119. Zanzonico, P. B. and Becker, D. V. *Effects of Time of Administration and Dietary Iodine Levels on Potassium iodide (KI) Blockade of Thyroid Irradiation by 131-I from Radioactive Fall-out* Health Physics Journal, Volume 78 No. 6, June (2000).

Further Reading

1. *An antibacterial, antiseptic action of plant oils has been described to be helpful in fighting biological toxins.* Journal Applied Microbiology, Volume 88 (2000).
2. BARC News Letter, Bhabha Atomic Research Centre, Trombay, Bombay, India. No.233, p 18, June (2003).
3. *Biosafety in Microbiological and Biomedical Laboratories*, fourth edn. JY Richmond, RW McKinney, eds (Washington, DC: US Department of Health and Human Services, Centers for Disease Control and Prevention, National Institutes of Health, Government Printing Office, May (1999). *Respiratory protective devices* part II; Final rule," *Federal Register 60,*) 30335-30398, June 8 (1995).
4. Biological activity of botulinum toxin depends upon iron, and metal chelators may be beneficial. Infection and Immunology, October (1989); Toxicon, July (1997).
5. *Chemical, Biological and Nuclear Terrorism*. Okumura T, Suzuki K, Fukuda A, *et al. Tokyo Subway Sarin Attack; Disaster Management,* Part 1*: Community Emergency Response*. Acad Emerg Med 5:613-7(1998); Davis, CJ. *Nuclear Blindness: An Overview of the Biological Weapons Programs of the former Soviet Union and Iraq*. Emerge Infect Dies 5:509-12(1999); Török TJ, Tauxe RV, Wise RP, *et al. Large Community Outbreak of Salmonellosis caused by Intentional Contamination of Restaurant Salad Bars.* JAMA 278:389-95 (1997); Tucker JB. Chemical/*Biological Terrorism: Coping with a New Threat.* Politics and the Life Sciences 15:167-184 (1996). Uncle Fester. *Silent Death*. 2nd ed. Port Townsend, WA: Loompanics Unlimited (1997); Ashraf H. *European Dioxin-contaminated Food Crisis Grows and Grows [news]*. Lancet 353:2049 (1999); Janofsky M. *Looking for Motives in Plague Case*. New York Times. May 28, A18 (1995); Federal Emergency Management Agency. *Federal Response Plan*. Washington, DC: Government Printing Office, 1999. Available at <<http://www.fema.gov/r-n-r/frp>>. Accessed February 3, 2000.)
6. *Crystal Structure of Anthrax Toxin Protective Antigen.* Nature 385, 833-38, 1997; Crystal Structure of the Anthrax Lethal Factor. Nature 414, 229-233, 2001; *Structural Basis for the Activation of Anthrax Adenyl Cyclase Exotoxin by Aalmodulin*. Nature 415, 317-402 (2002).
7. *Drinking Water and Health.* Vol. 3. Washington, DC, the National Academy of Sciences, National Academy Press, 1980.
8. *Guidelines for Preventing Transmission of Mycobacterium Tuberculosis in Health Care Facilities* (New York): Thompson Publishing Group, Inc., 130 (1994).

9. Guidelines for Iodine Prophylaxis following Nuclear Accidents states: "Stable iodine administered before, or promptly after, intake of radioactive iodine can block or reduce the accumulation of radioactive iodine in the thyroid. World Health Organization (WHO) Report, updated (1999).

10. Hazardous waste operations and emergency response; Final rule, *Federal Register 59*, 43268-43280, Aug. 22 (1994). Occupational exposure to blood-borne pathogens; Final rule," *Federal Register 56,* 64004-64182, Dec. 6 (1991); US Department of Health and Human Services, Centers for Disease Control and Prevention, National Institutes of Health, *Biosafety in Microbiological and Biomedical Laboratories*, fourth ed. JY Richmond, RW McKinney, eds (Washington, DC: US Government Printing Office, May (1999); *Guidelines for Preventing Transmission of Mycobacterium Tuberculosis in Health Care Facilities* (New York: Thompson Publishing Group, Inc., 1994) 130.

11. Huperzine A, a derivative of Chinese club moss, has been suggested as a pre-treatment against nerve gases. Annals Pharmacology France, January (2000); Huperzine A protects against nerve gas poisoning in a superior manner to physostigmine, a long-standing anti-nerve toxin drug. (Defense Technical Information Center Review, The Walter Reed Army Institute of Research, Volume 2, December (1996).

12. IP6 has been found to have similar iron chelating properties as desferrioxamine, a drug commonly used to kill germs, tumor cells or to remove undesirable minerals from the body. Biochemistry Journal, September 16 (1993).

13. Iron removal retards the growth of plague. Medical Hypotheses, January (1980).

14. KI4U, Inc., 212 Oil Patch Lane,Gonzales, Texas, 78629; Phone (830) 672-8734 has a large ranging of FAQs available in the internet describing very useful information for its consumers for taking adequate preventive and protective measures in situations where one has to face chemical, biological and radiological accidents or attacks. The readers are advised to connect them through internet, through their FAQs and or otherwise from the details.

15. Melatonin effect on anthrax toxin. New England Journal of Medicine. Vol. 274 on Page 1442, June 23(1966); Melatonin, a sleep-inducing hormone has been found to be able to help prevent lethal toxins from anthrax exposure. Cell Biology Toxicology, Volume 16 (2000).

16. Mustard gas work is its ability to bring about cell death by deleting the levels of glutathione. eMedicine Journal, April 9 (2001).

17. No adverse health effects were reported in men who drank water providing iodide at doses of 0.17-0.27 mg/kg of body weight per day for 26 weeks. Armed Forces Medical Journal, 4:725-728 (1953).

18. Oregano completely inhibited the growth of 25 different bacteria, such as Staphylococcus aureus, Escherichia coli, Yersinia enterocolitica and Pseudomonas aeruginosa. Journal

Food Protection, July (2001); Oregano has been shown to be effective in eradicating intestinal parasites in humans. Phytotherapy Research, May (2000); Wild oregano, which is quite different than the variety on most kitchen spice racks, has over 50 antibacterial compounds. Just one part wild oregano oil in 4000 dilutions sterilizes contaminated water. (London Times, May 8 (2001).

19. Occupational exposure to blood-borne pathogens; Final rule, *Federal Register 56,* 64004-64182 (Dec. 6, 1991).

20. Potassium Iodide as a Thyroid Blocking Agent in a Radiation Emergency: Almost complete (greater than 90%) blocking of peak radioactive iodine uptake by the thyroid gland can be obtained by the oral administration of ... iodide... *Federal Register*. Vol. 43 Friday, December 15 (1978); Potassium iodide, if taken in time, blocks the thyroid gland's uptake of radioactive iodine and thus could help prevent thyroid cancers and other diseases that might otherwise be caused by exposure to airborne radioactive iodine that could be dispersed in a nuclear accident. The Nuclear Regulatory Commission (NRC), July 1 (1998); Potassium Iodide as a Thyroid Blocking Agent in Radiation Emergencies. FDA document, November (2001); Potassium Iodide as a Thyroid Blocking Agent in Radiation Emergencies states: The effectiveness of KI as a specific blocker of thyroid radioiodine uptake is well established (Il'in LA, *et al.*, 1972), FDA document, November (2001); Potassium Iodide in Emergency Medicine.: The Nuclear Regulatory Commission (NRC), July 1 (1998); Potassium Iodide as a Thyroid Blocking Agent in a Radiation Emergency: Federal Register. Vol. 43 Friday, December 15 (1978).

21. Protection of the Thyroid Gland in the Event of Releases of Radioiodine. National Council on Radiation Protection and Measurements. NCRP Report NO. 55., Page 32: August(1979); Thyroid gland is especially vulnerable to atomic injury since radioactive isotopes of iodine are a major component of fallout. June, the New England Journal of Medicine. Vol. 274, 23(1966); Thyroid Doses of I-131 Received by Americans From Nevada Atmospheric Nuclear Bomb Tests. The NCI's 'worst case' estimate is that fallout from nuclear weapons testing likely generated from 10,000 to 75,000 cases of thyroid cancer, National Cancer Institute, NIH, Bethesda, Maryland, USA.

22. Phytic acid (IP6) derived from rice bran extract is the most potent naturally occurring iron chelator, and so has strong antioxidant and antibiotic action Free Radical Biology Medicine, Volume 8 (1990), JBC August 25 (1987).

23. There is no medicine that will effectively prevent nuclear radiations from damaging the human body cells that they strike. FDA document, (November, 2001).

24. (WHO) Guidelines for Iodine Prophylaxis following Nuclear Accidents. World Health Organization (1999).